THE WOMAN IN JEWISH LAW AND TRADITION

Also by Michael Kaufman

LOVE, MARRIAGE AND FAMILY IN JEWISH LAW AND TRADITION

THE ART OF JUDAISM

A TIMELESS JUDAISM FOR OUR TIME

A GUIDE TO JEWISH ART

THE WOMAN IN JEWISH LAW AND TRADITION

Michael Kaufman

JASON ARONSON INC.
Northvale, New Jersey
London

First Softcover Edition – 1995

This book was set in 10 pt. Schneidler by Lind Graphics of Upper Saddle River, New Jersey, and printed and bound by Haddon Craftsmen of Scranton, Pennsylvania.

10 9 8 7 6 5 4 3 2 1

Library of Congress Cataloging-in-Publication Data

Kaufman, Michael, 1933–
The Woman in Jewish Law and Tradition
Michael Kaufman.
p. cm.
Includes bibliographical references and index.
ISBN 1-87668-346-4 (hardcover)
ISBN 1-56821-624-6 (softcover)
1. Women in Judaism. 2. Woman – Legal status, laws, etc. (Jewish law) 3. Women, Jewish – Religious life. 4. Women, Jewish – History.
I. Title.
BM729.W6K38 1993
296'.082 – dc20 93-1230
CIP

Manufactured in the United States of America. Jason Aronson Inc. offers books and cassettes. For information and catalog write to Jason Aronson Inc., 230 Livingston Street, Northvale, New Jersey 07647.

To Marcia

"A good woman is like the Torah itself."

Yevamot 63b

בטח בה לב בעלה, ושלל לא יחסר
קמו בניה ויאשרוה, בעלה ויהללה
רבות בנות עשו חיל, ואת עלית על כולנה
שקר החן והבל היופי, אשה יראת ד' היא תתהלל
תנו לה מפרי ידיה, ויהללוה בשערים מעשיה.

Contents

Acknowledgments xix

Introduction: The Jewish Woman Today xxi

Some Things Never Change xxi
Women in the Classical World xxii
Women in Christianity xxiii
Women in Judaism xxv
In Contemporary Society xxvi
The Self and the Other xxvii
Gender Differences xxix
Natural Causes xxx
A Sociological Experiment Regarding Gender xxxi
Toward a Moral World xxxii
Jewish Literacy xxxiii

PART I FAITH AND MORALITY

1 Jewish Morality and Values 3

The Basis of Jewish Morality 3
The Jewish Idea: God–Not Reason–the Source of Morality 4

God as Role Model 4
The Unity of Jewish Ethical and Religious Teachings 5
Judaism as a Guide to Moral Living 6
Mitzvot: Divine Precepts, Not Personal Whims 6
Fulfilling an Exalted Act 7
Becoming a Light unto the Nations 8

2 Woman and Family in Jewish Life 9

Love, Judaism's Guiding Principle 9
Attaining Love of God by Loving People 10
"Walking" after God 10
Marriage as a Path to Giving 11
Achieving Wholeness through Marriage 12
Rabbinic Views Regarding the Single Condition 13
Why Marriage Is Optional for the Woman 13
Women's Exemption from the Duty of Procreation 15
The Greater Reward of the Woman 15
Singlehood as the Selfish State 16
The Jewish Idea of Marriage: Not Partnership but Merger 17
Marriage as a State of Transcendental Wholeness 18
Service to Society versus Self-fulfillment 18
The Family—Foundation for Jewish Life 19
Masculinity Plus Femininity Equals Humanity 19
How to Have a Successful Marriage 20

PART II MEN AND WOMEN: THE DIFFERENCES

3 Judaism and Gender Roles 23

Physiological and Psychological Differences 23
Why Judaism Has Role Divisions 24
The Nature of Judaism's Role Divisions 24
Role Differentiation in the Jewish Family 25
Which Role Is More Significant? 26
R. Samson Raphael Hirsch on Judaism's Role Divisions 26
Distinctive Traits of the Woman 28
Women's Understanding 29
Women: Wise, Judicious, God-fearing 29
Women: Mercy and Compassion 30
Women and the Golden Rule 31
The Influence of Women 32

Women as Torah Educators 32
Women as a Source of National Moral Strength 33
The Equality of Status at Creation 35
The Consequences of the New Relationship 35
The Jewish versus the Christian Attitudes 36
In the Torah: Man's Duties, Woman's Rights 37
Woman as the Enabler 38
Mother of a Sage 39
The Ignorant Shepherd and the Wise Young Woman 39
The Woman of Torches 40
A Woman of Valor 40

PART III WOMEN IN THE TORAH

4 **Women in the Bible and the Talmud** 45

Section 1: In the Bible

Biblical Women as Inspiration 45
The Mother in Ancient Israel 46
The Matriarchs: Spirituality, Power, and Influence 47
Sarah, Spiritual Paradigm 47
Sarah: Modesty and Reserve, Power and Influence 48
Rebeccah: Loving-kindness and Discernment 49
Rebeccah's Superior Insight 50
Rachel and Leah, Builders of the House of Israel 51
Ancient Marriage without a Dowry 51
Tamar–Forced to Take the Initiative 52
The Mother of Kings of Israel 53
Jewish Prophetesses 53
Huldah 54
Miriam 54
The Pivotal Role of Women in the Redemption 55
Deborah and Yael 56
The Song of Deborah 57
Hanah: Prayer and Devotion 59
Ruth the Moabite 60
Esther, Champion of the Jews of the Persian Empire 61
Judith, Savior of the Jews 62
Commemorating Judith on Hanukkah 63
Judith: The Holiness of Women's Sensuality 63

Section 2: In the Talmud

Queen Salome, Deliverer of the Jewish People 64
Salome Defends the Pharisees 65
Salome: Assuring the Continuation of Torah Study 66
Queen Helena: Aiding the Poor 66
Rachel Bat Kalba Savua 67
Rachel: Transforming a Shepherd into a Sage 68
Bruriah, Talmudic Scholar 69
Kimchit, Mother of High Priests 69
Ima Shalom, Yalta, and Bluria 70
Conclusion 70

5 Women in Jewish History 73

In the World of Torah Scholarship 73
Rashi's Daughters: Yocheved, Miriam, and Rachel 74
Namnah 74
The Mother-in-law of the Or Zarua 75
The Wife of R. Abraham Meir of Worms 75
Redel Isserlin 75
The Grandmother of the MaHarshal 75
Pomona da Modena 75
Bathsheba da Modena 75
Rebeccah Tiktiner and the *Techines* Composers 76
Royzil Fishel and Toiba Pann 76
Sarah Rebeccah Rachel Leah Horowitz 77
Hanah Katz 77
Sarah Bat-Tovim 77
Boula Ashkenazi 78
Beilah Falk 78
Edel Heilpern 79
Havah Bacharach 79
Osnat bat Samuel Barazani 80
The Mother of the Shach 80
Flora Sassoon, Torah Scholar 81
Hasidic Women of Renown 81
    Adel the Tzadikah 82
    Feige bat Adel 82
    Meirosh, Daughter of R. Elimelech of Lizhensk 82
    Yenta the Prophetess 83
    Malkah and Adel of Belz 83

Sarah, Mother of R. Aryeh Leib Sarahs 83
Freda, daughter of the *Baal HaTanya* 83
Perele Shapira 84
Hanah Havah 84
Nehamah the Tzadikah 84
Surele Horowitz-Sternfeld 84
Hanah Brachah 85
Malkah the Triskerin 85
Sarah Shlomtzi 85
Hanah Rachel, the Maid of Ludomir 85
Hasidism Joins the Jewish Mainstream 86
Benvenida Abrabanel, Leader of Italian Jewry 87
From Naples to Ferrara 87
Dona Gracia Nasi, Star in the Jewish Firmament 88
Imprisoned in Venice 88
Praise for a "Human Angel" 89
Aiding Scholars and the Needy 90
Taking on the Pope 90
Dona Gracia's Project: A Jewish State in *Eretz Yisrael* 91
"An Ornament to Her People" 92
Esther Kiera, Court Jewess 92
The Jewish Woman in the Italian Renaissance 92
Sarah Coppio (Copia) Sullam 93
Gluckel of Hameln, Memoirist Extraordinaire 95
Her Life and Times 95
Piety and Acts of Loving-kindness 96
Moral Directives 96
"Love One Another, Study Torah, Pray with Devotion" 97
Judith Montefiore: Devotion to the Jewish People 98
Supporting *Eretz Yisrael* 98
Rachel Morpurgo, Hebrew Poet 99
Rebecca Gratz, Communal Worker 100
Grace Aguilar, Voice of Her People 101
Urging Women toward Tradition 101
Her Marrano Heritage 102
Implanting Jewish Pride in Young Women 102
Beauty and Truth 103
Emma Lazarus, Poet of Her People 103
"Give Me Your Tried, Your Poor . . . Yearning to Breathe Free" 104
The Jewish Passion 104
The Influence of Persecutions of the Jews 105
Early Zionist 106

Sarah Schenirer, Educator of Jewish Women 107
The Bet Yaakov Idea 108

PART IV THE MARRIED JEWISH WOMAN

6 Women's Rights in Marriage **111**

The Jewish Idea of Marriage 111
Marriage in Judaism: A Legal Contract 111
Consent of Both Parties Required 112
The Husband's Ten Obligations to His Wife 113
The Wife's Four Obligations to Her Husband 113
The Woman's Choice: Dependence or Independence 114
A Jewish Document of Women's Rights 114
The *Ketubah*: A Unilateral–Not a Two-Way–Contract 115
Obligating the Man and His Estate for Her Support 116
Assuring that the Husband Fulfills His Obligations 116
The Importance of Possessing a *Ketubah* 117
The *Ketubah*: An Ancient Tradition 117
Ketubot from the Dead Sea Caves 117
Discovering an Ancient Treasure Trove 118
Variations in the Text of the *Ketubah* 119
The Origin and Purpose of the *Ketubah* 120
The Obligation of the Husband to Respect His Wife 121
A Guarantee of Rights and Privileges to the Wife 121

7 Sexuality and Marital Relations **123**

Harmonizing the Spiritual and the Biological 123
Humanization–The Jewish Approach to Sexuality 124
Mastering and Guiding One's Instincts 125
The Jewish View of Relations between Singles 125
Negiah–Touching, Hand-Holding, Kissing, Embracing 126
Lesbianism 127
Women's Sexuality 128
The Man's Obligation to "Gladden" His Wife 129
Humanization versus Depersonalization 129
The Need for the Woman's Consent 130
Protecting against Conjugal Neglect of the Woman 131
The Man's Obligation to Ensure His Wife's Satisfaction 132
What about Agreeing to Abstain? 133
The Need for Emotional Commitment 134

A Wife's Privileges 134
The Husband's Duty to Cater to His Wife's Needs 135
Guiding the Husband 136
The Wife's Satisfaction Takes Precedence 138
The Idea of Pleasure as an Incentive 138
Advocating Moderation 139
Mutual Privileges and Duties 140

8 **Femininity and Family Purity** 143

The Rules of *Niddah* and *Mikveh* 143
The Biblical Source for *Mikveh* and Family Purity 144
The *Mikveh*: A Medium for Living an Elevated Life 145
Family Purity: Concern for the Woman and for the Marriage 146
Consideration for the Woman 147
Separation: A Time for Intimacy of the Spirit 147
A Medium for Periodically Refreshing the Relationship 148
Assuring That They Don't Take Each Other for Granted 149
The Contemporary Revival of *Niddah* and *Mikveh* 150
The "Hedge of Roses" 150
Together Again 151
A Time for Tranquillity and Repose 152
Time and the Woman 153
The Health Benefits of the Family Purity Life-style 153
Is Family Purity the Same as Good Hygiene? 154
Purification and Cleanliness 155
The Importance of *Mikveh* in Jewish Tradition 157

9 **Birth Control, Abortion, and Jewish Demographics** 159

The First Commandment of the Torah 159
Birth Control: The Biblical Reference 159
The Jewish View of Contraception 160
Sterilization 161
When Contraception May Be Permissible 162
Abstinence 162
"Family Planning" 163
Birth Control: Dissimilar Jewish and Catholic Positions 164
Abortion 165
The Severity with Which Abortion Is Viewed 165
When Abortion Is Allowed 167
If the Fetus Has AIDS, Tay-Sachs, or Down's Syndrome 168

Where Catholics and Jews Differ on Abortion 169
The Church: The Fetus Is to Be Favored over the Mother 170
The Jewish View 172
The High Abortion Rate in Israel Today 172
The Massive Jewish Population Loss and Its Causes 172
Jewish Education Today 173
The American Jewish Family Today 173
Intermarriage 174
Jewish Demographic Losses 174
Assimilation and Personal Status Problems 175
Replenishment 176
The Lack of Concern for Jewish Posterity 177
"The Vanishing Jew" 177
The Future: A Revitalization from the Core 178

10 Divorce 181

The Jewish Discouragement of Divorce 181
When the Truth Need Not Be Said 182
"Bringing Peace between Man and Wife" 182
How R. Zusya Saved His Marriage 183
When Divorce Is the Only Option 184
Get: The Jewish Divorce and Its Execution 184
Judaism's Liberal Attitude toward Divorce 185
Husband and Wife (Not Courts) Decide on Jewish Divorce 186
Jewish Divorce Is Not Dependent on Apportioning Blame 187
The Power of the Rabbinic Courts to Aid the Woman 187
Maltreating and Abusing a Wife 188
Disrespect as Grounds for Divorce 189
Nine Instances When the Husband May Compel Divorce 190
Twenty Instances When the Wife May Compel Divorce 191
The Problem of the *Agunah* 191
Alleviating the Situation of the *Agunah* 193

PART V WOMEN IN CIVIL LAW

11 Civil, Criminal, and Inheritance Law 197

The Woman in Jewish Civil and Criminal Law 197
Women as Witnesses 198
Credibility in Court 199
Court Testimony 200

Inheritance Laws 202
Daughters Preferred in Support and Maintenance 203
Property Rights 204

PART VI WOMEN IN RELIGIOUS LAW

12 Religious Laws and Customs 207

Women's Exemption from Some Torah Precepts 207
Women Are Excused from Fulfilling Fourteen Positive Precepts 208
Women's Spirituality 209
Woman's Option to Perform the Exempted *Mitzvot* 210
Doing Exempted Precepts That Are Not Optional Ones 211
The Obligation to Fulfill All the Negative Precepts 212
Three Precepts Devolving upon Women 212

13 The Sabbath and the Festivals 213

A–The Sabbath 213

Kindling the Sabbath Lights 213
Precedence Accorded the Woman in Kindling the Lights 214
Hallah 215
Kiddush 216
The Three Sabbath Meals 217
Havdalah: Separating the Holy from the Profane 217

B–The Festivals 218

The Obligation of Men and Women to Keep the Festivals 218
The Man's *Mitzvah* to Please His Wife at the Festivals 219
Listening to the *Shofar* 219
Fasting on Yom Kippur 220
Dwelling in the *Sukkah* and the Four Species 221
Hakafot: Rejoicing with the Torah on Simhat Torah 221
The Hanukkah Lamp 223
Kindling the Hanukkah Lights 223
The Purim Festival 224
Reading the *Megillah*, the Scroll of Esther 224
Purim Gifts to Friends and to the Poor 225
Passover: *Hametz* and *Matzah* 226
The Four Cups of Wine 226
Counting the *Omer* 228

C–The Fast Days 228

D–Rosh Hodesh, the Woman's Festival 228

A Festival Presented as a Reward 229

14 Women and Prayer 233

A–Women and Prayer 233

The Place of Prayer in Judaism 233
Prayer: A Duty of Men and Women 234
Praying with a Congregation Is Preferable 235

B–Women's Congregations 236

Halachah and Women's *Minyanim* 237
Religious School Prayer Groups for Girls 237

C–*Aliyot* to the Torah for Women 238

"Kevod Hatzibbur" 238

D–Separation of the Sexes in the Synagogue 239

An Alternative Focus 239
Kaddish 240

E–Women and *Tefillin* 240

The Nature of *Tefillin* 240
Tefillin: Sanctity and *Kavanah* 241

F–Women and the *Tallit* 242

The *Mitzvah* of *Tzitzit* 242
Wearing a *Tallit* as an Optional Precept 243
Women's Exemption from *Tallit* and *Tzitzit* 243

G–Blessings and Benedictions 244

H–*Birchat HaMazon*: Grace after Meals 245

The Duty to Express Gratitude 245

I–"That He Has Not Made Me a Woman" 246

The Separate Benedictions for Men and Women 246

15 Torah Study and *Bat Mitzvah* 249

A–Torah Study and the Woman 249

The Importance of Studying the Torah 249
Teaching Torah to Daughters 250
Women and In-Depth Torah Study 252
The Example of Bruriah 253

B–Torah Study for Women in Modern Times 254

"Jews Should Strive to Emulate Their Forebears" 255
Jewish Insights and Modern Discoveries 255

C–*Bat Mitzvah* 256

Celebrating *Bat Mitzvah* Today 257

Notes 259

Glossary 301

Bibliography 307

Index 315

Acknowledgments

It is a pleasure to acknowledge my grateful appreciation to those who contributed to this work by giving generously of their time and suggestions.

First, R. Dovid Gottlieb, formerly associate professor of philosophy at Johns Hopkins University in Baltimore, and presently with Yeshivat Ohr Somayach and Neve Yerushalayim College for Women in Jerusalem, was kind enough to provide a critical analysis of the manuscript at different stages, and he stimulated me with his incisive comments.

I express my gratitude to R. Aharon Feldman, Rosh Yeshivah of The Center for Jewish Learning in Jerusalem, and R. Emanuel Feldman of Jerusalem, editor of *Tradition* magazine, who read an early draft and gave me the benefit of their thinking.

I am grateful to Dr. Tamar Frankiel, lecturer on comparative religion and author, whose book *The Voice of Sarah: Feminine Spirituality and Traditional Judaism* (San Francisco: HarperCollins, 1990) was the stimulus for a number of ideas that were incorporated into this work. Dr. Frankiel was kind enough to read portions of the manuscript and render helpful suggestions.

I express my thanks to Leah Abramowitz, Jerusalem writer, social worker, indefatigable community leader, *baalat hesed*, and mother of thirteen, who read the manuscript and offered valuable insights and comments.

Much of the material in the book was discussed with the many students with whom we are privileged to share our *Shabbat* table at our home in the

Jewish Quarter of the Old City of Jerusalem. Studying at Yeshivot Aish HaTorah and Ohr Someach, Neve Yerushalayim College for Women, Hebrew and Tel Aviv Universities, and Hebrew Union College, these students served as critical sounding boards, listening to my ideas and stimulating me with theirs. In particular, I benefited from the insightful thinking and fresh perspectives of Ian Kalsmith and Ariella Smith, who read parts of the manuscript.

I am indebted to Linda Kashani and Sara Nathan for their editorial assistance and their suggestions.

My publisher, Arthur Kurzweil of Jason Aronson Inc., believed in the necessity for this work and supported it. At Jason Aronson, the infinite patience and exacting care of my editor Muriel Jorgensen once again accompanied me and assured that the work was properly transformed from manuscript form to its present state.

My wife, Marcia, has a share in this book, having lived it with me. As my most important critic, her keen observations and penetrating ideas are reflected throughout this work. I treasure her friendship and support.

Last, without the invaluable help of our four youngest children, this work would, to paraphrase P. G. Wodehouse, have been finished in half the time—and for this I am indeed grateful. I thank Sasson, Simha, Rachel, and Ora for making sure, with their many interruptions and distractions, that as deeply involved as I was in this work, I would never forget where the true values and priorities of life lie.

While I acknowledge my indebtedness to all those who have extended themselves and contributed to this work, I retain sole responsibility for any errors.

The Western Wall, Jerusalem

Introduction

The Jewish Woman Today

SOME THINGS NEVER CHANGE

> Nothing has suffered so much from . . . distortions as the current conceptions of the Jewish woman. In total disregard of the clear and unmistakable testimony of the Jewish Bible, of every word of Jewish tradition, of every page of Jewish history . . . [there has been a] diffusion of the most groundless notions about the degradation and subjection of women in Israel and the laudation of the present day as striving above all for the liberation of the Jewish woman from the oriental yoke.[1]

Do these words sound familiar? No, they were not written yesterday. They were penned about 150 years ago by R. Samson Raphael Hirsch, the leading rabbi of nineteenth-century Germany. Yet their truth endures. *Le plus ça change, le plus c'est la même chose.*

Far from holding a marginal place in Judaism, women have had an extensive impact on Jewish history, to a degree unknown in other cultures. Their influence on the direction taken by the Jewish people has been immense and incalculable and has characterized every age in which Jews have lived. From the biblical period to modern times, it would be no exaggeration to say that Jewish women have shaped the Jewish experience.

Montesquieu introduced the idea that a society's level of civilization can be measured by its treatment of women, who embody society's standards of public and private morality.[2] It has become a commonplace of Western culture to measure a society's morality on this indicator. But there is hardly a nation, society, or religion that would come close to passing this test, and most would certainly not welcome an evaluation based on it. One exception is Judaism and Jewish civilization.

Yet most people are unaware of this. The status of women in the Jewish world, both past and present, has been misrepresented. The need for knowledge and guidance on the subject of Judaism and women is compelling. Contemporary Jews possess little authentic knowledge of the subject, and incorrect information abounds, distorting the popular image of women in Judaism. It is therefore imperative that the position of women in Judaism be set forth clearly.

Ever since women's role in society became an issue, Jewish women have become an issue. Although in contemporary times misconceptions are especially prevalent, it is obvious from R. Hirsch's statement that such fallacies have a long history. The Jewish attitude toward women has been repeatedly discussed and repeatedly diagnosed as oppressive. Usually the untruths are perpetuated out of ignorance, but occasionally out of malevolence.

The distortion of the image of the Jewish women has served many ideological purposes. Well-meaning theorists have at times accepted common misconceptions as fact and have succumbed to the rhetoric and social pressure of the contemporary feminist movement. Others intentionally present a skewed picture. For many the advancement of the status of women is to be attained by denigrating Judaism.

In short, the general assumption is that women are subjugated in Judaism. It has become an axiom that needs no proof or substantiation. Jewish women are oppressed, their status comparable to women in primitive societies. Their historical condition compares poorly with that of women in other, more enlightened early societies and religions. These popular assessments have resulted, in part, from a failure to carefully examine the position of women both in the ancient world and in Judaism. The actual status of women in the ancient societies popularly extolled for their egalitarianism belies the myths.

This work is presented in response to a discerned need for the exposition of the Jewish view and out of a conviction that this view has not been fully articulated in the past.

WOMEN IN THE CLASSICAL WORLD

Greece and Rome are universally considered to be the most advanced societies of the ancient world. These cultures, which existed contemporaneously with ancient Israel, were major influences that shaped Western civilization. Many Western scholars praise them as near ideal societies for women. Such appraisals ignore basic realities. In ancient Greece, the classicists' ideal of a utopian society, women were regarded with contempt. Generations of Greek writers directed their venom and vituperation at women. Nothing more illustrates the Greek attitude toward women than the common practice, enshrined in classical Greek law and condoned by custom, of "exposing" infant daughters–in other words, infanticide. Newborn baby girls were abandoned in the wilderness atop a mountain to die of exposure.

The most enlightened thinkers, such as Aristotle, regarded women as a subspecies that, although perhaps useful, did not deserve to survive. Describing the female as a "deviation" from nature, the noted Greek philosopher rationalizes her existence as "a necessity required by nature, since the race . . . has got to be kept going," but adds that "female offspring must of necessity be produced by animals."[3] Aristotle teaches, "We should look upon the female as being, as it were, a deformity, though one which occurs in the ordinary course of nature. . . ."[4] What should be done with such deformities? His solution is simple: "Let there be a law that no deformed children shall live. . . ."[5]

Those girls who managed to survive into adulthood were married off at a very young age with complete disregard for their wishes. They rarely saw their husbands, and they were kept in a locked women's pavilion, the *gynaeceum*, a kind of harem, which they could not leave without the authorization of the *gyneconomus*, a public official charged with enforcing the laws regarding women.

WOMEN IN CHRISTIANITY

Another subject that requires clarification is the history of women in Christianity. Christianity, in its many forms, is the major religion of the West, and it has influenced Western civilization more powerfully than any other force. More than any other single factor, Christianity has shaped societal attitudes toward the treatment of women in the Western world. Western civilization is a Christian civilization, and its mores are Christian mores.

Jews in the West have lived in a Christian society for the past two millennia, and many Jews have been assimilated into that society and adopted Christian values as their own. An examination of Christianity's historical attitude toward women–often presented as a paradigm of enlightenment–shows that Christianity has veered sharply from its Jewish roots, particularly in this regard, and has furthermore engendered a dramatic lowering of women's status.

Statements by Paul and others in the New Testament, the teachings of Augustine and his fellow Church Fathers, the quasi-scientific Aristotelian statements of Thomas Acquinas, many of the edicts and proclamations of the popes, and the teachings of the Protestant reformers Luther and Calvin, manifest an almost uniform, unabashed contempt for women.

Paul tells women to keep quiet and to be utterly obedient.[6] He tells the married woman to subordinate herself to her husband as if he were God,[7] for he–and he alone–"is the image and glory of God."[8] This is a selective reference to only the first part of the passage in Genesis–"God created man in His own image; in the image of God did He create him"[9] with an omission of the second part ("male and female He created them"). Paul thus misrepresents the Jewish idea propounded by the Torah that man and woman are equally created in God's image.

In the Gnostic gospels, which make up part of the New Testament Apocrypha, Jesus is quoted as declaring, "I have come to destroy the works of the female,"[10] while Simon Peter states, "Women are not worthy of life."[11]

These early Christian teachings provided the foundation upon which the Church built its antifemale philosophy. They were built upon and amplified by the early Church Fathers. Augustine wondered how a man could possibly love his wife, knowing what she is and what she represents, and concluded that he should love her as a Christian is commanded to "love our enemies."[12] The ascetic Church Fathers identified women with sexuality, which they equated with filth. Their horror of sexual relations became transposed into a horror of women.

For Augustine, the female represents sin, dirt, and inferiority, whereas the male represents the power and superiority of God. Origen sees women as epitomizing human weakness and a symbol of evil.[13] Tertullian finds women to be evil incarnate, "the devil's gateway" who "destroyed man, the image of God."[14]

Albertus Magnus (c. 1200–1280), the German philosopher and bishop of the Church–who attempted to destroy Jewish scholarship by authorizing the mass burnings of the Talmud in Paris in 1242–despised woman, calling her "a misbegotten man [who] has a faulty and defective nature in comparison with his. One must be on one's guard with every woman as if she was a poisonous snake and a horned devil."[15]

Albert's student, Thomas Aquinas (1225–1274), the most authoritative thinker of the Church, shares Albert's disgust, seeing woman as a retarded man, a defective being, and man as representing perfection. He wonders why woman was created at all and decides that "woman is intended for procreation,"[16] since "man can be more efficiently helped by another man in other works." Saint Thomas teaches that children should love their fathers more than their mothers, since "the father, in principle, is more excellent than the mother."[17]

The great Protestant reformer Martin Luther viewed women no differently from the Catholic saints. He praises man's intelligence and derides women's lack thereof, based on "scientific" evidence, of which the following is an example: "Men have broad shoulders and narrow hips, and accordingly they possess intelligence. Women [however] have narrow shoulders and broad hips . . . and a wide fundament to sit upon. . . ."[18]

The most blatant example of the revulsion felt toward women in the Christian world is the witch-hunts that took place between the fourteenth and seventeenth centuries. Authorized and endorsed by the Church, these hunts produced hundreds of thousands of victims, nearly all of whom were women, who were tortured and burned to death.

Thus Christianity provided the religious foundation and moral and social seal of approval for misogyny and maltreatment of women and for civil laws discriminating against them, severely limiting their rights while granting men virtually total control over them. These ideas were incorporated into Western and European legal systems and traditions and translated into accepted norms of behavior for men and women throughout the world. The near universal disdain and degradation to which women were subjected in Christianity provided the social and religious sanction for their debasement and oppression in the Western world.

WOMEN IN JUDAISM

Regrettably, many of the critics of women's status in Judaism are as unfamiliar with Christian thinking concerning women as they are with the original Jewish sources in regard to women that are crucial for the comprehension of women's status in Judaism.

George Foot Moore, a non-Jewish theologian, orientalist, and professor of theology and history of religion at Harvard University, who studied the Talmud and classical Jewish sources, examined the status of women in the ancient world and concluded that women hold a higher position in Judaism than in other societies. Jewish law is "consistently favorable to woman," he writes, and "the legal status of woman under Jewish law compares to its advantage with that of [the other] civilizations."[19] Moore sums up:

> The social and religious position of woman in Judaism is . . . a moral achievement. That it [has always existed and] was no recent achievement in our period is shown by the eulogy of the good wife and mother in Proverbs 31 (incorporated into the liturgy of the weekly Jewish Sabbath eve feast as the *Eishet Hayil* hymn in praise of the Jewish woman).[20]

Moore's conclusions comes as no surprise to those scholars directly acquainted with the Talmud, *Halachah*, and Jewish tradition. Significantly enough, one rarely finds references to Moore's classical work, *Judaism in the First Centuries of the Christian Era*, in studies on women in Judaism.

IN CONTEMPORARY SOCIETY

For thousands of years women have been subjected to oppression at men's hands. Their subordination derived in large measure from social systems dominated by men and from authoritarian structures. Feminism, a movement whose purpose is the attainment of political and economic equality, social status, and power, represents women's reaction against such discrimination practiced by men in the legal, social, and moral spheres. It also expresses the dissatisfaction of many women with their situation in society, and their desire to change it. Its success at significantly transforming popular attitudes toward women has won widespread admiration and support. Since the beginning of the twentieth century, feminism has had a broad and profound impact on society and its way of thinking about women, and it has effected substantial changes in the lives of many women.

In the feminist view, the basic understandings of human nature in society are essentially patriarchal, drawn from the perceptions of men. These are considered standard, while those of women are considered "other." In her classic work, *The Second Sex*, Simone de Beauvoir says that men have defined the absolute human type–the male–against which women are to be compared as the "other": "Thus humanity is male, and man defines woman not in herself but as relative to him; she is not regarded as an autonomous being. . . . She is the incidental, the inessential as opposed to the essential."[21]

Feminism therefore comprises not merely a search for equality but a determinator of the values by which women should live. A major social movement, it has made significant contributions to the universal betterment of the lot of women. Contrary to widespread belief, many of feminism's goals are entirely in accord with traditional Judaism. However, there are central feminist values that stand at opposite poles from Jewish values. In regard to the fair treatment of women, Judaism supports–in fact preceded–feminism in its fight for the fair treatment of women. But it considers many components of mainstream feminist ideology actually socially regressive and harmful to women and society.

Feminism is represented by more than one school of thought. The two leading groupings, although they share some broad goals, differ significantly from each other, the division based mainly along the following lines. The school of "equality feminism," which might be termed "masculofeminism," insists on the basic *equality*, or sameness of men and women, in all areas of life. Such equality is to be achieved by the emulation of male modes and methods. The second school, which we term "feminalism," emphasizes the essential feminality of women and the fundamental differentness, or basic *inequality*, of men and women. It urges women to cultivate their feminality, their uniquely feminine attributes, and strives to inculcate feminine values–which are viewed as superior to male values–into the community at large for the betterment of society.

The masculofeminist idea has dominated feminism since its modern incarnation, largely because political and economic equality were the major issues. This appears to be changing.

THE SELF AND THE OTHER

Central to masculofeminist ideology is an emphasis on the self. The family was perceived as an institution of confinement and restriction for the woman and, furthermore, as an instrument for an oppressive Jewish patriarchy. Bearing and raising children were viewed as an unnecessary burden preventing women from achieving economic self-sufficiency and self-development.

Much of Jewish tradition, family, and community were seen as primary instruments for the subordination of women. Concluding that women's "auxiliration" in Jewish life was inextricably linked to those institutions, many found the family to be unnecessary and possibly harmful. Self-development was promoted as a higher value than family or Jewish continuity.

Such an ideology is incongruous with the Jewish value system. At Judaism's core is the development of an other-directed consciousness. Judaism understands life as God centered. God is the source of all values for the Jew, who knows that he was placed in this world in order to better it and that he is answerable to God for his behavior. The Jewish value system derives from the quintessential teachings of Judaism–the Torah, the Talmud, the *Halachah*, and the legal and ethical teachings of the Jewish Sages, the transmitters of the Torah through the centuries. These are the Jew's primary sources.

In the Jewish value system, living a moral life is the noble goal, achieved through love of God and love of one's fellow. This involves embracing the Golden Rule[22]–performing acts of loving-kindness for others. A life based on giving is both an elevated, moral life and an eminently satisfying one. By fulfilling God's precept of love in daily behavior, the individual lives a life distinguished by the sanctification of God and the betterment of humanity. The Jewish ideal can be expressed as follows: people love God best when they love their fellows best. In the words of the Jewish Sages, "If you are pleasing to your fellows, you are pleasing to God."[23]

Performing *hesed*–serving the needs of the family, community, and others–is a fundamental obligation of the Jew and has always been a distinguishing characteristic of the Jewish people.[24] In Jewish thought, it is one of the three pillars that uphold the world.[25] Acting justly, loving *hesed*, and behaving humbly, the prophet Micah teaches, is what God desires.[26] Above all, Judaism says, God wants *hesed*.[27]

Jews are expected to concern themselves less with their demands on society and more with their contribution to society. Jews loyal to their tradition cannot easily accept a movement that prizes personal success over service to the community, individual rights over individual duties, and personal gratification over communal obligations. Selflessness, not selfishness, is the Jewish ideal. The "other" is the focus of Jewish concern. Jews are expected not to live for themselves alone; the needs of the community occupy their attention.

Life is meaningless, Judaism teaches, if it is not lived by constantly giving to others.[28] Self-fulfillment is not a Jewish goal; it is a satisfying and fulfilling by-product attained by giving to and helping others. There is an unmatched richness and joy derived from giving of oneself to benefit others that one can never achieve from pandering to oneself.

Judaism teaches that the very purpose of the creation of the world[29] and of humanity was for humans to do *hesed* for one another.[30] Consequently, the Jewish Sages teach, the Torah begins and ends with acts of *hesed*.[31] The entire Torah[32] is based on the commandment of *gemilut hasadim*, acts of loving-kindness. Giving charity and performing acts of loving-kindness for others are said to be the equivalent of all the 613 precepts of the Torah combined.[33] The Jewish approach is to ask, "What can I do for others? Who are those who require my aid? How can I use my resources and abilities to help them? How can I best be of service to those who require my aid? What can I do to further the purpose for which I was created?"[34]

The answer to these question begins with the family. Marriage and family are the foundations of Jewish life and society. They serve as the basis for Jewish viability and continuity and the framework for the nurturance and perpetuation of Jewish values. Men and women begin to learn about true giving when they leave the period of singlehood. In marriage, they forsake the independence and selfism of single people for the greater concern of the marital unit. Judaism teaches that it is in the married state that an individual can best live a life governed by *hesed*. The Sages find that the single life is an imperfect, selfish state and that human perfection is possible only through marriage. Marriage, the paradigm for mutual giving–and thus for a full Jewish life–is thus considered the ideal condition.

Those who marry demonstrate that they do not live for themselves alone but that they choose to live lives of continuous giving. This finds fruition in procreation, bringing children into the world and establishing a family, that institution which nurtures Jewish life and is the indispensable unit for Jewish continuity. Marriage also provides the framework for man and woman each to contribute their distinctly male and female qualities for the sake of the well-being of the family unit they have created.

Judaism's measure of the value of a life is how it will be valued before God.

Neither professional or financial success nor public recognition are important Jewish goals. Self-fulfillment is legitimate, but service to God and to one's fellow are the principal Jewish aspirations.

This is not to say that Judaism is ascetic or that it discourages aspiration to individual success in careers, professions, and interests. On the contrary, such effort is desirable. As long as the career, profession, or interest remains but a medium for and subordinate to the primary goal of building a Jewish home, it is compatible with Jewish values. But Jews, both men and women, are bidden to have their priorities clear: the happiness and welfare of the family unit take precedence.

The family is not a burden; it is the epicenter of the individual's happiness. In the Jewish view, no pleasure in life can remotely compare with the deep, abiding joy of family relationships. The time spent with the family comprises the most treasured moments of a person's life.

GENDER DIFFERENCES

Judaism postulates innate gender differences and is sensitive to their specific, noninterchangeable character. Traditional Jewish society is based on the essential dissimilarity of the sexes. Where there is insistence on gender *equality* and unawareness of, or lack of sensitivity to, the natural *inequality* of the sexes, men and women suffer, as both are forced to compete with members of the other sex on unequal terms.

The distinctive gender spheres in Judaism derive from gender differences. They relate to the public and private areas of life. Judaism teaches that the inherent disparities between the dominant inclinations of men and women are part of the grand design of the Creator that people fulfill the task set out for them in the world. Each finds satisfaction in his or her complementary role. This contributes to the harmony of the family unit.

The Sages identify character traits indigenous to each gender. Women typically possess more modesty, piety, greater judiciousness, wisdom, insight, and discernment than men. They are also more merciful, compassionate, and empathetic and are more concerned with others.

Many feminists believe that the man's more public role in Judaism is the all-important one: they identify the duties of men in the synagogue and public prayer as the real values of Judaism. Women's role, the private sphere—"building the faithful house of Israel"—is derided as of marginal significance.

While there is a general awareness of the importance of the Jewish family as a social institution, few appreciate its centrality and even fewer that home and family are far more important than synagogue and temple. It is paradoxical that the glorification of the public sphere and the deprecation of the private sphere is shared by both male chauvinist sexists and many feminists.

In addition, masculofeminists have long opposed attempts to ascribe innate gender-differentiated psychological and behavioral characteristics to men and women. For years it was argued that masculine and feminine traits are culturally determined, the result of social acculturation and environmental conditioning. Infant boys and girls, it was held, are equal at birth except for their physiological, reproduction-related differences. In this view, the newborn infant is, in the theory first promulgated by John Locke, a *tabula rasa*, a blank slate upon which society may inscribe anything it wishes, including masculinity or femininity.

As for man and woman, they are basically androgynous entities, possessing few, if any, uniquely masculine or feminine proclivities. Each can do what the other can. In child-rearing, therefore, the roles of mother and father are basically interchangeable.

As for the role divisions in Judaism, some feminists maintained that since these are based on the false hypothesis that men and women are innately different, they are simply the medium employed by a patriarchal society to subordinate women.

NATURAL CAUSES

In recent years, science has confirmed that men and women are profoundly different and fundamentally unequal. Extensive studies in the physical and behavioral sciences have substantiated the thesis of a predominately biological basis for sexually differentiated behavior in humans. These findings have replaced earlier popular theories assigning societal, cultural, and environmental influences the primary causal role in behavioral differences of men and women.

The findings demonstrate that anatomy is indeed destiny. Biologists, neurologists, and psychologists who examined the relationship of the brain to sexually differentiated human behavior have discovered that men and women are born with inherent, distinctive male and female character traits. Far from being a formless piece of clay waiting to be shaped by society, a newborn infant comes into this world with inborn masculine and feminine characteristics, which will determine many aspects of behavior throughout his or her life.

Although the findings did not entirely rule out cultural influences on the development of sexually differentiated behavior, researchers found overwhelming evidence linking such behavior to biology.[35] Societal conditioning is now being related to a lesser, supportive role in strengthening the existing natural masculine and feminine inclinations. A child is born with natural predilections toward gender-oriented behavior. Hormones produced early in fetal development profoundly influence behavioral gender differences. The cumulative evidence of genetics,[36] brain research,[37] sociology,[38] and psychology[39] confirm that the primary determinant of sexually differentiated behavior is biology and not culture. Natural proclivities determine that men excel in some activities and women in others.

As sociologist Dr. Carol Gilligan points out,[40] psychologists from Freud to Piaget have formed misperceptions of the female personality by treating women as if they were men. When women failed to develop in certain areas as men do, they concluded that something might be wrong with them, when what they failed to perceive is that they are merely different. Gilligan determines that men and women have different behavior orientations and perspectives in regard to nurturance, caring, morality, and justice. She finds that women "feel a responsibility to discern and alleviate the real and recognizable trouble of this world," whereas men's moral imperative "appears rather as an injunction to respect the rights of others."[41]

Kant, who was a misogynist, nevertheless admits that women are morally superior to men in that "they surpass men in the virtue of philanthropy or lovingkindness, for the origin of this is, in most cases . . . compassion, to which women are decidedly more susceptible."[42]

A SOCIOLOGICAL EXPERIMENT REGARDING GENDER

Social anthropology has reinforced scientific findings regarding the fundamental differences between men and women. The Israeli kibbutz is the long-lasting twentieth-century experiment of a community that aims to construct a democratic, totally egalitarian society dedicated to the equal treatment of men and women. Recognized as the most rigorous and extensive social experiment of its kind, its goal is to transform society and its institutions and create a new, sexually neutral society.

The kibbutz provides women with the means of pursuing full equality with men in occupation and education by relieving them of housework, child-care, and the nurturing and rearing of children. Children are raised in sexually neutral environments, provided with an egalitarian education, and taught by modern child education experts.

The kibbutz experiment has molded more than four generations. Yet to everyone's surprise, a gradual polarization has taken place: women have gravitated toward roles as wives and mothers and to stereotypically female occupations. In contravention to their socialization, education, and ideology, and against the wishes of their husbands–and in opposition to the economic interests of the kibbutz–the women have chosen to work at traditionally female occupations: nursing, child-care, nursery and school teaching, and social work.

Despite the intensive egalitarianism that permeated the environment in which they lived, women found it unnatural to perform "men's" work. Granted free choice, men and women gravitated toward occupations coinciding with their natural propensities. Writes sociologist Melford Spiro: "The emergence of sex-role differentiation represented a recognition on the part of men and women alike that there are important physical and psychological differences between the sexes, and that the occupational distribution of the sexes must take these differences into account."[43]

For more than three thousand years Judaism has postulated psychological gender differentiation, from the Sages of the Talmud and down through the ages. Judaism provides a way of life that is sensitive to, and halachic parameters that are uniquely responsive to, the divergent attributes of the sexes.

TOWARD A MORAL WORLD

Alexis de Tocqueville wrote in the 1830s, "No free community ever existed without morals and . . . morals are the work of women." In de Tocqueville's thought, women provide a counterpoint to the relentless competitive pressure of capitalist societies. Men "rushing boldly onward in pursuit of wealth" lead "tumultuous and constantly harrassed lives," and are apt to relinquish ideals for profit.[44]

Feminist Sylvia Ann Hewlett observes that men

> [traditionally] presided over a domestic universe where an entirely different set of values held sway. . . . Wives and mothers were engaged in the creation of a comfortable home; the care and nurturing of husband and children; the handing on of a cultural tradition; the teaching of values; and the maintenance of a complex web of social and familial relationships. These tasks clearly required a great deal of selfless labor, but they also encompassed a moral dimension. . . . Life was about tenderness, beauty, compassion, and responsibility to others. . . .[45]

Emma Goldman, early twentieth-century feminist and anarchist, concurs. However, she holds that women's morals have been compromised by undue influence from the selfish worlds of business and politics, where the central theme seems to be, "To take is more blessed than to give." Goldman stood at the forefront in the battle for women's rights. Although she asserted that the rights women were demanding were just and fair, she declared:

> . . . but after all, the most vital right is the right to love and be loved. Indeed, if partial emancipation is to become a complete and true emancipation of women, it will have to do away with the ridiculous notion that to be [a] . . . mother, is synonymous with being a slave or subordinate. . . .
>
> A true conception of the relation of the sexes . . . knows of but one great thing: *to give of one's self boundlessly*, in order to find one's self richer, deeper, better.

That alone can . . . transform the tragedy of women's emancipation into joy, limitless joy.[46]

In Jewish tradition the world is the family, and it is a giving, caring world, infused with concern for others. It is a world encompassing the Jewish moral dimension. The Jewish woman gives of herself in her capacity as wife and mother, and her children learn, by example, the tradition of giving. In the process, she finds herself, in Emma Goldman's words, richer, deeper, and better. She thereby attains fulfillment as a woman, as a marital partner, as a mother, and as the central figure in the family she has created, nurtured, and fashioned. By so doing, she enriches her life with purpose and forges a vital link in the ongoing chain of tradition, bonded to both past and future generations of Jews.

Dr. Tamar Frankiel, feminist scholar, teacher of comparative religion, and convert to Judaism, finds women in the Jewish tradition "models of spiritual insight and power, bold shapers of Jewish destiny." She discovers that they are achievers, multidimensional women possessing deep inner strength, "indisputably powerful and influential members of their families and communities." In her book *The Voice of Sarah,* Frankiel underscores that it is traditional Judaism that nourishes these Jewish women and is the very source of their strength.[47]

JEWISH LITERACY

Unfortunately, what many contemporary Jewish women lack is a Jewish education. Although they may be familiar with all areas of human knowledge, they are generally Jewishly illiterate. They may be as conversant with Socrates, Aristotle, and Plato as with Kant, Nietzsche, and Schopenhauer but possess only a Sunday-school knowledge of Judaism. Many of these women know little about Judaism and even less of the teachings of the Jewish Sages who gave civilization its moral soul.

So powerful is society's pressure on the individual that the Jewish woman is deprived of access to Jewish awareness unless she makes the effort to distinguish fact from fashion. Notwithstanding her intensive education in other disciplines, she has no idea of her importance as a Jew and as a woman. Her only hope of making her unique contribution as a Jewish woman to the creation of a better world is through profound search and research in Jewish tradition.

Once she acquires a Jewish knowledge, the Jewish woman can apply herself to the discovery of her essential femininity, her feminine spirituality, and her Jewish heritage. Through this process, she gradually implants in those close to her her own feminine and Jewish values. The woman as Jew and the

Jew as woman is a powerful being, potentially capable of achieving the transformation of society. Such women endow society with a fusion of the Jewish and the feminine. Society thereby becomes more humanized, more caring, more altruistic, more empathetic.

Such a redefinition of society's values leads to the subordination of the individualist, competitive prototype and to the development of a new model whose center of gravity is care and nurturance and that possesses a rich moral dimension encompassing goodness, truth, sensitivity, compassion, and interdependence. The feminalist school of feminist theory speaks of recasting society and creating a better, more compassionate world. Their inspired, transformative dream shares a transcendent vision with Judaism.

I

Faith and Morality

1

Jewish Morality and Values

THE BASIS OF JEWISH MORALITY

Judaism is founded on the principle of divine authority. God, the Creator and Ruler of the universe, created the world with order. God provided natural laws to govern the operation of the universe, and He provided humans with moral laws to govern their behavior.[1]

Both nature in its majesty and the Torah in its profundity are the products of divine revelation; the moral teachings of the Torah derive their imperative from the same divine legislator as the physical laws of the universe. Natural law and moral law are equally manifestations of God's will. Just as God's will determines the natural law, God's will determines what is good.

God, who is perfect, has created an imperfect human being. He nonetheless created humans in His own image. Apparently contradictory, this teaches that God imbued human beings with elements of His own Godliness and has bidden humans to utilize the godly elements within them to achieve moral perfection on their own.

When a Roman official, Turnus Rufus, taunted R. Akiva, the great second-century scholar and teacher, that the Jewish rite of circumcision is evidence that God created man as an imperfect creature, R. Akiva readily agreed that according to Jewish tradition "the handiwork of man is more pleasant than that of the Holy One." He then placed a sack of wheat and a row of pastry before the Roman official and asked him to make his choice.[2]

Circumcision and the other *mitzvot* provide a God-given opportunity for humans to complete God's work and thus attain perfection. The guide that God has given the Jew for attaining perfection is the Torah.

Judaism believes not only that God created man in an imperfect state, but also that God, who is perfect, intentionally created an imperfect world with humanity as its perfecting agent: men and women are God's instruments for the attainment of the moral completion of the universe.

THE JEWISH IDEA: GOD–NOT REASON–THE SOURCE OF MORALITY

Judaism rejects the idea of the autonomy of moral law, i.e., that reason and rationality are the sources of ethics. Judaism rejects also the related humanistic thesis that humans are the ultimate source of human values. Judaism does not subscribe to the concept of individual autonomy in moral values. Judaism rejects private ascertainment as immoral, private judgment of right and wrong based on personal reasoning and conscience as arbitrary and fickle, and potentially immoral. History has shown that no act is so evil, no perversion so vile, that the individual cannot rationalize it to suit his or her own desires.

Mortal and finite, limited in wisdom and understanding, humans look to the immortal, infinite, omniscient God, the source of wisdom and value, for guidance in building a moral society. This begins with an awareness of the primal obligation to revere God, expressed in the passage in Psalms: "The beginning of wisdom is reverence of God."[3] Implicit in this is not only belief in God but also its consequent impact on behavior.

The concept of belief in and obedience to one God is enshrined in the first of the Ten Commandments. *Anochi HaShem Elokecha* is less a declaration by God of His existence, as it is commonly translated, than it is the primal commandment that serves as the basic foundation of Judaism: "I, the Lord, shall be your God"[4] is nothing less than a divine imperative for the acceptance of the Creator as a personal God. It thus serves as the indispensable prerequisite for acceptance of the other nine commandments of the Decalogue and for the entire Torah as well.

GOD AS ROLE MODEL

Elsewhere, the Torah expresses this idea in the form of mutual commitment: "I shall be your God and you will be a people to me."[5] Jewish belief begins with acceptance of this divine imperative and manifests itself by faithful adherence to it through the performance of the *mitzvot*, God's precepts. Its acceptance is affirmed by the Jew in his twice-daily iteration of the fundamental Jewish prayer, the *Shema*, "Hear O Israel, the Lord Our God is One God."[6] All else flows from that acceptance.

By acknowledging God as their moral authority, Jews also assert that God is their moral role model. Inherent in acceptance of divine authority is the Jewish concept of following in God's ways, known as *imitatio Dei*, in accordance with the divine obligation of the Jew to "walk in God's ways."[7] The Jewish Sages teach that this requires nothing less than adopting God's ethical virtues as one's own: behaving as God behaves, with love, justice, mercy, and compassion,[8] and subordinating one's own moral judgment to the absolute moral values prescribed by the divine authority in the Torah.

Fundamental in Judaism, therefore, is the belief in an intimate relationship with the omnipotent God who is the source of all moral values. God as moral authority has provided a code of ethical and moral values and norms by which the Jew shall live. The guidelines and prescriptions for a Jew's moral behavior are expressed in the commandments of the Torah, which directly communicate the divine will to human beings.

THE UNITY OF JEWISH ETHICAL AND RELIGIOUS TEACHINGS

Judaism makes no distinction between "moral" and "ritual" commandments; all are moral manifestations of God, and all are equally morally binding and obligating. Jews understand that humans must obey God, the source of morality, through ethical conduct. The ethical teachings of the Bible are essential elements of the Torah. The Ten Commandments can be divided into *mitzvot bein adam laMakom*, duties toward God, and *mitzvot bein adam lahaveiro*, duties toward others.

While the Torah contains precepts involving both categories, it does not distinguish between ethical and religious precepts. The rules of ethical behavior, the *mitzvot bein adam lahaveiro*, are at the same time *mitzvot bein adam laMakom*, since their fulfillment implies obedience to God's will. The prophet Micah summarizes this succinctly: "He has told you, O man, what is good and what God requires of you: to do justice and love acts of lovingkindness and to walk humbly with your God."[9]

For Jews, faith in God is an essential introduction to a moral life; the absence of such belief leads, inexorably, toward immoral behavior. Belief motivates deed. Disbelief in God opens up possibilities of evil. Throughout the ages, people who have rejected God have performed unspeakable horrors.

At the same time, many of those who have proffered a belief in God, yet never performed the acts God wanted, have undertaken bloody and inhumane deeds in God's name. If belief in God is not a prelude to, and is not accompanied by, moral conduct, evil is therefore equally possible. This is the clearest evidence of the need for a close unity between religion and moral behavior.

In ancient religions and cults, and in many popular religions practiced today, no direct correlation exists between faith and a moral life. The result is cruel and immoral behavior among religious adherents.

JUDAISM AS A GUIDE TO MORAL LIVING

Judaism introduced the idea that religion is not merely spiritualized teachings but is indissolubly linked to moral living. As already pointed out, a major distinguishing characteristic of the Torah is the interdependence between God's ethical and religious requirements. Unlike most religions, Judaism is not limited to specific spheres of human activity, but involves all aspects of life. In linking faith to action, Judaism has developed a distinctive way of life in which all human activities, from the sublime to the mundane, are charged with religious meaning. This blending of behavior to religion turns the abstract theological concept of Judaism into a dynamic guide for moral living.

The centrality of ethics in the Torah has resulted in the inseparability of faith and action. Judaism emphasizes the unity of faith and deeds. Faith alone is not sufficient. Unlike many other religions, Judaism does not denigrate the act; action is not secondary to faith. On the contrary, "creed and deed" is the Jewish motto–action generated by faith.

The act is essential because it was commanded by God, and its proper motivation is faith in God, who directs behavior. Faith provides the motivation and moral framework for good actions, and it is these good actions that are the aim of faith. In Judaism, belief is important, but it is not enough. One must become a good person by acting in accordance with the Godly dictates of morality.

Belief in one Supreme Being is inextricably bound up with moral behavior. "The scoundrel said in his heart, 'There is no God,'" says the Psalmist, ". . . they have become corrupt, they have acted abominably, there is none who does good."[10] The Talmud explains, "No man deals dishonestly with his fellow unless he denies the fundamental truth [belief in God]."[11]

MITZVOT: DIVINE PRECEPTS, NOT PERSONAL WHIMS

In Judaism, faith requires belief in the truths taught in the Torah; deed obligates faithful adherence to the Torah's precepts. The 613 *mitzvot*, or precepts, are the means God provides through the Torah for the attainment of moral perfection. Each *mitzvah* is symbolically a single rung on a ladder 613 rungs high, reaching from earth to heaven. In Jewish thought, man ascends heavenward, as it were, by observing the *mitzvot*, through which he attains moral perfection, which is akin to Godliness.

Pirkei Avot, Chapters of the Fathers, the compendium of Jewish ethical teachings by the mishnaic Sages of the Talmud, begins: "Moses received the Torah from Sinai, and handed it to Joshua; Joshua to the elders; the elders to the prophets; and the prophets handed it to the Men of the Great Assembly."[12] This teaches that the Jewish system of ethical and moral teachings presented by the Sages derives from Sinai and has the same divine authority as the Torah itself. Indeed, they are the Torah itself.

Yet the *mitzvot* are not an end in themselves, but the means to an end–performing God's will in order to fulfill our purpose in life. The Jews observe the *mitzvot* because they are commanded to do so. Various elements in the Jewish nation–the *kohen*, the Levite, the Israelite, the man and the woman–are, at times, given distinct *mitzvot* to perform in order to fulfill the roles assigned to them as part of God's grand design. While all may wish to perform *mitzvot* not assigned to them, they refrain from doing so.

Consider the Sabbath. As fundamental a precept as its observance is, it is nevertheless a *mitzvah*–an obligatory precept–to desecrate the Sabbath in order to preserve a life. The essential is neither the keeping of the Sabbath nor its desecration, but obedience to God. Jews keep the Sabbath not because they think it is a good idea, but because God has commanded it.

FULFILLING AN EXALTED ACT

Divine authority is the source of all obligation to perform the *mitzvot*.

Jeremiah declares:

> . . . I did not command . . . concerning burnt-offerings or sacrifices, but this I commanded them, saying "hearken to My voice, and I shall be your God, and you shall go in the way that I command you so that it will be well with you."[13]

Jeremiah's message is not that God did not command the bringing of sacrifices, for this would contradict the Torah. Rather, he declares, in effect, "God commanded observance of the *mitzvot*, and the *mitzvot* include bringing sacrifices." While an individual may enjoy bringing sacrifices, Jeremiah says they must do so only for the purpose of fulfilling God's command, not for personal satisfaction. If their intention is to fulfill God's command, Jeremiah is saying, they surely would not violate God's other precepts.

The most exalted act a human being performs is the fulfillment of the Godly command, a *mitzvah*. Jeremiah cautions, however, that God does not want an individual to perform a *mitzvah* unless he is so instructed by God. Indeed, since the word "*mitzvah*" means commandment, it is no *mitzvah* if it is not commanded by God. Therefore, neither *kohen* nor Levite nor Israelite, neither man nor woman, is to perform *mitzvot* assigned to others because they derive satisfaction from performing these *mitzvot*.

The death of Aaron's two sons, Nadab and Abihu, illustrates the subtle distinction. Nadab and Abihu brought a sacrifice "they had not been commanded to bring."[14] Their death is understood by the Sages as divine punishment for their arrogance. Nadab and Abihu assumed that a holy act is a holy act, whether or not God had commanded it. Their punishment is interpreted as a solemn warning against personal whims and emotionally motivated impulses dictating the performance of a *mitzvah*.[15]

R. Samson Raphael Hirsch writes that the presumption of the two sons of Aaron bespeaks "sinful arrogance . . . perhaps they were so greatly taken with their own sense of self-worth as individuals that they felt sufficient unto themselves . . . each followed his own impulse."[16] Through the severe public punishment meted out to Nadab and Abihu, God dramatically demonstrated before the entire nation of Israel that Aaron's sons had not been imbued with the proper spirit of Judaism.[17] Performing a *mitzvah* not prescribed for one by God is not in consonance with submission to God's will. It is not what God wants.

BECOMING A LIGHT UNTO THE NATIONS

Judaism teaches that the world was created for humans, and their mission is to utilize the Godliness instilled in them by the Creator to bring moral order to the world. The Jewish people are intended to be *Or Lagoyim*, a light unto the nations.[18] But they can be so only when they use their *tzelem Elokim*, the divine image in which God has shaped humanity,[19] to disseminate to the peoples of the world the morality that God has vouchsafed to them through the Torah.

A fundamental prerequisite to satisfying the moral charge is obedience to God, i.e., fulfilling God's commands. Human moral value and human fulfillment are achieved by responding to the divine will. A Jew performing a *mitzvah* that he or she has been commanded obeys God by performing God's will and expresses by this act readiness to further God's plan.

2

Woman and Family in Jewish Life

LOVE, JUDAISM'S GUIDING PRINCIPLE[1]

"Love is the voice of God. Love is the rule of heaven!" declares the nineteenth-century Anglo-Jewish writer Grace Aguilar.[2]

God's embracing rule of love descended from heaven in the form of the Torah's Golden Rule. *V'ahavta lereyacha kamocha*, "Love your fellow as yourself."[3] Rabbi Akiva, the great first/second century C.E. Sage, taught that this verse "is a fundamental principle of the entire Torah."[4] It is a cosmic, all-embracing law governing all Jewish behavior.

The Golden Rule, Judaism's gift to the world, is a foundation of Jewish morality. In Judaism it is not merely a pleasant aphorism involving rote recitation and general good feelings about people and a lofty ideal. To fulfill this obligation Jews are obligated to live in a manner that enables them to perform *hesed*, acts of loving-kindness, for others. Like virtually all the Torah's precepts, the Jewish idea of love calls for the individual to translate the general governing concept into specific actions; the idea of love must be turned into acts of loving-kindness.

In the Bible, the Golden Rule is followed by the words, "I am the Lord." As stated in the previous chapter, the emphasis underscores that the source of the Golden Rule is God, from whom all moral law derives, and whom the Jew is also commanded to love. The precept to love and cleave to God is part of the prayer recited immediately after the *Shema*, the twice-daily prayer of allegiance to God. The words, "Hear O Israel, the Lord our God is One God" are followed by *Ve'ahavta*, "And you shall love the Lord your God with all your soul and with all your might."[5]

ATTAINING LOVE OF GOD BY LOVING PEOPLE

How does one love God? This is not an abstract concept nor a mere ecstatic feeling in Judaism. The individual must exemplify the idea in his or her daily behavior. To begin with, Jews have to perform certain acts that, among other things, serve as mnemonic devices to ensure that the principles of the *Shema* become deeply etched into their consciousnesses. They are told to enclose the words of the *Shema* in their *tefillin*, the phylacteries worn by Jewish men during daily morning prayers, to insert them into *mezzuzah* cases and affix them to the doorposts of their homes. Jews are also directed to diligently teach the principles of the Torah to their children.

The Jewish people express love for God by observing God's Torah (lit. the "Teaching," or "Instructions") and by emulating His attributes. On several occasions the Bible employs the phrase "those who love Him and observe His precepts."[6] To the Jew, observing God's precepts is a *sine qua non* for loving God. As discussed, the Bible also states that man was created *betzelem Elokim*, in God's image. This is mentioned three times in the Torah,[7] emphasizing both God's profound attachment to humans and that God has endowed human beings with attributes of Godliness.

The Jew is obligated to strive to become Godlike in his or her behavior. The Torah declares, "You shall be holy, because I, the Lord your God, am holy."[8] In creating humanity in His image, God gave human beings the ability to discern right from wrong and directed them to strive to hallow themselves through their behavior.

"WALKING" AFTER GOD

Elsewhere, the Torah teaches, "You shall walk after the Lord your God, and Him shall you revere, and His precepts shall you observe, and Him shall you serve and to Him shall you cleave."[9] Perplexed about the possibility of "walking" after God, the Sages ask, "Is God not a consuming fire?" They reply that this command means that a Jew should emulate God's attributes by behaving as God does: a Jew is to give with love, justice, mercy, and compassion. The Sages explain that the Torah begins with an act of *hesed*, loving-kindness, the provision of clothing for Adam and Eve in Genesis,[10] and closes with an act of *hesed*, God's burial of Moses, in Deuteronomy,[11] in order to teach humans that love should be the guiding principle in their lives. Just as

God is constantly performing *hesed* for humans, God wants humans to emulate God and do acts of *hesed* for one another. According to Maimonides, emulating God, *imitatio Dei,* is the goal of all creation: "It is the aim of everything to become, according to its faculties, similar to God in perfection."[12]

The Jewish idea is that love of God and true faith in God inevitably entail fulfilling God's wishes. One demonstrates love of God through love of one's fellow and service to society. Acting kindly toward others also emanates from love of God. "Love your fellow" is another way of saying "Love God." The two are inseparable. One loves the Godly virtues of one's fellow—that person's goodness—and by fulfilling God's precept to love others one thereby expresses love for God who so commanded. This is a fundamental concept of Jewish existence: God requires that people extend themselves to others in order to attain love of God.

R. Judah Loew of Prague (1525–1609), known as the *MaHaral,* expresses it this way: "The love of people is at the same time the love of God. For when we love one we necessarily love His handiwork."[13]

The hasidic teacher R. Levi Yitzhak of Berditchev adds: "Whether a man loves God can be determined by the love he bears towards his fellow."[14]

MARRIAGE AS A PATH TO GIVING

In the biblical description of the creation of the first human, we are told "He created them male and female."[15] Jewish thought interprets this to mean that Adam was originally a single androgynous being, a hermaphroditic compound of man and woman, who was later separated by God into separate male and female entities.

In Jewish thinking, the purpose of the division was to prevent a self-contained egocentricity and instead direct humanity to community and to acts of *hesed.* The message is that one lives not for oneself alone and benefits not oneself alone; one must direct one's attention outward and must love and give to others. God would not have created a being in His own image, with its encompassing connotations of love, mercy, and compassion, had that being been meant to remain alone. A single person is an entity devoted to self-gratification.

Prior to the separation of Adam into separate male and female entities, God declares that the single state is not a good one: *Lo tov heyot haadam levado,* "It is not good for man to be alone." *Ehehseh lo ezer kenegdo,* "I'll make a helpmeet for him."[16]

In the Jewish view, the single person is an incomplete entity who lacks the wholeness that God ordained for humanity. In a profound existential sense, Adam's descendants yearn for a return to the original state of oneness that existed in humanity's primordial stage before separation. An individual achieves wholeness only when rejoined with his other half through marriage. Only a married couple can re-create the original unity.

ACHIEVING WHOLENESS THROUGH MARRIAGE

The Sages teach:[17] "A man without a wife is not called a man, as it is written, 'He created them male and female . . . and he called their name Adam (man).' "[18]

Only through marriage is a male able to attain the status of manhood. The *Zohar* declares: "A man is not called a man until he unites with a woman in marriage."[19]

The Rabbis say elsewhere: "A man without a wife is not a complete human being."[20]

The *Zohar* explains:

> The Holy One Blessed be He does not dwell, nor is He to be found at all, with that which is imperfect. He can be found only with one who has attained true oneness. . . . A person can be considered one and whole . . . and without defect . . . when he is joined together with his complementary partner and is thereby hallowed by the elevated sanctification of *kiddushin*. He who has not married a woman . . . remains but half a person – and his [intended] life's partner remains but half a person. . . .[21]

In the single, or defective, state, a person possesses only the potential for attaining completion and for giving completion to another. The *Zohar* makes this clear:

> Soul and spirit, male and female, are intended to illuminate together. One without the other does not radiate and is not even termed a "light." Only when they are attached to one another are they called a "light."[22]

Thus, Jewish teaching views man and woman as indispensable to each other. The desire for marriage emanates from the unconscious yearning in man and woman to return to the original, primordial state of oneness. Furthermore, in Judaism the man and the woman are seen as incomplete in themselves, but each provides elements that can give completion to the other. Interestingly, it is the woman who is seen as possessing the characteristics that can provide perfection.[23] As the supremely perfecting element, woman is essential to the perfect wholeness of humanity.

The Jewish idea is that marriage thus brings two incomplete beings to the state of wholeness in which they can establish real communion with God. It creates out of two individual, complementary entities a single, mystical superentity of transcendental significance, through which, in the words of the Sages, "heaven and earth embrace."[24]

RABBINIC VIEWS REGARDING THE SINGLE CONDITION

The single person, the Sages teach, lacks joy, blessing, good, and even Torah,[25] all the elements necessary for well-being. The Midrash says:

> And the Lord God said: "It is not good for man to be alone. . . ."[26] R. Jacob learned: Every man who has no wife lives without good, without help, without happiness and without forgiveness.
>
> Without good, as it is written, "It is not good for a man to be alone."
>
> Without help, as it is written, "I shall make a helpmeet for him."[27]
>
> Without happiness, as it is written, "And you shall rejoice, you and your household."[28]
>
> Without blessing, as it is written, "to bring blessing to your household."[29]
>
> Without forgiveness, as it is written, "And I shall forgive you and your household."[30]
>
> R. Simon said in the name of R. Joshua ben Levi: Even without peace, as it is written, "And peace will be with you and peace will be with your household."[31]
>
> R. Joshua of Sichnin said in the name of R. Levi: Even without life, as it is written, "See life with the wife that you love."[32]
>
> R. Hiya bar Gamda said: He is not even a complete person, as it is written, "And He blessed them and He called their name Adam."[33]
>
> And some say: He even diminishes the Divine Image, as it is written, "For man was created in God's image,"[34] and immediately afterwards it is written, "And be fruitful and multiply."[35]

The woman has an equal need to achieve completion, as we learn in the following Midrash:

> A woman has no tranquility except with a husband, as it is written [in relation to Ruth's singlehood in the Book of Ruth] "And Naomi said: My daughter, let me seek for you tranquility, which will be good for you."[36]

The Talmud refers to the woman's need for wholeness: "A woman is an incomplete being who concludes a covenant [of marriage] only with the one who can transform her into a completed vessel."[37]

WHY MARRIAGE IS OPTIONAL FOR THE WOMAN

Judaism considers marriage as voluntary and optional for the woman. Unlike the man, she is exempt from the duty of procreation.[38] There are several reasons for this. Marriage and procreation entail seeking a mate. A certain aggressiveness is required; the Sages consider these characteristics to be more appropriate for the male, and not in harmony with the reserved and modest character of women.

The process is thus described in Scripture: "Therefore shall a man forsake his father and his mother and cleave to his wife."[39] It is the man who is bidden to actively search for a wife, and not vice versa. The Talmud explains:

> Why did the Torah state "When a man will take a wife,"[40] and why did it not state the reverse? Because it is in the nature of a man to actively pursue the woman and it is not the nature of the woman to actively pursue the man. If a person loses something, who seeks out whom? It is the one who loses something who seeks it out and not vice versa.[41]

The Torah teaches that woman was created by being taken from man. The unmarried man thus feels more incomplete than the unmarried woman, and therefore is the more active one in pursuit of his mate. In every generation man repeats the saga of Adam, his primogenitor, and follows his instinct to find the woman who will make him whole.

Another reason that Judaism makes marriage voluntary and optional for women is that in principle, the Torah does not impose burdens that are too difficult to bear. As Scripture puts it: "The ways [of Torah] are those of sweetness."[42]

Recognizing that pregnancy and childbirth may jeopardize health, the Torah would not categorically require woman to experience discomfort and place herself in a potentially precarious situation that might compromise her well-being. This commitment must be made of her own free will; she is not directed to make it by fiat.[43] Therefore, the command to procreate is not equally incumbent upon the woman as upon the man.

There are some sages in the Mishnah and Talmud who nevertheless maintain that a woman is equally obligated to fulfill the command to procreate,[44] basing their view on the verses in Genesis: "Male and female He created them. God blessed them and said to them, 'Be fruitful and multiply, fill the earth and master it.' "[45]

In addition, they cite[46] the passage in Isaiah: "For thus says the Lord, Creator of the heaven: He is God who fashioned the earth and created it; He did not create it to be a waste: He fashioned it to be inhabited."[47]

The predominate view in the Jerusalem Talmud is that women are included in the obligation to marry and procreate.[48] This view is supported by the medieval Tosafists, who see the passage in Isaiah as having universal implications that include women in the obligation to procreate and populate the world.[49]

WOMEN'S EXEMPTION FROM THE DUTY OF PROCREATION

The final halachic ruling, however, is that women are exempt from the command to procreate.[50] Maimonides concludes that a woman may, if she wishes, even marry a eunuch or remain unmarried. This view is shared by other codifiers of Jewish law.[51] Yet Maimonides and R. Joseph Caro advise women to disregard this exemption and marry to avoid facing male impudence and immorality. They therefore make it incumbent upon Jewish parents to arrange marriages for daughters as well as for sons.[52]

Marriage, then, is the preferred state for women, but Jewish law does not mandate it. *Halachah* encourages the woman to marry, but does not condemn her if she chooses to remain single.

The Rabbis were aware, however, that women are often more interested in marriage than men. "More than a man wants to marry, a woman wants to be wed."[53] The Jewish woman has always chosen marriage and children because her wish for children is greater than that experienced by men. This need overrides any desire she might have to take advantage of her halachic option to remain single. Rachel's plea poignantly captures the pain of the barren woman: "Give me children, for if not I shall surely die."[54]

Consequently, one might say that while a man has a natural inclination to seek completion simply through uniting with a woman, for a woman this is insufficient. For her personal fulfillment, she needs children as well. Because of this, Jewish law provides that a woman married to a sterile man can seek legal recourse through the rabbinic court to force a divorce.[55] Although she is excused from the *mitzvah* of procreation and cannot use her husband's sterility as automatic grounds for divorce, the court respects her wishes on this point and allows both this factor and her desire for children to constitute valid grounds for divorce. It is the woman's right to bear children and raise a family. Maimonides further explains that the law respects the woman's desire to have children at her side "when she is old."[56]

Comments one observer:

> The release of the Jewish woman from the commandment of procreation has made possible the evolvement of a concept of woman as a personality and not as a child-bearing machine. Certainly woman is involved in the commandment to preserve the race, but it is her privilege to determine whether she becomes involved or not. The rabbinic opinion on this subject and its formulation in Jewish law may have been the first stage in the full emancipation of Woman.[57]

THE GREATER REWARD OF THE WOMAN

While Jewish law exempts the woman from the command to marry and bear children, by marrying she enables her husband to procreate. Her reward for the *mitzvah*, therefore, is greater than that of her husband, in accordance with the rabbinic principle,[58] *Gadol ham'aseh yoter mei-ha'oesh*, "Greater is the enabler of the act than its actual performer."[59]

R. Nissim Gerondi, the fourteenth-century Spanish commentator on the Talmud known as the *Ran*, notes: "Although she is not personally commanded regarding procreation, she nevertheless performs a *mitzvah* in marrying because she thereby assists her husband in the fulfillment of his *mitzvah* of procreation."[60]

Men and women who did not marry have been regarded as unfortunates in Jewish tradition. Those who deliberately refrained from marrying were considered as having failed in one of humankind's fundamental purposes: propagation. The Sages teach that procreation is the *raison d'être* for the creation of the world.[61]

A life without children, the Rabbis say, is a life devoid of life. As they phrase it: "A childless person is like one dead."[62]

The Talmud declared that in the afterlife a man will have to account for not having married and had children:

> When a man is brought before the ultimate tribunal for the final judgment, he is asked: Did you deal honestly in your business dealings? Did you set regular hours for the study of Torah? Did you fulfill your duty of procreation?[63]

The commandments of marriage and procreation apply, of course, only to those who are capable of them. When natural or other circumstances prevent fulfillment of these obligations, the Sages regard the situation with compassion.

SINGLEHOOD AS THE SELFISH STATE

Judaism regards the deliberate intent to remain single as unforgivable selfishness. Selfless love is a fundamental principle of the Torah[64] and a pillar upon which the world rests.[65] The Sages speak of a man who chooses to remain single with uncompromising severity:

> R. Eliezer says: He who does not marry and engage in procreation is as if he has shed blood. . . .
>
> R. Jacob says: It is as if he has diminished the Divine Image. . . .
>
> R. Ben Azai says: It is as though he has shed blood and diminished the Divine Image. . . .[66]

The premium that Judaism places on human life is universally known; bloodshed ranks among the major crimes in Judaism. Murder, as well as incest and idolatry, is a cardinal sin, forbidden even at the cost of one's own life. A corollary to this is the person who is able to create life and does not use this potential. He causes the diminution of life. On the other hand, a person who does marry and have children contributes to the increase of life, a primary Jewish value.

The *Zohar* teaches:

> When is a man called complete? . . . When he is joined with his mate in unity, in joy and in affection, and there issues from their union a son and a daughter. Only then is man complete below like the Holy Name above, and the Holy Name becomes attached to him.
>
> However, if a man is unwilling to complete the Holy Name below, it is better for him that he had not been born, for he has no portion at all in the Holy Name. And when his soul leaves him in this world it will never join him again, because he has diminished the likeness of his Master. . . .[67]

In Jewish thought, people who do not marry are not willing to transcend their own egocentricity and selfism for the sake of their fellow human being. People who deliberately remain single increasingly enclose themselves in a circle of isolation and gradually become less involved in interpersonal relationships and more self-absorbed. Persons who do not marry and have children have, in part, severed themselves from the rest of human history. Married individuals, in contrast, are compelled to break down the barriers separating them from humanity. Marriage does not survive if one partner insulates himself or herself. Intimate contact with another human being must eventually breach such defenses.

Judaism teaches that human love should flow first toward a spouse and children, then to one's own people, and ultimately to all of humanity. Persons who marry in essence construct a bridge connecting themselves with the human community. Their tools are the acts of loving-kindness essential to the Jewish home and spirit.

THE JEWISH IDEA OF MARRIAGE: NOT PARTNERSHIP BUT MERGER

In Western society marriage is often perceived as a kind of business partnership. Each side contracts with the other to provide certain goods and services, with each party exacting specific obligations from the other. The failure of either partner to fulfill its side of the agreement is grounds for the dissolution of the partnership, which means a divorce.

Jewish tradition approaches marriage not as a partnership or cooperative organization, but rather as the merger of two separate but complementary entities. A new being is formed, a single marital entity. Man and woman are profoundly different. When they marry, they are considered complementary halves of the same unit, neither half more important than the other. The division of labor by both parts of the marital unit is based on their unique and different capabilities, with the aim of maximizing the effects of the unit's efforts.

Ideally, the man, who is the physically stronger and more outgoing, is the initiator. The empowerer, the one who makes the success of the household and all its goals possible, is the woman. In her role as *ezer* she emulates God, who is referred to as *Ezer*,[68] the One who makes it possible for an undertaking to be fulfilled.

MARRIAGE AS A STATE OF TRANSCENDENTAL WHOLENESS

This relationship is intimated at the beginning of married life, when the bride is termed *kallah*, or completion. A word with the same root, *Vayechulu*, is employed in Genesis to declare that God had completed the creation of the world.[69] Jewish tradition considers a wedding to be the commencement ceremony that marks the emergence of two people from the preparatory cocoons in which they had existed in a nascent, incomplete state, and their metamorphosis as *hatan* and *kallah*, bride and groom, into a new state of transcendental completeness in marriage.

A man has the tendency to become engrossed in his outgoing role as initiator and builder. In the process he may lose sight of his deeper, underlying purpose—of the real reason he toils so doggedly. The means to an end—his work—becomes, for him, the end itself. The inner life of the family and its essential sense of purpose and meaning are provided by the woman, the *ezer*, or helpmeet. She has the ability to provide a more spiritual environment for the family, which makes life profoundly more fulfilling for all the members of the family. That "*ezer*" refers to the spiritual element is evident from Eve, who was the "*ezer*" in the Garden of Eden, despite the fact that in the Garden of Eden Adam and Eve were fully supplied with all their physical needs.

Woman, the Talmud tells us, was granted a *binah yeteirah*, an extra understanding,[70] above that granted to man. This higher level of understanding gives her a clearer awareness of the underlying goals of life and of what is entailed in creating a family and a nation. It is she who instills in her family love and concern for others and a desire to serve humanity.

SERVICE TO SOCIETY VERSUS SELF-FULFILLMENT

The Jewish scale of values places contributions to society above fame or fortune. Judaism teaches that a major purpose in life is to help others. This transcends the "me" of self-gratification; the individual is expected to ask himself or herself, "How can I best contribute to society?"

There are people who devote their entire lives to to seeking honor and fame. Yet how true the popular saying, "It is by God decreed, fame shall not satisfy the highest need."

Humans do have a need for achievement and self-fulfillment. The person who seeks fame is wrapped up in his own ego, however, and therefore will never achieve true satisfaction. The need for fulfillment can truly be met only by contributing to humanity in a meaningful way.

The Jewish ideal can be summed up as follows: If you can be either a good social worker or a top football player who will reap wealth and fame, Judaism will unhesitatingly recommend the path of social work. A life devoted to love and service to others transcends the struggle for personal fame and achievement because it is directly contributing to society.

THE FAMILY–FOUNDATION FOR JEWISH LIFE

To achieve God's purpose, Judaism teaches, each person must share those unique personal qualities with which he is endowed with the world. In the end, precisely such altruism will yield satisfaction and true pleasure. Such is the nature of the human being created in God's image that he or she derives greater pleasure from the giving of his or her skill and efforts to others than from the seeking of personal benefit.

The family, the basic institution of human life, is the foundation of Jewish life. The family is the cornerstone of Jewish existence and continuity. In Judaism's perception, no meaningful human life can exist without the family. When individuals marry and become parents, they confirm that they do not live for themselves alone, that self-gratification is not their ultimate value, that they are living for others as well as for themselves. They rise above the animal in their nature, which seeks only self-satisfaction.

When an individual learns to subordinate personal needs and interests for the needs and interests for those of his or her family, only then does selfism end and humanity begin. The family is the beginning of humanity.

MASCULINITY PLUS FEMININITY EQUALS HUMANITY

Family life requires that husband and wife, with their distinct male and female characteristics, make their unique contributions to the family's structure. The family relationship depends on it. Such a symbiotic, mutual relationship between the couple is not incidental to Jewish family life: it is integral to it, an absolute requisite for the maintenance of Jewish family life and Jewish continuity.

The separate and distinct male and female qualities that husband and wife offer are necessary for a secure family structure. When this vital structure is disturbed, the family comes apart. When the guiding purpose that a woman provides as *ezer kenegdo* disappears, the family is lost.

In the animal kingdom, in most instances, the male and female are drawn together to copulate, but do not remain together. On the other hand, if humans beings are compatible, they desire to stay together. This desire derives from the fulfillment each provides to the other as complementary elements of a single entity and from their yearning to revert to their primordial oneness. Because of this, the man and woman must learn to give to each other as if they were separate organs of the same body. Adam called Eve "bone of my bone, flesh of my flesh."[71] This is the level of oneness a Jewish couple strives to achieve.

Thus, citing the verse in Genesis, "Therefore shall a man leave his father and mother and cleave to his wife and shall be as one flesh,"[72] R. Ovadiah ben Jacob Sforno (c. 1470–1550), the Italian commentator on the Torah, explains, "They should endeavor in all their activities to achieve that wholeness that was intended by God with the creation of man as if the two were actually one."[73]

HOW TO HAVE A SUCCESSFUL MARRIAGE

The Jewish idea is that the two members in the fused marital entity learn to think of themselves as a "joint personality," rather than as separate selves, as they were when they were single. This is not a magical transformation, but rather a process that involves continual learning. The idea of marriage as merger does not mean the loss of their individualities, but a combining of the two. Interweaving the two characters allows a married couple to confront the outside world from a position of considerably increased strength. This completed marital personality is a greater force than the sum of its two constituent parts. The Sages emphasize this: "Husband and wife together are greater as a unit than both of them are as individuals."[74]

From its inception, Judaism has perceived marriage as a necessary and optimal human institution. Marriage involves turning the focus away from the self to the other–giving to spouse and children and to others, finding fulfillment through living an other-directed life.

Intended for the welfare of men and women, as a medium for procreation, for the creation of a family, and for mutual companionship and security, its success is largely dependent on the realization by the married man and woman of their individual roles in the marital entity.

II

Men and Women: The Differences

3

Judaism and Gender Roles

PHYSIOLOGICAL AND PSYCHOLOGICAL DIFFERENCES

Judaism takes the straightforward position that men and women are fundamentally different, not only physiologically but psychologically as well. In keeping with the cosmic design of the Creator, neither their bodies nor their psyches function identically.

Although men and women share certain characteristics that are embedded in the general human condition, their dissimilar psychological traits, no less than their dissimilar biological ones, clearly delineate each sex. The Talmud says: "What is characteristic of men is not characteristic of women, and what is characteristic of women is not characteristic of men. . . . Women are a people unto themselves."[1]

The differentness emanates from God, and, therefore must be good. Infants are not clean slates upon which society, parents, and teachers inscribe masculinity or femininity. In the Jewish view, children are born with inherent, distinct characteristics–physiological, behavioral, and psychological. The Creator implanted these so as to grant each of the sexes unique abilities in the various realms of human endeavor, in order for men and women to complement each other.

Thus, in Judaism's view, biology is indeed destiny. Men and women are dramatically and innately different, in their patterns of thought and behavior, in their perceptions of themselves and the world, and in the roles they most naturally and easily assume.

WHY JUDAISM HAS ROLE DIVISIONS

This cognizance lies at the root of Judaism's role divisions of the tasks, privileges, and obligations assigned by the Torah and by Jewish law. The roles prescribed for men and women in the Jewish tradition correspond to their intrinsic characters.

Such dissimilarities and differing roles do not make either gender superior or inferior to the other. The psychological and physiological diversities in their makeup provide for a functionally complementary and harmonious role division of the sexes.

God surely had His reasons, for among higher animals the protracted internal and external care and nurturance of the newborn through the mother's body indicates that the mother–child relationship is the most basic, nature-oriented unit of society. The family, which is centered around this relationship, is the primary social institution to evolve in the civilized community. While the family plays a central role in the structure of society in general, it is particularly significant in Jewish society, where it is the vital medium for the transmission of tradition and the preservation of the Jewish people.

Family life requires that both husband and wife make their distinct contributions to the family structure. While building a Jewish home is certainly a joint endeavor of husband and wife and each possesses characteristics and interests associated primarily with his or her partner,[2] the fundamental differences of their psyches and the inherent disparities of their dominant inclinations dictate a natural role division based primarily on gender. This is in accordance with the grand design of the Creator that each fulfill the task set out for him or her in this world. Each finds personal human fulfillment primarily through his or her complementary family role. This, in turn, ultimately provides satisfaction and harmony within the family unit.

THE NATURE OF JUDAISM'S ROLE DIVISIONS

Separate roles derive from differences in the psyche, which in turn stem from natural, instinctual inclinations. These influence the respective abilities of men and women in specific areas and functions in life. In relation to the family, the differing, complementary roles of men and women derive from the need to provide for, nurture, and protect the family as a vital cell in the Jewish national body.

The two main tasks in the family are the nurturance of the family unit and intrafamily relations on the one hand, and the financial support and maintenance of the family and extrafamily relations on the other. Intrafamilial responsibilities require personalities with sensitivity, perception, gentleness, and flexibility. Women manifest these qualities *par excellence.* The male personality, having an abstract and analytical mentality weaker in these spheres, possesses the rigor and forcefulness necessary to represent the family in extra-familial confrontations. The man is also not circumscribed; the dynamics of home and family are not dependent on his constant involvement. Naturally, he thus assumes the public, communal role.

This division of the woman as mother, nurturer, and homemaker and the man as provider, warrior, and defender is not an arbitrary one, nor is it based on physical considerations alone. When cultural influences are removed and men and women are given the option, both sexes continue to seek roles suited to their inherent proclivities.[3]

While each gender also posseses those traits primarily associated with the other, and each can perform tasks primarily associated with the other–at times even *better* than the other–the generalization that men and women are more comfortable and more capable in their characteristic roles nevertheless holds true.

ROLE DIFFERENTIATION IN THE JEWISH FAMILY

Judaism sees this complementary relationship as integral to the maintenance of Jewish family life. It constitutes the basis for the smooth functioning of the family. When ripples disturb this foundation, the family begins to disintegrate. The same values are no longer there. The unique contributions that the man and the woman have to offer disappear, the family structure erodes, and the family itself falls apart.

Tamar Frankiel, author of *The Voice of Sarah: Feminine Spirituality and Traditional Judaism*,[4] finds the separate spheres for men and women to be one of Judaism's greatest strengths. Frankiel was formerly a Christian who had taught comparative religions at Stanford and Princeton universities and the University of California at Berkeley and had devoted most of her life to the study and objective analysis of religions. She discovered in Judaism a way of life that satisfied her as a feminist and fulfilled her spiritual needs as a woman.

After determining that there was an intimate affinity between Judaism and feminine spirituality, Frankiel converted to Judaism and became an observant Jew. She was drawn to the Jewish faith in large measure because of Judaism's acute awareness of, and its accommodation to, the essential differences between the sexes. Frankiel found that Judaism's role differentiation, with its complementary spheres for men and women, allows the Jewish woman to develop in her natural, feminine manner. This, in turn, she found to be a source of the contentment and power of Jewish women.

For the proper functioning of society, it is necessary for men and women to have an understanding of their roles. Judaism grants husbands and wives delicately balanced responsibilities in different realms in accordance with their natural tendencies. These separate spheres provide for a smooth functioning of the family, and are, in large measure, responsible for the legendary strength of the Jewish family and the vital role the family has played in Jewish survival and continuity.

WHICH ROLE IS MORE SIGNIFICANT?

There is a popular witticism about a woman describing role divisions in her family: "I am in charge of the 'minor' tasks – decisions on finances, the conduct of the household, the education of the children, and planning for the future. His are the 'major' ones – deciding on a proper foreign policy for the country, whether the government's taxation principles are fair, and which government ministries are not properly fulfilling their functions."

Underlying this story is both a commonsensical awareness by women that their function in the external-internal division of family responsibilities, their task in the home, is ultimately the more significant one. The question is, does this conception correspond to reality? Or do people see the woman's role as insignificant and believe that the public role of the man is the more important one?

The general formula for male and female divisions in Judaism could be stated as follows: man's role is to confront the external sphere of existence, woman's is to direct the inner sphere, the one relating to the home, the bastion of Jewish strength and continuity. To the woman is assigned the task of molding the character and personality of the individual during childhood

R. SAMSON RAPHAEL HIRSCH ON JUDAISM'S ROLE DIVISIONS

R. Samson Raphael Hirsch presents the Jewish view according to Genesis:

> For the performance of Man's task of building up the world, [God] reckoned on the harmonious cooperation of both sexes. . . . "It is not good that man should be alone" – the . . . task is too great for one; it requires essentially two human beings who can share the work and carry it through, compensating for each other's deficiencies. "I will provide for him a helpmeet (*ezer kenegdo*)." A helpmeet is that kind of assistance which through taking over a part of the work . . . allows the . . . partner to concentrate his attention on the [other]. . . . This is the

> essence of the division of labor. If . . . the whole work is to be carried out as efficiently as possible, then it is essential that their powers and abilities should be of different kinds, and yet so interrelated as to supplement one another, one being strong where the other is weak.
>
> This is forcibly indicated in the added word *kenegdo* (lit. opposite him). *Neged* assigns to an object a different place, but one determined by the position of the other. It places the woman forthwith on a footing of equality with the man, while giving to each a different sphere of activity, so that the man cannot fill the position of the woman nor the woman that of the man. Both . . . by their cooperation consummate the human task. This partition of the human task in society is no mere matter of agreement; the woman has from the very beginning been created *kenegdo* [so that both can supplement each other's] activity. They are fashioned for one another and for carrying out the same task together. . . . That is the deep design of God in the founding of marriage.[5]

Jewish law takes care to rule out potentially harmful ambiguities in the psychological development of the growing child. It clearly defines the responsibilities incumbent upon the members of each sex, while allowing for a certain overlap where each can participate to some extent in functions primarily associated with the other gender. In such a climate, maturing young people develop a thorough understanding of their identities, both as members of their respective genders and of the Jewish people. With their natural inclinations allowed to flourish, they follow natural and healthy paths to adulthood and become mature individuals with a strong sense of purpose in life.

R. Samson Raphael Hirsch contends that the molder of character occupies the more significant role in Jewish development.

> According to God's word, the center of gravity of the spiritual and moral human-to-be is the spiritual and moral character and influence of the mother. Even at the highest level of society, when the divinely written history of the Jewish state lists the kings of Judah–the men who brought blessing or curse upon their people–it never fails to name the mother, to credit or blame her . . . surely in order to teach us that if one of them "did what is righteous in God's eyes" and the other did "what is evil in God's eyes" all this is rooted in his mother's lap, her heart, her glances and her words. . . .[6]

If R. Hirsch is correct that it is the woman's influence that moves history even in the external sphere, then perhaps our commonly accepted interpretations of historical events could bear reexamination.

In Hebrew, the word "father," *av*, is spelled with the first two letters of the alphabet, *aleph* and *bet*, indicating that he is to set the pace. *Em*, the Hebrew word for mother, is made up of the first and middle letters of the alphabet, *aleph* and *mem*, indicating that she is to unify the family, as the center unifies the whole.

DISTINCTIVE TRAITS OF THE WOMAN

"Nothing is more dear to God than modesty," teaches the Midrash, "it is a trait especially beloved by God."[7]

Modesty, or *tzeniut*, is one of the three character traits considered central to Jews.[8] The modest person demonstrates that he or she lives with a constant awareness of the presence of God.

Tzeniut nurtures an awareness of privacy, a knowledge that the inner space takes precedence over the external. Sensitivity to *tzeniut* affects both attitude and behavior: speech, dress, appearance, and comportment. *Tzeniut* is incumbent upon all Jews. However, women surpass men in sensitivity and privacy.[9]

King David teaches: "*Kol kevudah bat melech penimah*, All glorious is the princess within."[10]

This verse expresses the Jewish attitude toward the private nature of women. *Rashi*, the great eleventh-century commentator, relates this verse to the reserve and modesty of women and their relationship to the palace of Judaism – the home.[11]

Sarah, the mother of the Jewish people, personified the idea of privacy.[12] When the angels visit Abraham and ask where Sarah is, he replies, "In the tent."[13] *Rashi* comments: "*Tzenuah hi*," She is a private person.[14] Although he was the public person and she the private, Sarah surpassed Abraham in prophetic power.[15] Can one postulate from Sarah a correlation between privateness and spiritual power?

The Sages teach that God created woman from a hidden part of man to demonstrate that she was to be *ishah tzenuah, ishah tzenuah*, a modest woman.[16] The double use of the Hebrew phrase emphasizes the extent to which inwardness is essential to femininity. The Talmud says further:

> God said: I will not create her from the head so that she will not be prideful; nor from the eye so that she should not be seductive; nor from the ear so that she should not be an eavesdropper; nor from the mouth so that she should not eavesdrop; nor from the heart so that she should not be jealous; nor from the hand so that she should not be acquisitive; nor from the foot so that she should not wander about; but from a part of the body which is hidden, so that she should be modest.[17]

The Talmud instructs men to be grateful for their women. A heretic once spoke to R. Gamliel. He accused God of being a thief, since He stole one of Adam's ribs in order to create Eve. Barthea, R. Gamliel's daughter, overheard the conversation. She asked her father whether she might reply. She said to the unbeliever: "Please give me a gold ducat." "Why do you need a gold ducat?" he asked. Replied Barthea: "Thieves came in the night and stole a liter of silver and left a liter of gold instead." "And this is thievery!" exclaimed the heretic. "Would that such thieves would come to my house every night!" At this R. Gamliel's daughter responded: "Was it not therefore a marvelous thing that God did and substituted a wife instead?"[18]

WOMEN'S UNDERSTANDING

The Talmud teaches: "It is the way of a woman to stay at home, and the way of a man to go out to the marketplace and [there] he will learn *binah* (understanding) from others."[19]

To attain his wisdom, a man must go to the external world, to the "marketplace." *Binah* is a characteristic that women innately possess and need not go out to acquire. The Talmud teaches: "The Holy One granted woman with *binah yeteirah*, a greater understanding, than He gave to man."[20]

Men are directed to ask, and follow, their wives' counsel: "*Ittecha gutza gahin vetilhash lah*, If your wife is short bend down and whisper in her ear [consult with her]."[21]

Elsewhere the Sages take for granted that intelligent men take the counsel of their wives.[22]

Alexander the Great was defeated only once, and that by women, says the Midrash:

> When Alexander of Macedon arrived at Kartigna,[23] the country inhabited entirely by women, its leaders came out to greet Alexander and said: "If you make war against us and defeat us, your name will go forth in the world as one who laid waste a province of women. If, however, we make war on you and defeat you, your name will go forth in the world as of one whom women made war against and defeated, so that henceforth you will be ashamed to face any king." Humbled, Alexander left, but before he did so he wrote upon the city gate: "I, Alexander of Macedon, was a fool until I came to the principality of Kartigna and learned wisdom from women."[24]

Apocryphal or not, the story dramatically illustrates the esteem in which the wisdom of women was held by the Rabbis: "The continued existence of the world depends more on women [and their wisdom] than on men."[25]

WOMEN: WISE, JUDICIOUS, GOD-FEARING

The Sages teach that in order for a man to understand his wife, he must understand women in general. Thus men should know that women are wiser and endowed with a keener understanding and a sharper sense of judgment than men. From the words of the Shunamite woman in regard to the prophet

Elisha, "Behold, the man of God is holy,"[26] the Rabbis determine that the woman is a better judge of guests than the man.[27]

A man should look for judiciousness in his marital partner: "He who has found a judicious wife has found everything."[28]

A woman is more keen in financial matters. The Talmud teaches: "The woman is more economy-minded than the man."[29]

Women are industrious: "A woman cannot just sit idle."[30]

The woman can be relied upon to be more faithful than the man.[31] This may relate to the conviction of the Sages that men do not feel shame as sensitively as do women.[32] Women are more concerned with chastity.[33]

The Sages find women to be more spiritual than men.[34] Women, the Sages teach, preserve their husbands from sin.[35] They are more sacred and have a more powerful faith: "*Benot Yisrael kedoshot vetehorot hen*–The daughters of Israel are holy and pure."[36]

The woman is more zealous to performs God's will. She will observe her religious obligations more swiftly.

The Midrash teaches:[37]

> Women's faith is stronger than that of men. It was the men among the Israelites who complained in the desert and said, "Let us appoint a leader and return to Egypt."[38] However, the women said, "Grant us a portion among our father's brothers."[39]

Women observe their *mitzvot* more stringently than what is required of them.[40] The Talmud upholds women as exemplars of zealous observance, citing these examples:

Women extend the period of abstention from work on the Sabbath through Saturday night instead of concluding observance at nightfall.

Women abstain from work on *Rosh Hodesh*, the minor festival celebrating the beginning of each month.[41]

Women love *Eretz Yisrael* more and are more desirous of living there than men.[42] *Rashi* teaches that the punishment given to the Israelites of wandering forty years in the wilderness and dying there, having rejected *Eretz Yisrael*, was not extended to the women. The reason, says *Rashi*: "Because they loved the Land of Israel."[43]

WOMEN: MERCY AND COMPASSION

The Talmud compares men and women and finds women consistently more merciful and quicker to extend acts of charity and human kindness.[44] The Sages state: "*Nashim rahmaniyot hen*–Women are [naturally] compassionate."[45]

They add, matter-of-factly, "A woman is more compassionate than a man."[46] The mercifulness of a woman is integral to her being, and results in greater charity.[47] Solomon's paean to the virtuous woman speaks of her charity: "Her hand is stretched out to the poor."[48]

This trait of women is recognized in heaven. The Talmud relates that when R. Abba Hilkiya, the tannaitic Sage, was asked why his wife's prayer for rain was answered before his prayer, he replied that when a man gives charity it is usually money; whereas a woman usually gives food, since she is approached in her home.[49] Giving a hungry person a coin is not equal to giving the person food to eat.

The greater the anonymity, the greater the level of charity, teaches the Talmud. Mar Ukba, the third-century talmudic sage and Babylonian exilarch, was known to be very charitable and very sensitive to the pain felt by the poor. Once Mar Ukba and his wife even ran into a furnace from which the fire had just been swept in order to avoid being discovered by a recipient of their charity. The simmering embers burned Mar Ukba's feet. His wife told him, "Stand on my feet and be protected." So he did, and the embers did not burn her feet. The rabbis determine that her level of charity was greater than his, and in her merit he was protected.[50]

WOMEN AND THE GOLDEN RULE

The Sages teach that women extend more *hesed*, acts of selflessness and loving-kindness, to others. Women are more hospitable, more considerate of the stranger, and more empathetic to the needs of others.[51]

Women initiate and participate in communal charitable endeavors more than men. The Talmud tells of women conducting campaigns for the support of people confined to the Cities of Refuge[52] and of noble Jerusalem women personally proffering medicines to the dying in order to ease their misery.[53]

Women cope with adversity and pain more successfully than men. Their faith is stronger in the face of personal tragedy. The Talmud tells of the mishnaic scholar, R. Meir, and his learned wife Bruriah, whose two sons died on the Sabbath. Bruriah did not inform her husband of their death on his return from the Yeshivah, because she did not want him to grieve on the Sabbath. When the *Havdalah* was performed at the close of the Sabbath, she broached the matter: "Some time ago a man left something in my trust; now he has called for it. Shall I return it to him or not?" "Return it, of course," R. Meir replied. Whereupon Bruriah showed him their dead sons. R. Meir began to weep, and Bruriah asked: "Did you not tell me we must give back that which we have been given in trust? 'The Lord gave and the Lord has taken away.' "[54]

THE INFLUENCE OF WOMEN

Women exercise a powerful influence on men's lives. R. Joshua ben Hananiah's greatness must be attributed to his mother, say the Sages.[55] Further, the Midrash relates:

> A pious couple was unable to have children. They said: "We are of no use to the Holy One," and they divorced. The man then married a wicked woman, and she made him wicked. The woman married a wicked man and she made him righteous. The lesson: All depends upon the woman.[56]

A woman's influence on a man is expressed in a noteworthy passage in the Talmud: "The woman assists the man. . . . She enlightens him and enables him to stand firmly on his own feet."[57]

The talmudic sage R. Elazar ben Azarya, when offered the exalted position of *Nasi*, president of the *Sanhedrin*, the supreme court of Israel, replied that he wished to consult with his wife.

The Midrash comments on God's decision to give the Torah to the women first:

> The Holy One Blessed be He said to Moses, "Go speak to the daughters of Israel [and ask them] whether they wish to receive the Torah." Why were the women asked first? Because the way of men is to follow the opinion of women.[58]

Women have a greater affinity for aesthetics, teach the Sages,[59] and beauty is primarily their domain.[60] This is not merely a secondary characteristic of women, but an integral part of their nature.[61] There are indeed legal obligations imposed upon men to fulfill their wives' aesthetic needs.[62]

WOMEN AS TORAH EDUCATORS

The Sages cite the woman's superior insight and intuition[63] as the basis for her vital role as Torah educator of the young. The passage, "Thus shall you speak to the House of Jacob,"[64] which precedes the giving of the Torah at Sinai, refers to the women, whom God addressed before the men.

The Sages find it noteworthy that God asked Moses to address the women first: "*Shehen mizdarzot bemitzvot*. Because they are are swifter in the performance of *mitzvot*."[65]

> Greater is the reward that the Holy One promised to women than to men[66] . . . for it is the women who send their children to school, watch over them to study the Torah, encourage them with kind words and watch them when they

> slacken their efforts in Torah, and teach them to fear sin while they are still young. Thus it is the righteous women who are responsible for the continuation of Torah and reverence of God. . . .[67]

King Solomon alludes to the importance of the mother's role in Proverbs: "Hearken my son to the ethical discipline of your father and do not forsake the Torah teaching of your mother."[68]

The twelfth-century Spanish commentator R. Abraham ibn Ezra explains: "For it is the woman who is wise; she guides her child in the proper path."[69]

The Torah expects the Jewish mother to lay the foundation for her child's moral life during the impressionable years by instructing the child to walk in the ways of the Torah. Her task is one of gentle guidance and tactful encouragement of the budding young Jewish personality. Perhaps this is why the Torah enjoins children to revere their fathers.[70] Indeed, the Talmud states that children are known to honor their mothers more than their fathers.[71] The father's role is more disciplinary, which is the external aspect of education. This is in keeping with his external, public personality.

WOMEN AS A SOURCE OF NATIONAL MORAL STRENGTH

Women are a source of moral strength to the Jewish people in the face of adversity, declare the Rabbis. It is in the merit of pious women retaining their righteousness in the face of adversity that the Jews were redeemed from Egypt. It is always due to the women that the Jewish people merit redemption from exile.

Women's faith and keener discernment[72] have manifested themselves particularly during the critical points of Jewish history. God's greater faith in the Jewish woman, expressed in His offering women the Torah first,[73] was justified very shortly thereafter. When the men's faith weakened after Moses delayed coming down from Mount Sinai,[74] the Jewish women had both the good sense and the courage to refrain from participating in the creation of the Golden Calf.[75] The Midrash elaborates:

> The women were occupied with protecting Jewish principles at a time when the men were transgressing them. When Aaron said, "Remove your wives' gold earrings,"[76] the women turned down their husbands' requests and objected before them. . . . And the women refused to join their husbands in participating in the sin of the golden calf. . . .[77]

The men did not follow the moral example of the women:

> The men saw that the women would not consent to give their earrings to their husbands. What did they do? Until that hour the earrings were also in their own ears, after the fashion of the Egyptians and after the fashion of the Arabs. They broke off their earrings . . . and gave them to Aaron.[78]

In many other instances the Jewish woman's sense of morality contrasted dramatically with her male counterpart. When the ten spies returned from their surreptitious surveillance of the Promised Land and urged the people to turn back to Egypt and not risk the hazardous military campaign of conquering it, the men called for the election of new leaders who would take them back to Egypt. But the women were unaffected by the spies' warnings, thus demonstrating faith and courage: "The women drew near to request portions of *Eretz Yisrael*."[79]

The biblical account of the forty-year journey to the Promised Land reads like a litany of complaints by the former Egyptian slaves against God and Moses and Aaron. The Sages underscore that the women were not involved in any of the uprisings of the people. They served "at all times . . . [as] the . . . saviors of the Jewish spirit."[80]

In all, there are more than 300 statements in the Talmud and Midrash about women, ranging from the commendatory to the laudatory. There are some atypically negative comments. "Happy is he who has sons; woe to one who has daughters."[81] "He who follows his wife's advice will end in Gehinom."[82] A woman is arrogant,[83] talkative and gossipy,[84] snoopy,[85] lazy,[86] gluttonous,[87] hard,[88] light-minded,[89] inclined to witchcraft,[90] an unclean seductress,[91] and a complex being, peculiar unto herself.[92] And then, suddenly, the Sages teach: "Nothing that You created in woman was created in vain."[93] This statement does not appear paradoxical to one familiar with the Talmud and accustomed to being presented with the facts of down-to-earth reality side by side with a sublime vision of Godly purpose. There is no contradiction.

As for men, they are excitable, especially when their money is at stake,[94] vain,[95] greedy,[96] quarrelsome,[97] injudicious,[98] spendthrifts,[99] whining and complaining,[100] prone to oppressive pessimism,[101] less discerning than women,[102] more sinful than women,[103] more brazen,[104] less merciful and compassionate,[105] more easily swayed than women.[106] Men like to intimidate others,[107] cause trouble and distress, and incite their fellows to forsake the path of life for the path of death.[108]

The Talmud teaches that human beings, man *and* woman, must see each other clearly, without illusions. The powerful bond that unites a Jewish couple is based on realism and on a frank acceptance of human weakness. Their dedication to one another and to God is based on their growing awareness of their own and each other's inner selves, for better and for worse.

Ishto kegufo, a man's wife is like his own body.[109] This is a legal as well as a philosophical principle of Judaism.[110] Also, *baal ke'ishto*, a husband is like his wife, and *ishah kebaalah*, a wife is like her husband.[111] These and other passages in the Talmud teach the interdependence of man and woman.[112]

In the Talmud, wives do not consider themselves subjugated. Women freely, clearly, and at times sharply speak their minds. Jewish law grants women preferential treatment in deference to their lesser physical strength and to their greater obligation in the Jewish home. They are exempt from certain precepts because of their absorbing responsibilities as wives, mothers, and educators of children. Women who are not preoccupied in these roles often adopt certain traditionally male-oriented precepts and activities. But the higher prestige is accorded to the womanly sphere.

Nowhere in Scripture, Talmud, or rabbinic literature is there indication that woman's primary role as foundation in the Jewish household and educator of children is less significant than that of the man's, whose duties lie primarily outside the home.

THE EQUALITY OF STATUS AT CREATION

The account of Creation in Genesis emphasizes the equality of men and women, as well as their differentness. The key passage reads:

> And God created Adam in His own image, in the image of God did He create him. Male and female He created them.[113]

At Creation, Adam is humanity in both its male and female aspects. Equally created and equally directed by God, both of these form the complete human conception–Adam. The sexes are neither superior nor subordinate to each other, but are elevated over other forms of life and granted authority over them. Both equally represent God's image on earth.

The act of deviating from a divine command, in other words, partaking of the Tree of Knowledge–of Good and Evil–effects a revolution in the Creation, the repercussions of which are felt in all existence. The human condition is radically altered. Adam and Eve were punished:

> To the woman He said: I will increase your travail in pregnancy; in travail shall you bear children; and your longing shall be for your husband, and he shall rule over you. And to the man He said: Because you hearkened to your wife's voice and ate of the tree which I commanded you not to eat, the ground will be cursed for your sake; with travail shall you eat of it all the days of your life.[114]

THE CONSEQUENCES OF THE NEW RELATIONSHIP

The woman's new dependence on the man is a result of the dramatically altered relationship of humanity to the earth following Adam and Eve's disobedience to God. Man and woman are no longer able to transcend nature and the physical realm of existence; they have become part of it. Before, humanity was immortal, and not subject to the laws of entropy. Now, humanity has become rooted in the physical reality. Heretofore, the earth freely gave its food; now humanity must toil to bring forth food. Previously, woman freely and effortlessly bore children; now she must labor to bring them forth. The added labor and increased effort and duration of childbearing have diminished her physical competitiveness, and the result is a reliance upon man. Man has become transformed into breadwinner for the childbearing and child-rearing woman.

Woman's forced dependence on the man seriously undermines the position of the woman in the world and the equality with which man and woman were created. Consequently, the Torah is concerned that man's misuse of his breadwinning role to the detriment of the woman may alter the original equality between the sexes. It therefore reinforces woman's position to reduce the *de facto* imbalance in the man's favor.

After Eve's transgression, the Torah declares the man the dominant partner in the relationship. However, there is hardly any mention of this in the Talmud or in the writings of the Sages. The Talmud refers to R. Bava ben Buta blessing an obedient wife,[115] and there is a midrashic passage referring to the proper wife as the one who performs her husband's wishes,[116] but these are the only references that even hint at any kind of male dominance. *Halachah,* while referring to these statements,[117] nevertheless obligates the husband to honor and respect his wife.[118] Thus, an awareness is manifested of the reality of the general human condition, while, simultaneously, legal and moral guidelines are presented to assure that women are accorded status and are not subjugated.

In Jewish law, a man may not insist that his wife accompany him in a move from village to city or vice versa, or move to another country, even for major economic reasons. Yet, there are instances where the wife may compel her husband to live in another city or country.[119] (Either may compel the other to move to *Eretz Yisrael.*)[120]

THE JEWISH VERSUS THE CHRISTIAN ATTITUDES

Nowhere in the Torah is the wife directed to be subject to or subordinate to her husband as Christianity directs wives to be.[121] Nowhere does the Torah stipulate that the man be the "head" of the woman, as does the New Testament.[122] The Torah does not direct the woman to relate to her husband as she relates to God, as Christianity directs.[123] Nor does it compel the woman to show obedience to her husband and remain silent before him as the New Testament repeatedly does.[124] Such a notion is utterly incompatible with

Judaism. The word "*kenegdo*," or opposite him, in the account of Creation,[125] indicates a balanced partnership of a complementary nature. Judaism requires the woman, like the man, to be subordinate to God. Directives to the woman are sprinkled liberally throughout the New Testament.[126] Their effect has been to undo the rights given to women by the Torah at Sinai, when clear guidelines were provided for the status and treatment of the woman 1,500 years before the advent of Christianity.

IN THE TORAH: MAN'S DUTIES, WOMAN'S RIGHTS

In its concern with offsetting the naturally dominant position of the male, the Torah's guidelines mention only the rights that woman has in marriage. In regard to the man, the Torah lays down only the duties that he has toward his wife. It says nothing of the man's rights in marriage, nor of the obligations of the wife.

Certainly a Jewish husband has marital rights, as has the Jewish wife marital obligations. Yet these are only scantily implied in the Torah and elaborated on somewhat in the Talmud. The Torah is acutely concerned that the woman's position be not lowered to one of obeissance or subjection to the man. It is concerned to buttress the woman's position so that she enjoys equality in fact, and not only in theory.

The man is physically the stronger and the more outgoing, and therefore the initiative for marriage and divorce is placed primarily in his hands. It is the woman, therefore—and not the man—who requires protection. For this reason, it is the wife who receives the *ketubah*, the marital protective writ, from her husband, and it is the husband who thereby legally and religiously obligates himself to his wife.

R. Eliyahu KiTov, a mid-twentieth-century Jerusalem teacher, remarks:

> It is easy to understand why the Rabbis did not engage in empty talk about "women's equal rights." . . . The Jewish people, living as it does according to God's laws and the Torah, never denies woman her rights and would not be able, even if they wanted to give woman more rights than she possesses. Man and woman are king and queen. Each has different tasks and different sorts of rights. . . .
>
> Man is the revealed part of the world, woman its secret part. Man conquers and woman gives him the strength to do so. Man is the trunk of the tree, woman the hidden well from which the tree draws its sustenance. Man's activities are broad, all-embracing and visible—and this is his advantage over woman. But woman's activities are of more lasting value and her influence is more permanent—and this is her advantage over man.[127]

WOMAN AS THE ENABLER

In her position as *ezer kenegdo*, the Jewish woman is the enabler. Enabling the Torah education of her children, enabling the Torah study of her husband, she is seen as the motivating–or causal–factor in the study of Torah, Judaism's supreme value.

Is this fair? Is woman's significance in this regard that she enables someone else to achieve spiritual gains? And what of her own spirituality? Is her spirituality negligible, insignificant? Furthermore, the idea of "enabler" implies that it is someone else who becomes "able" as a result of her efforts, and not she, the enabler.

The Talmud conveys the opposite message: "*Gadol ham'aseh yoter mei-ha'oseh*–Greater is the one who causes a good deed to be performed than the one who actually does it."[128] In Judaism, enabling is not a secondary act–it is a primary one. The one who induces the performance of a *mitzvah* is not considered as ancillary; that person is the empowerer–the primal cause.

It is the operative principle in charity. Great is the giver, and greater yet is the one who causes the giver to give.[129]

In a talmudic discussion about *olam haba*, paradise, the Talmud teaches:

> Greater is the reward that the Holy One Blessed be He has made to women than that made to me, as we find, "Rise up, you women who are at ease, hearken to my voice; daughters of good faith, listen to my word."[130] Why are women selected for this special merit? Because they take their children to the synagogue to study Torah, they motivate their husbands to study Torah by allowing them time in the House of Study, and they wait up for their husbands to return from the House of Study, and they allow them to go and study Torah in another city.[131]
>
> The Sages add: Thus the righteous women are responsible for the continuation of Torah and reverence for God. For it is they who remind their husbands, when they return from work, tired and weary, to study Torah and give charity.[132]

"Motivating" and "responsible" imply either mutuality or greater power. "Allow"–and this term is used repeatedly–is clearly a reference to power.

The Talmud teaches that the entire process rests on the woman's will. If the woman wills it, there is Torah study. If the woman does not will it, there is no Torah study, regardless of the man's wish. Anecdotal evidence abounds in support of the talmudic thesis that if the wife does not will it, it will not happen.

God enables human beings and strengthens them by His will. So, too, a wife enables her husband and strengthens him by her will. Enabling is an act of *hesed*, generosity and loving-kindness. God's creation of human beings and granting them strength is considered a supreme act of *hesed*. Indeed, all God's deeds on behalf of humans are acts of *hesed*.

The woman's gift of strength to the man is pure *hesed*. She herself is exempt from the precept of studying Torah. She does not need it. For the man's sake, in order to fulfill his need for Torah study, she obliges him to persevere—and she empowers him to do so.

As God, with no expectation of "payment," gives strength to the weary,[133] so too the woman, with no expectation of payment, gives her man the strength to persevere in his toil of studying Torah.

Hesed is at the heart of Judaism—the means for fulfilling the precept of loving one's fellow, the great rule of the Torah.[134] *Hesed* involves love of God, the most sublime duty of the Jew. The Midrash teaches: The inner meaning of the precept that "you shall love the Lord your God with all your heart, with all your soul and with all your might,"[135] is that "you shall *cause* the name of God to be loved by others."[136]

MOTHER OF A SAGE

The Talmud tells of R. Yossi's mother, who would bring his crib to the academy so that when he grew up he would be accustomed to the sounds of Torah study.[137] Did R. Yossi's father not contribute to the development of the great sage? Did he not at least provide for the family's sustenance? Might he not even have fulfilled the *mitzvah* of teaching his son Torah? Yet the Talmud does not mention him at all in relation to R. Yossi's spiritual development. It is his mother's efforts that brought it forth.

THE IGNORANT SHEPHERD AND THE WISE YOUNG WOMAN

R. Akiva was discovered by Rachel. He was an ignorant shepherd employed by her father, the rich Calba Savua. With deep insight, Rachel sensed a powerful potential in the illiterate shepherd. She proposed marriage to Akiva on condition that he go and study Torah, and then married him against her father's will. Calba Savua disinherited her, and she lived a life of isolation, poverty, and deprivation. Beginning at the age of forty, Akiva studied with great intensity. He developed the potential that Rachel had seen and went on to become one of the greatest sages and scholars of history. It was Rachel who altered the course of the shepherd's life. By her will he became the intellectual giant, the legendary R. Akiva, whose teachings have profoundly influenced the spiritual life of the Jewish people for two millennia. R. Akiva told his students: "*Sheli veshelachem shelah hu*—Whatever I have achieved and whatever you have achieved is due to her."[138]

THE WOMAN OF TORCHES

"And Deborah was a prophetess, the woman of Lapidot who judged Israel at that time."[139]

What is *eishet Lapidot*, "the woman of Lapidot?" ask the Sages. Was her husband named Lapidot? No, she was "the woman of torches–*lapidot*" (*lapid* is Hebrew for torch; plural *lapidot*). This refers to Deborah's custom of preparing wicks and bringing torches to the Temple and to public houses of Torah study and of kindling their lamps. This earned her the popular title of "the woman of the torches."

Deborah enabled the continuation of prayer and Torah study. This was her greatness, the Sages teach.[140] Her great prophetic status notwithstanding, she personally pursued the mundane task of kindling torches. With her prophetic power she accurately assessed the premium that God placed on enabling Torah study. She devoted herself to this as to the most sublime of tasks.

A WOMAN OF VALOR

R. Samson Raphael Hirsch comments on King Solomon's ode to the Woman of Valor in Proverbs:

> Even if from all the past history of our womanhood, the word of the Sacred Scriptures would have preserved for us nothing else but this one glorious testimonial, this one hymn in itself would be a most forceful refutation of the fable fabricated by inconceivable thoughtlessness that the Jewish woman of ancient history had been enslaved and degraded. . . .[141]

George Foot Moore, the Christian theologian, orientalist, and professor of theology and history of religion at Harvard University, comments:

> The social and religious position of woman in Judaism is . . . a moral achievement. That it [has always existed and] was no recent achievement in our period is shown by the eulogy of the good wife and mother in Proverbs 31.[142]

Nothing in the ancient literature of any people in the world attests to the dignity and worth accorded the woman as does this remarkable ode to the Jewish woman in The Book of Proverbs:

> Who can find a woman of valor?
>   She is more precious than gems.
> Her husband's heart trusts in her
>   and there will be no lack of gain.
> She repays his good, but does him no harm
>   all the days of her life.

She seeks out wool and flax,
and works with willing hands.
She is like a merchant ship,
she brings food from afar.
She rises while it is yet night
and provides food for her household and tasks for her maidens.
She considers a field and buys it;
from her earnings she plants a vineyard.
She girds her loins with strength
and makes her arms strong.
She perceives that her enterprise is good;
and her lamp is not snuffed out at night.
She puts out her hand to the distaff,
and her palm holds the spindle.
She opens her hand to the poor,
and extends them to the destitute.
She fears not frost for her household,
for she has clothed them all in fine wool.
She makes her own tapestries;
but her clothing is of fine linen and purple.
Distinctive in the councils is her husband,
when he sits among the elders of the land.
She makes cloaks to sell,
and delivers belts to the peddler.
Strength and dignity are her garb,
and smiling she faces the future.
She opens her mouth with wisdom,
and the teaching of lovingkindness is on her tongue.
She looks after the conduct of her household,
and does not partake of the bread of idleness.
Her children rise and praise her;
her husband also, and he exalts her:
"Many women have done excellently,
but you surpass them all."
Charm is deceptive, beauty is vain,
but the God-fearing woman is deservant of praise.
Acclaim her for her accomplishments!
and let her deeds hail her at the gates.[143]

The Jewish woman is praised for all she does and is – her work, her caring, her love, her compassion, her wisdom – with which she sustains the family and sees it through. This paean of love and gratitude is an integral part of the Sabbath eve liturgy that precedes the festive Sabbath meal. Every Friday evening in the Jewish home, as the family sits around the table at the start of the weekly Sabbath eve feast, the husband and the children sing this 3,000-year-old hymn of praise to the *Eishet Hayil*, the Jewish wife and mother.

III

Women in the Torah

4

Women in the Bible and the Talmud

Section 1: In the Bible

BIBLICAL WOMEN AS INSPIRATION

Though we may analyze the position of the Jewish woman and compare her to women in other societies, the only way to capture the essence of what she stands for is to turn to Judaism's source–the Bible. The Jewish people look to the heroes of the Bible as sources of inspiration. In every age the men and women of the Bible are viewed as paradigms to be emulated by Jews, their character traits to be studied.

The four Matriarchs–together with the three Patriarchs–are considered to be the founders of the Jewish people. Even in biblical times, the Matriarchs, the mothers of the Jewish people, were singled out in the Bible as examples to be emulated. Ruth, for example, is blessed that she be "like Rachel and Leah, the two of whom built the House of Israel."[1] To this day Jewish parents bless their daughters at the Sabbath eve feast that they should be like Sarah, Rebeccah, Rachel, and Leah.

The blessing given to Ruth emphasizes the significance of the role of the woman in the Bible as mother. Indeed, Ruth became the grandmother of King David, from whom, according to tradition, the Messiah will issue. These biblical heroines believed that their most important mission was to raise and nurture the next generation of the House of Israel.

THE MOTHER IN ANCIENT ISRAEL

Women had a primary role of the utmost significance in ancient Jewish society. Child bearing and raising children were highly regarded functions and were seen as essential to the survival of the Jewish people. Women who fulfilled this role served an importance that is perhaps difficult to understand in modern times. In view of the high death rate that must have existed for women in childbirth in ancient times, we may appreciate the significance of the blessings in Psalms given to the "man who walks in God's ways":

> Your wife will be as a fruitful vine
> Within your house;
> Your children will be as olive shoots
> Around your table.
>
> Lo, so shall the man be blessed
> Who reveres the Lord:
> May God bless you from Zion
> And may you see the good of Jerusalem
> All the days of your life.
> And may you see children born to your children,
> And may there be peace upon Israel.[2]

The welfare of Israel is related to fecundity. Motherhood is associated with joy. The Psalmist sings:

> He gives the barren woman a home.
> He makes her the joyous mother of children,
> Praise be God.[3]

Just as fertility is associated with blessing, barrenness is associated with punishment for transgressions.[4] In gratefulness for life, which woman grants, and in recognition of her crucial role in building the House of Israel, the mother was treated with immense respect. Children were commanded to honor[5] and revere[6] mothers, as they were expected to act toward their fathers. The manner in which the Jew is expected to express filial honor is exemplified by King Solomon. When his mother, Bathsheba, entered the royal chamber,

> the king rose from his throne and went forward to meet her. He bowed down before her. He sat on his throne and had a seat brought for the king's mother, and she sat on his right.[7]

All of Solomon's actions in relation to his mother's entrance illuminate the extraordinary respect with which the mother was held in the Bible. The mother was seen as both granting life and exerting the greatest influence on the children's character and development. Judaism sees motherhood as the most creative human act–and as the very essence of femaleness.

It is not merely the physical process of bringing children into the world and nurturing them to which we refer, although many women experience intense spirituality in the process of childbirth and raising children. Through motherhood women are seen as transcending the present dimension, because it serves as a means for women's physical/spiritual link between past, present, and future. Through motherhood and through the nurturing and rearing of children and thus through personal involvement in the coming generation, women are able to shape the future; they utilize their influence on their children to bend the future to their will.

Mothers' importance in Jewish thought might thus be understood from the frequent mention of the mothers of kings throughout the Bible. Significantly, the mothers are almost always identified by name, although they play no role in the associated biblical narrative. Thus, women exerted a powerful influence on and forged major changes in the direction and destiny of the Jewish people through their roles as mothers and *materfamilias*.

We here examine some heroic figures in the Bible and the Talmud to determine their historical and religious significance and the character traits they exhibited.

THE MATRIARCHS: SPIRITUALITY, POWER, AND INFLUENCE

Sarah, Spiritual Paradigm

In the biblical story of Abraham, the Patriarch is obviously the central figure. He is the first one to recognize God as Creator of the universe, while his wife Sarah, the first Jewish mother, is seemingly a background figure. However, Sarah, as she appears in the Torah and in rabbinic writings, is a fascinating, multidimensional and influential figure, a woman of strength and confidence, and a powerful model of women's spirituality.[8]

Perhaps the most significant statement characterizing both God's assessment of Sarah and the relationship between Abraham and Sarah is the passage in which God, speaking to Abraham, says: "In everything that Sarah says to you, hearken to her voice."[9] Comments R. Samson Raphael Hirsch:

> Listen to the voice of Sarah even if the content of her words do not appeal to you. Trust her judgement. Her insights are deeper than yours, just as in general women have a more profound insight into human nature than men.[10]

Elsewhere, the Torah says: "And Abraham listened to the voice of his wife Sarah."[11] *Rashi*, the French medieval commentator on the Torah, comments that she was a prophetess.[12] Moreover, the Sages determine that Sarah was superior to Abraham in this respect; her power of prophecy was greater.[13]

Sarah was a woman of power. Sarah's spiritual powers were such that she could effect significant changes in her environment. When Abraham and Sarah went to Egypt, the Torah says:

> And the Egyptians saw that the woman was very beautiful, and then Pharaoh's ministers saw her and they praised her before Pharaoh, and she was taken to Pharaoh's palace. . . . And God caused Pharaoh and his household to be afflicted with great plagues *al d'var Sarai eishet Avraham,* because of Sarai, Abraham's wife.[14]

Of the affliction, the Midrash relates that Pharaoh was afflicted with a kind of skin disease or inflamatory gonorrhea affecting his ability to have sexual relations.[15] The Midrash relates, on the basis of the phrase *al devar Sarai,* literally "because of the word of Sarai" (Sarah's earlier name), that Sarah instructed an angel to smite Pharaoh accordingly, and her instructions were followed to the letter.[16]

Sarah: Modesty and Reserve, Power and Influence

Abraham played a very public role in going out to the unbelievers in his generation, preaching monotheism and teaching them to follow in the ways of God. However, Sarah (whose name means chieftainness or princess), unlike her husband, was a private person who was reserved, preferred to be in the background, and personified the Jewish ideal of *tzeniut,* modesty.[17] Sarah was not a pretty accessory to Abraham; she was a spiritually powerful person who taught the principles of monotheism to women. She was so successful in her work that eventually Abraham established a separate tent for her activities.[18]

She performed her tasks with modesty and reserve inside their home,[19] seeking guests, welcoming them, preparing food for them, and performing acts of loving-kindness for others. Abraham is considered to have "brought light" into the world through his conversion to monotheism, against the accepted belief of an entire generation of idol-worshippers. The light that Sarah brought, that of the Jewish home, was symbolized by a light that burned in her tent throughout her life.

When an aged Sarah eventually gave birth to Isaac in fulfillment of God's promise, it is as if God, through this miracle, concluded a separate covenant with Sarah, as he had done with Abraham through circumcision. It is through

Isaac that the Jewish people would be perpetuated. By this act God established a maternal line, whereby Sarah's son Isaac, whom Sarah had carried and delivered–and not Hagar's son, Ishmael, who had also been circumcized–would continue the Jewish line.

In her quiet way, Sarah made her power and influence felt in the household. When she realized, long before her husband did, that Ishmael's behavior and his proximity to Isaac were a threat to the development of Isaac's character as a founder of the Jewish nation, Sarah did not hesitate to approach Abraham and bid that he act upon the matter immediately. When Abraham, however, hesitated to send his son Ishmael away with the boy's mother Hagar into the solitary desert, God came to the Patriarch and told him to hearken to Sarah's request.[20] Sarah's insight, God indicated to Abraham, was better than his, and her understanding of the situation was deeper than Abraham's. The wife and mother, the Torah teaches here, is often gifted with greater perception and wisdom, what the Talmud calls the *binah yeteirah*, or greater discernment of women.[21] God's advice to Abraham has been repeated countless times by the Rabbis, as sage counsel to all generations of Jewish husbands from Abraham's time to our own.

Rebeccah: Loving-kindness and Discernment

Eliezer, Abraham's servant, went on a mission for his master, to search for a wife for Abraham's son Isaac. Abraham abjured Eliezer not to look for a woman among the idolatrous Canaanites, whose women were morally corrupt. He was to seek purity of character, which would be manifested through *hesed*, the performance of acts of loving-kindness. In the words of R. Samson Raphael Hirsch:

> How [was he] to fill the gap left in the house of Abraham by the demise of Sarah? Not by her wealth, not by her physical charms, not by her intellectual attainments would he recognize her, but by her character, by the goodness of her heart, by her readiness to help others, in a word by her *gemilut hesed*, by that trait which is the outstanding characteristic of the sons of Abraham and Sarah. . . . That [would be] the maiden in whom he would recognize the heaven-sent spouse of Isaac the worshipper of God.[22]

Rebeccah more than demonstrated this trait when she not only offered water to Eliezer, who was tired from his long trek though the desert, but made numerous trips to the well to feed all his many camels as well. It was the trait of *hesed*, more than any other, that made her worthy of being part of Abraham's household, and a Matriarch of the Jewish people.

Rebeccah followed in Sarah's footsteps, demonstrating the same keen insight into her children and into the future. Commenting on the verse, "And

Isaac took her into the tent of his mother Sarah,"[23] *Rashi* says that she modeled herself after Sarah. According to Jewish tradition, as long as Sarah lived, a cloud representing the *Shechinah*, the Spirit of God, hovered over the tent, which vanished when Sarah died, and returned when Rebeccah entered it. The Midrash says that the candle that burned in the tent throughout the week was snuffed out when Sarah died and was rekindled only when Rebeccah came into the tent.[24] Similarly, the tent was always wide open for hospitality as long as Sarah lived, but was closed when she died, and with Rebeccah's entry the tent was opened again and the hospitality renewed.

Rebeccah's Superior Insight

Rebeccah, like Sarah, was a prophetess who received prophetic insights to which her husband Isaac was not privy. With her superior insight she understood that although her son Jacob was spiritually inclined, his twin, Esau, the hunter, possessed a wicked nature, although he demonstrated piety in his father's presence. Rebeccah realized that Esau was morally and spiritually unfit to receive his father's blessing, to carry on the heritage of Abraham and Isaac and to be one of the forefathers of the Jewish people.

Without consulting her husband, who may have been unaware of Esau's nature and was close to him, she acted against his wishes and maneuvered the matter so that Jacob, the younger of the twins, would receive Isaac's blessing. As the personification of truth, Jacob's nature revolted against deception of any kind, and he objected to his mother's strategem. Yet Jacob acceded to his mother, bowed to her greater wisdom and prophetic vision, and the scheme succeeded.

Events bore out the truth of Rebeccah's wisdom and foresight. Esau was found to be a murderer and idolator and one unsuited to be a founder of the Jewish people. As Sarah had decided to separate Isaac from Ishmael against Abraham's wishes, so Rebeccah recognized more than her holy husband did that the influence of a wicked sibling on Jacob would mold his character in a negative way.

Despite the pain of a mother at having the son whom she loves leave her, Rebeccah's deep faith and her vision that Jacob was destined to follow in the spiritual footsteps of Abraham and Isaac convinced her that the difficult decision was the best one. She arranged for Jacob to flee from Esau and travel to her family, where he would develop without the influence of his brother and where he would not marry Canaanite wives as had Esau, an act that Rebeccah considered an abomination.

In their concern for the spiritual welfare of their children and their destiny, Sarah and Rebeccah manifest a deep awareness of the values that Judaism has ever since considered important in life–not material gain, not great wealth, but bringing children into the world, being concerned with and providing for their spiritual well-being, and molding them into moral human beings.

Rachel and Leah, Builders of the House of Israel

In a virtual replay of what had occurred with his mother, Jacob recognized that Rachel, whom he had met at the well when he reached Haran, was destined to be his future wife through her act of *hesed* in giving water to him and his camels.

When Jacob had completed the seven years of labor he was to perform for Rachel's father, Laban, for Rachel's hand in marriage, Rachel and Jacob arranged secret signs between them so that Jacob would know that the heavily veiled bride was indeed Rachel. True to his crafty nature and to Jacob's fears, the wily Laban planned to substitute Leah for Rachel as Jacob's bride, with a subsequent explanation that in his circles it was unheard of for a younger sister to be married before the older one. Rachel, who very much wanted to wed Jacob, in a supreme act of altruistic *hesed*, revealed the secret signs to Leah in order to save her sister from ignominy and embarrassment; whereupon Jacob worked an additional seven years for the privilege of marrying Rachel.

It was Rachel's *hesed*, more than any shown by the three Patriarchs, that caused God to redeem the Israelites from Egyptian bondage. Many years later when the Israelites were in exile, according to the Midrash, the Patriarchs in heaven interceded with God to redeem the Jews. One by one, Abraham, Isaac, and Jacob approached the Heavenly throne to plead with God to take the Jews out of exile on the strength of the Patriarchs' respective merits: Abraham brought up his willingness to sacrifice his only son Isaac when he was tested; Isaac his readiness to be sacrificed; Jacob the great suffering he had undergone all his life. Yet by all their pleas God was unmoved. But when Rachel came forward and reminded God of her readiness to lose her future husband, Jacob, to sacrifice her happiness, and even her place as one of the Matriarchs of Israel rather than to cause her sister embarrassment, God instantly responded to her prayer.

ANCIENT MARRIAGE WITHOUT A DOWRY

It was standard practice in ancient times for marriages to involve dowries that would be turned over to the groom by the father of the bride. No dowry was given to Jacob with his wife. Indeed, he had to work seven hard years for the hand in marriage of each of the sisters, and after fourteen years of service at no pay, which left him as poor as he was when he started, he had to work another six years in order to establish himself economically and be enabled to support his wives and his children. R. Hirsch points out that devoting all these years to work for his wives demonstrates how unlike "oriental degradation" was the nature of Jewish marriage and the Jewish home.[25]

The greatest source of fulfillment for both Rachel and Leah was in giving birth to children and rearing them. Because Leah was less loved, God compensated her with the gift of motherhood, and she bore seven children. But Rachel's greatest source of sorrow and deprivation was in being barren for many years. Both sisters felt a profound fulfillment of destiny through the life-giving process. God answered Rachel's prayers and gave her a child.[26] Rashi comments that this was God's reward to Rachel for her selflessness in giving Leah the secret signs with Jacob so that Leah could marry Jacob first.[27]

Rachel was eventually to give birth to two children, and Leah and Rachel gave to Jacob their handmaidens, who bore additional children. Interestingly, Jacob did not name any of his children. The fact that all the children were named by Rachel and Leah illuminates the position that the women occupied in the household. Similarly, Jacob did not decide to return home to *Eretz Yisrael*—even after having been directed to do so by God—until he had first discussed the matter at length with Rachel and Leah, and they had agreed.[28]

TAMAR—FORCED TO TAKE THE INITIATIVE

From its beginning Judaism has expressed cognizance of the sexuality of both men and women and an awareness of its power. As a fundamental human trait provided by God for the purpose of the continuity of the race, humans were directed to use their sexuality in order to further God's aims. With the candor that distinguishes the entire Bible, the early leaders of the Jewish people are depicted as human beings, with all their strengths and weaknesses. Yet the Torah is never merely a book of stories—always, there are moral lessons to be derived from the lives and acts of Israel's founding fathers and mothers.

Jacob and Leah's son Judah married Shua, and they had three children, Er, Onan, and Shelah. Er, who married Tamar, the daughter of a priest, died as a young man, and Judah arranged a levirate marriage for Tamar with Onan, the customary procedure in biblical times whereby the brother of a man who dies childless marries the widow in order for children to be brought up in the name of the deceased. Unhappy at the prospect of fathering children who would not be his own, Onan "spills his seed" so that Tamar would not conceive. Whereupon God punished Onan and he died. With Shelah too young to fulfill his levirate duty, Judah asked Tamar to await Shelah's maturation.

After waiting a considerable length of time and seeing that Judah was not acting on her behalf, the twice-widowed Tamar decided to move on her own. According to the Midrash, Tamar had been foretold that she would bear a son of the seed of Judah.[29] Since Shelah, Judah's only living son was not being married to her, Tamar took the initiative to have Judah father her son.

THE MOTHER OF KINGS OF ISRAEL

Upon learning that Judah was embarking on a journey, she exchanged her mourner's clothes for attractive garments and went to a crossroad where she knew Judah would pass. She disguised herself as a harlot and seduced him as he came by. Not knowing she was his daughter-in-law, Judah came to Tamar. He promised her a sheep as payment, and pending receipt of the sheep Tamar took his cloak, staff, and signet ring as security. When a servant returned with the sheep there was no one there.

Upon learning, three months later, that his daughter-in-law Tamar was pregnant, Judah became furious at the shame she was bringing to the family, and in accordance with the custom of the times he called for her to be brought before him for judgment so that she could be put to death. This punishment conformed to the legal code of the time for sexual immorality committed by a priest's daughter. Tamar sent him his cloak, staff, and ring and asked Judah to recognize them, saying: "I have conceived by the one to whom these belong."[30]

Judah realized that he had wronged Tamar by not having married her to Shelah as he had promised. She then joined him, and she gave birth to twins, Peretz and Zerah. Boaz, who married Ruth, was a direct descendant of Peretz,[31] and King David was the grandson of Boaz.[32] *Rashi* cites the Sages to underscore that Tamar, who was forced to forthrightly take matters into her own hands, was a chaste, modest woman. God rewarded her, and she was destined to become the mother of kings in Israel.[33]

JEWISH PROPHETESSES

The term *neviah*, prophetess, is applied to five women in the Bible—to Miriam,[34] Deborah,[35] the wife of Isaiah,[36] Huldah,[37] and Noadiah.[38] Additionally, Hanah is considered a prophetess,[39] as are Sarah,[40] Abigail,[41] and Esther.[42] A total of twenty-three prophetesses are listed by the Sages.[43] One biblical passage assumes the natural presence of prophetesses along with prophets.[44] Indeed, the Sages stress that there were as many prophetesses in Israel as there were prophets.[45]

The prophet Micah gave equal status to Miriam as a leader alongside Moses and Aaron.[46] Ezekiel complains of unworthy female prophets as he does of unworthy male prophets.[47] When Deborah spoke to the people with the authority of prophecy it was in terms different from those used by the male prophets of Israel.[48]

HULDAH

Huldah[49] was the major prophetess, and an influential one. A contemporary of Jeremiah, she spoke in a basically similar style[50] as that of her male counterpart, and in their time she may have been as well known as he. It was thought that she preached mostly to women.[51] Huldah was said to have headed an academy for the study of Torah in Jerusalem.[52]

King Josiah consulted Huldah "to inquire of the Lord" when the Torah scroll was found in the Temple. The Sages say Huldah was consulted rather than Jeremiah because as a woman she was considered to be more compassionate and therefore more likely to intercede on behalf of the people than would Jeremiah.[53] The proud, dignified answer of the prophetess was that misfortune could not be avoided. God would judge the nation because the people had forsaken God and were serving idols.[54]

However, the destruction of the Temple would not take place, she said consolingly, until after the death of Josiah, who had repented. In view of Huldah's prophecy and the imminent destruction of the Temple, Josiah hid the Temple treasures and ritual appurtenances in order to guard them against their being taken by the enemy.

MIRIAM

In the Torah we find women playing significant roles in politics and government[55] and being renowned for their wisdom[56] Their influence is clearly seen at critical points. The Talmud reports that Miriam the prophetess, later to lead the women as Moses led the men, shaped the courageous response of the Jewish nation to Pharaoh's decree to drown all Jewish infant boys that were born in the Nile:

> "And a man of the house of Levi [Amram, father of Moses, Aaron, and Miriam] went and took a daughter who was a Levite."[57] Where did he go? R. Judah bar Z'vina said, "He went after the advice of his daughter" [Miriam].
>
> Amram was the *gadol hador*, the most learned and esteemed of his generation, and all followed his guidance. When he saw that Pharaoh the wicked king commanded every Jewish male son to be drowned in the Nile, he said: "We are all laboring for nothing." [Our sons will be drowned upon birth.] He thereupon

> divorced his wife [Yocheved]. Whereupon all the Jews followed his example and did likewise.
>
> Then Miriam said to him: "Your act is worse than Pharaoh's! He decreed only that male children not be permitted to live, but you decreed the same fate for both male and female children! . . . It is uncertain whether or not Pharaoh's decree will be fulfilled. However, there is no doubt that your decree will indeed be fulfilled." [If there are no married Jewish men and women there will be no Jewish children.] Whereupon Amram remarried Yocheved and all the other Jewish husbands then remarried their wives.[58]

Thereafter, a boy was born to Amram and Yocheved whose name was Moses, who was destined to lead the Israelites out of Egyptian bondage to freedom. When Pharaoh decreed that all Jewish male children be drowned in the Nile at birth, the God-fearing Jewish midwives Shifra and Puah arranged to save many of the children[59] and then fed them. The Sages say that as a result of the efforts of these women for the Jewish nation, they were destined to have many illustrious descendants, and the royal line of Israel was established.[60]

Miriam, Moses' sister, watched in hiding over her infant brother as he was placed in a tiny ark in the water to escape Pharaoh's soldiers. When he was removed from the water by Pharaoh's daughter, Batyah, according to tradition it was Miriam who arranged for his own mother Yocheved to be his nurse.[61]

THE PIVOTAL ROLE OF WOMEN IN THE REDEMPTION

The Sages sum up the piety of the Jewish women during the time of the Egyptian bondage by saying: "In the merit of the righteous women who lived in that generation the Jewish people were redeemed from Egypt."[62]

When the Jews crossed the Red Sea, Miriam led the women in praising God:

> And Miriam the prophetess, the sister of Aaron,
> took a timbrel in her hand; and all the women went
> out after her with timbrels and with dances. And
> Miriam sang to them:
>
> Sing you unto the Lord, for He is highly exalted:
> The horse and his rider has he thrown into
> the sea.[63]

According to tradition, in Miriam's merit a miraculous well was created during twilight on the eve of the first Sabbath[64] that accompanied the

Israelites during their journey through the desert.[65] Like Moses and Aaron, Miriam, too, died by the kiss of God.[66]

The Talmud relates that the wife of On ben Pelet saved her husband from death during the Korah rebellion against Moses by persuading him to leave Korah.[67]

Generally, women in the Bible demonstrated more piety and foresight than men. Often, when the men were drawn to sin, the women refrained from it. For example, the women did not participate in the sin of the golden calf.[68] Nor did they wish to return to Egypt when the spies returned from *Eretz Yisrael* to report that the land was unconquerable,[69] nor did they join the men in any of the sins committed en route from Egypt to the holy land.[70]

During the period of the conquest of *Eretz Yisrael*, Achsah, daughter of Caleb ben Y'funeh, had the wisdom and foresight to ensure that the land she and her husband would acquire in the arid Negev desert would have water sources, a fact mentioned twice in the Bible.[71]

DEBORAH AND YAEL

Women of the Bible played central roles in the deliverance of the Jewish people. Though they did not seek power or public roles, when it was necessary for the survival of the Jewish people, they did not hesitate to take active leadership. Yet they did so while maintaining their distinct, feminine traits.

In the period following the conquest of the land of Israel, there were many such women. During the period of the Judges, Yael was such a heroine. She alone killed the dreaded general Sisera, who was waging war on Israel. As Sisera was fleeing the battlefield, she lay in wait for him in her tent, and she invited him in, offering him food and drink until he fell asleep, then killed him with a tent peg. With their leader dead, the morale of the Canaanites fell, and the Israelites were victorious.[72]

In the *Song of Deborah* Yael is praised, "Blessed be Yael among the women. . . . She is blessed more than the women in the tent."[73] To which *Rashi* comments that she was blessed even more than all the Matriarchs.[74]

Deborah herself is a prime example of the tendency of women, when a specific need arises, and when they are best qualified to do the task, to leave the private realm to serve the nation in public positions. These women are praised for doing so. Deborah was a prophetess who served as Judge, the leader of the nation. When the Canaanites attacked the Israelites, it was she who galvanized General Barak–who refused to go to battle unless she joined him–to mobilize an army of 10,000 men, which utterly routed the Canaaite enemy. The Midrash states that Deborah rebuilt a number of small towns that were destroyed by Sisera and converted them into large metropolises.[75]

THE SONG OF DEBORAH

In The Song of Deborah, Deborah and Barak sing:

When men let grow their hair in Israel,
When the people offer themselves willingly,
Bless the Lord.

Hear, O you kings; give ear, O you princes:
I, to the Lord will I sing;
I will sing praise to the Lord, the God of Israel.

Lord, when you did go forth out of Seir,
When You did march out of Edom,
The earth trembled, the heavens also dropped,
Yes, the clouds dropped water.
The mountains quaked at the presence of the Lord,
Even did Sinai at the presence of the Lord, the God of Israel.

In the days of Shamgar the son of Anat,
In the days of Yael, road travel ceased,
And the travellers travelled the byways,
Until you did arise, Deborah,
You did arise a mother in Israel.
They chose new gods;
Then was war in the gates;
Was there a shield or spear seen
Among forty thousand in Israel?
My heart is toward the lawmakers of Israel,
Those among the people who offered of themselves,
Bless the Lord.

You that ride on white asses,
You that sit on rich cloths,
And you that walk by the way tell of it;
Louder than the voice of archers by the watering troughs!
There they shall rehearse the righteous acts of the Lord,
Even the righteous acts of His rulers in Israel.

Then the people of the Lord went down to the gates.
Awake, awake, Deborah!
Awake, awake, utter a song;
Arise, Barak, and lead your captives, O Son of Avinoam.

Then made He a remnant to have dominion over the nobles and the people;
The Lord made me have dominion over the mighty.
Out of Ephraim came they whose root is in Amalek;
After you, Benjamin, among your peoples;
Out of Machir came down lawmakers,
And out of Zebulun they that handle the marshall's staff.

And the princess of Issachar were with Deborah;
As was Issachar so was Barak;
Into the valley they rushed forth at his feet.
Among the divisions of Reuben
There were great resolves of heart.
Gilead abode beyond the Jordan;
And Dan, why does he sojourn by the ships?
Asher dwelled at the shore of the sea,
And abides by its bays.
Zebulun is a people that jeopardized their lives to the death,
And Naphtali upon the high places of the field.

The Kings came, they fought;
They fought the kings of Canaan,
In Taanach by the waters of Megido;
They took no gain of money.
They fought from heaven,
The stars in their courses fought against Sisera.
The brook Kishon swept them away,
That ancient brook, the brook Kishon.
O my soul, tread them down with strength!

Then did the horsehoofs stamp
By the prancings, the prancings of the mighty ones.
"Curse you Meroz," said the angel of the Lord,
"Curse you bitterly the inhabitants thereof,
Because they came not to the help of the Lord,
To the help of the Lord against the mighty."

Blessed above women shall Yael be,
The wife of Heber the Kenite,
Above women in the tent shall she be blessed.
Water, he asked, milk she gave him;
In a lordly bowl she brought him curd.
Her hand she put to the tent pin,
And her right hand to the workmen's hammer;
And with the hammer she smote Sisera, she smote through his head,
Yes, she pierced and struck through his temples.
At her feet he sank, he fell, he lay;

At her feet he sank, he fell;
    Where he sank, there he fell down dead.

Through the window she looked forth and peered,
    The mother of Sisera, through the lattice;
"Why is his chariot so long in coming?
    Why tarry the wheels of his chariots?"
The wisest of her princesses answer her,
    Yes, she returns answer to herself;
"Are they not finding, are they not dividing the spoil?
    A slave-woman, two slave-women to every man;
To Sisera a spoil of dyed garments,
    A spoil of dyed garments of embroidery for the neck of every spoiler?"
May all your enemies so perish, O Lord;
    But may they who love Him be as the sun when it goes forth in its might.[76]

The *Zohar* states that Deborah and Hanah were two women who composed praises to God unequaled by those written by men.[77]

HANAH: PRAYER AND DEVOTION

Hanah was married to Elkanah and was childless. She prayed to God with such fervor that Eli, the *kohen gadol* (high priest) thought her to be drunk. Her prayer, recited silently, "in her heart, only her lips moved, but her voice could not be heard,"[78] became the paradigm for prayer for the thrice daily *Amidah* prayer. When her prayer for a son was answered, Hanah fulfilled the vow she had made when praying and brought her young son, Samuel, to Eli, to serve God.

In a joyous prayer of thanksgiving, Hanah sings:

My heart exults in the Lord,
    My horn is exalted in the Lord;
My mouth is enlarged over my enemies,
    Because I rejoice in Your salvation.
There is none as holy as the Lord;
    For there is none beside you;
Neither is there any rock like our God.

Speak not too much proud talk,
    Let not arrogance escape your mouth;
For the Lord is a God of knowledge,
    And by Him actions are weighed.

The bows of the mighty were broken,
And those who stumbled are girded with strength.
They who were full hired themselves out for bread,
And those who were hungry ceased;
While the barren ones bore seven,
She who bore many children has languished.

The Lord causes one to die and revives the dead,
He brings down to the grave and raises up.
The Lord makes poor and makes rich;
He brings low and he raises up.

He raises up the poor from the dust,
He lifts up the poor from the dung-hill,
To cause them to sit with princes,
And inherit the throne of glory;
For the pillars of the earth are the Lord's,
And he has set the world upon them.

He will keep the feet of His holy ones,
But the wicked shall be made silent in darkness;
For not by strength shall man prevail.

The contenders against the Lord shall be dissected,
Against them will He thunder in heaven;
The Lord will judge the ends of the earth;
And He will give strength to His king,
And exalt the horn of this annointed.[79]

RUTH THE MOABITE

Ruth, a Moabite princess who had been married to an Israelite–who had come to Moab during a famine in Israel–was an exemplar of loyalty, modesty, and personal courage in choosing to leave her birthplace, country, and familiar world to follow her mother-in-law, Naomi, to Israel to adopt a foreign land, a foreign people, and to await an unknown destiny.

Her words were destined to become the classic pledge of loyalty of the Bible: "Where you go I will go, and where you stay I will stay. Your people will be my people, and your God my God."[80] According to some of the Sages,[81] her action was greater even than that of Abraham, who left his homeland and family in response to God's command.

Yet the act that was considered greatest of all was Ruth's decision to pursue Boaz. Boaz, a wealthy landowner and the leader of his generation of Jews, was the only kinsman of her late husband who was able and willing to redeem her, in accordance with the custom of the times, in a levirate marriage, and at Naomi's urging she sought him out.

Ruth, who took upon herself the task of supporting both herself and Naomi–both were poor–had been gleaning grain droppings from Boaz's fields. Following the counsel of her mother-in-law entailed Ruth's setting aside her natural feminine modesty and reserve and appearing before Boaz at night at his threshing floor to remind him of his duty to redeem her late husband's estate[82] and to wed her, according to biblical statute, in order to assure the perpetuation of her late husband's name.[83]

Boaz, who was eighty at the time, was acutely aware of the sacrifice her action entailed for her, and he knew that she was doing it out of piety. Indeed, the Sages praise Ruth for her modesty. Boaz said to her: "Be blessed of God, my daughter; you have made your latest act of kindness greater than in the first, in that you have not gone after the younger men, be they poor or rich."[84] Boaz married Ruth, and their son Oved became the father of Yishai, the father of King David.

ESTHER, CHAMPION OF THE JEWS OF THE PERSIAN EMPIRE

Esther, the daughter of Abigail, was destined to become the queen of the Persian Empire and the savior of the Jewish people. Yet never did she seek power or political prestige for their own sake, or enjoy them for their own sake.

The story takes place at about the sixth century B.C.E. Chosen by King Ahasuerus in a beauty contest above all the maidens of the land to be his queen, Esther's reluctance to assume the position was apparent, but she complied with the request of her uncle Mordecai, one of the leading Jews in the realm, to participate in the contest. At Mordecai's behest she kept the fact of her Jewishness secret. She also continued practicing Judaism clandestinely.

When Haman, the anti-Semitic vizier of the king, persuaded the king to sign a decree calling for the annihilation of the Jews in the Persian Empire, Mordecai sent a message to Queen Esther asking that she approach the king to have the decree annulled. When she was reluctant to do so, since court rules required her to come to the king only at his initiative, Mordecai rebuked her, telling her that when the Jewish people are in danger personal concerns and considerations must be set aside, saying: "And who knows, at a time like this, whether the decree will not also reach the highest levels of royalty?"[85]

Rising to the occasion, Esther called on the Jews of Shushan to fast with her for three days, after which she approached the king, doing so in full awareness that to approach the king without being summoned meant possible death. Esther was successful in bringing about Haman's downfall through a brilliant plan, which pitted King Ahasuerus and Haman against each other and aroused the king's jealously of Haman. Haman was hanged on the same gallows he had prepared for Mordecai.

Esther, the savior of the Jewish people in the Persian Empire and the greatest of all Jewish heroines, has been acclaimed at Purim celebrations year after year, with little girls dressing up in royal robes as Queen Esther. The event is celebrated annually by Jews through the observance of the festival of Purim, the merriest feast of the Jewish year, at which time the Esther Scroll, the biblical Book of Esther, is read in the synagogue to the accompaniment of much merriment and rejoicing.

JUDITH, SAVIOR OF THE JEWS

Judith of Bethulia saved the Jewish people in the early Second Temple period at around the sixth-fifth century B.C.E. by deceiving the Assyrian General Holofornes, whose army was about to conquer all of Judaea, and by then killing him. As described in the Apocrypha in the Book of Judith, during the siege by Holofornes' army of the Jews of Bethulia, the Jews were about to surrender because of a lack of water. The young, aristocratic, and pious widow Judith prayed and then decided on a bold and courageous course of action. At great risk, she went to the enemy camp to see Holofornes.

Judith was taken to Holofornes, and she told him that she would be his adviser and help him to defeat the Jews without any loss of his soldiers, since the Jews were weakened because they were not properly observing the Torah. Attracted by her great beauty and intelligence, Holofornes invited her to stay on as adviser. At a private feast with Holofornes, she proferred cheese to him so that he became thirsty, and then he drank a great deal of wine, which put him to sleep. Whereupon she removed his sword, cut off his head, and returned with it to Bethulia so that the Jews could display it on the walls to the Assyrian army at morning. She then incited the Jewish soldiers to attack the Assyrians.

Realizing that they were deprived of their commander-in-chief, the Assyrian officers and soldiers lost their morale, panicked, and fled, pursued by the Jewish soldiers, who defeated them. A prayer of thanksgiving was pronounced by all Israel for Judith's act and for their deliverance:

> You are the exaltation of Jerusalem, you are the great glory of Israel, you are the great eminence of our nation. You have done all this with your own hand; you have done Israel good, and God is overjoyed. The Omnipotent God bless you forever.[86]

When Judith died at the age of 105, she was mourned by all Israel for seven days.

COMMEMORATING JUDITH ON HANUKKAH

To commemorate Judith's act, special foods are eaten during the eight-day Hanukkah festival. It is customary for Jewish women to remember Judith every evening during Hanukkah by refraining from performing any work in the home while the Hanukkah lights are burning.[87] The story of Judith was a popular subject for paintings during the Renaissance, and Judith holding aloft the head of Holofornes is a scene that was frequently used on Hanukkah lamps during the sixteenth to eighteenth centuries.

JUDITH: THE HOLINESS OF WOMEN'S SENSUALITY

In the Apocrypha, Judith is depicted as a modest, somewhat retiring, apparently passive and inwardly focused mourning widow who, when circumstance demanded, transformed herself into an attractive, captivating woman – and risked her life – in order to save the Jewish people. Tamar Frankiel perceives Judith as a Jewish prototype who brings together femininity and spirituality. Frankiel finds that the story of Judith – like those of Tamar, Ruth, and Esther – demonstrates that the essence of a woman's strength and femininity is derived from her spirituality and that Judith utilized her feminine power and her sexuality for a transcendent good.[88]

Upon seeing this representative of Jewish womanhood in her beauty, intelligence, and strength, Holofornes' soldiers exclaimed: "Who can despise these people, when they have such women among them?! For it is not right to leave even one alive, for if we let them go they will be able to beguile the whole world!"[89] Frankiel sees the Jewish idea of women's sexuality as a medium, not to achieve a worldly purpose or to exploit man's vulnerability, but as a strong dimension of the female that is the very essence of womanhood and can be used to elevate humanity.

To Frankiel, Judith demonstrates that women's physical being and sensuality are both powerful and holy, and she goes so far as to compare woman's body to the holy Temple. In her moving prayer before going out to Holofornes, Judith begged the "God of Simon" – not the God of Abraham, Isaac, and Jacob – to protect the sanctuary in Jerusalem from pollution and defilement by Holofornes' army, just as Simon, Jacob's son, avenged the pollution and defilement of his sister Dinah.[90] Frankiel understands this as indicating that for Judith there was an equivalency between the holiness of the Temple and that of a woman's body.[91]

Women have direct access to the power of sanctity, Frankiel feels. However, when a woman uses her sensuality in the service of holiness – to achieve a special destiny and to save the Jewish people – she must regard herself as holy, *and she must be holy as well*. Frankiel emphasizes that Judith, Esther, Ruth, and Tamar had also to be chaste, modest, and pious in the Jewish manner.

Concludes Frankiel:

> The feminine models in Judaism tell us that sex used any other way than for holiness is dishonest to God, dishonest to the purpose of our feminine being. The woman who knows her sexuality and her inner, spiritual self can recognize her true purpose in life, can act with power and confidence at any moment, and can thereby affect her own destiny, the destiny of her people, and that of the whole world.[92]

Section 2: In the Talmud

A number of women are mentioned in the Talmud and Midrash, who, like their biblical forebears, have served as sources of moral inspiration up to this day.

QUEEN SALOME, DELIVERER OF THE JEWISH PEOPLE

If there is a single individual who can be considered responsible for the very existence of the entire Jewish nation, it is Salome, known as Shlomzion HaMalkah. Toward the end of the period of the Second Temple, Salome (Shlomzion) Alexandra (139–67 B.C.E.), queen of Judaea and wife of Aristobulus I and then Alexander Yannai, was held in great affection by the Jews. Salome was the last independent ruler of Judaea. Her authority was greatly respected by Israel's neighbors, and her reign was characterized as peaceful.

A strictly observant Jewess, Salome's piety and religiosity so powerfully provoked God's beneficence that during her reign, the Sages say, the Land of Israel was exceedingly fertile. The grains of wheat, oats, and lentils grew to extraordinary size, and specimens were kept so that future generations would be able to see what piety by one individual could achieve.[93]

Salome's husband, King Alexander Yannai,[94] was heavily influenced by the aristocratic and heretical Sadducean party that came into being around 200 B.C.E. The Sadducees, who accepted the authority of the Written Torah only, in its literal sense, rejected the Oral Torah and tradition. The Sadducees worshipped an anthropomorphic God who, in their theology, very much resembled a human king; in essence, they tried to bring God down to human level.

The Pharisees, on the other hand, represented the normative Jewish view. They sought to elevate man to the Godly heights of a supernatural, spiritual, and transcendent God by the traditional Jewish understanding that man was to imitate God's noble attributes. The Sadducees, a relatively small group composed primarily of the wealthier elements of the population – merchants, priests, and aristocrats – were under the influence of Hellenism and Greco-Roman culture and religion. They claimed the authority of their aristocratic geneology.

SALOME DEFENDS THE PHARISEES

The Pharisees, who represented the religious beliefs, traditions, practices, and social and moral values of the Torah, had the support of the vast majority of the Jewish people and claimed the authority of the Sinaitic tradition. The Sadducees controlled the Kohanic priesthood and the Temple hierarchy and the majority of the Sanhedrin, the Supreme Court, which had become dissolute and was effectively nonexistent.

The Pharisees opposed the occupation by the king of the additional post of *kohen gadol*, or high priest, and were severely persecuted by the king. On one occasion Yannai deliberately flouted tradition during the Temple service on Succot, directing insult at the Pharisees and at religious tradition. His act provoked furious response by the people, who pelted the king with their *etrogim*, citrons; whereupon the king ordered 6,000 Jews killed within the Temple precints. The king then embarked on a ruthless persecution of the Pharisees. Large numbers were put to death, and many of the surviving leaders, including the remaining Torah scholars, were forced to flee the country. Torah study and scholarship were the hallmarks of the Pharisaic tradition, but these became virtually nonexistent in Israel with the disappearance of the Torah scholars from the country, and the very future of the Jewish people was threatened.

Salome convinced her husband that he was wrong in favoring the Sadducees and in persecuting the Pharisees, and she arranged for a reconciliation between her brother, R. Simon ben Shetah, the great Sage and respected rabbinic leader of the people, and Alexander Yannai. Thereafter R. Simon was constantly in the king's presence. Salome also arranged for the return to *Eretz Yisrael* from exile of the Pharisees, including many great Pharisaic scholars, such as R. Judah ben Tabbai. These scholars had fled the country during the Sadducean persecutions, which had left "the world desolate" because of a lack of Torah.[95] Salome arranged for the ascendancy of the Pharisaic party to the leadership of the country, entrusting them with the management of the country, but she refrained from persecuting the Sadducees. The study of the Torah, which had ceased, was restarted, and Salome saw to the reinstitution of the tradition of the study of the Oral Torah.

SALOME: ASSURING THE CONTINUATION OF TORAH STUDY

Salome also reestablished the Sanhedrin and had R. Judah ben Tabai and later her brother, R. Simon, appointed as its *nasi*, or head.[96] R. Simon ben Shetah, one of the greatest scholars of the Second Temple period, was instrumental in "restoring the Crown of Torah to its original glory and splendor."[97] With the help of R. Judah ben Tabbai the Sanhedrin was eventually purged of Sadducees, and incorrect literal interpretations of the Torah's penalties ("an eye for an eye") were replaced with the traditional interpretation of the Oral Torah.

Neglected Jewish customs and traditions were renewed. R. Simon arranged for compulsory education for the young, introduced school attendance for children, and organized high schools for those over age sixteen. He arranged for the enactment of important laws and a number of significant rules of judicial legislation and rabbinic enactments. These included the institution of the written *ketubah*, or unilateral marriage contract, for the protection of the married woman, and the undertaking in it that all of the husband's property is mortgaged as security to ensure his fulfillment of his obligations to his wife. R. Simon's close connection with the queen, his commanding position in the Sanhedrin, his enormous erudition, and his acceptance by the greatest scholars of his day had an enormous impact on the religious life of the period and on succeeding generations of the Jewish people. Upon the death of Alexander Yannai and the ascendancy of Salome to the throne, she arranged the consolidation of government by the Pharisees, and the Pharisees became responsible for the spiritual life of the Jewish nation.

Salome's accomplishments were of transcendent and far-reaching significance. It is not easy to measure the dimensions of her contribution to Jewish existence, but there can be no doubt that it was both extraordinary and crucial. The Pharisaic Judaism based upon the validity of both the *Torah Shebichtav*, the Written Torah, and *Torah Shebaal Peh*, the Oral Torah, which Salome championed and made supreme, is essentially normative Judaism. With the destruction of the Temple in 70 C.E., Judaism was continued by the synagogues and the schools and seminaries for Torah study that had been established by the Pharisees, the lineal descendants of whom flourish to this day.

Salome, by her acts, assured both the continuity of Torah and Torah study among the Jewish people and the continued existence of the Jewish nation.

QUEEN HELENA: AIDING THE POOR

Helena, the first-century C.E. queen of Adiabene in Syria, converted to Judaism together with her son Izates in about 30 C.E., moved to Jerusalem, and made major gifts to the Temple, including a golden menorah. She was extremely pious and meticulous in the observance of the *mitzvot*.[98] She was scrupulous in her observance, even to the extent of eating in a *sukkah*, the temporary hut used by Jews during the eight-day fall Sukkot festival (which is a time-dependent *mitzvah* from which women are ordinarily exempted[99]) and had a large *sukkah* built in Lod that was frequented by the rabbis.[100]

In 45–46 C.E., when the populace of *Eretz Yisrael* was suffering from a severe famine, Helena sent her attendants to Alexandria and Cyprus for large supplies of food and grain, which she distributed to the needy.[101] When her son Izate (who became king of Adiabne) learned of the famine, he likewise sent a great sum of money to the Jewish leaders in *Eretz Yisrael*. Her husband, Monobaz, was said to have spent all his treasures and those of his ancestors during the years of famine.[102]

The historian Josephus, a contemporary of Queen Helena, writes: "She left a very great name that will be famous forever among all our people for her benefaction. When her son Izates (who became king of Adiabne) learned of the famine, he likewise sent a great sum of money to leaders of the Jerusalemites."[103] Helena's mausoleum, together with an inscription, has been identified in the "Tombs of the Kings" outside Jerusalem.[104]

RACHEL BAT KALBA SAVUA

Rachel was the daughter of Kalba Savua, one of the richest people in Jerusalem at the end of the first to the beginning of the second century C.E. Her husband, Akiva, was a poor, unlearned shepherd. Rachel perceived in Akiva enormous potential. Her influence transformed him into a towering talmudic sage, one of the greatest Jewish scholars of history.

R. Akiva frequently referred to all that Rachel had done for him.[105] When R. Akiva presented Rachel with a magnificent gold diadem with a depiction of Jerusalem on it, the wife of a colleague of his complained to her husband as to why he didn't give her such a fine present. He replied: "Had you done for me what Rachel did for Akiva, I too would have given you a headdress of gold!"[106]

R. Akiva's deep love for Rachel can be seen in his saying, "Who is truly wealthy? . . . He who has a wife who is comely in her deeds."[107]

Although the Talmud, which brings us the story of Rachel and R. Akiva, does not give us much background information about Rachel, we piece together from her actions a vivid picture of her nobility of character. She, the young and wealthy aristocrat, discerned the greatness and inner nobility that lay buried within the untutored shepherd. He was more than twice her age and in his own words, an absolute *am haaretz*, or ignoramous. Rachel suffered years of poverty, privation, and isolation, content in the unshaken belief that her husband would one day be a great *talmid hacham*, a Torah scholar.

RACHEL: TRANSFORMING A SHEPHERD INTO A SAGE

Rachel persuaded the shepherd to leave his sheep and to become a pupil, learning the *aleph-bet* from the scholars whom he loathed. (R. Akiva said: When I was an *am haaretz*, if I would have a scholar in my hands I would bite him as if I were a donkey!"[108]) Rachel's father, fiercely opposed to the match, disinherited his daughter,[109] leaving the new couple to face dire poverty. She and the poor, ignorant Akiva had nowhere to go. To aggravate matters, he found the learning tedious and painful. He became exceedingly frustrated in not being able to understand his studies. More than once he felt he must stop studying and go back to the sheep, and were it not for his wife's patient encouragement and insistence he would have returned to the shepherd's life.

So poor were they that Akiva kneaded the dough of his teachers for their bread. At one time he earned his livelihood by picking a bundle of wood every day, half of which he sold, while the other half provided faggots for his light while studying; the neighbors complained of the smoke he was making.[110] The Talmud tells that Elijah once came to Akiva and Rachel dressed as a poor man. He begged them for some straw upon which his wife, who had just given birth, could sleep.[111] His purpose in coming was to console them by showing them that there were those who were even poorer than they.[112]

Despite their privations, Rachel did not complain, but continued to encourage Akiva to learn Torah. At one point, she cut off her hair and sold it in order to buy food.[113] Much later, when Akiva became a renowned scholar and they were reconciled with Rachel's father, R. Akiva presented Rachel with the gold diadem to console her for her hair that she had sold for Akiva to be able to continue studying Torah.

The Sages say that on the final day of judgment God will sit as judge. He will ask people why they did not study Torah. If people answer that they were too poor, God will point to R. Akiva and say, he was able to do so. Should the poor protest that they had to support their families, God will remind them that Akiva, too, had a wife and child and yet he managed to study. But the severity of the punishment will be mitigated at the end, when the poor offer their final defense: our wives were not as great as Rachel![114]

Rachel sent her husband away from home to study with scholars, among them R. Nahum of Gamzu, R. Eliezer ben Hyrcanus, and R. Joshua ben Hananyah. Studying intensively day and night, Akiva eventually became a brilliant scholar and returned home after twelve years, bringing with him twelve thousand students.

Approaching his dwelling, he overhead an interfering neighbor chiding Rachel for having permitted her husband to leave her for so long. To which Rachel replied that if Akiva would take her advice he would stay away and study Torah for another twelve years. Immediately R. Akiva turned around and went back to the academy with his students. When he returned home after twelve more years with 24,000 students, Rachel pushed her way through the huge crowd, and, to the annoyance of his students, threw herself at his feet. R. Akiva spoke sharply to his students, who were unaware of her identity: "*Sheli veshelachem shelah hu*–Whatever I have achieved and whatever you have achieved, we owe to her."[115]

R. Akiva became an intellectual giant whose rulings and teachings had a profound impact on the Jewish people. It was on the merit of his wife, Rachel, that he was able to realize his potential, and therefore it is to her vision that the Jewish people is indebted.

The daughter of R. Akiva and Rachel, in keeping with the values she had absorbed from her mother, made a similar sacrifice for her own husband, R. Simon Ben Azai. He, too, became one of the great Sages of the Talmud.

BRURIAH, TALMUDIC SCHOLAR

Bruriah (first to second century C.E.), was the wife of the mishnaic Sage R. Meir, and the daughter of R. Hananyah ben Teradyon, who was martyred by the Romans.

A brilliant scholar whose opinions are quoted throughout the Talmud, Bruriah distinguished herself, the Talmud reports, by studying 300 *Halachot*, religious laws, each day.[116] Her views on religious, scholarly, and secular matters were respected by the Sages of her day, and decisions in law were made in accordance with her opinion.[117] The Sages acknowledged her expertise in Jewish law, praising her with the accolade, "Bruriah has spoken well."

Bruriah was self-assured and confident in her knowledge. She chided the talmudic Sage R. Jose HaGalilee for phrasing a question to her in an inordinately lengthy style. She criticized a sectarian concerning the interpretation of a verse from the prophets.[118] She disparaged the excessively quiet manner of study of one of her father's pupils, pointing out that only when one studies aloud can the meaning be clear.[119]

According to *Rashi*, Bruriah was overly self-confident. She was put to a test by R. Meir and as a result was led astray, with tragic consequences.[120]

Bruriah exerted considerable influence on R. Meir and served as his spiritual support. Her moral stature can be seen in her rebuke to R. Meir, who prayed for the death of some people who were causing difficulty and distress: "The scriptural verse[121] does not say that sinners shall be destroyed, but that sins will be ended and the wicked will then disappear. Pray for them rather that they should repent of their evil ways." The Talmud reports that he followed her advice and prayed for them and they did indeed repent.[122]

KIMCHIT, MOTHER OF HIGH PRIESTS

Kimchit lived during the last years of the Second Temple. She is described as the mother of seven sons, each of whom became a *kohen gadol* (high priest) in the Temple in Jerusalem. These included Simon (reign 17–18 C.E.) and Joseph (reign 44–47 C.E.). When asked to explain the great merit that had earned her such reward, she explained that it was her *tzeniut*, her intense, inner-directed modesty in dress; she was never immodestly clothed, even in her own home.

The Talmud praises her family, saying "All flour (*kemah*) is good, but the flour of Kimhit is the best."[123]

IMA SHALOM, YALTA, AND BLURIA

Ima Shalom (late first to early second century C.E.) was the daughter of the great sage R. Simon ben Gamliel, the wife of R. Eliezer ben Hyrcanus, and the sister of Raban Gamliel, the *nasi*, or head of the Jewish community in *Eretz Yisrael*.

Her husband had been excommunicated by her brother, Raban Gamliel, and the dissension between the two was a source of great distress to her. Upon seeing her husband in supplication and sensing that he was praying to God regarding his pain over his excommunication, she exclaimed "You have just killed my brother!" Immediately thereafter the sound of the *shofar* was heard announcing the death of her brother, the *nasi*. When her husband asked how she could have known, she replied, "I have a tradition from my paternal grandfather that 'all gates [of heaven for receiving petitions] are closed except for the gate of wounded feelings.' "[124]

The Talmud relates how Ima Shalom concocted a ruse that was successful in exposing a dishonest judge.[125]

Yalta (late third to early fourth century C.E.) was the daughter of the exilarch, or head of the Jewish community in exile, in Babylonia, and the learned wife of R. Nahman. She is mentioned in the Talmud on several occasions in relation to learned discussions.[126]

Bluria, the convert, would present learned queries to R. Ishmael for discussion.

The mother of Ben Zaza was chosen to deliver the eulogy for R. Ishmael.

R. Samuel's daughters quoted and interpreted Jewish law.

The prayer for rain by R. Aba Hilkya's wife was accepted, though R. Hilkya's was not.[127]

CONCLUSION

It is the popular belief that Jewish women in ancient times were passive figures, discriminated against by men. This belief is most powerfully refuted by the Bible and Talmud. The women described in the pages of those works are archetypes, but they were real enough; and they were neither mere appendages, nor were they female revolutionaries.

They were strong women, good wives and mothers who functioned within the framework of the Jewish family, modest in nature and of noble trait, with a character distinct from their husbands, a deep, abiding faith in God, and a loyalty to their people and to their religious tradition, who drew their spiritual sustenance from the inner world of that tradition.

5

Women in Jewish History

In every age Jewish women have left an indelible mark on Jewish history. Undoubtedly, it is in her private role in the home that the Jewish woman has exercised the greatest influence. Through the powerful position she occupies in the Jewish family, particularly in her critical capacity as the educator who molds the character and behavior of the children, the Jewish woman has shaped, to an incalculable degree, the history of the Jewish nation and through it the history of the world.

Because of their essentially private role, Jewish women have shunned the public limelight. At times, however, they have assumed leadership roles in response to the needs of their nation, so that the limelight came to them in spite of their desire to avoid it. We shall here discuss a few of these extraordinary Jewish women, who, for the most part, lived in their inner roles, but have also left their marks in the public annals of Jewish history.

IN THE WORLD OF TORAH SCHOLARSHIP

Women are exempted from the obligation to study Torah. (See Chapter 15.) There have been a number of traditional Jewish women, however, who were strongly motivated to learn and impart Torah knowledge. While living as fully observant Jews, these women attained high levels of scholarship and were influential in the development of their husbands or children into notable Torah scholars.

RASHI'S DAUGHTERS: YOCHEVED, MIRIAM, AND RACHEL

The three daughters of *Rashi* (R. Solomon ben Isaac of Troyes, 1040–1105) the great French rabbinic authority, biblical exegete, and commentator on the Torah and the Talmud, were Yocheved, Miriam, and Rachel. They helped out in their father's small business–he was a wine merchant–and made it possible for *Rashi* to produce the prodigious scholarly output that made him the principal interpreter for Jews of the Torah and the Talmud of all time.

All three were students of their father's as well, and they would faithfully put *Rashi*'s thoughts down on paper, especially in his later years, and would sometimes reply in their father's name to questioners who wrote to the French sage requesting halachic decisions. Yocheved, Miriam, and Rachel all married men who became great Torah scholars, and they and their sons, virtually all of whom distinguished themselves as brilliant students of Torah as well, formed the school of talmudic scholars known as the *Tosafot.*

Yocheved married R. Meir ben Samuel, who studied at the Torah academy in Mainz with *Rashi.* They had one daughter, Hanah, who was a teacher of Torah laws and customs. Hanah married R. Samuel of Dampierre, *Rashi*'s student, and had four sons, all of whom became famous scholars: Isaac, known as the *Rivam*; Samuel, known as the *Rashbam*; Solomon; and the greatest of them all, Jacob, who was known as the *Rabbeinu Tam.*

R. Jacob's wife, Miriam, was known as a scholar who replied to questioners in their city and who was in touch with various rabbis concerning her *responsa.* Their four sons and their daughter all were distinguished students of Torah. Miriam was a respected scholar whose opinions were often quoted and who was known to question difficult talmudic passages and to explain the teachings of the *Tosafot.* Her son R. Matityahu Treibish was the rabbi of Paris.

Rashi's daughter Miriam married the talmudic commentator R. Judah ben Nathan, known as the *Rivan,* and their son R. Yom Tov also became an important Torah scholar.

Rachel married the scholar R. Eliezer. Their son R. Shemaya was a disciple of *Rashi* who composed original commentaries on various talmudic tractates.[1]

NAMNAH

Namnah, daughter of R. Samuel ben Ali, the Gaon and head of the *yeshivah* in Baghdad in the twelfth century, was known to be so well versed in Talmud that *yeshivah* students would come and sit outside her house, listening at the window to her teachings–hearing, but not seeing her, because of her modesty.[2]

THE MOTHER-IN-LAW OF THE OR ZARUA

So knowledgeable was the mother-in-law of R. Isaac ben Moses of Vienna, known as the *Or Zarua*, the great rabbinic authority of Germany and France of the thirteenth century, that the learned Sage would quote halachic rulings in her name.

THE WIFE OF R. ABRAHAM MEIR OF WORMS

The wife of R. Abraham Meir of Worms (fourteenth century) delivered learned Torah discourses before the congregation every Sabbath.

REDEL ISSERLIN

Redel, the daughter-in-law of R. Israel Isserlin (fifteenth century), the foremost German rabbinic scholar of his era, was said to have studied Torah under R. Yudel Sofer and was reputed to be as well versed in the Talmud as the best of the *yeshivah* students.

THE GRANDMOTHER OF THE MAHARSHAL

Similarly, the grandmother of R. Solomon Luria of Poland (sixteenth century), the great rabbinic authority known as "the teacher of rabbinic scholars," would deliver Torah lectures to students while concealed behind a curtain.

POMONA DA MODENA

Pomona da Modena of Ferrara, Italy (fifteenth-century), was a pious woman who was said to be as well versed in the Talmud as any man and was honored by R. David of Imola with a detailed halachic *responsum* that could have been understood only by a scholar. Her son R. Abraham ben Jehiel Modena celebrated her piety with more than a thousand liturgical poems that he composed between 1536 and 1552.

BATHSHEBA DA MODENA

Another member of the family, Bathsheba (or Fioretta), mother of the physician Mordecai (Marco) Modena, and ancestor of many scholars, including the erudite R. Aryeh (Leone da) Modena and the kabbalist R. B'rachiah da Modena, was also a talmudic scholar of note.

She would devote much of her time to Torah study, with an intense weekly learning schedule, and was said to have been particularly well versed in the works of Maimonides. The credit for the love of the learning of the Torah among members of her family was largely attributed to her.

REBECCAH TIKTINER AND THE *TECHINES* COMPOSERS

In the early 1500s, Rebeccah bat Aaron Meir Tiktiner (c. 1490–c. 1550), a Polish moralist, wrote *Meneket Rivkah*, a Yiddish compilation of ethical teaching of the Jewish sages. It was first published in Prague in 1609, more than half a century after her death, and republished in Cracow in 1618. *Meneket Rivkah* followed upon Rebeccah Tiktiner's translation into Yiddish of Bahya ibn Pakudah's eleventh-century ethical work, *Hovat HaLevavot*, Duties of the Heart.

Meneket Rivkah means "Rivkah's Wetnurse." In the introduction to the work the publisher writes that the author is an important woman, knowledgeable in *Halachah*, Jewish law, and a learned expositor of Torah. He explains that the book's biblically derived title[3] is called *Meneket Rivkah* "so that the author's name will be remembered, and is in homage to all women–in order to demonstrate that a woman can create a fine ethical work, and can explicate these matters as well as many men."[4]

In 1719, Gustavo Georgio Zeltner, a German Lutheran priest, published a study of Rebeccah Tiktiner's work in Latin in a booklet titled "The Polish Rebeccah."

Rebeccah Tiktiner also wrote Yiddish poetry and *techines*, Yiddish for *techinot*, pious liturgical supplications and prayers usually used by women. *Techines* were usually written by men. There were many that were composed by women, however, and these served as a medium for expressing their spirituality as Jews.

Techines usually included special prayers to be recited by women at the time of the execution of a *mitzvah* associated with women, such as Sabbath and festival candle-lighting, the separation of the dough at the time of baking bread in commemoration of the Temple tithes, immersion in a *mikveh* (ritual bath), and so forth. These frequently called upon the Matriarchs, Sarah, Rebeccah, Rachel, and Leah, for divine intercession on behalf of the woman and her family.

ROYZIL FISHEL AND TOIBA PANN

Rebeccah Tiktiner is also known to have composed a popular festival song, *Simhat Torah Lied*. Other women also published works in this genre. Royzil (or

Raysel) Fishel of Cracow is known for a poem written as a preface to Moses Stendel's translation of the Psalms in 1588. Fishel was also a printer-typographer.

Toiba Pann (circa 1700) published a long poem in which she portrays the state of the Jews of her time.

SARAH REBECCAH RACHEL LEAH HOROWITZ

In the early 1700s the Polish Sarah Rebeccah Rachel Leah Horowitz, daughter of R. Yukel Segal Horowitz, wrote *techines* in which she pleads with women to attend synagogue more frequently and to express their emotions while praying, and in this way their prayers would bring the Messiah and the redemption.

Sarah Rebeccah Rachel Leah Horowitz urged women to rest on the Sabbath, not just from work but from speaking words that should not be uttered. Specifically, she recommended that on the Sabbath only words of Torah should be spoken and Torah should be studied. For those who could not study Torah she urged reading the Torah in Yiddish translation, for it was necessary to learn how to observe God's precepts.

HANAH KATZ

Hanah Katz published a *drashah*, a rhymed homiletical sermon for women, and a Sabbath prayer, *Tefillah LeShabbat*.

SARAH BAT-TOVIM

Sarah Bat-Tovim is the seventeenth-century Ukrainian author of *Shloshah She'arim*, "Three Gates," a popular small book of *techines* in Yiddish that were recited with the execution of various "women's *mitzvot*." Sarah Bat-Tovim was from Brisk (Brest-Litovsk), and her father Mordecai was a grandson of the rabbi of Brisk.

Although she grew up in a wealthy home, she is recorded as being impoverished in her old age and forced to wander homeless from place to place. Sarah Bat-Tovim attributes her suffering as punishment for her "great sin"–conversing in the synagogue during the prayers when she was younger.

Shloshah She'arim deals with three sets of *mitzvot* for women that are included in the acronym *HANAH*: *Hallah*–the separation of the dough from the bread when baking, *Niddah*–Family Purity and *mikveh*, and *Hadlakat Haner*–kindling the Sabbath lights; and also *techines* for the welcoming of Rosh Hodesh, the monthly New Moon festival, and for the lighting of the candles for Rosh HaShanah and Yom Kippur.

Much of the work is written in rhyme. As in many of the women's prayers of supplication, these call on God for aid in the merit of the Matriarchs: Sarah, Rebeccah, Rachel, and Leah. So popular a classic was Sarah Bat Tovim's *Shloshah She'arim*, that in the nineteenth century a number of men and women published *techines* under her name.

Much of the creative literature these women produced was in the genre of lyrical poetry rather than scholarship. They reflect the deep emotions of their creators and are genuine expressions of profound deep piety and spirituality and the desire to teach Jewish spirituality to women. These works mirror the experiences of the Jewish people, their times of joy and happiness and their trials and misfortunes.

BOULA ASHKENAZI

Boula Eskati (or Ishkati) Ashkenazi (1520–1605) was a well-known physician in Turkey who specialized as a woman's doctor and gynecologist. She attained fame when she cured the sultan Ahmed I of smallpox. She was said to have learned medicine from her husband, R. Solomon Ashkenazi, the learned scholar, physician, and diplomat, who, like his father Nathan and their son Nathan, had studied medicine in Padua.

Boula Ashkenazi was influential in the Turkish court, and on several occasions used her influence to intercede with the sultan on behalf of the Jews, saving them from deportation and exile.[5]

BEILAH FALK

Of Beilah, wife of R. Joshua Falk (c. 1555–1614), Polish *rosh yeshivah* and halachic authority and author of *Me'irat Enayim* and *Derisha U-perishah*, her son wrote:

> Every day, winter and summer, she would promptly rise several hours before daylight and recite many prayers and supplications with great devotion. She had the key to the women's section of the synagogue and would be the first to enter and the last to leave, an hour or two after the congregation left. Upon concluding her prayers, she wouldn't waste any time, but would devote her time to study the Torah diligently, the weekly scriptural readings along with Rashi's commentary.
>
> As all of my father's students knew so well, whenever Torah discussion would be held at our table, my mother would join the discussion. At times, in

words sweeter than honey, she would add her own original interpretation to a passage. She was especially well-versed in laws concerning women, and indeed her knowledge in this area approached that of a halachic authority.[6]

Not everyone agreed with Beilah's conclusions on *Halachah*. The *Magen Avraham* commentary to the *Tur, Yoreh De'ah*, responded to one halachic opinion of hers regarding the Sabbath candlelighting procedure with a curt dismissal;[7] whereupon the rabbinic authority R. Ezekiel Landau, known as the *Noda BeYehudah*, writing in *Daqul MeRevavah*, declared: The law follows the opinion of the *Derishah's* wife. . . . Was she not a woman "whose heart was uplifted by wisdom?"[8]

EDEL HEILPERN

R. Samuel Eliezer Edels (1555–1631), the Polish rabbinic authority and *yeshivah* dean, was known as the *MaHarshah*. He produced a powerful commentary on the Talmud that is considered an indispensable accompaniment to intensive study by serious students of the Talmud. He was one of the greatest talmudic commentators of the sixteenth and seventeenth centuries.

So influential to the young Samuel Eliezer's development as a scholar and teacher was his mother-in-law, Edel Heilpern, a wealthy woman who supported him and his *yeshivah* with its many disciples for some twenty years, that he became known as R. Samuel "Edel's."

HAVAH BACHARACH

Havah Bacharach of Prague (1580–1651), granddaughter of R. Judah Lowe ben Bezalel, the famed *MaHaral* of Prague, was distinguished for her Torah learning. It is reported that she had an extraordinary knowledge of Hebrew and rabbinical literature, uncommon in her day. Havah Bacharach wrote commentaries on the Midrash and the Aramaic Targum, and her opinions were sought on a variety of learned topics.

Married to R. Abraham Samuel ben Isaac Bacharach, rabbi of Worms, she was the female progenitor of a celebrated line of learned rabbis and scholars, beginning with her son, R. Moses Samson Bacharach. Her grandson, the famed talmudic scholar R. Yair Hayim ben Moses Samson Bacharach, is known as the *Havat Yair*, after the title of his important work of *responsa*, published in 1699. The title comes from a biblical passage,[9] and means "the tent-villages of Yair." However, the Ashkenazic Hebrew pronunciation, "Haves Yair," means the Yair of Havah, thus constituting a remarkable tribute to his distinguished and learned grandmother Havah.

At the age of seventy-one, having set out on a journey to fulfill her lifelong yearning to come to Eretz Yisrael, Havah Bacharach died in Sofia.

OSNAT BAT SAMUEL BARAZANI

In the seventeenth century there arose a remarkable Kurdish woman, Osnat bat Samuel Barazani (c. 1590–c. 1670), who became the *rosh yeshivah*, head of the rabbinical academy in Mosul, Iraq. A brilliant Torah scholar and poet, Osnat was taught by her father, R. Samuel Barazani, who was a learned rabbinic scholar and poet of note and the leader of Kurdistan Jewry. She married her cousin, Jacob ben Abraham, a noted scholar and her father's successor. Describing her upbringing, Osnat wrote:

> as the daughter of the King of Israel . . . I was raised by scholars; I was pampered by my late father. He taught me no art or craft other than heavenly matters.[10]

When her husband died, Osnat Barazani's knowledge and brilliance was such that she succeeded him as *rosh yeshivah* and became the chief teacher of Torah in Kurdistan. She wrote letters of spiritual support and exhortation to various communities and letters requesting financial aid for her *yeshivah*. The famous Kurdish rabbi, kabbalist, and *paytan* (liturgical poet) Phineas Hariri of Harir addressed a letter to Osnat Barazani in terms of respect and veneration reserved for great rabbis and Torah scholars.

Osnat Barazani was referred to as *tanna'it* (the feminine of *Tanna*, the term used for the tannaitic Sages of the Talmud), and was famed throughout the country. She was a kabbalist and mystic. Tales were told about her of miracles she was reputed to have wrought. Osnat Barazani authored a commentary on Proverbs that has apparently been lost.

Osnat Barazani's son Samuel, whom she had taught and reared, assisted her in conducting the *yeshivah*, and he later became a rabbi in Baghdad. One of her descendants David Barazani was one of the outstanding scholars of Kurdistan in the eighteenth century.

THE MOTHER OF THE SHACH

The *Shach*, R. Shabtai ben Meir HaCohen (1622–1663), who produced one of the most important commentaries on the Code of Jewish Law, would frequently quote his mother.[11]

FLORA SASSOON, TORAH SCHOLAR

In more recent times, Flora Sassoon of London (1859–1936) achieved renown as a Torah scholar of note. Her husband, Solomon, was a scholar and Talmudist. However, Flora was often consulted on questions of Jewish law. Religiously observant, whenever traveling she is said to have included in her entourage a *minyan*, a quorum for prayer, and a *shohet*, an authorized slaughterer for kosher meat, so that she would have kosher food.

In 1924 Flora Sassoon delivered a learned discourse on the Talmud at Jews' College in London, and in 1930 she published an essay on *Rashi*. Flora and Solomon's son David Solomon Sassoon was also a scholar as well as a bibliophile, amassing an exceptional collection of Hebrew and Samaritan books and manuscripts.

HASIDIC WOMEN OF RENOWN

Hasidism, founded by R. Israel, known as the *Baal Shem Tov* (1698–1760), in Eastern Europe in the eighteenth century, stressed joy, prayer, and the individual and represented an important historical movement for change and revival in the Jewish life of Europe.

The most honored individuals in the Jewish community have always been the Torah students and scholars. There was no pursuit considered worthier than the study of Torah. Understandably, many Jews who were uneducated and could not aspire to be Torah scholars were attracted to this new folk movement that stressed piety more than learning, and Hasidism rapidly grew. Women in particular found the stress on the individual and the idea that devotion to God and spirituality are as important as Torah study very attractive.

At the inception of Hasidism, most normative Jews did not accept the hasidic innovations–although today Hasidism is universally accepted, although not necessarily adopted, by all Jews. Many were critical of unusual customs being introduced by revolutionary *hasidim* at the time and deplored what they perceived as eccentric behavior on the part of some of the leaders of the new movement. However, a number of pious women who had nonnormative tendencies saw innovative Hasidism as a means of expressing their spirituality in ways that were unacceptable in normative Judaism.

Charisma was important to a movement in which allegiance to a leader and reverence for a sublime personality were central aspects. People would come to the hasidic *rebbe* with questions and problems and request advice on all sorts of matters, ranging from those of a personal nature, such as marriage, to matters of a livelihood. They would also come for requests for intercession with God on their behalf, in the belief that the prayers of a *tzadik*, a righteous one, were especially efficacious before God.

The *Baal Shem Tov* had on a number of occasions expressed the thought that the prayers of women were most acceptable to God. It was understandable, if not totally expected, that the hasidic movement with its new standards for spiritual leadership and its innovative tendencies would generate some charismatic women who would rise to leadership in some communities. Some women became *tzadikot*, "righteous ones," and hasidic rabbis and spiritual leaders, or *Admorot*, the equivalent of hasidic "rebbes" or *Admorim* (acronym for "Our master, teacher, and rabbi").

Notable among the women in early Hasidism was Hanah (c. 1705–c. 1760), wife of the *Baal Shem Tov*, who was widely known for her piety.

Adel the Tzadikah

The first *tzadikah* was Adel (Hodel) (d. 1786), the daughter of the *Baal Shem Tov* and of Hanah, who is venerated by *hasidim* and is the subject of many legends. Adel was said by the *Baal Shem Tov* to be "from the treasury of the purest of souls," and he said that her name was an acronym for the passage *Eish Dat Lamo*, "[At His right hand was] a fiery law unto them."[12] Famed for her piety and wisdom, Adel was considered one of the learned disciples of the *Baal Shem Tov*. She distributed amulets and remedies for the sick.[13]

Adel, who was married to R. Yehiel Ashkenazi, was the mother of some of the outstanding early hasidic rabbinic leaders, R. Moses Hayim ben Adel of Sodilkow, R. Baruch ben Adel of Medzibezh, and R. Israel "Der Tuter" ben Adel–all of whom were popularly identified with their mother.[14]

Feige bat Adel

Adel's daughter, known as Feige bat Adel (d. c. 1805), who was married to R. Simha ben Nahman of Gorodenka, was an illustrious personality in the early hasidic movement. She was considered to be a mystic who was blessed with divine inspiration. Feige was the mother of R. Nahman of Bratslav, the brilliant hasidic leader and founder of Breslaver *Hasidut*, and is said to have had a profound influence upon him.[15]

Meirosh, Daughter of R. Elimelech of Lizhensk

Meirosh, daughter of R. Elimelech of Lizhensk (d. c. 1810), a significant figure in the early hasidic movement, was an outstanding Torah scholar to whom many would come to hear Torah discourses and lectures on the essence of hasidic thought.[16]

Yenta the Prophetess

Yenta, known as "the Prophetess," was the daughter of an unassuming eighteenth-century Galician town-dweller who married a student of the *Baal Shem Tov*. After meeting the *Baal Shem Tov* and observing his humble manner, his piety, and his simplicity, she began to conduct herself in an extraordinarily pious manner and adopted ascetic customs that were foreign to Judaism. Her unconventional behavior included idiosyncratic behavior, such as separating herself from her husband, immersing herself in the *mikveh* (ritual bath) several times a day, and praying with a *tallit*, the men's prayer garment.

The *Baal Shem Tov* said of Yenta that "she has eyes that see and ears that hear," and called her "Yenta the Prophetess." Thereafter that was the name she was known by. Petitioners came to her from far and wide for her blessings.

Yenta lived modestly, and she accepted food rather than money from her petitioners, distributing the food to the poor. Hasidic legend has it that she performed miraculous acts.[17]

Malkah and Adel of Belz

Malkah, daughter of R. Isachar Ber of Sokol and wife of R. Shalom Ber Rokeah, founder of the Belz hasidic dynasty (1779–1855), was famed for her piety and would give religious counsel to visitors.

Her daughter Adel was married to R. Isaac Rubin of Sokolov, who did not call himself *Admor* and was reluctant to practice as a hasidic rebbe. However, Adel, like her mother, conducted herself as a *tsadikah*, receiving petitioners and granting blessings. All she lacked, her father R. Shalom quipped, was a *shtraimel*, the fur hat worn by *hasidim* and their rabbis.[18]

Sarah, Mother of R. Aryeh Leib Sarahs

Sarah, the mother of R. Aryeh Leib Sarahs (i.e., son of Sarah) (eighteenth century), the near legendary hasidic Sage, is also the subject of hasidic stories, although she is not considered one of the *Admonot*. Her son R. Aryeh Leib Sarahs is unique in that he is always associated with his mother.

Freda, Daughter of the *Baal HaTanya*

Freda, daughter of R. Shneur Zalman of Lyady (1747–1812), founder of *Habad* Hasidism and known as the *Baal HaTanya*, is revered by followers of the

"Lubavitcher" *hasidim*. Freda is known to have written a number of treatises based on her father's teachings and to have related his Torah teachings to her brother R. Dov Ber, known as the "Middle Rebbe."[19]

Perele Shapira

Perele Shapira, daughter of R. Israel, known as the *Maggid* (itinerant preacher) of Kozienice (early nineteenth century), was a *tzadikah* of whom R. Elimelech of Lizensk said, "the Divine Presence reposes upon her."[20] She wore a *tallit katan*, a four-cornered garment with *tzitzit*, fringes, at all times, and a *tallit* and a *gartel*, a beltlike sash worn over the clothes by *hasidim* at prayer.[21]

Hanah Havah

Hanah Havah was the daughter of R. Mordecai Twersky of Chernobyl (1770–1837), who also fathered eight sons, all of whom became *Admorim*, hasidic rebbes. Of his daughter Hanah, R. Mottele said, she is the equal of any of them: "She has had the Holy Spirit from her birth."

Many *hasidim*, and even *Admorim*, would discuss hasidic teachings with Hanah Havah, and she would give ethical discourses accompanied by parables. She received petitioners for blessings.[22]

Nehamah the Tzadikah

Nehamah (d. 1935), daughter of R. Hayim Halberstam (1793–1876), founder of the Sanzer dynasty of *hasidim* known as the *Divrei Hayim*, also had eight brothers who became *Admorim* and luminaries in the hasidic movement. She was revered as "Nehamah the *tzadikah*," and *hasidim* came from far and wide to consult with her.

Surele Horowitz-Sternfeld

Sarah ("Surele") (1838–1937), daughter of R. Joshua Heschel Teumim Frankel of Tarnopol, Galicia, was a highly learned woman who was treated like a hasidic "rebbe" by her followers. Married to the *Admor* R. Hayim Samuel Horowitz-Sternfeld of Hantshin, it was to her, however, that *hasidim* turned for blessings. Conducting herself as an *Admorah*, she received homage from them, and she would prescribe remedies for the sick.[23]

Hanah Brachah

Hanah Brachah, daughter of Sarah and R. Haim Samuel, was a famed and brilliant scholar. Married to R. Elimelech of Grodzisk, she was known to wear a *tallit katan*, and many *hasidim* came to receive her blessing.[24]

Malkah the Triskerin

Malkah, daughter of R. Abraham Twersky, the *Maggid* of Trisk (1806–1889), was known far and wide as "Malkele the Triskerin" and was famed for her brilliance and her Torah knowledge. She conducted herself as a *tzadikah* and would receive *hasidim* for audiences and blessings twice daily.[25]

Sarah Shlomtzi

Sarah Shlomtzi (d. 1947), daughter of R. Mendele of Ziditshov, was renowned as a scholar who would deliver Torah discourses from her room, dressed in a *tallit katan*. She received petitioners who came to her for blessings.

Hanah Rachel, the Maid of Ludomir

The most famous of all such hasidic *Admorot* was the *tzadikah* Hanah Rachel Webermacher (c. 1805–1892), known as the "Maid of Ludomir." The only child of Monesh Webermacher of Ludomir in the Ukraine, an established businessman, Hanah Rachel received a good education in Torah and *mitzvot*. She was known to pray with fervent devotion and great ecstasy and unconventionally observed several customs associated with men, such as wearing a *tallit katan*.

Hanah Rachel studied, and became proficient at, Midrash, *Aggadah*, and the ethical works of the Sages. Deeply emotional and sensitive, she was unable to commit herself to marry and establish a family, although she had been promised in marriage to a fine young man. Her nonnormative behavior included retreating often into solitude and excessive meditation and reciting of Psalms.

Once, while undergoing a serious illness, Hanah Rachel had a religious occurrence during which she experienced a spiritual ecstasy; she said she received a "new soul." Her marriage plans were put off, and she donned a *tallit* and *tefillin* (leather cubes containing parchment inserts bearing passages from the Torah and worn on the forehead and upper arm by men during weekday morning prayers), which she wore all day. She also recited the *Kaddish* prayer for the dead, usually recited by men, for her father.

Hasidim built a synagogue for her–known as the Green Schul, because of its color, together with a small apartment for her adjoining it. She began to teach Torah intensively, at first only to women, but soon men also began coming to listen. During the traditional Sabbath Third Meal–the *Seudah Shelishit*–her door would be opened and she would deliver a discourse–usually on hasidic thought and *musar*, Jewish ethics–to her *hasidim*, who would be seated at tables in the synagogue.

Her fame spread throughout the Jewish world, and many Jews, including numerous rabbis, flocked to Ludomir from all over Europe to present their problems to her to receive counsel and blessing from the Maid of Ludomir.

Although many proposals of marriage were made, Hanah Rachel did not marry, hence her title, "the Maid of Ludomir." Finally, at the age of forty she did marry, but the marriage was not a good one and they divorced.

With her marriage, her power as a teacher waned, her students became fewer in number, and popular interest in "the Maid" plummeted. She continued to study, however, devoting in particular considerable time to the study of Kabbalah and Jewish mysticism, especially conjectures regarding the coming of the Messiah.

Hanah Rachel Werbermacher subsequently settled in *Eretz Yisrael*, where she continued her studies, delving into the practical Kabbalah and being occupied in activities that she hoped would hasten the coming of the Messiah.[26] Together with a man who was studying Kabbalah, the two decided on a course of action that they believed would bring the Messiah. They set a date for the event. As he was about to set out for the rites, the young man was greeted by a man at his door who requested hospitality. He was unable to leave for the meeting with Hanah Rachel because of the *mitzvah* of caring for the wayfarer, and so the event did not take place. According to hasidic lore, the wayfarer was none other than Elijah the Prophet, considered to be the forerunner of the Messiah, who did not wish the Messiah to come just yet.

HASIDISM JOINS THE JEWISH MAINSTREAM

Hasidism gradually merged into the Jewish mainstream. Normative, nonhasidic Jews have adopted hasidic (and fundamentally Jewish) teachings regarding fervor and emotional involvement in worship. Hasidism has adopted the tools of intellectual and legal rigor and exactitude.

By and large there is mutual acceptance, although clear differences remain. It is perhaps significant that with the normalization of Hasidism, the occasional tendency for female leadership has disappeared. The woman as the center of the home, as the shaper of the private space, today constitutes an equally prestigious role in hasidic and nonhasidic communities.

BENVENIDA ABRABANEL, LEADER OF ITALIAN JEWRY

One of the unique characteristics of the Jewish community in the Italian Renaissance was the degree of influence exerted by a number of Jewish women on political events and on significant institutions in Jewish life. A striking exemplar of this is Benvenida Abrabanel (Abarbanel, Abravanel) (c. 1490–1560), a central figure in a distinguished family of Spanish/Portuguese Jewish exiles, probably the most important Jewish family of the age. The Abrabanels were the leaders of the Jewish community of Spain in the fifteenth century and that of Italy in the sixteenth century.

Both by birth and marriage, Benvenida was uniquely trained for the position she was to occupy as a significant personage in the leadership of the Italian Jewish community. She was the daughter of Jacob Abrabanel, whose brother R. (Don) Isaac was the greatest rabbinic figure, biblical exegete, and Jewish philosopher of his era, as well as a distinguished statesman who was business agent and financier to Queen Isabella of Spain (he lent her 1,500,000 maravedis) and the man who led Spanish Jewry into exile in 1492.

Benvenida's husband was her cousin, Don Samuel Abrabanel, the son of Don Isaac and the distinguished head of Neapolitan Jewry, who was considered the most eminent Jew in Italy of his day. Don Samuel had built a considerable fortune in banking in Naples. The Jewish poet Samuel Usque said of Don Samuel that "he deserves to be called thrice great–he is great and wise in the Torah, great in nobility and great in wealth" and that he combined in himself all the characteristics that, according to Jewish tradition, merit the gift of prophecy[27]–and Bievenida was said to have shared his qualities.[28]

From Naples to Ferrara

Benvenida Abrabanel was a warm, pious woman, loved and revered by the Jews of her generation as wise, courageous, and genteel. Don Pedro de Toledo, the Spanish viceroy of the Kingdom of Naples, thought so highly of her that he permitted his daughter to be on the closest of terms with Benvenida so that she might learn from her–indeed, she called Benvenida "mother"–and when the daughter became Grand Duchess of Tuscany, she continued to turn to Benvenida for counsel.[29]

When the Jews were expelled from Naples in 1541, the Abrabanels moved to Ferrara, where Bevenida conducted the family banking business after the death of her husband. Under her leadership, the bank-and-loan business grew and flourished, and to help her with the management she took her sons Jacob and Judah and her sons-in-law Isaac (son of Don Samuel's brother, Judah "Leone Ebreo" Abrabanel) and Jacob (also her nephew) into the business.

In Ferrara she lived in magnificent style; their palatial home was thronged with servants and was a center of Jewish and cultural life in Ferrara. Deeply religious and very concerned with her people and their sufferings, Benvenida Abrabanel was active in Jewish communal and charitable endeavors and was a munificent patroness of Jewish learning and scholarship. She was a major financial supporter of David Reubeni, the messianic pretender who many Marranos believed was their deliverer from suffering and persecution, sending him vast sums of money and presenting him with many rich garments and a costly silk banner embroidered with the Ten Commandments that she made for him with her own hands.[30]

Benvenida is reported to have personally provided the funds for the ransom of more than one thousand Jewish captives.[31] The chronicler Immanuel Aboab describes Benvenida as "one of the most noble and high-spirited matrons who have existed in Israel since the time of our dispersion. Such was the Senora Benvenida Abrabanel, a pattern of chastity, of piety, of prudence and of valor."[32]

DONA GRACIA NASI, STAR IN THE JEWISH FIRMAMENT

One of the most remarkable figures in all Jewish history is the stateswoman Dona Gracia Nasi (c. 1510–1569). Gracia was born shortly after the expulsion of the Jews from Spain and Portugal to a Portugese converso (Marrano) family originally known as Benveniste – probably of Spanish origin – who had been forced to adopt Christianity in 1497, but whose members continued to practice Judaism clandestinely while ostensibly living as Christians.

In 1537, following the death of her husband, Francisco Mendes, also a converso, who had established a fortune in precious-stone dealing and banking, Dona Gracia left Portugal with her family, including her nephew Joseph Nasi, for Antwerp, where she headed a bank. There she began to work actively to finance and help the flight of poor conversos from Portugal by setting up a fund for this purpose and also to halt the activities of the Inquisition.

Living as a Christian in Antwerp, Gracia mingled with the highest level of society and had many intimates among the nobility. When the Regent of the Netherlands, Mary of Hungary, the sister of King Charles V, invited Dona Gracia to her palace and asked for her consent for her daughter Reyna ("Malkah") to marry Don Francisco d'Aragon, one of the nobles in court, Dona Gracia told her she would rather have her daughter dead.[33] Now suspected of being a secret Jewess, Dona Gracia was forced to flee to Venice in 1545.

Imprisoned in Venice

Shortly after her arrival in Venice and still living secretly as a pseudo-Christian and occupied with efforts at helping conversos, she was denounced to the authorities as a Judaizer and arrested, and all her property was confiscated by the Inquisition. After many months of internment, she was released from prison following the intervention of Turkish diplomats arranged by her nephew Joseph Nasi, and then moved to Ferrara.

Once in Ferrara, she finally threw off her Christian mantle and her Christian name, Beatrice de Luna, and became known by her Jewish name, Gracia Nasi. She openly continued her work to help Jews suffering from the Inquisition and established a secret organization that operated in the form similar to that of the underground railway that was to be organized several centuries later in the United States. It was to spirit Jews out of Spain and Portugal from "station" to "station" to freedom and reestablish them elsewhere.

The name Dona Gracia Nasi became known far and wide throughout Europe, and Jews everywhere sang her praise.[34] She also financed and encouraged scholarship and became a patroness of Jewish scholars. In 1551 a medal was issued in her honor.

The Ferrara Spanish Bible, which she financed, was dedicated to her as "Her Highness the Senora Dona Gracia." The rabbis in Ferrara praised Dona Gracia as

> the noble princess, the glory of Israel, the wise woman who builds her house in purity, with her hand sustains the poor and needy. . . . Many are they whom she has rescued from death . . . when they were languishing in a dungeon and were given over to death. She has founded houses wherein all may learn the Torah of God. She has given to many the means whereby they may not only live, but live in plenty."[35]

Praise for a "Human Angel"

The Italian poet Samuel Usque, who dedicated a work to her, refers to Dona Gracia as "Divine Mercy" revealed in human form and compares her to the biblical Miriam and Deborah. He writes, in part:

> The Lord hath sent her down in our days from the midst of his holy angels, and united every virtue in one person, and for thy happiness is it that He hath placed this soul in the lovely form of the blessed Jewess Nasi. She it is who, at the beginning of the dispersion (of the Marranos), gave strength and hope to thy perishing sons, made hopeless by their want of means to escape the fire, and encouraged them to go forth on their pilgrimage
>
> With bountiful hand did she succor those who had already set out on their wanderings . . . and who, weakened by poverty and overcome by the perils of the sea passage, were in danger of going no further, and strengthened them in their need. She did not withhold her favor even from her enemies. With her pure

hand and her heavenly will has she freed most of this nation (of Marranos) from the depths of endless misery, poverty and sin, led them into safe places, and gathered them together into obedience to the precepts of the true God. Thus did she become thy strength in thy weakness.[36]

In 1552, on a visit to Venice, Dona Gracia was again arrested and imprisoned and once again was released upon the demand of Sultan Suleiman the Magnificent. In 1553 Gracia Nasi accepted the sultan's invitation and relocated to Constantinople, seat of the Ottoman Empire, where she founded a base for business–spices, wool, shipping, ship building, and international banking. It became a world headquarters for her activities on behalf of persecuted Jews everywhere.

Aiding Scholars and the Needy

In the palace in which she established herself in Galata on the banks of the Bosphorus, Dona Gracia became known far and wide for helping the poor, feeding an average of eighty poor people there every day,[37] and daily distributing charity and largesse to the needy Jews of Constantinople.

She also supported Torah scholars and Torah study. Every day she received at her magnificent residence rabbis and scholars and provided them and their institutions with financial support. She contributed huge sums for the advancement of Torah learning and set up foundations for the provision of fixed financial support for rabbis and Torah scholars all over the world.

Gracia Nasi established synagogues and *yeshivot* in Constantinople and elsewhere and a synagogue and a *yeshivah* for advanced studies in Salonica, and she provided endowments for Torah scholars. A *yeshivah* and synagogue she founded in Galata near her home became the central synagogue there.[38] Upon the circumcision of her nephew Joseph Nasi, when he threw off his cloak of pseudo-Christianity and publicly returned to the Jewish fold, she gave her daughter Reyna to him in marriage.

Taking on the Pope

In her efforts to rescue endangered Jews, Dona Gracia even pitted herself fearlessly against the powerful pope, Paul IV. Like many of his predecessors and successors, Pope Paul instituted odious anti-Jewish measures. In 1555 he issued a Papal Bull that called for vicious anti-Jewish action in the Papal States in Italy. The Jews in Ancona were segregated in a ghetto, prohibited from owning real property, and restricted to dealing in second-hand clothing. The pope hated the Marranos in particular and sought them out.

Upon learning that Pope Paul IV had imprisoned 100 conversos of Ancona with the intention of burning them all and had already had 24 (or 26) burned to death at the stake between April and June 1555—a tragedy still mourned throughout the Jewish world in elegies that are recited on the Fast of the Ninth of Av—Dona Gracia immediately went to work. She persuaded Sultan Suleiman to put an attachment on ships from Ancona at all Turkish ports and to importune the pope to release the remaining Marrano Jews who had Turkish citizenship, threatening him in a letter (on March 9, 1556) that unless he did so reprisals would be taken against Christians living in Turkey.

Dona Gracia then organized a boycott to punish the pope, influencing many rabbis—including R. Joseph Caro, author of the *Shulhan Aruch*, The Code of Jewish Law—to sign a letter to Jewish merchants against doing business with the important Adriatic port under the threat of *herem*, or excommunication. The boycott had a telling effect upon Ancona's commerce during the eight months it was in effect, but because some rabbis, fearing that Jews under the control of the pope would suffer, did not go along with the letter, the boycott did not achieve the maximum success it could otherwise have had. Dona Gracia's boycott was, however, the first attempt by Jews to utilize international economic power against persecutors of the Jews, and it was the precursor of other such efforts in the years to come.

Dona Gracia's Project: A Jewish State in *Eretz Yisrael*

The indefatigable and versatile Dona Gracia's plans to aid her people appeared to be limitless. She had long set her sights on setting up a state for Jews, a refuge for the Jewish people to where they could escape and live in peace. In 1558–1559, she had her son-in-law Joseph Nasi arrange to obtain from Sultan Suleiman the Magnificent various concessions in the ruins of Tiberias and seven surrounding villages. In exchange for the payment of an annual fee to the sultan of 1,000 ducats, she also obtained the express privilege that only Jews should dwell in Tiberias and the surrounding area, the idea being that this would be the nucleus for the establishment of a Jewish state in *Eretz Yisrael*.[39]

Due to illness, Dona Gracia was unable personally to supervise the project. She made available to Joseph Nasi all the funds that would be needed to bring the project to fruition, requesting that he also build a house for her near the Sea of Galilee. Whereupon Joseph sent his agent to Tiberias and sent word to Jewish communities everywhere of Dona Gracia's plan and invited them to settle in Tiberias.

Within a year houses were built, including a palatial residence for Dona Gracia, streets were paved, and a *yeshivah* was set up in Tiberias. The town was revitalized, and the walls around it were rebuilt in 1564–1565. The nucleus for silk manufacturing was set up in order to make the community self-sufficient. Interested as Joseph Nasi was in the success of the project, it was not as pressing a matter for him as it was for his mother-in-law, and he never got around to visiting Tiberias to oversee the project. Dona Gracia became ill and was unable to come to Tiberias.

"An Ornament to Her People"

In the spring of 1569 Dona Gracia Nasi died. She was mourned throughout the Jewish world, and elegies were composed by rabbis and read to their communities. Dona Gracia Nasi was undoubtedly one of the outstanding Jewesses of all time. The historian Heinrich Graetz describes Dona Gracia ("a name which her Jewish contemporaries pronounced only with admiration and love") as "a noble Jewish lady, an ornament to her people by her grace, her intelligence, her character, and greatness of kind, one of those beings whom Providence seems to place in the world from time to time that the likeness of man to the Divine Image may not be quite forgotten."[40]

ESTHER KIERA, COURT JEWESS

In the last quarter of the sixteenth century Esther Kiera (c. 1545–1600), a court Jewess in the powerful Ottoman Empire, distinguished herself and exercised extraordinary sway and influence in the royal court on behalf of the Jews.

The wife of the rabbi and merchant R. Elijah Handali, Esther Kiera was a close friend of the sultana Safiyeh (or Baffa), who was the favorite wife of the sultan and who was in charge of the royal harem. Esther Kiera exercised a decisive influence on court affairs. So important a figure in the court was she that Christian countries such as Venice that wished to win support for anything would require her services as a go-between. Catherine de Medici made use of her services, as did people in the Ottoman Empire who wanted to advance themselves or gain favor with the court.

In the Jewish community Esther Kiera provided aid for the poor, fed the hungry, provided substantial support for rabbis and Jewish scholars, and financed the publication of works by Rabbis Samuel Shullam and Isaac Akrish and the astronomer and historian Abraham Zacuto. She aided the Jewish merchants when they were faced with difficulties on the part of the government and was influential in mitigating a decree that would have destroyed the Jewish communities of the Ottoman Empire.[41]

Involved in court intrigue in which her power was weakened, she was killed by enemies in 1600.

THE JEWISH WOMAN IN THE ITALIAN RENAISSANCE

Jewish women distinguished themselves in a number of fields during the period of the Italian Renaissance. There were even Jewish women physicians in Italy. One Jewish woman physician, Perna, was licensed to practice in Fano in 1460,[42] and another, Virdimura di Medico of Catania, who sought to work with the poor, was authorized to practice in Sicily in 1736.[43]

A Talmud Torah school for the instruction of Torah to girls was established in Rome in 1475,[44] indicating that religious teaching for girls was part of the life of the Jews at that time. Mention is made by the would-be king of the Jews, David Reubeni, of a woman teacher who taught Torah to the daughter of a Roman Jew.[45]

Poems were written in Hebrew in honor of women, indicating that Jewish women at the time were literate in Hebrew–that they would be able to read and understand the poems. There were also translations of the prayer book for women in Judeo-Italian beginning in the sixteenth century.

As mentioned, Pomona de Modena was well versed in Talmud, and she was honored by R. David of Imola with a detailed *responsum* on Jewish law.[46] There were also women scribes who transcribed a number of rabbinic treatises. As early as the thirteenth century, Rome was known to have a Jewish copyist, Paula, a member of the Anavim family, whose name appears as a copyist on various manuscripts. Paola dei Piatelli (Ana), wife of Jehiel ben Solomon of Rome, is considered to have been an outstanding scholar.[47] Some women had mastered the *Shulhan Aruch*, the Code of Jewish Law, and the laws of *shehitah*, ritual slaughter of animals for kosher food, sufficiently to perform the role of *shohet*.[48] While it would hardly be what one would call a typically feminine occupation, it is one that is permitted by *Halachah*.

SARAH COPPIO (COPIA) SULLAM

In Italy there emerged an exceptional Jewish poet in the person of Sarah Coppio (Copia) Sullam (c. 1590–1641). Born into a wealthy Venetian family, she lived in Venice all her life and received an intensive Jewish religious education. By her fifteenth year, in addition to Hebrew and Italian, she could read Latin, Greek, and Spanish, had studied the classics and science, and was already known for her sonnets.

Sarah Coppio was graced with a charming personality. On marrying the learned Jacob Sullam in 1614, the social graces and cultural accomplishments of the poetess made their home in the Venetian ghetto a place where Jewish scholars would gather for discussions. In the words of one observer, Sarah Coppio Sullam had a "noble heart and penetrating understanding, striving after high ideals . . . and surpassed her sex and even men in her period in knowledge."[49] When the brilliant Venetian rabbi and scholar R. Judah Aryeh (Leone da) Modena published one of his works, he concluded that the most fitting person he could dedicate it was Sarah Coppio Sullam and provided a dedication with melodious Hebrew verses in her honor.

An admiring letter she wrote to Ansaldo Ceba, a Genoese monk, for a verse epic he published about Queen Esther, initiated a lengthy correspondence between the two. The correspondence was characterized both by its remarkably high literary level and by conversionary zeal on the part of the monk to convince her to forsake Judaism for Christianity. Deeply religious, Sarah responded with caustic sonnets with which she defended, and declared pride in, her faith.

In 1621 a priest (later Cardinal) Baldassar Bonifaccio attacked her in a pamphlet, accusing her of denying the immortality of the soul. It was a charge that in the Catholic Venice of the time could have had serious consequences, including not only fine and imprisonment, but the Inquisition could have sentenced her to the dungeon and torture, and possibly even to being burnt at the stake.[50]

Sarah lost no time in writing her reply, which she made public two days after publication of the pamphlet, in the form of a spirited Manifesto dedicated to her father's memory on the significance of the immortality of the soul in Jewish belief, proclaiming that the soul is "incorruptible, immortal and divine." She affirmed that the Ten Commandments were given by God and that she clung to them "with my faith and also perform [them] with my acts." She proudly declared that she was a Torah-observant Jew, loyal to Judaism and Jewish tradition, and challenged the priest to observe his Christian teaching "as well as I observe the laws of Judaism."

The work is notable and is characterized by its wit, its courage, and its inexorable logic. She also published two sonnets in which she expressed deep pride in her faith, one of which is a psalmlike Jewish prayer in which she alludes to the false accusations of the priest Bonifaccio:

O Lord, You know my inmost hopes and thought,
    You know when e'er before thy judgment throne
I shed salt tears, and uttered many a moan.
    It was not for vanities I sought.
O turn on me Thy look with mercy fraught,
    And see how envious malice makes me groan!

The pall upon my heart by errors thrown,
    Remove: illume me with Thy radiant thought.
At truth let not the wicked scorner mock,
    O'Thou, that breathed in me a spark divine.
The lying tongue's deceit with silence blight.
    Protect me from its venom, Thou My Rock,
And show the spiteful slanderer by this sign
    That Thou dost shield me with Thy endless might.[51]

GLUCKEL OF HAMELN, MEMOIRIST EXTRAORDINAIRE

Gluckel (pronounced "glickel") is a feminine diminutive derived from *gluck* ("glick" = luck), which means happiness, joy, or good luck. Gluckel of Hameln, Germany (1645–1724), wrote her memoirs. It is our good luck that Gluckel's autobiography has been preserved for posterity and is with us, for it is a significant classic work, a vital source of information about Jewish life and culture in Central Europe in the seventeenth and early eighteenth centuries.

Gluckel, daughter of Beila and Leib Pinkerle (Pincherle), began writing her memoirs in 1690–1691, when she was forty-six, after the death of her first husband, Hayim Segal, in order to "while away her long and melancholy nights" and to inform her children about their family and lineage. She later married Hirsch Levy, who was the president of the Jewish community of Metz.

What unfolds in her autobiography is an invaluable font of information about her own family's daily life and that of their close circle and also a panoramic cross-section of Jewish history of the period in such places as Altona, Hamburg, Hameln, Berlin, Metz, Hanover, and Amsterdam.

While her family was better off than most, in many ways her life was typical of those of girls and women of her time. Gluckel was betrothed at twelve and married at fourteen in Hameln, a small town in Hanover, known to children the world over as Hamelin and made famous by the Pied Piper. Judging by her memoirs, written in Yiddish, the Judeo-German language written in Hebrew letters and containing a substantial sprinkling of Hebrew words, Gluckel was intelligent and knowledgeable and had a traditional Jewish respect for scholarship and learning.

Her Life and Times

Gluckel had received her education with other girls in a *heder,* a traditional Jewish school, where she was taught the Hebrew language, the Bible, Jewish ethical works, and mathematics, and apparently, the rudiments of other subjects, such as history and geography. Based on references in her memoirs to various Jewish works of literature popular at the time and the mention she makes of moralistic stories, she was well read. We gather from her memoirs that apparently neither her education nor her knowledge were unusual for Jewish girls and women in her area at the time.

In all their years together, her husband Hayim–whom she referred to as the crown of her life, her beloved, her dearest and most precious friend–consulted with her regarding all his business decisions. And although she had twelve children, Gluckel was able to successfully conduct the business after his death.

She conducted an array of business transactions, ran a stocking factory, engaged in trading on the Exchange, and attended commercial fairs in different parts of the country, traveling in uncomfortable wooden wagons on rutted, muddied roads in the cold of winter – in an age when any kind of travel was time-consuming and was fraught with the greatest of dangers.

Piety and Acts of Loving-kindness

Life was difficult and insecure, with the fear of pogroms against the Jews constantly present. Gluckel was a religious woman of deep piety and faith in God, who believed fervently in the coming of the Messiah and the redemption that would put an end to Jewish exile and suffering. In expectation of the imminent arrival of the Messiah, her family kept two large casks at the port of Hamburg, one filled with nonperishable food and the other with clothing, and in this way they could quickly set sail for the holy land when the time came.

Gluckel read *techines* frequently and was undoubtedly influenced by them. She was gifted with an excellent memory, a kind, pleasant temperament and disposition, and a desire to fulfill the *mitzvot* of *hesed,* the performance of acts of loving-kindness for others, something she also urged upon her children.

Gluckel was a warm, good mother. Interspersed throughout the memoirs, which were written for her children and grandchildren, are moral directives – notwithstanding her disclaimer that hers is not a book of morals – designed to serve as a kind of ethical testament and to influence them in their behavior to be good, observant Jews in the classical Jewish tradition.

Moral Directives

Gluckel writes:

> This is not a book of morals . . . for . . . we have the Holy Torah, from which we may learn what is useful and what will lead us from this to the future world. We must hold fast to the Torah. As an example: a ship full of passengers sailed the seas. A passenger on deck leaning towards the waves fell overboard and began to sink. Seeing this, the captain threw a rope and called to him to hold it tight and he would not drown. We, in this world of sin, are as if we swim in the sea, not knowing at which moment we may drown. . . . But gracious God threw us a rope for our guidance, to which to hold fast and so save ourselves. This is our holy Torah. Hold tight to it and you will not drown.[52]
>
> The Torah guides us to the rewards for obeying the Commandments and the punishment for sinning, "therefore choose life."[53] God forbid that we should not serve our Creator but live after the desire of our hearts. . . . As soon as the poor human dies he must render his account to his Creator. Therefore well for us that we can prepare our accounts while we yet live. . . . So one should follow

this path: as soon as he has committed a great or minor sin, repent immediately and do penance, as our teachers of morals have written; so that the sin may be blotted out of His Book of Records and a merit be marked in its place. . . . Almighty God is merciful, for, indeed . . . only out of His great mercy and lovingkindness He has done this for us, as a father has mercy on his children . . . [and] we are His children. . . .

So, my beloved children . . . be penitent, charitable and pray, and God will protect you, for His mercy is great. . . . If it is a merit to obey the commandments enjoining us to honor our parents, how much more so should we heed our Heavenly Father who created us and our parents? He gave us life, food, drink, clothed us, and sees to all our needs with a full hand. . . .

My dear children, be devout and good. Serve the Lord God with all your heart as well if things go well with you as when, God forbid, all is not well. We have to bless God for good, so also must we for evil. Remember, everything comes from the Lord. Should, God forbid, children and dear friends die, do not grieve too much, for you did not create them. . . . When should a person grieve? When a day passes in which he has not performed a good deed. . . . We were created only to serve God and observe His commandments and to hold fast to His Holy Torah, "for that is your life and the length of your days."[54]

"Love One Another, Study Torah, Pray with Devotion"

People should love one another, for it is said, "Love your neighbor."[55] This is a principal point. But we seldom find in these times that a person loves another with all his heart. . . . Moreover, set aside a fixed time for the study of Torah. . . . Then diligently go about your business, for providing for your wife and children is likewise a *mitzvah*–the command of God and the duty of man. We should put ourselves to great pain for our children, for on this the world is built.

Your prayers should be said with devotion and awe. And at the time of prayer, do not stand talking with anyone, leaving the Creator waiting until you have finished. . . . After praying, study a page of Torah according to your ability. Do everything with diligence, and support your wife and children honestly. And especially that you should do honest business with Jew or gentile, lest by not doing so, God forbid, you desecrate the Holy Name. If one has another's money or goods in hand, one must be more careful than with his own, so that one should not do an injustice to another.

The first question in the future world will be: have you dealt honestly? If you have acted as a rogue, stolen so as to gather riches, God forbid, and after giving your children fine dowries left them great inheritance–alas! and woe! to those evildoers who enrich their children and lose their share in the world-to-come.

Put your trust in God. Pray that He should . . . bring us good tidings soon, and send us our Messiah speedily, in our our own time. Amen.

Some of Gluckel's children became, or married, noted rabbis. (Her memoirs were transcribed by her son Moses, Rabbi of Baiersdorf.) While bringing up her orphaned children, she decided that when they were all married off she would leave to settle in the holy land.

Gluckel's work is unique and a classic, an important work of Jewish literature and the first autobiographical work by a Jewish woman. Gluckel beautifully reconstructs Jewish life of a period, bringing that millieu to the attention of those living in later periods and giving them an insight into the way Jewish women and mothers lived.

JUDITH MONTEFIORE: DEVOTION TO THE JEWISH PEOPLE

Judith Montefiore (1784–1862), wife of Sir Moses Montefiore, the great nineteenth-century Anglo-Jewish leader, statesman, and philanthropist, had a profound influence on her powerful husband and was a moving force involved in all his endeavors.

Born to Levi Barent Cohen, a leading Dutch-English businessman, and his wife Lydia, Judith Montefiore was a well-educated and highly intelligent and talented woman. Fluent in a number of languages and knowledgeable of Hebrew, she was skilled in music and art and knew well the history of the Jewish people. Her family was observant–her mother Lydia wrote in a last testament to her daughters that they should never forget that they were Jews and should keep their religion and should always bear in mind their Father in Heaven and learn from Him. Judith was a pious and devout woman. She married the equally observant Moses Montefiore, a highly respected businessman of Italian origin, in 1812, and they set about living a life devoted to the Jewish people and Jewish causes everywhere.

Their efforts were joint ones, with Judith being a full partner in all their endeavors. The two traveled together to *Eretz Yisrael* and other lands, often braving danger in order to do so, and participated mutually in efforts to save and protect Jews who were at risk from oppression and persecution.

Supporting *Eretz Yisrael*

Judith Montefiore was a powerful force for the establishment of Jewish communities throughout *Eretz Yisrael* in the nineteenth century, in the years before the advent of modern-day Zionism, setting up communities so that they might eventually become self-sufficient and nurturing their growth by providing financial support during their formative years.

The Montefiores sent a doctor to Jerusalem and set up a medical dispensary in the city. They subsequently established a maternity clinic and a credit bureau for the poor in the city and a girls' school and a hospital. They introduced a printing press and put up a textile factory–and provided raw materials and expert teachers of spinning and weaving–and helped establish a number of agricultural colonies in *Eretz Yisrael*. They founded *Yemin Moshe*, the first Jewish quarter outside the walls of Jerusalem's old city.

A diary Judith Montefiore left of their first–of many–visits to the holy land, in 1827 and 1838, movingly describes *Eretz Yisrael* and its inhabitants. She writes on returning from her first visit that during the previous century only six European females were said to have visited the country during the previous hundred years.

The outbreak of serious blood libels against the Jews of Damascus and Rhodes prompted swift action by the Montefiores in 1840. Similar efforts were undertaken on behalf of the Jews of Russia in 1846, of Morocco in 1863, and of Romania in 1867.

At her death in 1862 following the Montefiores' fiftieth wedding anniversary, all ships in British harbors lowered their flags in homage to a great lady. Moses Montefiore established the Judith Lady Montefiore College at Ramsgate, England, in her memory and wrote in his diary: "May I become more and more deserving of the blessed happiness of being again her companion in Heaven."[56]

RACHEL MORPURGO, HEBREW POET

Rachel Morpurgo (1790–1871), an Italian Hebrew poet, lived in Trieste. Born Rachel Luzzatto, she was related to the illustrious eighteenth-century ethicist, poet, and mystic R. Moses Hayim Luzzatto, the *Ramhal*, and her contemporary, R. Solomon David Luzzatto, the noted Italian Bible commentator, philosopher, and scholar known as the *Shadal*.

Growing up in the scenic Adriatic city, Rachel received a fine Jewish education that stressed ethical teachings. At the age of twelve Rachel is said to have been studying Bahya ibn Pakudah's classical moralistic and pietic work *Hovat HaLevavot* (Duties of the Heart) in Hebrew.

She began writing Hebrew poetry in her late teens, and her poems quickly won praise and gained her wide popularity. Her poems were often based on Jewish historical events or on the travails of the Jews and the hope for the coming of the Messiah, the redemption of her people, and the rebuilding of *Eretz Yisrael*. In one sonnet (translated into English in free verse), she writes:

> He who bringeth low the proud, has brought low all the kings of the earth. . . . He has sent disaster and ruins into fortified cities, and sated with blood their cringing defenders.
>
> All, both young and old, gird on the sword, greedier for prey than the beasts of the forest; they all cry for liberty, the wise and the boors; the fury of the battle rages like the billows of the storming sea.

> Not thus the servants of God, the valiant of His host. They do battle day and night with their evil inclinations. Patiently they bear the yoke of their Rock, and increase cometh to their strength.
>
> My Friend is like a hart, like a sportive gazelle. He will sound the great trumpet to summon the Deliverer.[57]

A deeply religious person, Rachel Morpurgo saw her poems as a means of instilling Jewish spirituality in her readers. In a poem entitled "The Dark Valley," she writes:

> O dark valley, covered with mist, how long will you keep me bound with chains. Better to die and abide under the shadow of the Almighty, than sit desolate in seething waters.
>
> I discern them from afar, the hills of eternity, their ever enduring summits clothed with garlands of bloom. O that I might rise on wings like the eagle, fly upward with my eyes, and rise my countenance and gaze into the heart of the sun.
>
> O Heaven, how beautiful are thy paths, they lead to where liberty reigns, forever. How gentle the zephyrs wafted over Thy heights. Who has words to tell?[58]

An admirer of Morpurgo's, R. Vittorio Castiglioni, chief rabbi of Rome, in 1890 published a collection of her works entitled *Ugav Rahel,* Rachel's Harp. R. Castiglioni quotes one of Rachel Morpurgo's last poems, where she writes a kind of poetic *vidui* confessional, acknowledging her sins, concluding: "I served my Creator with willing heart, I thank Him for all He has done for me."[59]

REBECCA GRATZ, COMMUNAL WORKER

Rebecca Gratz (1781–1869) was one of twelve children of Michael and Miriam Simon Gratz of Philadelphia, who were among the founders of Mikveh Israel, the first synagogue in Philadelphia. A dedicated communal worker, Rebecca Gratz was active in establishing Jewish educational institutions and in social organizations aiding Jewish women and Jewish orphans.

Rebecca Gratz concludes her last will and testament, in the age-old Jewish tradition, by pronouncing the solemn *Shema Yisrael* declaration of the Jewish faith:[60]

> I commit my spirit to the God who gave it, relying on His mercy and redeeming love, and believing with a fine and perfect faith in the religion of my fathers, "Hear, O Israel, the Lord our God is one Lord."[61]

GRACE AGUILAR, VOICE OF HER PEOPLE

In the first half of the nineteenth century the Anglo-Jewish writer Grace Aguilar of London (1816–1847), scion of a noble Portuguese Jewish family of Marrano extraction, produced exceptional books about Judaism, novels related to Jewish themes, and books addressed primarily to Jewish women.[62]

Instructed in Hebrew and in Jewish studies by her learned mother, Sarah, Grace Aguilar was Jewishly knowledgeable and was a deeply committed, religiously observant Jew. She attended Bevis Marks, the leading Sephardi synagogue in London, of which her father was president. She was a prolific writer, almost all her works being about Jewish religious and historical themes and most expressing a deep and abiding yearning for Zion.

Grace Aguilar wrote most of her books for women, whom she constantly urged to study and learn about Judaism. Her goal was to convey to them Jewish traditions and values. She was extremely successful in influencing in particular large numbers of American Jewish women through her writings.

She gained fame with the publication of a learned work, *The Spirit of Judaism: In Defense of Her Faith and Its Professors*, when she was twenty-one. In the book's opening pages Aguilar expresses the wish that her work "be permitted to find some response in the gentle minds of her own sex, to awaken one lethargic spirit to a consciousness of its own powers, its own duties . . . for to them is more especially entrusted the regeneration of Israel."[63]

Urging Women toward Tradition

Setting forth her view that the goals Jewish women should strive for are within the framework of the traditional role Judaism sets forth, Grace Aguilar writes:

> [The author's] aim is to *aid, not* to dictate; to *point* to the Fountain of Life, not presumptuously to *lead*; to waken the spirit to its healing influence, to rouse it to a sense of its own deep responsibilities, *not* to censure and judge.[64]

A considerable portion of the work is given over to a discussion of the significance of the *Shema*, the important Jewish prayer in Deuteronomy proclaiming the unity of God and the precept to love God. For not observing the Torah the Jewish people were punished by the destruction of the Temple in Jerusalem and their dispersion throughout the world, Grace Aguilar declared. She expressed the firm belief in the coming of the Messiah and the ultimate redemption of the Jewish people.

In a spirited defense of Judaism against Christian attacks, she describes the Jewish understanding of God as a God of truth, love, justice, and mercy, and emphasizes the Jew's duty to perform God's commands and to walk in God's paths by performing acts of love and social charity for others.

Spirit was followed by *The Jewish Faith: Its Spiritual Consolation, Moral Guidance and Immortal Hope*, in which Judaism and its traditions are explained in the form of letters to a friend whose religious Jewish convictions she wished to encourage.

Her Marrano Heritage

The travails of her people had a deep impact on Grace Aguilar. Her most important novel was *Vale of Cedars*, a book rooted in family traditions and based on the lives of fifteenth-century Spanish Jewish Marranos, pseudo-Christians who practiced their Judaism in secrecy under the constant fear of discovery, which would be followed by incarceration, torture, and death by public burning by the Catholic Inquisition. The work vividly conveys the milieu and atmosphere of the period.

An immediate popular success, it was especially widely read by Jewish girls. The book was reprinted many times in the nineteenth century and was translated into a number of languages. Like Grace Aguilar's other novels, *Vale of Cedars* was edited by her mother, Sarah Aguilar.

She also expresses her sentiments about Sephardi Jewry and their travail in *Song of the Spanish Jews* and *Records of Israel: Two Tales* and wrote a number of songs and sketches about Jewish life and traditions. She also translated from the French the work about Judaism by the former Marrano Don Isaac Orobio de Castro, *Israel Defended*.

Implanting Jewish Pride in Young Women

Among the books Grace Aguilar wrote for young Jewish women was *Women of Israel*, which consists of biographical sketches of biblical Jewish women. Its intention was to implant in Jewish girls pride in their Jewish heritage and a desire to live full Jewish lives and build traditional Jewish homes, in the process defending the role of Jewish women in Judaism.

She was well versed in the Scriptures and studied Torah and Jewish law extensively. Concerning the position of the woman in Judaism, Grace Aguilar writes: "[I have] scanned every statute, every law [of Judaism] . . . and the result of such examination has been, we trust, to convince every woman of Israel of her immortal destiny, her solemn responsibility, and her elevated position, alike by the command of God, and the willing acquiescence of her brother man."[65]

She wrote a short history of the Jews in Great Britain, *History of the Jews in*

England, published in her work *Chambers' Miscellany*. Her *Sabbath Thoughts and Sacred Communings* consist of reflections on the Torah and on religious matters in general.

Beauty and Truth

A deeply honest and sensitive person, Grace Aguilar viewed beauty and truth as essentially related elements. In her work *Amete and Yafe*, Truth and Beauty, she writes, "Truth is the vital breath of beauty; Beauty the outward form of truth."[66]

Very ill most of her life, she died when was 31. In her short life Grace Aguilar managed to publish eight books and numerous poems. Prior to her death more than one hundred women who were grateful for all they had learned from Grace Aguilar's writings wrote and signed a letter to her, in which they said:

> Dearest Sister: Our admiration of your talents, our veneration for your character, our gratitude for the eminent services your writings render our sex, our people, our faith, in which the sacred cause of true religion is embodied. . . .
>
> You, dearest Sister . . . have taught us to know and appreciate our dignity; to feel and to prove that no female character can be . . . more pure than that of the Jewish maiden, none more pious than that of the woman in Israel.
>
> You have vindicated our social and spiritual equality with our brethren in the faith; you have, by your own excellent example, triumphantly refuted the aspersion that the Jewish religion leaves unmoved the heart of the Jewish woman.
>
> Your writings place within our reach those higher motives, those holier consolations, which flow from the spirituality of our religion, which urge the soul to commune with its Maker and direct it to His grace and His mercy as the best guide and protector here and hereafter. . . .[67]

EMMA LAZARUS, POET OF HER PEOPLE

The finest Jewish poet of the nineteenth century was the American Emma Lazarus (1849–1887). Emma Lazarus was a gifted, perceptive writer who was a loyal defender of her people. Much of her work manifested a deep love for Jewish ideals and values.

Born in New York to a wealthy traditional family of Portuguese extraction, Emma Lazarus was educated at home in Jewish religious and secular studies by private tutors, although it wasn't until she was thirty that she undertook to learn Hebrew. She began writing verse in her teens and published her first major volume of poetry, *Poems and Translation*, when she was only seventeen. It attracted the attention of the poet Ralph Waldo Emerson, who became an admirer of her work and wrote to her.

She also published essays on Emerson and on the American poet Henry Wadsworth Longfellow. By her twentieth year Emma Lazarus had already made her mark on American literature, her lyrical poems characterized by a sensitivity for the beautiful and for the downtrodden.

Intensely proud of her Jewish heritage and identity, Emma Lazarus was inspired to take up her pen to write about her people upon reading George Eliot's *Daniel Deronda,* which called for a Jewish national revival. She began by translating into fine English and publishing in the periodical *The Jewish Messenger* the poems of some of the classical medieval Spanish Jewish poets such as Judah HaLevi Solomon ibn Gabirol and Moses ibn Ezra and the Jewish poems of Heinrich Heine.

Her second collection of poems, *Admetus and Other Poems,* included the poem "In the Jewish Synagogue at Newport," which was reprinted in the *The Jewish Messenger.* It evokes the sounds that reverberated in the synagogue when it was filled with prayers and the glories of the Jewish past.

"Give Me Your Tired, Your Poor . . . Yearning to Breathe Free"

Emma Lazarus is best known for her sonnet *The New Colossus,* written in 1883, which is engraved on a plaque at the base of the Statue of Liberty in New York Harbor and which gained her lasting fame. It was motivated by seeing Jewish refugees from the Russian pogroms of 1881 who were in quarantine on Wards Island in New York. The sonnet reads, in part:

> Give me your tired, your poor,
>   Your huddled masses yearning to breathe free,
> The wretched refuse of your teeming shore,
>   Send these, the homeless, tempest-tossed to me.
> I lift my lamp beside the golden door.[68]

Although modest and unassuming in demeanor, Emma Lazarus was moved to express anger and indignation at the established American Jews who, concerned with their own status, looked down with contempt and disdain on the new wave of poor, traditionally garbed Jews who were being washed up on the shores of the New World, and rejected them as not being of their kind.

The Jewish Passion

Emma Lazarus wrote poems glorifying the Jewish festivals, especially Hanukkah and the spirit of the Maccabees. In *Gifts* and *Birth of Man,* she glorifies the Jewish passion for truth – and its sad consequences:

"O World-God, give me Wealth!"
the Egyptian cried . . .

"O World-God, give me Beauty!"
cried the Greek . . .

"O World-God, give me Power!"
the Roman cried . . .

"O God, give me Truth!"
the Hebrew cried.

His prayer was granted; he became the slave
Of the idea, a pilgrim far and wide,
Cursed, hated, spurned, and scourged with none to save.

The Pharaohs knew him, and when Greece beheld,
His wisdom wore the hoary crown of old.

Beauty he hath forsworn, and wealth and power.
Seek him today, and find him in every land,
No fire consumes him, neither floods devour;
Immortal through the lamp within his hand.[69]

Emma Lazarus' Jewish heritage was dear to her. Among her historical and religious poems, the most powerful is *The Epistle,* which is based on a letter written in the fourteenth century by Joshua HaLorki of Spain to his teacher, Solomon HaLevi, who became the apostate Paul (de Santa Maria) of Burgos and persecuted the Jews of Spain. The former disciple doubted the sincerity of the conversion to Christianity of his former teacher, and, as Emma Lazarus expresses it in her poem:

On this side, death and torture, flame and slaughter,
On that, a harmless wafer and clean water.[70]

The Influence of Persecutions of the Jews

Emma Lazarus tenders an excellent presentation of the Jewish position in the world through the person of *Rashi* in an epic poem, *Rashi in Prague*. In *Dance to Death,* she tells the story of the martyrdom of a Jewish community in Germany during the horrible massacres of the Jews during the Black Death in 1349.

Learning of the pogroms against the Jews that were taking place in Russia and coming into contact with East European Jewish immigrants who had escaped the pogroms, she devoted the last years of her life to aiding Jews and to a vigorous espousal of the cause of her people. She became enraged at the detractors of the new wave of Russian-Jewish-refugee immigrants who were being spewed out in the latter part of the nineteenth century on the shores of New York, and she responded vigorously to anti-Semitic attacks in American periodicals such as *Century* magazine. In her responses Emma Lazarus praised the Jews as pioneers of progress who were the victims rather than the perpetrators of massacres.

In *Crowing of the Red Cock* she writes:

Coward? Not he, who faces death,
Who singly against the world has fought,
For what? A name he may not breathe,
For liberty of prayer and thought.[71]

In passionate Jewish poems such as *The Banner of the Jew*, she cries out:

Where is the Hebrew's fatherland,
His cup is gall, his meat is tears,
His passion lasts a thousand years.[72]

Elsewhere, she points an accusing finger:

Each crime that wakes in man the beast
Is visited upon his kind,
The lust of mobs, the greed of priests,
The tyranny of kings combined.[73]

Early Zionist

In her book *On the Shores of Babylon*, published in 1887, Emma Lazarus comforts the Jew and expresses love for the Jewish people, raising high the ideas of a Jewish homeland in *Eretz Yisrael*, where a religious and cultural refuge for the Jews would be built with close ties to the United States, a country that was already becoming just such a refuge.

Emma Lazarus saw *Eretz Yisrael* as the ultimate home of the Jew, however, and not as a temporary refuge. In February 1883, decades before the idea of political Zionism was popular, she wrote in *Century* magazine: "I am fully persuaded that all suggested solutions other than [the return of the Jews to *Eretz Yisrael*] are but temporary palliatives."[74] Emma Lazarus called for a Jewish leader to rise up and take the Jewish people there:

Oh, deem not dear that martial fire,
Say not the mystic flame is spent,

With Moses' law and David's lyre.
    Your ancient strength remains unbent,
Let but an Ezra rise anew
    To lift the banner of the Jew.[75]

She attains her heights in her poem *The New Ezekiel*, where, recalling the biblical prophet, she calls for a new spirit to revive the bones of Israel and rebuild them in a living, vigorous body:

The spirit is not dead, proclaim the words . . .
    I open your graves, my people, saith the Lord,
And I shall place you in your promised land.[76]

Emma Lazarus was one of the finest American poets of her age, a brilliant writer who skillfully presented the story of her people and their travail and their yearning for spiritual respite in their homeland. At her death the renowned poet John Greenleaf Whittier wrote: "Since Miriam sang of deliverance and triumph by the Red Sea, the Semitic race has had no braver singer. . . ."[77]

SARA SCHENIRER, EDUCATOR OF JEWISH WOMEN

In the early years of the twentieth century, a remarkable Jewish woman, Sarah Schenirer (1883–1938), a seamstress in Cracow, Poland, revitalized Jewish education for girls in Europe. Deeply interested in Judaism as a young girl, Sarah contributed to the household income by sewing clothes during the day, and in the evenings and on the Sabbaths she studied Torah.

Living in Vienna with her family during World War I, Sarah Schenirer thought about the extensive Jewish educational opportunities for boys available in Poland, and was troubled by the low level of religious Jewish education for girls in that country, linking this to a growing inclination to assimilation among young Polish Jews. She writes that she was dismayed when she witnessed the many *hasidim* who would flock to their *rebbes* during the fall festivals to be inspired by Torah, while

> we the wives and daughters stay home with little ones. Our festival is an empty one, bare of Jewish intellectual involvement. For our women have never learned anything about the spiritual content that is absorbed within a Jewish festival. The mother goes to *schul*. The services ring faintly into the fenced and boarded women's gallery. There is much crying by the elderly women. The girls look on them as being of a different century. Youth and desire to live a full life shoot up violently in the strong-willed young personalities. . . leaving behind them the

wailing of the older generation, they follow the urge for freedom and self-expression. Further and further away from *schul* they go, further away to the dancing, tempting light of a fleeting joy.[78]

The Bet Yaakov Idea

Sarah Schenirer decided to return to Poland with a new idea for the Jewish education of girls. She came back to Cracow in 1917 and organized a group of girls into a class of 25 girls in a one-room school, where they were taught traditional Jewish studies with an emphasis on Torah, ethics, and morality and were given industrial skills. By the end of 1918 there were 80 girls, and the school had expanded into a three-room apartment. Heartened by the support for her work by leading Polish rabbis, she traveled to other communities, encouraging them to open similar schools for girls.

By 1929 there were 147 such religious Jewish girls' schools in Poland and an additional 20 schools in Latvia, Lithuania, and Austria, in a network known as Beth Jacob. The Beth Jacob school system came to include a teacher's seminary, founded in 1931, and post-graduate courses. At the time of her death in 1938 there were 248 such institutions, with some 36,000 students in Poland alone, as well as an extensive system of summer camps and the teachers' seminary. By the end of the 1940s there were Orthodox Beth Jacob schools in eight countries, including Israel and the United States.

The list of Jewish women in history continues to grow as Jewish women confront the challenges of their age. Theirs is a balancing act. Nourishing their families physically and spiritually, providing the moral center of gravity, they are frequently called upon to fulfill other roles. They are in demand as teachers, as organizers, as scholars, as community leaders. The litmus test of their success remains, as it has always been among Jews, the harmony of the home and the well-being of the family.

IV

The Married Jewish Woman

6

Women's Rights in Marriage

THE JEWISH IDEA OF MARRIAGE

The Hebrew word for betrothal, *kiddushin*, means sanctification. The purpose of a Jewish marriage is to unite a man and a woman in a shared spiritual bond. *Kiddushin* sanctifies their life together so that they may undertake the holy tasks of procreation and the education of children. From its inception, Judaism has viewed marriage as an institution designed to enhance equally the welfare of men and women. Out of their mutual companionship, security, and happiness, they create a *mikdash me'at*, a sanctuary in miniature.

Marriage provides public recognition of a person's transition from single status to another status, higher than the previous. Marriage provides a framework, hallowed by tradition, for two people to live together in privacy and intimacy.

Marriage is an institution that incorporates various elements–social, psychological, economic, and biological. Judaism raises marriage above all its elements, however, by consecrating the husband-wife relationship on the spiritual foundation of *kiddushin*, thereby allowing holiness to permeate all aspects of the married relationship. Judaism thus creates a "sanctuary" out of a worldly institution.

MARRIAGE IN JUDAISM: A LEGAL CONTRACT

Within the marital relationship, women are accorded certain rights. These rights are founded upon three principles: divine decrees; human duties; and privileges; they entail, moreover, ethical and moral proprieties. Judaism has embodied these principles in religious law to provide a legal foundation for marriage. Jewish religious law provides for legal acts and instruments to contract the marital relationship and to terminate it.

The term *kinyan,* literally, acquisition, is used metaphorically in the Bible and in rabbinical writings to indicate the establishment of a close and intimate relationship. The Bible states, *Am zu kanita,* "This people that you have acquired,"[1] indicating God's establishment of a special relationship with the Jewish people. The Talmud teaches:

> The Holy One, Blessed be He, has five *kinyanim* in this world: Torah, Heaven and Earth, Abraham, the Jewish people and the Temple.[2]

Here again, the term *kinyan* is used to express a deep and intimate bond. In the framework of marriage, *kinyan* is both an expression for the warmth that the marriage relationship offers and the term for the ceremony that legally changes a couple's status.

A traditional Jewish marriage, with its accompanying legal terminology, can be compared to other, mundane, commercial transactions. Unlike most contracts, which are bilateral, the Jewish marriage contract is unilaterally executed, but it requires the consent of the second party. A man "takes" or "acquires" a spouse.[3] *Kinyan* ("taking" or "acquiring"), the legal ceremony marking the change in title or status, provides the marital relationship with its legal foundation.

A major difference between a Jewish marital contract and a commercial transaction, one in which legal title is transferred, is that the former includes mutual legal responsibilities. The man, recognized as the more public one, is the party who takes the initiative and "acquires" a wife.[4] It is he who must write a *ketubah,* the Jewish marriage document, which places obligations on him in her favor. The woman "acquires" a husband who is obligated to her, while she simultaneously places herself under obligation to him.

CONSENT OF BOTH PARTIES REQUIRED

A woman cannot be married without her freely given consent.[5] While it is technically possible for a father to arrange a marriage for a young daughter, this was frowned upon, and such arrangements were generally limited to certain countries and periods in history when girls of marriageable age were forced to marry non-Jewish men unless they were affianced. Maimonides teaches: "Although a man is permitted to commit his minor or young maiden daughter in marriage to whom he likes, it is improper to do so, for [if he does so he violates] a precept of the Sages that a man is forbidden to arrange a marriage for his daughter while she is a minor; she must first mature and say: He is the one I want."[6]

The legal contract of a Jewish marriage is validated only when the consent of both parties has been obtained and the contract has been properly executed, accepted, and attested to by two witnesses.

THE HUSBAND'S TEN OBLIGATIONS TO HIS WIFE

The marital relationship in Judaism transcends the dry legal contract. It includes interpersonal responsibilities as well. When the marriage is performed, the groom recites the traditional marriage formula that refers to marriage as "sanctification" and ends with the words: "according to the laws of Moses and Israel." At this time, the couple is considered to have accepted all Jewish laws and traditions concerning the relationship between husband and wife.[7]

Maimonides delineates the fundamental Jewish principles that govern the marital relationship:

> When a man marries a woman . . . he assumes ten obligations toward her and acquires four obligations from her.[8] The husband's obligations are:[9]
>
> 1. To supply sustenance and maintenance;
> 2. To supply clothing and lodging;
> 3. To provide conjugal relations;
> 4. To provide the *ketubah* sum (an amount to be paid out in the event of death or divorce);
> 5. To procure her medical care;
> 6. To ransom her if she is taken captive;
> 7. To provide her suitable burial;
> 8. To provide her sustenance after his death from his estate, and to ensure her right to live in his house;
> 9. To provide for the maintenance of her daughters after his death;
> 10. To provide that her sons shall inherit her *ketubah* sum.[10]

THE WIFE'S FOUR OBLIGATIONS TO HER HUSBAND

The woman, in turn,[11] in exchange for her sustenance, (1) relinquishes the earnings from her labor; (2) gives to her husband any objects she may happen to find, and (3) cedes to her husband, during her lifetime, the profits from her property (but not the property itself) for the benefit of the household as a whole;[12] and (4) acknowledges that her husband has the right to inherit her estate.[13]

The primary reason for the husband's ten obligations is to provide his wife with security. The wife's four obligations are, however, designed only for the establishment of goodwill and to compensate her husband for some of his obligations toward her. The woman has the option of unilaterally abrogating her obligation to supply her husband with her earnings and becoming financially independent.[14] She thus has the right to keep her income if she wishes.

The husband, however, does not have a similar right; he does not have the option to abrogate his responsibility for her sustenance should he so decide. Maimonides rules:

> If a woman decides, "I do not wish to be sustained by you and I do not wish to give over my earnings," we accede to her wishes, and she is not to be compelled otherwise. However, if the husband says, "I shall not support you and I shall take none of your earnings," he is not to be heeded.[15]

THE WOMAN'S CHOICE: DEPENDENCE OR INDEPENDENCE

According to the Torah, a woman has the legal right to retain her earnings and still be fully supported by her husband.[16] This, however, was seen as a potential cause for marital discord, granting the woman the opportunity to benefit without contributing to the household. To balance this inequity, the Sages granted the woman the option of a trade-off, the choice between financial dependence and financial independence. A woman opting for independence would reimburse her husband for her food, but would receive his support for such expenses as clothing, cosmetics, and personal needs.

Even when the woman opts to contribute her earnings to the family finances, however, the Sages frown on the husband making use of his wife's earnings. "He who looks to his wife's wages," they admonish, "will not find blessing."[17]

A JEWISH DOCUMENT OF WOMEN'S RIGHTS

Concern for the married woman is reflected in the *ketubah*, the legal document that the Jewish groom hands his bride under the marriage canopy during the wedding. A basic precondition for a valid Jewish marriage, the *ketubah* enumerates the essential obligations that a husband assumes toward his wife, both during their marriage and in the event of its dissolution.

The *ketubah* is read aloud to the guests at the wedding, and the husband's obligations, outlined in the *ketubah*, are thereby publicly proclaimed. This demonstrates that these obligations are a matter of public record and accountability and are not merely a private matter between husband and wife. The husband thus becomes bound by Jewish law, morality, and community pressure to treat his wife appropriately.

The financially dependent role of the wife within marriage leaves her vulnerable to a variety of potential evils. While most societies relegated a wife to a position of penniless, utter dependence, the *ketubah* guaranteed a wife rights and privileges. In Jewish marriage, the woman has neither been helpless nor heavily dependent on her husband's goodwill. It is the *ketubah,* in large measure, that is responsible for her strong position.

THE *KETUBAH*: A UNILATERAL–NOT A TWO-WAY–CONTRACT

The *ketubah* is a unilateral agreement, binding only on the husband; it is not a mutual marriage contract obligating both parties. Its essential function in Jewish marriage is to serve as a protector of the woman's rights,[18] and for this reason it is a prerequisite to a Jewish marriage.[19] If the document that the bride and groom execute is a bilateral agreement obligating the bride and groom to fulfill certain commitments to each other, it is not a *ketubah,* even should it so be labeled. It is not the traditional guardian of the rights of the woman in marriage that the *ketubah* is. Whatever the benefits a two-way marriage agreement may appear to offer, such a contract does not fulfill the role of a *ketubah,* and it does not have the binding validity in Jewish law of a *ketubah.* A *ketubah* is the husband's *unilateral* guarantee of the rights of the woman in marriage, and in divorce. A ketubah is designed for the protection of the woman alone, not of her husband.

A husband not bound by an established set of unilateral obligations could employ any number of weapons, ranging from financial deprivation to neglect, with which to humiliate or mistreat his wife during their marriage and even after divorce. By focusing on the husband's legal and economic responsibilities toward his wife, the *ketubah* protects her.

The psychological benefits of the *ketubah* are equally weighty. The *ketubah* bestows on the wife a sense of her own worth and dignity by granting her legal and financial rights. The husband is not tempted to regard his wife as a helpless dependent, because she is protected by the *ketubah.* The *ketubah* corrects these potential imbalances in marriage by forcing the husband to fulfill certain basic responsibilities toward his wife. A husband obligates himself in the *ketubah* to provide his wife several elementary guarantees, including financial support and maintenance, as well as sexual relations. The *ketubah* has proven its effectiveness. Even when living among societies that denied women any semblance of independence or status, the Jewish wife was able to maintain her dignity and self-respect.

OBLIGATING THE MAN AND HIS ESTATE FOR HER SUPPORT

The *ketubah* obligates the man to provide for the woman after a divorce and, in the event of his death, requires his estate to be used for her maintenance. The financial arrangements outlined in this legal document serve to protect the woman from undue economic hardship[20] in the event of her becoming widowed or divorced.

The *ketubah* sum has been compared to alimony, but they are different. The *ketubah* amount, on the dissolution of marriage, is paid out in a single sum and is not, as is alimony, paid out in installments. The basic sum the Sages decided upon was 200 *zuzim* (100 *zuzim* for a divorcee),[21] a sum that could provide support for the wife and her children for one year.[22]

To ensure the proper fulfillment of his marital pledges, the *ketubah* binds the man to legally mortgage as security all his present and future assets,[23] including even "the shirt on his back."[24] So essential to the document was this financial obligation that the amount itself became known as "the *ketubah*," and "*ketubah*" thus became both a legal and a financial term.

In addition to the basic sum of the *ketubah*, the husband is required to provide an additional sum of his own. In the event of divorce or of his death, this amount, representing the bride's dowry and the total value of her personal belongings, becomes her possession.

The wife maintains ownership of the property she brings to the marriage, according to the terms of the *ketubah*. In the event of divorce, her former husband is obligated to pay her certain compensatory sums.

ASSURING THAT THE HUSBAND FULFILLS HIS OBLIGATIONS

Should the man fail to live up to the obligations outlined in the *ketubah*, the wife can request that the rabbinic court either compel him to carry out his obligations or force him to grant her a divorce. The husband cannot easily initiate divorce proceedings that are contrary to her interest. Dissolving the marriage requires his fulfillment of a number of legal obligations outlined in the *ketubah* in addition to the outlay of substantial sums of money.

Historically, the *ketubah* also provided security for the woman, ensuring that her husband would not treat her as a mistress or servant girl to be sent away according to his whim, and that he would not leave her when her attractiveness began to wane.[25] Since the basic biblical requirement for divorce is a relatively simple act on the part of the husband, the financial, economic, and legal provisions of the *ketubah* are specifically designed to complicate the divorce procedure and protect the woman.[26]

One of the safety mechanisms afforded by the *ketubah* is the husband's commitment, in the event of divorce, to pay his wife the *ketubah* sum. The heavy payment itself acts as a deterrent against any impulsive act. Thus, while maintaining the possibility of terminating a bad marriage, the *ketubah* constrains a man from deciding hastily on a divorce by imposing a heavy financial burden on him.

The *ketubah* makes divorce a lengthy process by bringing in complex legal provisions and financial adjustments. It also serves to some extent as a deterrent to a potentially exploitative husband. Indeed, the expense and complexities involved might motivate both parties to invest in efforts in improving the marriage rather than turning to divorce.

THE IMPORTANCE OF POSSESSING A *KETUBAH*

The Sages placed such importance on the *ketubah* that they ruled that "it is forbidden for a man to reside with a woman even one hour without a *ketubah*."[27]

Jewish law requires the woman to ensure that she not only receives a *ketubah*, but that she keeps it in a safe place at all times. If it is lost, destroyed, or misplaced, she must have it replaced.

THE *KETUBAH*, AN ANCIENT TRADITION

The *ketubah* dates back to ancient times; the marriage agreement referred to in the third to the second centuries B.C.E. in the aprocryphal Book of Tobit, "And he took paper,[28] wrote a contract, and signed it; then they began to eat"[29] – is probably a *ketubah*.

But the *ketubah* predates this reference as well. One of the earliest Jewish manuscripts discovered to date is a *ketubah* from 440–420 B.C.E.,[30] belonging to a woman named Mibtahya. The document is part of a remarkable collection of Judaic-Aramaic *papyri* unearthed early in this century at Elephantine and Aswan in southern Egypt, where a community of Jewish soldiers and their families settled following the Babylonian exile in 586 B.C.E.

While the text of the *ketubah* as we know it had not yet become formalized 2,400 years ago, the ancient contract bears a striking resemblance in many details to the one used today.

KETUBOT FROM THE DEAD SEA CAVES

In March 1961 Israeli archaeologist Yigael Yadin and a team of volunteers were exploring a cave in Nahal Hever, a canyon near the Dead Sea.[31] The cave, located in a rugged and forbidding area of the Judaean Desert, was situated on an almost vertical rock face, with the entrance about a hundred meters down a cliff and the canyon floor a sheer drop of 200 meters below. The cave could be reached only by carefully climbing over narrow ledges and jumping over dangerous crevices while holding onto a rope.

Jewish fighters led by the near legendary Simon Bar Kochba had occupied this large cave during the revolt against Rome in 132–135 C.E. They had obviously chosen it for its remoteness, relative inaccessibility, and ease of defense. The clear remains of a large Roman siege camp on the plateau above testified to the importance and size of the Jewish contingent of men, women, and children who had inhabited the cave.

In the spring of 1960 Yadin's team had made a monumental discovery in this same cave: letters written by Bar Kochba and signed with the apellation "President of Israel." Also found were other documents, bronze vessels, and textiles, in addition to the skeletal remains of Jewish fighters and their families.

In 1961 Yadin returned for a more thorough exploration of the Nahal Hever cave. It was Wednesday, the first day of the second search, and the noted archaeologist divided the volunteers into small work groups, assigning each a different portion of the cave to systematically explore it in its entirety.

About three in the afternoon, Yosef Porat, a restive young volunteer with a heightened sense of curiosity, left his assigned work group to search with another. "Just before I reached them," he later reported, "I trod on a stone which wobbled suspiciously. So I removed it, and under it I saw this crevice full of finds." Brimming with excitement, he hurried to Yadin, who described the event in these words:

> I rushed back with him. In the cave this was not an easy thing. First one had to crawl through the narrow tunnel . . . then jump like an acrobat over the huge and pointed boulders. . . . We just ran. . . . Hope and doubt tumbled over each other in my mind. . . . When I approached . . . I saw a crevice between big stones . . . and below it was still another crevice about a meter deep. Inside it I could see quite clearly a basket made of palm fronds . . . filled to the brim. . . .[32]

DISCOVERING AN ANCIENT TREASURE TROVE

Among other finds, the men discovered a leather pouch containing a bundle of ancient papyri. Carefully opening what turned out to be a woman's purse, Yadin was astounded to discover a veritable treasure trove of ancient documents belonging to a much-married woman, Babata. On the back of one of the documents was the inscription: "The *Ketubah* of Babata, the daughter of

Simon." Another *ketubah* in the collection was that of Shlomzion, daughter of Judah.

The significance of the *ketubah* of Babata, the date of which is not decipherable, but which Yadin fixes between 128 and 130 C.E. and that of Shlomzion, dated at 128 C.E., together with two other, less well-preserved *ketubot* dating from 117 C.E. (discovered in the Wadi Murabaat in the Judaean Desert by French archaeologist *Père* Roland de Vaux), is that they were written at the time of the compilation of the Mishnah. With the exception of the *ketubah* of Mibtahya of the fifth century B.C.E., they are the oldest known existing *ketubot*.

Despite the antiquity of these documents, their wording indicates that they followed an accepted format, the general framework of which may have been used by Jews for a considerable period of time even before the fifth century B.C.E. In fact, the *ketubah* is traced by some to the Torah itself,[33] which declares that the woman is entitled, as her minimum requirement from her husband, to the basic provisions of food, clothing, and conjugal rights.[34]

VARIATIONS IN THE TEXT OF THE *KETUBAH*

An interesting variation in the Babata *ketubah* is the opening statement that the marriage is declared valid "according to the laws of Moses and the Jews," and not "Moses and Israel," the formula that appears in the Tosefta and is used even today in *ketubot* and for the betrothal ceremony at Jewish weddings. The term "Moses and the Jews" is, however, in accordance with the wording for the betrothal in the Jerusalem Talmud and for the proposal formula of a number of contemporary *ketubot*. The *ketubah* of Shlomzion, daughter of Babata's second husband by a previous marriage, is dated 5 April 128 C.E. Here, too, the text contains clauses remarkably similar to those in use today. Shlomzion's *ketubah* is written in Greek, which may indicate that some of the Jews of that period had assimilated to some degree. This is confirmed by the wording of the proposal formula, which is executed "according to Greek law." Babata's *ketubah*, however, is in Aramaic, the *lingua franca* of Israel of her day and the language traditionally used in *ketubot*, even today.

Aramaic was chosen as the language for *ketubot* and other legal documents during the period when large numbers of Jews lived in Babylon, where Aramaic was spoken.[35] While their dates since talmudic times were usually written in Hebrew, Aramaic was generally preferred for the text, as it was for other legal documents, because of its international character. Subsequently, Hebrew began to be reserved for sacred texts, leaving Aramaic for secular ones.

A *ketubah* that may be found at University College, Cambridge, England, dated 922 C.E., comes from Mantaura, the Lydian city in the Meander Valley in Asia Minor, then part of the Byzantine Empire. This *ketubah* was uncovered in the *genizah* (a repository for books or ritual objects that have become unusable) of the Elijah Synagogue in Fostat, Old Cairo, at the end of the nineteenth century. This *genizah* brought to light many important early Jewish documents, including hundreds of fragments of *ketubot*.

Pioneering studies on the *ketubot* found in the Cairo *Genizah* were done by S. Asaf and S. D. Goitein. M. A. Friedman produced a major study of the Cairo *Genizah ketubot* by analyzing 78 fragments of 65 *ketubot* located in 10 separate libraries. The fragments date from 993 to 1100. His examination of these fragments – which follow the *ketubah* format used in *Eretz Yisrael* – has provided a wealth of information on the nature and contents of the *ketubah* and its development.

The *ketubah* fragments testify to the rich diversity of the traditional *ketubah* itself. They are particularly revealing in relation to the status of the Jewish woman, especially during the classical *Genizah* period of the tenth to the thirteenth centuries. Almost every fragment contains some unique element. The *ketubot* essentially conform to the formulation of the Babylonian *Gaonim*, with many containing minor conditions and special clauses that are highly informative of the relationship between men and women of that period. Both the *Genizah ketubot* and those of the Bar Kochba period 800 years earlier show evidence of a continued line of uninterrupted tradition.

THE ORIGIN AND PURPOSE OF THE *KETUBAH*

The *ketubah* in its modern form probably dates back to the first century B.C.E. when, as indicated in a historic *Baraita*[36] (a Tannaitic statement not included in the Mishnah), the Sanhedrin (Supreme Court of 70), under the leadership of its president R. Simon ben Shetah, the sister of Salome (see Chapter 5) formally defined the contents of the *ketubah* and specified the duties to which it obligates the groom and the security he must provide for the fulfillment of his obligations and had the *ketubah* committed to writing. From this we learn of its purpose in relation to the couple's marriage or divorce and in the event of the husband's demise.

Before this ruling of the Sanhedrin, a man could put aside a sum of money for his wife in the event of his death or of a divorce. But if he were to lose or hide the money, his wife would not be legally protected. Bereft of her rightful *ketubah* sum, she could become destitute. The Sanhedrin legislated, therefore, that a husband's entire estate is to be mortgaged through the *ketubah* and considered as collateral for the *ketubah* sum in order to guarantee the fulfillment of his obligations as specified by the *ketubah*. In this way a wife would be able to collect the sum due her just as she would any contractual debt.[37] In the event of the woman's becoming widowed, they ruled that the *ketubah* is to protect her; her wealth is to be returned to her, and she is to receive the *ketubah* amount as well as an additional sum of money.

As mentioned, another important function of the *ketubah* is to deter the husband from severing the marital bonds too easily, "so that it should not be considered easy to send her away."[38] Since in Judaism marriage is seen as a permanent union, the *ketubah* is a vital instrument circumscribing and making it difficult for the husband to divorce his wife, by placing in her hands a variety of legal means designed to protect her from possible abuse and to safeguard her rights. Today, therefore, through a rabbinic ordination dating from the tenth century, a man may not divorce his wife against her will.[39] Still, a *ketubah* is a required obligation.

THE OBLIGATION OF THE HUSBAND TO RESPECT HIS WIFE

The significant legal and psychological benefits the *ketubah* brings to the Jewish marriage have contributed substantially to the stability of the Jewish family. The obligation to which the contract commits the husband serves to create in him a sense of responsibility and respect for his wife that is the cornerstone of a healthy, enduring relationship.

The difference in approach between Jewish tradition and other religions regarding the relationship between husband and wife is underscored as early as the marriage ceremony itself. The traditional marriage vows of the church, in accordance with the New Testament's obligations of wifely obedience and subjection to her husband, require the woman to pledge to "honor" and "obey" her husband.[40] The Torah, on the other hand, obligates the husband to give his wife a *ketubah* at the wedding ceremony, a solemn written obligation to protect her rights in marriage.

Historically, societies dominated by men have delegated the overriding position of strength within marriage to the husband, by permitting him to control the family's finances. Judaism, however, has always recognized the vulnerability of the woman. Bound to the home by social norms and the realities of childbearing and motherhood, she has been dependent on her husband for sustenance and protection.

A GUARANTEE OF RIGHTS AND PRIVILEGES TO THE WIFE

The structure of marriage itself makes the wife susceptible to a dependent role. Throughout history, the woman's status has been vastly inferior to the man's. She has been relegated to a position of utter economic dependence on the husband and left devoid of possessions. Among Jews, the *ketubah* has served as an enlightened instrument comitting the husband to certain fundamental responsibilities and guaranteeing a wife inalienable rights and privileges. The *ketubah* raises woman's status, placing a substantial measure of control in her hands. The Jewish woman has maintained her dignity within the family. Her position and her dignity are bolstered by the *ketubah,* in stark contrast to the degradation of married women in most traditions.

In the Jewish perception, the man does not need to be further strengthened by laws and legal instruments; it is the woman who is in need of this. By obligating a husband to a strict set of responsibilities toward his wife, the *ketubah* thus balances the potentially uneven structure of marriage.

There are, in addition, many other rights of the woman in marriage that are not dependent on the *ketubah.* Should a man decide to relocate his family to another city–or to another neighborhood in the same city–that is not as desirable, the wife can prevent him from doing so. She can also force her husband to relocate when she wishes to leave an area that is undesirable and move to another domicile. If she wishes to leave the Diaspora and reside in *Eretz Yisrael* she can unilaterally force him to settle there–a right he also shares. She also has an array of privileges regarding satisfaction in marriage and relating specifically to conjugal fulfillment and neglect.

Long before the concept of women's rights became popular, through the *ketubah* and through a series of laws designed to protect the woman in marriage, Judaism established a check-and-balance system of *human* rights.

7

Sexuality and Marital Relations

HARMONIZING THE SPIRITUAL AND THE BIOLOGICAL

Sexual attraction between male and female is a fundamental aspect of human nature created by God to ensure the propagation of humankind. Sexual desire is seen in Judaism as a divinely given procreative impulse through which humans fulfill God's command to procreate.[1]

As a God-given impulse, sexual desire cannot be regarded as sinful, shameful, or unnatural,[2] but is viewed as a natural experience. The power of this drive, an integral part of being human, impels procreation and ensures the preservation and continuation of the human race. It is also the God-given means for the creation of a family, the ideal social framework for the life of the Jew.

This Jewish view differs radically from classical Christian doctrine, which considers sexual desire to be a necessary evil, a compromise with morality tolerated because of the need for procreation. These concepts are foreign to Judaism. Judaism is incompatible with the classical Christian belief that the sexual act is a debasing experience from which holy people abstain. Judaism recognizes that sensual desire stems from the same divine source as a human being's most ethereal and spiritual components.

The Torah uses the term *kedushah,* holiness, to refer to proper sexual conduct. To be imbued with holiness, sexual activity must be performed in a licit manner that reflects elevated human conduct. The Jewish ideal of holiness requires both renunciation of the illicit and sanctification of the licit. Merely avoiding forbidden sexual relations does not constitute holiness. Holiness requires participation in sanctioned and sanctified marital relations.

The concept of these relations as *kedushah* requires that they be conducted in a decidedly human fashion. Within the context of marriage, sexual relations, performed with restraint, respect, and sensitivity for one's partner, and with *kavanah*, proper intent, fulfill a commandment of God.

When regulated by the religious bonds of marriage and when conducted in a human manner and invested with proper intent, the act is viewed in Judaism as the essence of life and an expression of the noblest human creative impulse. Marital relations are a *mitzvah* a commandment of God, notwithstanding the intensely physical nature of the act. Fulfillment of this *mitzvah* provides that spiritual and transcendental experience that leads to *kedushah*. Judaism views sexuality as a means of sanctifying that which would otherwise be an act of physical gratification only.

HUMANIZATION–THE JEWISH APPROACH TO SEXUALITY

The Jewish approach to sexuality is characterized simply by humanization. According to Jewish belief, an individual human being, created in God's image, realizes his or her fullest potential by behaving in a humanistic way, differentiating himself or herself from animalistic behavior and tendencies. Humans fulfill their obligations to their Creator, to themselves, and to their fellows when they behave decently and with compassion. This approach to human conduct extends especially to sexual behavior, an area where there is a compelling need to set guidelines for behavior.

The key to the humanization of the sensual drive is human mastery of it. Jews are expected, through self-discipline in thought and action, to humanize and take responsibility for–but not to suppress–their natural physical urges.

The sexual drive of humans can both raise them to the highest level of holiness and can also debase and corrupt them. Sexual temptation and infidelity can also wreak havoc in the structure of the family and the community. During the Jewish wedding service, the man tells the woman, "Behold, you are sanctified to me."[3] The Hebrew word here for "sanctified" is *mekudeshet*, the root of which is *kadosh*, holy. In the Bible, *kedeshah*, harlot,[4] has precisely the same root, but its meaning is exactly the opposite–"one who has perverted her holiness." Judaism teaches that the same faculty that produces lofty holiness can also produce degradation.

Judaism requires that the sexual drive be properly channeled, to differentiate human beings from lower orders of creation. In the words of R. Samson Raphael Hirsch:

> No single one of the powers and natural tendencies which are given to man is either good or bad in itself, from the most spiritual down to the most sensuous. They are given to him for beneficial purposes to accomplish God's will on earth.

The divine Torah gives them a positive aim and a negative limit. In the service of this purpose indicated by God and within these limits set by God everything is good and holy. Separated from these purposes and outside these limits, coarseness and evil begins.[5]

God has given sensuality an appeal to your senses, not that it should master and direct you, but that you should direct it.[6]

MASTERING AND GUIDING ONE'S INSTINCTS

The oft-repeated biblical injunction to be holy is directed exclusively to the Jew. This command usually refers to those laws that regulate the human's strongest physical instincts: the instincts for self-preservation and self-perpetuation. These instincts are intrinsic to all creatures and are essential to their existence and propagation. Only the human being is endowed with the ability to master these instincts, however, and only the Jew is commanded to exercise this mastery.

The Sages teach that for the moral individual seeking holiness, mastery over his sexuality is a compelling goal. When the power of moral direction over the sensory nature is absent and free reign is given to the body's elementary urges, human beings lower themselves to the same level as the animals. Mastered by their desires, humans cannot rise above those components that make up their lowest common denominator, which they share with animals.

Humans share certain characteristics with animals. However, humans can choose to rise above animals. Alternatively, they become more brutalized than the animal. Animals lack human consciousness and conscience. Humans are rational beings endowed with free will and a soul. Unlike animals, humans can, through the reasoning process of rational beings, both form and amend beliefs and ideas. When humans do not act rationally, but are prompted solely by desire, they subvert their humanity.

The rational human being experiences a moral and spiritual imperative unknown to the animal. There exists a desire to elevate oneself above the animal, and, as a rational being, to exercise control over impulses and to begin the ascent to holiness. Humans must utilize the rational, human faculties and become free of dependence on and submission to primal urges. However, a Jew is forbidden to stifle the God-given inclinations, only to master them and harness them to God's will.

THE JEWISH VIEW OF RELATIONS BETWEEN SINGLES

Recognizing the sexual relationship as the most intensely personal and intimate human experience, Judaism teaches that marriage is the only proper framework for such relations. Only an institution that provides a binding legal and religious commitment of a publicly recognized nature can support and sustain such a relationship. Marriage teaches that individual actions unfold within a social structure.

Marriage provides a universally recognized framework powerful enough for the most intense human relationship, because its obligations are not merely derived from a contractual relationship between partners but are imposed by the institution. Marriage also provides a universally accepted framework for bringing children into the world and rearing them.

Judaism does not sanction sexual activity that lacks the long-term covenant of marriage. Intimate relations within the marital structure are desirable and holy; sexual behavior and relations outside of marriage are considered in Judaism as undesirable, undermining the human aspiration for holiness.

To avoid the overstimulation of the sexual drive and reduce the risk of premarital sexual involvement, social relations between unmarried men and women are governed by rules of conduct designed to minimize social contacts that might lead to sexual stimulation. Jews are encouraged to avoid situations in which their self-discipline will be tested. Any physical contact between unmarried men and women–and between men and women married to others–is, therefore, proscribed by Jewish law. Traditional Judaism recognizes the power of sexual desire and the ease with which it can be aroused, particularly in men. Male sexuality is seen as a strong force that must be contained in the interest of women and of social order. Judaism provides clear behavioral guidelines to hold biological drives in their appropriate place.

The Sages consider a "platonic" friendship between man and woman as a transitional relationship, in which instinct gradually prevails. The strength of physical desire transforms into a physical relationship what was formerly one of friendship and camaraderie between a young man and woman.

NEGIAH–TOUCHING, HAND-HOLDING, KISSING, EMBRACING

The Sages therefore impose limitations on a relationship between a single man and single woman to ensure that the relationship remains social. That point of limitation is physical contact (Hebrew: *negiah*). While society at large may accept certain physical acts as expressions of affection to which no sexual overtones are attached, the Jewish view is that no form of physical contact between a man and a woman, whether it be hand-holding, embracing, or kissing, can be guaranteed to remain casual for long. Physical contact between members of the opposite sex will often progress beyond the casual stage.

The human touch has the power to arouse physical desire and to transform dramatically the nature of a relationship. Recognizing this, the Jewish view holds that self-control is feasible so long as there is no physical contact. It is true that no two people, upon exposure to external stimuli, will have the identical threshold of response. Then, too, there may be individuals for whom physical contact with members of the opposite sex does not provoke a sexual response; nevertheless, the single gauge of *negiah* was established by the Sages as a standard for all Jews.

Judaism regards biological sex drives as serving a dual function: two separate individuals are drawn together in order to fulfill their basic desire of perpetuating themselves, to engage in the physical act of sexual union; additionally, this union establishes an intense emotional bond between two individuals that allows them to merge their separate selves into a unified entity—an indispensable condition for the creation of a viable family.

Since this intimate act is an expression of love and a vehicle for fulfillment, it is reserved for one's life-partner in marriage. Judaism considers single men and women to be in a state of preparation for marriage. This "preliminary" state requires as substantial a measure of restraint, self-discipline, and self-control as does marriage itself, and in this sense it is an ideal preparation for marriage.

The Jewish rules of conduct for single men and women express a keen awareness of the nature of the sensual drive and of the stimuli that activate it. To ease self-control, young people avoid confrontations—i.e., unnecessary social contacts between men and women and situations and settings where erotic thoughts and sensual desire are often inevitable. Judaism holds that constant exposure of an individual to such situations turns sexuality into an obsession and demoralizes the unmarried man or woman. The mind and the heart are forced to surrender to instinct and passion.

Humans who are slaves to their passions subordinate their reason to their instinct and erase the difference between themselves and animals. An animal knows no restraints; it copulates as freely as it eats. A human being who is governed by passion rather than by reason is animal-like in behavior. Coitus is a depersonalized act; one has relations with a thing, not a person. Seeking only to gratify their desires, these humans exploit another person in the process. It is not a loving, giving relationship, but a taking one, in which one individual uses another in order to gratify his or her desires.

LESBIANISM

Lesbianism is prohibited by Jewish law. Judaism perceives physical relations between members of the same sex as a perversion of nature and of the divine order. In Judaism procreation is a major—though not the only—purpose of sexual relations. Since homosexual activity cannot result in offspring, it frustrates the natural function of human sexuality.

Homosexuality is also seen as damaging family life and is perceived in Jewish tradition as intrinsically repulsive, *prima facie*. Unlike homosexual relations between men, which are specifically prohibited in the Torah as an "abomination,"[7] a capital offense comparable to incest and relations with animals,[8] lesbianism is not expressly mentioned in the Torah. Lesbianism is forbidden[9] on the grounds of its inclusion in the general biblical prohibition against imitating the immoral practices of the Egyptians and the Canaanites.[10] It is therefore a punishable transgression. Maimonides expresses the law as follows:

> Women are forbidden to engage in lesbian practices with one another, since the act is one of the abominable practices of the Egyptians that we were warned against doing.[11] As the Torah declares: "You shall not emulate the practices of the land of Egypt."[12] What did they do? A man would marry a man and a woman would marry a woman, or a woman would marry two men. Although such acts are prohibited, one is not flogged for the transgression, for there is no specific negative biblical precept regarding it, and [in such acts between women] intercourse is not involved. Consequently, such women are not disqualified from marrying members of the priesthood on the grounds of prostitution, nor is such a woman forbidden to her husband, for it is not prostitution. However, she is to be flogged because she transgressed. And a man should give heed lest his wife do this, and do what he can to prevent known lesbian women from visiting and her from going out to them.[13]

WOMEN'S SEXUALITY

Age-old traditions, lately challenged by modern Western thought, have granted all conjugal rights to the husband while ignoring the needs and wants of the wife. Judaism is often erroneously included in a blanket condemnation of these. Some of these traditions are often referred to as part of a "Judaeo-Christian heritage." This term is a misnomer, a heritage of either Judaism or Christianity but rarely both. Judaism and Christianity are antithetical in so many respects than one can seldom hyphenate the two terms. It is in their differing views on sexuality and marriage in particular that the contradictions between them are most blatant.

The Torah and the Talmud reveal a sensitivity of female sexuality. The Sages teach that the woman's drive is a more powerful one and that her passion is greater than that of the man.[14] The married woman is granted a greater right to fulfillment than is her husband; the obligation is placed on the man to provide his wife with fulfillment.

A newly married Jewish man acquires not only the right of sexual congress with his wife but also a strict sexual responsibility. In the *ketubah*, the Jewish marriage contract, the groom, on the basis of a biblical precept, agrees to provide his wife with *onah*, or marital relations. This obligation is distinct from the *mitzvah* of *piryah verivyah*, procreation.[15] This is underscored by the fact that Jewish law requires a husband to have conjugal relations with his wife during pregnancy and at other times when conception is not possible.[16] In the words of the Sages, "the *mitzvah* of *onah* and the *mitzvah* of *piryah verivyah* are two separate things, and neither is dependent on the other."[17]

THE MAN'S OBLIGATION TO "GLADDEN" HIS WIFE

Onah, the husband's duty to have marital relations with his wife, is one of the three fundamental obligations he undertakes upon marriage, along with providing his wife sustenance and clothing.[18]

Judaism teaches that the two separate *mitzvot* are fulfilled with different *kavanot*, intentions. For the *mitzvah* of procreation, the intent is that the act should result in "proper, fitting and pure children . . . who fulfill God's commands."[19] To fulfill the *mitzvah* of *onah*, the husband must concentrate on giving his wife pleasure,[20] in accordance with the biblical directive, *Vesimah et ishto*, And he shall gladden his wife.[21] The duty of *onah* is stated thus in the Torah: "*She'erah, kesutah ve'onatah lo yigra*, He shall not neglect her need for food, clothing and *onah*."[22]

The Talmud condemns the man who does not carry out his conjugal responsibilities: "He who neglects his marital duties to his wife is a sinner."[23]

When the act is performed with the proper *kavanot*, it is a selfless, giving one. When stripped of these *kavanot*, the sexual relationship becomes one in which each partner uses the other as a vehicle for personal pleasure, and one's partner becomes a depersonalized object providing the same physical gratification obtainable from autoeroticism. Such a relationship is not only unholy but debasing.

HUMANIZATION VERSUS DEPERSONALIZATION

In Judaism conjugal relations are not seen as a physiological experience or a mechanical-hedonistic exercise but as an intensely human activity to which personal involvement and a committed relationship between the participants is an absolute precondition. Depersonalization means dehumanization. Without the personal involvement and commitment the act of intimate union becomes dehumanized, the participants debased.

The Sages employ the term *devar mitzvah*, an act of kindness extended by one person to another, to refer to conjugal relations. Relations conducted in a manner of a *devar mitzvah* are intensely human and personal, an act of sanctification.

Humans' ability to rise above the impersonal, elementary, instinctual level of biological impulse and their control and direction of the biological imperatives so that they can become expressed in a giving mode define their humanity. Judaism teaches that the transformation of physical union from an impersonalized act into a committed, personalized act marks human beings' humanization and their elevation above the animal.

THE NEED FOR THE WOMAN'S CONSENT

While it is a man's right and obligation to participate in relations with his wife, the scope of his demands is restricted by the simplest laws of human courtesy. Explains the Spanish rabbinical authority R. Abraham b. David (c. 1125–1195), the *Ravad*:

> The *onah* specified by the Sages is solely for the purpose of satisfying the desires of the wife. The husband is not free to fulfill his duty to her without her consent. . . .[24]

Jewish law prohibits sexual compulsion in any form.[25] Therefore, though a man may ostensibly have relations with his wife whenever he desires,[26] he may exercise his privilege only with her freely given consent. He may not exact marital relations contrary to his wife's wishes.[27] A husband may not force his wife to engage in conjugal relations or even approach her in a manner that may appear threatening or frightening.[28] The rape of one's wife is considered an abomination and is strictly forbidden,[29] regarded as an abhorrent act that will be reflected in the character of his children, who will be termed *benei anusa*, children of a raped one.[30]

The Jewish idea of a man's conjugal obligations toward his wife extend far beyond the laws forbidding cruel or brutish treatment of the woman and include positive obligations for decent, respectful behavior. The Torah explicitly details the husband's duties and the wife's privileges. However, even specific privileges provided for the husband are granted only so that he can better carry out his duties to his wife. This is illustrated in the scriptural stipulation that a newly married man is not to be drafted for military service for one year:

> He shall not go out to military service, nor shall he be impressed for any service; he shall be free for his home for one year and he shall cause his wife to rejoice.[31]

The first year of marriage is a critical period when the basic foundations for a lasting relationship are built, a year for establishing mutual trust, learning about commitment and devotion, and allowing the ripening of new love. Although the husband obviously benefits from a year of deferment from military duty, the scriptural command was not designed for his happiness, but for his wife's. He is granted this privilege in order to "cause his wife to rejoice." In the words of the Sages, he must accomplish this with "a matter of a *mitzvah*,"[32] a talmudic euphemism for marital relations.

The Torah recognizes that the success of a marriage and the development of a secure Jewish home depend in large measure on the wife. Since the family is recognized as the vital unit in the Jewish nation, it is therefore seen to be in the national interest that the husband be excused from military service for the first year of marriage in order to build the foundation of a family based on mutual love. Only when his family life has a solid foundation may he be called on to serve his nation in a military capacity.

PROTECTING AGAINST CONJUGAL NEGLECT OF THE WOMAN

According to some codifiers, the principle of making one's wife "rejoice" extends beyond the first year of marriage to last all of the couple's married life. The word *onah* literally means season. Thus, "he shall not neglect her . . . *onah*"[33] exhorts a husband not to neglect his wife through a lack of frequency or regularity in their marital relations. This is the Jewish legal prohibition against conjugal neglect.

This law is restated as a positive commandment in the scriptural injunction *Vesimah et ishto*, "And he shall cause his wife to rejoice."[34] The two complementary expressions of the law are often combined in talmudic terminology as *simhat onah*, "seasonal gladness."[35]

R. Isaac of Corbeil, the thirteenth-century codifier of Jewish law, author of *Sefer Mitzvot Katan* (*Semak*) teaches:

> "To cause his wife to rejoice"—as it is written, "And he shall cause his wife to rejoice."[36] The negative formulation is, "He shall not neglect her *onah*."[37] And behold how important is this positive *mitzvah* . . . for even when his wife is pregnant it is a *mitzvah* to cause her to rejoice when she is desirous. . . .[38]

These laws and various talmudic statements[39] reflect an acute awareness of a woman's sexuality and her need for physical fulfillment. Mortimer Hunt in *The Natural History of Love* points out that Western societies did not acknowledge that women had sexual desires. Until recently, one would be accused of "casting vile aspersions on womankind" if he suggested that women feel sexual desire or, worse, experience sexual pleasure.[40] Comments Dr. David M. Feldman in his work *Health and Medicine in the Jewish Tradition*, "While this may have been true in the Western world, in Jewish culture and tradition both sexual desire and sexual pleasure of women are not only acknowledged but made into a religious concern for men. 'To fulfill her desire' is one of the two purposes of the *mitzvah* [of marital relations]."[41] This has been the Jewish approach for thousands of years and is incorporated into Jewish law.

There is undoubtedly a considerable inequality in Jewish law between the conjugal rights of the woman and those of the man, the scales being tilted one-sidedly in favor of the woman. Yet the nature of the physical relationship often intrinsically places the initiative in the hands of the man. Thus, the woman's preferred status in this regard may be seen as a means of establishing equity.

THE MAN'S OBLIGATION TO ENSURE HIS WIFE'S SATISFACTION

Jewish law grants women some measure of control over her frequency of sexual relations within the marriage. The husband is obligated to ensure his wife's satisfaction. To clarify the responsibilities of the husband, the Sages prescribed tables of minimal frequencies for cohabitation that have been incorporated into Jewish law. These timetables are based on the husband's profession and occupation, the amount of physical labor his occupation entails, and the amount of time his occupation requires him to be absent from home.[42] Each situation is to be determined individually, "each man according to his strength and his occupation."[43] Another factor in the frequency of marital relations is the desire of the individual woman, the Sages add.[44]

A man is forbidden to deny his wife conjugal relations.[45] A husband who denies his wife sexual relations because of ill health is given six months to regain his health. If, at the end of this period, he is still unable to have satisfactory relations with his wife, she is entitled to a divorce, and he is required to pay the *ketubah* sum.[46]

This and other options granted the woman in Jewish law allow her a considerable amount of control over the physical aspect of her marriage. Indeed, a husband, without his wife's freely given assent, may not have relations with her.[47] Her consent may not be in response to any overt or subtle pressure.[48]

A woman may prevent her husband from embarking on a distant business journey if it will adversely affect their conjugal relations.[49] Moreover he may not travel at all for business without her permission, if it will diminish the frequency of their conjugal relations.[50] Even with his wife's consent, a husband may not absent himself for more than thirty days,[51] and prior to embarking upon the journey a man is required to have relations with his wife.[52]

Jewish law also allows a woman to prevent her husband from changing his profession if the change will reduce the frequency of their marital relations.[53] However, she may not compel him to change his profession to one that might increase the frequency of their sexual relations.

The obligation that a man provide satisfaction to his wife is quite stringent, a strict legal requirement. Impotence[54] or other inability to fulfill conjugal obligations or conscious neglect of the needs of one's wife constitute valid grounds for divorce.[55] In addition, a woman is entitled to financial compensation for the period during which she suffered from her husband's neglect.[56]

The woman's personal taste is a valid factor in Jewish marriage law. If a woman is so physically repelled by her husband that she cannot bring herself to cohabit with him, she is also entitled to a divorce.[57] According to Maimonides, her claim of his impotence is considered sufficient grounds, and no further substantiation is required on her part.[58] Maimonides explains:

> If a woman says, "My husband is repugnant and I cannot willingly be intimate with him," we compel him to divorce her forthwith, for she is in no way like a captive who is compelled to be intimate with the one she hates.[59]

WHAT ABOUT AGREEING TO ABSTAIN?

Should a woman tell her husband prior to marriage that, although he is obligated to provide her with her sustenance, she has her own source of income and wishes to forgo his support, the marriage is still considered a valid one according to Jewish law. Should she, however, stipulate before the marriage that she will accept support from him but wishes to abstain from conjugal relations, the marriage is considered null and void. An abstinent marriage is contrary to the Torah. Judaism does not recognize any mutual agreement to abstain from marital relations.[60] Neither may the husband, in the name of a so-called higher spiritual goal, deny his wife her conjugal rights. Judaism calls for the sanctification of life, conducting oneself in an elevated fashion within the regimen of a regular daily life; it does not encourage the pursuit of a "holiness" that removes one from the realm of human interaction.

If a man has made a religious vow to abstain from marital relations, and if the period of abstinence exceeds one week, the vow itself is legal grounds for the woman to obtain a divorce.[61] Withholding conjugal relations or using the sexual relationship in order to manipulate one's partner is strictly forbidden.[62]

The physical side of marriage is, in Judaism, one facet of a complex relationship; it is not something to be considered separately. The Torah teaches that husband and wife must strive for a total emotional commitment that finds expression in their physical relationship. Their closeness must be expressed continuously and not only when they desire physical satisfaction. Physical intimacy must reflect devotion and must be matched by emotional intimacy. The *Shulhan Aruch*, the Code of Jewish Law, declares that "a man may not drink of one cup and look at another,"[63] meaning that "a man may not think of another woman while having relations with his wife."[64]

THE NEED FOR EMOTIONAL COMMITMENT

Judaism holds that a man owes his wife respect as a sensitive human being; she is not an object for his pleasure. For this reason, if a man is contemplating divorce he is forbidden by Jewish law to engage in sexual relations with his wife.[65] The same applies to a man who hates his wife[66] and to a man who has had a bitter argument with his wife. In such a case, the man may not have relations with her before becoming reconciled with her.[67] The Sages summarize the rule: "A man may not cohabit with his wife unless there is love and peace between them."[68]

Each of the instances cited here is a situation of potential sexual exploitation. Physical intimacy that lacks emotional commitment may provide momentary physical gratification, but it will leave a residue of shame and loathing. With the depersonalization of the woman, both partners are degraded, and their relations are compared to acts of prostitution.[69]

Just as a husband is required to cause *his wife* to rejoice, so too must *he* be joyous during intimacy. As mentioned, the Sages refer to the *mitzvah* of marital relations as *simhat onah*,[70] the joy of *onah*, because mutual joy is an indispensable element of the act.[71] They teach that the *Shechinah*, the Divine Presence, joins the husband and wife when they unite in love, but they add that if there is no joy between them, God will not be present, since the *Shechinah* dwells with a couple only when there is gladness between them.[72]

Emotional involvement, in the Jewish view, is not incidental to conjugal relations; it plays a central role in marital intimacy—as it does in all aspects of the marital relationship. The married couple is expected to achieve emotional intimacy before their physical relationship is consummated; physical oneness must be accompained by emotional oneness. Jewish law stipulates that a man may have conjugal relations with his wife only when she is coherent,[73] and not when either partner is drugged or intoxicated,[74] lethargic, or sad,[75] or when the woman is asleep.[76]

A WIFE'S PRIVILEGES

In addition to a man's basic obligation to have regular sexual relations with his wife, he is also required to satisfy her whenever she indicates a desire.[77] The Talmud states:

A man is obliged to cause his wife to rejoice with a *devar mitzvah* (lit. "a matter of a *mitzvah*," i.e., conjugal relations) even at times other than the usual ones for *onah*[78] if he perceives that she desires him.[79]

Maimonides maintains that such a right is not limited to the woman alone and that the man too can exercise his conjugal rights according to his desires.[80] Other codifiers disagree, however, maintaining that the privilege of having a desire for conjugal relations satisfied at times other than the usual ones is enjoyed by the woman only. They point out that the Torah singles out the woman for this privilege by specifically obliging the man to satisfy his wife with the *mitzvah* of *onah*, without mentioning a reciprocal obligation for the woman:

> She is not obligated to him at every time if she does not wish to . . . for she is not like a captive slave to fulfill his needs every time he so desires. . . . However, *he* is *obligated* to fulfill the *mitzvah*.[81]

Judaism understands the woman's conjugal needs to be at least of equal importance to the man's and encourages her to take the initiative in intimate relations.[82] The Sages praise the piety of the woman who intimates her desire for conjugal relations, comparing her to the matriarch Leah.[83] They bless such a woman, proclaiming:

> Every woman who requests of her husband a *devar mitzvah* will be rewarded with children greater even than those who lived in the generation of Moses.[84]

However, Jewish women are advised to be tactful and modest[85] and not brazen[86] in indicating their desire for intimacy.[87] Men are instructed to be understanding of the woman's sensitivity and exercise greater subtlety in this regard. The Talmud states, "A woman indicates her desire by her heart while a man does so verbally; this is a fine quality among women."[88]

Jewish law teaches that a man must strive to anticipate his wife's desires and endeavor to fulfill them without waiting for her to signal them.[89] This thoughtfulness will endear him to her and promote her happiness.

THE HUSBAND'S DUTY TO CATER TO HIS WIFE'S NEEDS

A Jewish husband does not fulfill his obligations to his wife regarding conjugal relations through participation in the physical act of coitus. He must also cater to his wife's emotional needs. By going through the motions and participating perfunctorily in a mechanically executed act, the husband does not satisfy the *mitzvah* of *onah* because he does not cause his wife to rejoice. The Sages emphasize at every turn that the husband's duty to satisfy his wife in this regard extends beyond the basic requirement of participating in cohabitation.[90]

It is in this respect, perhaps more than in any other, that Judaism's consideration for the woman's needs is apparent. The sensual nature of the woman, her sexuality, must be regarded with great sensitivity and care. The Sages were acutely aware of the urgency of male desire, and they were concerned that a husband's lack of self-control might result in his disregard of his wife's needs and in his maltreatment of her.

Out of concern for the woman, the Sages provide detailed guidelines to the husband on how to treat his wife. The man is obliged to foster intimacy and warmth between himself and his wife and properly prepare her for sexual relations. Through intimate conversation[91] and appropriate foreplay[92] the husband must arouse his wife with warmth and tenderness and stimulate her psychologically, emotionally, and physically. Closeness, affection, placation, and soothing words are some of the terms the Sages use to indicate how the Jewish husband must draw near to his wife through sensitivity, tenderness, and endearment in order to establish the proper atmosphere and engage in the appropriate preliminaries. In the words of the Sages:

> With coitus alone, he does not fulfill the *mitzvah*. He must, in addition, participate in all of the various forms of *krevut* (lit. "closeness" or "intimacy") with which a man gladdens his wife.[93]

GUIDING THE HUSBAND

The *Igeret HaKodesh*, the "Epistle of Holiness," a thirteenth-century guide to moral family life, dealing in particular with the ways in which a Jewish man should behave in intimate relations with his wife, offers this advice to the husband:

> You should first engage her in conversation, beginning with words that will draw her heart to you and put her mind at ease and thus gladden her. In this way your mind and heart will be in harmony with hers. . . . Speak to her charming and seductive words which will arouse in her passion, love, desire and *eros*. Also, speak to her of matters that are appropriate and worthy to inspire her intentions for the sake of Heaven . . . words that will elicit reverence for God, piety and modesty. Tell her of pious women who gave birth to fine, God-fearing children. . . .
>
> Win her over to you with words of love and seduction and with words that inspire reverence of Heaven, modesty and pure thoughts. . . . Do not compel her or force her in any way, for the *Shechinah*, the Divine Presence, cannot abide such a union. Quarrel not with your wife, and certainly do not strike her on account

> of these matters. . . . As our Sages taught,[94] just as a lion tramples and devours his prey and has no shame, so a boorish man strikes and copulates and has no shame.[95]

R. Jacob Emden (1697–1776), the German rabbi and halachic authority, provides additional insights:

> A man should first calm his wife's mind . . . and should begin by bringing his wife into the proper mood by speaking soothing words that attract her heart and soothe her mind and cause her to rejoice, so as to fuse her mind with his and her intent with his.[96] He should speak to her with words that arouse her desire, her love and her passion. He should also speak to her of reverence for Heaven and of loving-kindness and of modesty, and about righteous Jewish women. . . . He should cause her heart to rejoice so that her desire will be aroused in holiness and in purity. . . . They must embrace and kiss before uniting in love, so that he will inspire her passion and arouse the desire between them. . . . When her passion becomes evident in her breathing and is reflected in her eyes, then they should make love to one another.[97]

Setting the mood through appropriate conversation is considered an indispensable part of marital relations;[98] the Sages go so far as to declare that one who fails to do this is to be considered as though he had raped his wife.[99]

The Rabbis use the term *tashmish vechol avizerayhu*, coitus and all its components, to express the total picture of the requirements involved in the obligations of the Jewish husband relating to marital relations and that they extend beyond the act of coitus. By engaging in proper relations with the requisite emotional involvement, the conjugal act becomes a highly satisfying physical and emotional experience that will truly gladden the heart of his wife and cause her to rejoice.

Initiating intimacy is not relegated to the husband alone. The Sages suggest that a woman should properly prepare her husband for relations by enticing him erotically[100] and by engaging him in conversation designed to arouse his desire for her.[101] The Talmud provides guidelines for the woman to arouse her husband skilfully so that his passion is progressively heightened and culminates in coitus.[102]

The quality of the act is important. Cohabitation is forbidden when either partner or both are clothed, or when separated by a sheet and there is not a complete unity of the flesh during relations. Such relations–termed "in the manner of the Persians" by the Sages–are said to denote disrespect and lack of affection for one another[103] and is considered a diminution of the fulfillment of the marital obligation. Nachmanides determines that the three minimal obligations of a Jewish husband to his wife, spelled out in Exodus, *she'erah, kesutah, ve'onatah,*[104] *all* refer to the quality of intimate relations.[105]

Conjugal relations without love and affection are considered no different from the relations of a harlot with a client.[106] One sage intimates, from a mystical perspective, that the character of a couple's children who will be the issue of the conjugal relations will be determined by the quality of the act and the intents of husband and wife at the time of conception.[107]

THE WIFE'S SATISFACTION TAKES PRECEDENCE

While a woman has the option to take initiatives to increase her husband's satisfaction, it is the man who is duty-bound to "cause his wife to rejoice" and not vice versa. It is the man who must give his wife physical and emotional satisfaction, and her gratification takes precedence over his own. The Talmud is effusive in its praise[108] of the man who places his wife's satisfaction before his own, and the Sages state that he will be rewarded[109] if he permits his wife to attain fulfillment before him.[110]

The *Igeret HaKodesh* provides a general guideline for the man:

> When you join with her, do not hasten to arouse her passions. When her mind is completely at ease you may unite with her in the way of love; and arrange it so that you allow her to attain satisfaction first. . . .[111]

The fourteenth-century Spanish ethicist R. Isaac Aboab stressed the need for the husband's consideration of his wife in this regard: "At the time of *onah*, a man should not intend for his own pleasure alone; he should be concerned with fulfilling his wife's pleasure as well."[112]

One codifier goes as far as to state that during conjugal relations the man should not seek to derive any pleasure for himself from the act, but to be concerned with giving his wife pleasure because this is his obligation.[113]

The Talmud relates that Ima Shalom, the wife of R. Eliezer, said that during intimacy her husband was *domah kemi shekefa'u shed*, like one who was forced by the devil. (The commentaries explain that he was behaving in a manner "as if against his will," so as to avoid being overcome by his own desire and to concentrate on pleasing his wife so that she could attain satisfaction.)[114] When Ima Shalom asked her husband why he behaved as he did, he told her that in this way he could focus solely on her–that "thoughts of another woman would not arise in me" at the time.[115]

The Sages view the physical pleasure as an essential part of intimacy that is to be *mutually* enjoyed; the Talmud employs the expression *guf nehneh miguf*, "one body has pleasure from another."[116]

THE IDEA OF PLEASURE AS AN INCENTIVE

The physical pleasure derived from sexual intimacy is the incentive God provided for man and woman to perform the act in order to procreate. R. Jacob

Emden maintains that the pleasure involved in conjugal relations is the inducement to participate in an act that might otherwise seem too physical and therefore might cause people to recoil.[117]

Maimonides reminds us that, while physical pleasure is important, it is not the only goal:

> The purpose of marital relations is the perpetuation of the species, and not only the pleasure of the act. The enjoyment of the act was given to living beings in order to induce them to participate in coitus so as to inseminate. This is proven from the fact that following semination passion subsides while physical pleasure from the act immediately recedes. . . . If pleasure was the entire purpose, it is obvious that the enjoyment of the act would continue after semination for as long as one desired.[118]

The twelfth-century German pietist and ethical teacher R. Judah HeHasid in his *Sefer Hasidim* says that enjoyment of relations should be mutual and that a husband may derive pleasure from the act so long as he is also concerned about providing pleasure to his wife. Referring to the scriptural verse, "He who has found a woman has found a great good and has obtained favor from the Lord," he indicates that it is no easy matter to find sexual compatibility:

> All these matters pertaining to conjugal relations must take the wife's desires into consideration as well as his own. If a man succeeds in finding a wife whose desires coincide with his own in these matters, then he has indeed "obtained the favor of the Lord," and to him the verse "God has favored your acts" applies.[119]

R. Isaiah di Trani (d. 1270), the Italian talmudic commentator and author of the *Tosafot Rid*, says that the pursuit of pleasure is in itself a legitimate reason for conjugal relations when a pregnancy constitutes a physical hazard to the woman.[120]

Cohabitation in moderation is also seen in Judaism as a healthy expression of a physical need and a medium to provide relief of physical pressure.[121] R. Emden expresses the conviction that such activity also provides relief for married people from psychological tension, "dissipates melancholy, soothes nervousness and temper, and gladdens the soul."[122]

ADVOCATING MODERATION

However, Maimonides, a major codifier of Jewish law and a philosopher who was also a renowned physician, was concerned about possible physical debilitation resulting from sexual excess, and he counseled moderation.[123] The Sages point out that in certain respects, the two great physical needs of human beings, food and sexual activity, are similar. Just as hunger often becomes intensified with eating, so too is the desire for sexual activity intensified by frequent indulgence. With both activities nonindulgence, or moderate indulgence, tempers the appetite.[124] Maimonides[125] and the other codifiers[126] advise against sexual excess, noting that even though his wife is accessible to him, "a man should . . . not be constantly with her [conjugally] like a rooster. . . ."[127] In other words, a person should at all times be the master of his desires, never a slave to them.

Marital relations are also forbidden in times of famine.[128] According to Maimonides, however, the prohibition applies only if one has already fulfilled the obligation of bringing children into the world.[129] The Sages derive their prohibition from the principle that at a time when the community suffers, one should empathize and share that pain in a personal way.[130]

MUTUAL PRIVILEGES AND DUTIES

In the area of conjugal rights in marriage, Jewish law contrasts sharply with the tradition that has for centuries dominated the Christian world. In the words of researchers Masters and Johnson: "The concept bolstered by ancient laws that sex is a husband's right and a wife's duty has made and continues to make for marriages in which sexuality is exploited and dishonored."[131]

Judaism's conception of the marital relationship is dramatically different. If anything, there is a strong case in Jewish law for the opposite principle: conjugal relations are a wife's right and a husband's duty.

Taken as a whole, however, Judaism views marital relations as a set of mutual privileges and duties, with particular concern for the woman's needs. The burden of obligation is on the husband, who must be sensitive to his wife's needs and must constantly strive to satisfy them, ahead of his own. Far from being sexually exploited, the Jewish wife is to be treated reverently, and her needs are to be responded to and satisfied as fully as possible.

In the Jewish perception, marriage is the crucial stage in the path of human sanctification of life. The urgency of the sexual drive, therefore, is neither denied nor condemned, but is accepted as a gift from God, to be properly channeled into relations within marriage. Central to the marriage relationship, sexual relations are understood to be a medium through which the partners in marriage communicate love for one another.

The operative principle, in the Jewish view of sexual relations is that they are called a *mitzvah*, a divine command. Intimacy between husband and wife, with restraint and concern for one's partner, constitutes a holy act that sanctifies the name of God.[132] Thus, a purely physical human function, common to animals, is imbued with a spiritual dimension.

Judaism requires that husband and wife provide physical and emotional gratification to each other, conducting their relations in a manner that will contribute to the strengthening of the matrimonial bond.[133] A higher purpose is mentioned: "Proper physical union can be a means of spiritual elevation," declares the author of the *Igeret HaKodesh*.[134]

Judaism transforms and elevates the physical act between a man and woman from the primal level of physical gratification to the exalted planes of sanctity and purity. This level attains its sublime peak as it becomes a joyous affirmation of the noblest of human emotions: love, devotion, and honor.

8

Femininity and Family Purity

THE RULES OF *NIDDAH* AND *MIKVEH*

The laws of Family Purity, *Taharat HaMishpahah,* are a central aspect of the Jewish sanctification of marriage. *Taharat HaMishpaha* requires a couple to abstain from marital relations and all physical contact and intimacies that may lead to them during the woman's menstrual period and for seven days after its cessation.

During this period the woman is called a *niddah,* or menstruant. At its end, she bathes thoroughly and immerses herself in a *mikveh* (lit. a gathering of waters). The *mikveh,* designed according to specific and ancient guidelines, is a specially constructed ritual pool with a natural water source. Prior to her immersion in the *mikveh,* the woman bathes and then recites the following blessing: "Blessed are You, O God, King of the Universe, who has sanctified us with His precepts and has commanded us to observe the *mitzvah* of *tevilah,* ritual immersion." After immersion, husband and wife renew their physical relationship.

A life-style built around the use of the *mikveh* is a crucial factor in differentiating the Jew from the non-Jew. Immersion in a *mikveh,* therefore, is a vital procedure in the conversion to Judaism; in fact, it is the most important rite in the halachic process by which a non-Jew becomes a Jew. In Judaism, the laws of Family Purity are regarded as among the most essential *mitzvot,* called *gufei Torah,* or *gufei halachot,* whose observance distinguishes practicing Jews from nonobservant ones. That these regulations have traditionally been held to be of extreme importance to Jews of all ages can be seen by the rigorous adherance of the Jewish people to the laws of *niddah* and *mikveh* throughout history, even under difficult and dangerous conditions.

One meaning of the word *mikveh* is hope or trust, or Source of Hope or Trust–an appellation of God, who is called the Hope of Israel. The word *mikveh* appears twice in the Bible; in the phrase *mikveh mayim*, a gathering of waters,[1] and once on its own.[2] Arachaeologists have discovered *mikvaot* ("mikvehs") dating back to the period of the Second Temple (fifth century B.C.E.–first century C.E.) in ancient Israel. The *mikvaot*, located on the outside of the Temple's southern and western walls, are close to two of the major ramps that lead up to the Temple Mount and were undoubtedly used for immersion by people purifying themselves prior to ascending to the Temple. *Mikvaot* dating to the talmudic period (second–eighth centuries C.E.) have been unearthed adjacent to a number of ancient synagogues throughout Israel.

It was no surprise to discover *mikvaot* at Masada, the renowned Judaean Desert fortress near the Dead Sea that was defended by religiously observant Jews. The *mikvaot* were discovered by the late archaeologist Yigael Yadin during his excavations in the 1960s.[3] A group of notable Jerusalem rabbis visited the site of the excavations at Masada and, after careful and awed examination, pronounced the *mikvaot* there to be "in scrupulous conformity with the injunctions of traditional law."[4]

THE BIBLICAL SOURCE FOR *MIKVEH* AND FAMILY PURITY

The law of marital abstention during the period of *niddah* (menstruation and the week following it) derives from this scriptural passage:

> And if a man lies with a woman when she is unwell and uncovers her nakedness, he has exposed the source of her blood and she has exposed the source of her blood, both of them shall be cut off from their people.[5]

Significantly, it is the Torah portion of *Kedoshim* (Holy Ones), in the Book of Numbers, that introduces the section on *niddah*:

> And the Lord spoke to Moses, saying: Speak to the Congregation of Israel and say to them: *Kedoshim tiheyu*–"You shall be holy, for I, the Lord your God, am holy."[6]

This all-encompassing scriptural passage introduces the section dealing with *niddah*.[7] It illuminates the fundamental aspiration of Judaism. The Jew is provided with a basic guideline for the conduct of his life: to pursue the path of godliness. Consecrated by the teachings of the Torah and the fulfillment of *mitzvot*, he is to mold himself into a moral, ethical, and holy being.

God says, as I am holy, you should be holy. The principle is: following in God's path, *imitatio Dei*, God asks the Jew: strive to become holy because I am holy. By achieving human holiness you become godly.

In certain religious persuasions, holiness is attained by, in effect, removing oneself from life. Judaism rejects this. The Torah is called *Torat Hayim*, a teaching of life. The purpose of life and the Jewish ideal is the sanctification of the self by bringing sanctity into everyday life. Therefore, the ascetic tradition and the accompanying renunciation of sex common to other religious disciplines are foreign and even repugnant to Judaism.

Judaism rejects these as actual impediments to the achievement of personal sanctification. The Jew is directed to be not the slave of his desires but their master. It is not through the stifling of his human drives that the Jew attains holiness, but through his dominance of them. The laws of *niddah* serve as a notable medium for the Jew to help attain that mastery and to channel those drives in accordance with God's will.

THE *MIKVEH*: A MEDIUM FOR LIVING AN ELEVATED LIFE

In preparation for *kiddushin*, the sanctification of marriage, *Halachah* requires that a bride immerse herself prior to her wedding. This act marks her transition from the status of *niddah* to the status of permitted woman. A married woman is similarly required to undergo immersion before resuming physical relations with her husband at the end of her period of *niddah*. Her husband is forbidden to approach her physically before she has undergone this experience of transition.

The *mikveh* serves as a profoundly symbolic medium for the transformation of sexual relations. Judaism understands that the laws of *niddah*, properly observed, are a medium for elevating sexual relations from an act of self-gratification to a meaningful, blessed *mitzvah* devoted to the service of God—a joyous, sacred physical-spiritual union of body and soul. Through the rituals of *niddah* and *mikveh*, the Jewish husband and wife affirm that their relations, pleasurable as they might be, are neither sinful nor in any way shameful, but are a positive, holy act performed in the service of God.

Ritual immersion prior to participation in a religious act denotes both a rebirth[8] and an elevation of status. The biblical consecration of Aaron and his sons as *kohanim* (priests) required their immersion in a *mikveh* as a first step.[9] Through this act they were both "reborn," and their status was elevated. Immersion in a *mikveh* also signifies the "rebirth" and change of status of a convert.

Blood taboos abound in primitive societies. Some critics have theorized that the laws of *niddah* reflect these taboos. These theories indicate an unawareness of the reality of *Halachah*. Menstrual blood does not contaminate. A menstruating woman may participate in Jewish rituals and touch a Torah scroll, and so forth, contrary to popular myth. The rules prohibit conjugal relations and proscribe all acts of physical intimacy lest they lead to such relations. They express and enhance the Jewish idea of the sanctity of marital relations.

FAMILY PURITY: CONCERN FOR THE WOMAN AND FOR THE MARRIAGE

The laws of *Taharat HaMishpahah* are divine statutes of the Torah for which no reason is given and that the Jew is commanded to accept on faith alone. The most notable other set of laws in this category is *kashrut*, the dietary regulations. Both sets of laws are associated in the Torah with the command to be holy. The reasons for these laws are deemed beyond human intellectual capacity and are therefore not given. While these laws strengthen the bond between God and His people, the manner in which they do so is not obvious. Yet we know that their observance sanctifies the Jew by regulating his two strongest drives—hunger and sex.

The Sages say: *Vekidashtem bitevilah*, And you shall sanctify yourselves through immersion in the *mikveh*.[10] Enjoy the lawful pleasures of this world, Judaism teaches, but do not be the slave to your desires. Exercise a measure of self-control in order to be elevated above the level of the animal.

One may certainly attempt to discern the reasons behind these statutes. But observant Jews are aware that their conclusions can at best be tentative. So they cannot alter any of these rules should they conclude that the reasons they have postulated no longer apply. While they can speculate about the statutes' reasons, they cannot determine with certainty the statutes' ultimate rationale. R. Aryeh Kaplan, a twentieth-century scholar, explains:

> We do not observe the commandments because logic demands it, but simply because they were given by God. The required basis is the relationship between the commandments and their Giver. This is higher than any possible human wisdom.[11]
>
> This may be one reason why a convert to Judaism must immerse in the *mikveh*. The convert's first step into Judaism involves a ritual the explanation of which is not apparent and obvious, and therefore, he must reaffirm the initial acceptance of the Torah, declaring [as did the Jews at Sinai], "I will do and I will hear." To abandon his gentile identity and to assume Jewish identity, he is required to participate in a ritual that is inexplicable to one who does not accept the basis of Judaism. . . . The fact that we are required to observe certain

commandments without awareness of their reason does not mean that there is no logic in their observance. The reasons involve deep concepts which are not immediately obvious. . . .[12]

CONSIDERATION FOR THE WOMAN

In seeking to understand the significance of the laws of Family Purity,[13] two of the reasons that suggest themselves are concern for a healthy marital relationship and consideration for the woman.

The required abstention from marital relations, physical contact, and intimacies that may lead to them for twelve to fourteen days each month provide a medium through which Jewish couples can develop a strong, healthy relationship rooted in a mutual attachment that is nonsexual.

The period of physical separation hallowed by Jewish law and tradition emphasizes that the physical relationship, though essential and important, is not all. A healthy marital relationship must be based on other components as well. It is considered especially important that mutual love and devotion be expressed generously, in a nonphysical manner, by both partners during the *niddah* periods of physical separation. When physical expressions of love are forbidden, husband and wife are freed to develop an enduring relationship based on fellowship of the spirit. It is an ideal preparation for that later period in married life when physical attraction wanes and potency weakens so that the bond must be expressed in other ways.

Aron Barth, a mid-twentieth-century Israeli thinker, comments:

> Marriage, according to the Torah, is a true and perfect partnership requiring love and fellowship of the spirit, not only fellowship of the flesh. Physical love can find expression according to the laws of the Torah only during half the life of a married couple. Half of married life passes without fellowship of the flesh; hence there can be no marriage according to the Torah unless there is a fellowship of the spirit. Herein lies the secret of the exemplary family life with which Jewry has been blessed for so many generations.[14]

SEPARATION: A TIME FOR INTIMACY OF THE SPIRIT

One of the blessings for a newly married couple, recited during the wedding ceremony and at the week of celebrations following the wedding, refers to the bride and groom as *re'im ahuvim,* beloved friends. Warmth, friendship, and companionship are vital ingredients in the Jewish view of marriage; these are enhanced during the couple's monthly physical separations. Referring to *niddah* as a period in which husband and wife live together as "brother and sister," R. Samson Raphael Hirsch points out that this does not detract from the intimacy. On the contrary, it has the effect of "making this intimacy still more intimate and raising it constantly, spiritually and morally."[15]

The Sages teach that a husband fulfills the *mitzvah* of *onah*, his duty of marital relations with his wife, and that of *vesimah et ishto*, "And he shall gladden his wife" when he causes his wife happiness during the *niddah* separation period, through intimacy of a nonphysical nature:[16]

> Marital relations are not the only means of performing this *mitzvah*; all kinds of intimacies through which a man gladdens his wife are a *mitzvah*, for all of these intimacies cause her joy.[17]

The Sages teach: "The *mitzvah* of *Taharat HaMishpahah* and, in particular, the laws of separation, train one to understand that the fundamental link between the members of a couple is founded on spirit, emotion and mutual understanding–and is not merely a physical tie."[18]

A married couple *needs* this purely emotional interaction that might otherwise be neglected when the physical relationship dominates their consciousness. Women need words of love. For the woman, the pleasure derived from physical relations is often tied to emotional intimacy. A physical relationship that lacks warmth and tenderness can render continual relations unfulfilling–if not unendurable–for the woman. Therefore, the days of enforced physical separation serve as an opportunity for renewal of the couple's emotional intimacy. When conjugal relations are again permitted, the wife, as well as her husband, can derive full physiological and emotional satisfaction from their resumption. In early talmudic times, R. Akiva objected to a ruling that forbade women from making themselves physically attractive, wearing cosmetics, or adorning themselves with jewelry and fine clothes during *niddah*. The law was suggested as a means of discouraging desire that could lead to physical intimacy. "Such a rule," said R. Akiva, "would cause a woman to be unattractive to her husband and lead to a loss of marital love, and ultimately to divorce."[19]

R. Akiva's amendment of the law regarding women's adornment during the *niddah* period was far-reaching. It underscored that a woman is not an object for gratification of a husband's desire; her attractiveness and companionship can be appreciated at all times without thoughts of physical intimacy. It is therefore halachicly permitted for the woman to make an effort to dress attractively and adorn herself during her period of separation from her husband.[20]

A MEDIUM FOR PERIODICALLY REFRESHING THE RELATIONSHIP

Marriages suffer when sexual relations gradually becomes monotonous. What was exciting when the couple began their life together often becomes a mechanically executed routine. Sensitivities are dulled by repetition and repletion. The idea of expressing love physically, or in other ways, becomes tedious. The novelty of the experience, the early awesome wonder at the pleasure it provided, the couple's fascination with each other – all these wane with time, familiarity, and the satiation of physical desire.

The freshness of the early period of marriage grows stale through perpetual accessibility. The indifference and boredom may imperil the marriage itself. Often, couples look outside the marriage to rediscover the thrill and excitement that they have lost in the marriage. The eyes that once regarded a spouse with delight may now begin to rove, longing for new excitement.

Here the periodic abstinence required by the rules of Family Purity serves a crucial purpose. Denying the married couple the right of constant access heightens mutual attraction and maintains a continuous fascination. The Sages understood this:

> Why did the Torah require a period of seven days of separation? Because by becoming overly familiar with his wife [marital relations become routine and] repulsion sets in. The Torah therefore ordained seven days of separation so that she will be as beloved [by her husband on the day of her immersion in the *mikveh*] as she was at the time she entered the bridal canopy.[21]

ASSURING THAT THEY DON'T TAKE EACH OTHER FOR GRANTED

This enforced separation ensures that the Jewish husband and wife will not take each other for granted. Humans have a natural craving for the forbidden. "Stolen waters are sweet."[22] A dull book becomes a best-seller the moment it is banned. Recognizing this, the Torah, through the rules of Family Purity, makes the husband and wife periodically forbidden to each other. This inaccessibility heightens longing. There is a recurrence of the desire the couple felt on their wedding night. Forbidding, for a substantial period each month, marital relations or even the slightest physical contact, the *niddah* interval is a built-in means of monthly renewal. The marriage bond tightens, preserving between husband and wife an ever-fresh physical and emotional relationship.

Husband and wife move in different circles during their daily activities. They can easily lose touch with each other. The observance of the laws of *niddah* ensure a constant awareness of the woman's monthly bodily cycles. The changes that *niddah* observance mandates for the couple's relationship draw the couple together, even as other demands upon their time and energy draw them apart.

There is no temptation so prevalent and insistent as that of an ever-present, beloved spouse. Mutual agreement or voluntary abstinence, no matter how sincere, could never assure absolutely that marital relations would not take place during the proscribed period. Yet, the strict religious sanctions proscribing all physical contact between husband and wife during this period and the requirement for immersion in the *mikveh* prior to the resumption of marital relations serve as an absolute and refined deterrent. The *niddah* rules thus effectively preserve the woman's fundamental freedom by protecting her from sexual demands at a time when she requires a measure of solitude and distance.

THE CONTEMPORARY REVIVAL OF *NIDDAH* AND *MIKVEH*

No doubt this helps account for the contemporary revival in the practice of *niddah* and *mikveh* among Jewish women today, many of whom have little or no religious background and are not otherwise religious observant. Many young Jewish married woman who observe neither *Shabbat* nor the *kashrut* rules have enthusiastically taken up the Family Purity rules and its attendant separation.

In the words of one feminist observer, "otherwise non-observant women are observing *mikveh* as a way of creating space for themselves and a separation from their husbands, providing each partner a measure of autonomy within the marriage."[23]

It is a way women have seen to affirm women's independence and to assert that they do not have the status of a sex object. Comments Gila Berkowitz, who has written about the subject:

> At the heart of *mikveh* law is the concept that a woman is a complete individual. Every month the practicing woman and her husband are reminded that she is more than an appendage to him, that she does not exist to serve his sexual needs. Yet this system also allows enough time together for the couple to grow sexually.[24]

THE "HEDGE OF ROSES"

The Sages termed the refined deterrent of the Family Purity regulations "a hedge of roses," in reference to a poetic image in *Song of Songs* of a woman's body as a "heap of wheat hedged with roses."

The Sages teach:

> When a man marries a woman . . . and he approaches her, and she tells him, "I have seen blood as red as a rose," he separates from her at once. Who held him back and would not let him come to her? What kind of an iron wall separates

them? What kind of serpent bit him? What scorpion stung him–to prevent him from drawing near to her?–The words of the Torah, that are as soft as a rose.[25]

The image of the "hedge of roses" is particularly apt. In the same way that a hedge of roses, though pleasing to the senses, should not be touched on account of its thorns, a woman, though still desired, is forbidden to her husband during this period. Mandated by the rules of the Torah, the couple's parting is not angry or resentful. The couple observing the *niddah* rules recognizes that the separation represents simultaneously fealty to Jewish tradition and consideration for each other. Rather than isolating them, the separation, paradoxically, brings them closer both spiritually and emotionally. The interval during which they are physically apart is a passing discomfort that is almost a pleasure; it is a loving time, the end of which is, nevertheless, eagerly awaited.

At the end of the *niddah* period, it is the wife's obligation to go to the *mikveh* on the proper night, and it is the husband's obligation to join her afterward. Delaying their physical reunion longer than required is indicative of an asceticism upon which Judaism frowns. The Jew is admonished neither to add to nor detract from the words of the Torah.[26] It is also not acceptable to defer immersion in the *mikveh* as a means of avoiding marital relations.[27]

TOGETHER AGAIN

Desire is heightened by the pattern of monthly separation and reunion. Human beings are naturally restless and eager for change. The Jewish rules of *niddah* and *mikveh* twice each month effect considerable change in the marital relationship. The onset of the woman's menstrual period brings a sudden halt to the satisfaction of their physical desire for twelve days. The anticipation that the separation engenders reaches its climax the night of the woman's immersion in the *mikveh*. This act marks the transition of the couple's physical relationship from one of heightened anticipation to one of union and fulfillment.

Only about two weeks later, however, just before the first twinge of boredom begins to set in once again, the couple is separated by the onset of *niddah*. These periodic changes, however predictable, provide a heightened sense of drama in the intimate relations between a husband and wife, making both the marriage and the marital partner more precious to each.

The periodic abstinence also provides, especially after long years of marriage, psychological benefits for the couple. Though long familiarity and their years together take their toll and tend to lessen their attractiveness for each other, this effect is considerably diminished by their periodic unavailability for physical union. On the night of the woman's visit to the *mikveh*, she becomes once again the beloved bride she was when they married, and he the beloved groom. Following her immersion in the *mikveh*, the relationship regains a freshness reminiscent of her original immersion on the eve of her wedding and provides the opportunity for a renewed courtship between the two. On the night of their reunion, the two relive the original joy and rapture of the early days of marriage.

Not surprisingly, among families observing the Jewish rules of Family Purity, incidence of marital infidelity is rare, and the level of divorce is considerably below the norm.

A TIME FOR TRANQUILLITY AND REPOSE

Underlying the concept of *niddah* and *mikveh* is Judaism's concern that the woman should not become a sex object, that is, a medium for the gratification of the passions of her husband, who may disregard her emotional and physiological needs. A man's libido is such that there are no distinct periods of time when he is more or less prone to sexual arousal. A woman's body, however, functions in accordance with an inner feminine rhythm that at different times affects her both psychologically and physiologically. There are certain times, corresponding to her unique biological body clock, when she feels an upsurge of desire and a readiness for physical intimacy. Alternately, there are times when, in response to the monthly physical upheaval in her body, she requires nothing more than rest–physical tranquillity accompanied by mental and emotional repose.

The laws of Family Purity are synchronized to these fundamental needs of the woman. The woman's immersion in the *mikveh* comes at a time that harmonizes with her body's recovery and her readiness both physically and emotionally to engage in conjugal relations. At this time her husband is not only permitted to join her, but is *obliged* to do so.

The laws of *Taharah* thus enrich the physical relationship between husband and wife by humanizing it. The union is thereby prevented from becoming one of autonomous physical satisfaction, or a form of onanism with a partner. The *niddah* laws, by requiring periodic abstention, provide a framework in which the husband expresses supreme consideration and concern for his wife as an individual, and the wife asserts this truth.

Relates one woman who observes the Family Purity regulations:

> I like the feeling of twelve days of separation. It's the moment of truth in our relationship, when we have to relate to each other as human beings and we don't have sex to gloss over problems. At that time my body is entirely mine, my bed is mine, my emotions are entirely my own. . . . *Mikveh* is like a honeymoon every month. . . .[28]

TIME AND THE WOMAN

Why are Jewish women exempt from the observance of many of the time-related *mitzvot*, all of which are required of men?[29] R. Norman Lamm postulates this rationale: the Sabbaths and festivals in Judaism teach that the holiness of time is superior to the holiness of space. The holiness of space refers to places or things that are holy: a synagogue, the Land of Israel, a Torah scroll. The holiness of time refers to the sanctity of many of the *mitzvot*, and in particular those relating to the Sabbaths and festivals.

The prime holiness is that of time—"And the Lord blessed the Sabbath day and sanctified it."[30] From the time-related *mitzvot* man is taught an awareness of the sanctity of time. However, R. Lamm points out, "women are excused from observing these commandments for the simple reason that they do not need them."

> A woman does not *need* the time-conditioned commandments, because she is already aware of the sanctification of time in a manner far more profound, far more intimate and personal, and far more convincing than that which a man can attain by means of the extraneous observances which he is commanded. For a woman, unlike a man, has a built-in biological clock. The periodicity of her menses implies an inner biological rhythm that forms part and parcel of her life. If this inner rhythm is not sanctified, she never attains the sanctity of time.
>
> But if she observes the laws of Family Purity, then she has, by virtue of observing this one *mitzvah*, geared her inner clock, her essential periodicity, to an act of holiness. By the observance of this single commandment, she is made conscious of the holiness of time to an extent far more comprehensive than that attained by a man. A woman, therefore, does not need the time-oriented commandments to remind her of the holiness of time, whereas a man, who does not possess this inner periodicity, must rely upon these many commandments to summon him to the sanctification of time. The laws of Family Purity are, therefore, a divine gift to woman, allowing her to attain this highest of all forms of sanctity.[31]

THE HEALTH BENEFITS OF THE FAMILY PURITY LIFE-STYLE

Considerable evidence has been found which indicates that the laws of *Taharat HaMishpahah* accord women tangible benefits as well. Scientific studies have concluded that there are medically salutary effects that derive from a life-style shaped by these ancient laws. Prominent among these is the significantly lower incidence of cervical cancer among observant Jewish women and their consequently lower mortality rate from cancer of the uterus.

Professor David M. Serr, director of the Department of Obstetrics and

Gynecology at the Sheba Medical Center in Israel and professor of obstetrics and gynecology at the Tel Aviv University Medical Center, writes:

> Medically, socially and hygienic-wise, the couple practicing Family Purity rituals is healthier in some important aspects than the couple which does not practice this way of life. . . . It is undisputed statistically that Jewish women suffer less from cancer of the cervix, a rapidly fatal disease, than non-Jewish women. . . . Other possible medical complications of non-observance of Family Purity laws may involve infections of the male and female genito-urinary tracts.[32]

Dr. Moses Tendler, rabbinic scholar and professor of biology at Yeshiva University, cites a definitive study on the epidemiology of cervical cancer which presents evidence that at certain times in a woman's life her "cervical lining is uniquely sensitive to the cancer-producing potential of human sperm."[33]

It can be deduced that the Family Purity rituals are directly responsible for the substantially lower cancer rate among Jewish women because the cancer rate among Jewish women has risen sharply in ratio to the slackening of these observances by Jewish women. Dr. Tendler comments:[34]

> The general pattern of the sex life of the Jew with its prescribed abstinence after the birth of a child, its abhorrence of sexual promiscuity, and its lesson of moderation, is now considered the key factor in protecting the Jewish woman against cervical cancer. . . . However, she is fast losing her "superiority." During the last fifty years, the ratio of cervical cancer incidence among non-Jewish and Jewish women dropped from approximately 20-to-one to 5-to-one. Since the evidence of this disease among the normal population has not changed significantly during this period, the evidence shows that there was a four-fold increase in the incidence of this disease among Jewish women. . . . A leading investigator of this disease summarizes these statistical results as follows: "The increasing difference in incidence of cervical cancer between Jew and gentile may in some way be due to the liberalization of attitude toward ancient religious laws, with associated decline in its observance."[35]

Dr. A. Shechter of Beilinson Hospital in Petah Tikvah, Israel, comments that in modern Israel the rate of cancer of the cervix among the general population is already not appreciably different from that among non-Jews. He adds that "among religious Jewish women who observe the rules of *niddah* and have sexual relations with only one man, however, the rate is, of course, quite low."[36]

IS FAMILY PURITY THE SAME AS GOOD HYGIENE?

Niddah observance provides obvious hygienic benefits even if it has taken science many centuries to realize this.[37] Traditional Jewish laws regarding

Family Purity should not, however, be confused with regulations regarding health and hygiene. Since the beginning of their existence as a people, Jews have incorporated laws of hygiene into their daily lives. Jews are *commanded* to keep themselves clean.

Jewish respect for cleanliness and hygiene has proven advantageous throughout history. During periods when plagues ravaged disease- and dirt-ridden populations, laws of cleanliness and hygiene kept the Jews well protected.[38] These advantages are considered a natural benefit of living a life governed by the Torah and its precepts, a way of life intrinsically designed for human happiness, contentment, and good health, both physical and spiritual.

The obvious advantages of hygiene and good health are not, however, the reasons that Jews observe the laws of Family Purity. They are also not the reason that Jews observe the dietary laws of *kashrut*. The recently discovered medical and practical benefits that these laws confer on their adherents are secondary considerations. Jews observe *Taharat Hamishpahah* and *kashrut* because the Torah commands them to do so. Traditional Jews, believing that the divine plan is a good one, are not amazed when science, medicine, and nature coincide to confirm that God, the Creator of the world, knows what He is doing.

The late Jerusalem scholar and ethicist R. Eliyahu KiTov provides this insight:

> If menstrual separation were practiced by the Jews because of the many medical authorities who currently recommend such separation, human nature might militate against the constancy of such practice. For human nature is so constituted that the soundest of medical advice often fails to prevail against the temptations of instinct and inconvenience. Such advice is best heeded when reward is immediately tangible and exceeds the inconvenience entailed. Where, however, such reward is intangible and distant, while inconvenience is immediate and pleasure beckons on the other hand, then medical advice often goes unheeded. What cannot be assured in the absence of police and courts can, however, be assured through the sense of obedience to the divine commandment which attends the observance of the laws of menstrual separation on the part of the Jewish people.[39]

PURIFICATION AND CLEANLINESS

The laws of *niddah*, like those of *kashrut*, are religious and are intended for purification and sanctification, not for sanitation and cleanliness. In Jewish law, however, a bath and thorough cleansing of all parts of the body are indispensable preliminary preparations for ritual immersion in the *mikveh*. This preparatory physical cleansing of the body is an absolute precondition for spiritual purification by *tevilah*, ritual immersion, not a substitute for it. One cannot substitute for the other. Thus, while a *mikveh* is designed for ritual immersion only, the procedures related to *mikveh* actually provide both spiritual purification and bodily cleansing.[40]

Immersion in a *mikveh*, a ritual hallowed by Jewish law and tradition, is regarded in Judaism as a religious act imbued with profound spiritual symbolism. It requires a benediction thanking God the Purifier "Who sanctified us with His precepts and commanded us regarding *tevilah*." In the words of R. Akiva:

> May you be praised, O Israel: Before Whom are you purifying yourselves? Who purifies you? Your Father in Heaven. . . . Just as the *mikveh* purifies the impure, so does the Holy One, Blessed be He, purify Israel.[41]

R. Samson Raphael Hirsch discusses the nature of natural water in a *mikveh* as a spiritual agent:

> The water must not be contained in a vessel but must still be in its primitive state; for instance, gathered in a natural hollow in the ground. Being underwater was the original condition of the world.[42] Also, water, in contrast to dry land, is that part of the world on which human domain did not establish its realm. So, finally, the world of water is that sphere where no impurity reaches. . . . So that immersion in the element of water expresses a complete departure from the realm of humanity subject to impurity and is a return to original conditions; it completely breaks off connection with the past and introduces a quite fresh, pure future.[43]

One who immerses in the *mikveh* is enjoined to have pure intentions. Body and soul then combine in this ritual.

The Jew is commanded to obey the laws of Family Purity with devotion. He and she are aware that these acts are endowed with profound significance, though they have but a limited understanding of the reasons for the laws. Maimonides provides a thoughtful comment:[44]

> Immersion in the *mikveh* as a means of freeing oneself from impurities is one of the *hukim*, the statutes of Scripture about which human understanding is not deemed capable of forming a judgment. . . . Impurity, therefore, is not like an adhesion of mud or filth that can be washed off with water: it is a divine scriptural decree, and is dependent on the intention of the heart. Therefore, the Sages have said, if someone had immersed himself without the proper intention, it is as if he had not immersed himself at all. . . .
>
> Even though nothing outwardly happens to his body, one becomes pure by immersing himself, if he sets his heart on purifying himself. Similarly, he who sets his heart on purifying his soul from impurities, i.e., evil ideas, his proper intent to purge himself from evil counsel and to purify himself, result in

> applying to him the Scriptural passage, "And I will sprinkle clean waters upon you and purify you of all your impurities."[45]

Purification is a spiritual concept, and immersion in a *mikveh* is a physical act effecting a spiritual transformation. The married woman's immersion in the natural waters of the *mikveh* prior to resuming marital relations has been compared to the *kohen*'s immersion in the *mikveh* prior to entering the Sanctuary for the Temple service in Jerusalem. On Yom Kippur, the climax of the Temple ritual was the entry of the *kohen gadol*, the high priest, into the *Sanctum Sanctorum*, the Holy of Holies. Five times during this day, before each major service, he would immerse himself in a *mikveh*. The immersions were symbolic acts of purification that had the effect of raising his spiritual status to allow him to enter the Holy of Holies, a place to which entry ordinarily was strictly forbidden.

Both of these acts are of a consecrated nature and thus require prior *mikveh* immersion: the Jewish woman preparing for marital relations and the *kohen* preparing for participation in the Temple service. The woman's *Sanctum Sanctorum* is her own body, and she must experience intimacy in a state of holiness. In the words of Maimonides, "Purification of the body leads to sanctification of the soul."[46]

THE IMPORTANCE OF *MIKVEH* IN JEWISH TRADITION

A common lack of knowledge among Jews of the traditional regulations and procedures relating to *niddah*, *mikveh*, and Family Purity have resulted in many taking these laws lightly and their consequent nonobservance of them. In Jewish law they are considered fundamental, their transgression of major import.

The overriding importance Judaism ascribes to Family Purity can be seen in the severity of the punishment cited in the Torah for violation of the *niddah* laws—*karet*, premature death,[47] one of the severest penalties in the Torah, reserved for incest[48] and other major violations[49] of the Torah. Intimate relations with a woman who is a *niddah* is considered to be sexual immorality. We find a passage equating such an act with adultery:

> If a man is righteous and would accomplish justice and charity . . . he will not defile his neighbor's wife, nor will he approach a woman who is a *niddah*.[50]

Although the concept of community in Judaism is popularly associated with a synagogue, according to Jewish law, a *mikveh* is more important. Building a *mikveh* takes precedence over building a synagogue, or even over acquiring a Torah scroll.[51] A community may sell a synagogue or a Torah scroll to provide funds for building a *mikveh.*

As long as a group of Jews has no communal *mikveh,* they do not constitute a community according to Jewish law,[52] no matter how many and varied the Jewish institutions they boast. Ordinarily, a synagogue is the very symbol of a Jewish community, the place of assembly where Jews pray for their own, for their family's, for their community's well-being. Yet, if there is no *mikveh,* that synagogue is considered an empty symbol of community.[53]

In establishing the principle that Family Purity takes precedence over such important religious concepts as community prayer and Torah scholarship, the Sages dramatically underscore the *mikveh's* indispensability for the spiritual health of the Jewish family and the continued survival of the Jewish nation.

Discussing the effect of the observance of *Taharat HaMishpahah,* the late chief rabbi of England, J. H. Hertz, writes:

> By the reverent guidance in these vital matters which these laws afford, Jewish men have been taught respect for womanhood, moral discipline and ethical culture. As for Jewish women, they were, on the one hand, given protection from uncurbed passion; and on the other hand, taught to view married life under the aspect of holiness.[54]

9

Birth Control, Abortion, and Jewish Demographics

THE FIRST COMMANDMENT OF THE TORAH

The first commandment of the Torah is procreation: *"Peru urevu,"* Be fruitful and multiply.[1]

Throughout history, people have sought to limit the size of their families through different forms of birth control, with varying degrees of success. In recent years the development of ever more effective methods of preventing conception and aborting fetuses has made their use both popular and controversial. The issue of abortion in particular has generated acrimony and emotional debate in American society.[2]

Procreation is a major factor in Jewish life. Although there are a number of reasons for marriage–among them companionship, security, emotional fulfillment, and the avoidance of sin–nevertheless, bringing children into the world, creating a family, and thereby perpetuating Judaism and the Jewish people are undoubtedly the most important reasons.

In the Jewish world, discussion of these subjects involves both Jewish law and Jewish ethics and is made even more complex by being linked, inextricably, to the issue of Jewish demography.

BIRTH CONTROL: THE BIBLICAL REFERENCE

The *Ravad,* R. Abraham ben David of Posquieres, France, a twelfth-century rabbinic scholar, wrote *Baalei HaNefesh,* a handbook on relations between husband and wife based on talmudic sources. The work declares that there are four primary purposes of marital relations: the first and most important is procreation; the second is the benefits they are said to bestow on both mother and child during pregnancy; the third is the *mitzvah* of *onah*, a husband's duty to satisfy his wife when she indicates her desire for him; the fourth is avoidance of thoughts of sin.[3] R. Isaac Aboab, writing in the fourteenth century in the *Menorat HaMaor*, includes in the fourth the purpose of physical release for the man.[4]

Procreation, though the most important purpose of the marital act, is clearly not its sole aim. One might therefore assume that Judaism is permissive in regard to birth control. This is not the case. Birth control in Jewish law is intimately related to the subject of *hotzaat zera levatala*, "bringing forth seed in vain," or *hash'hatat zera*, "the destruction of seed." The sole biblical reference to what may be considered birth control appears in Genesis in regard to Onan, whom God punished with death. He "spilled his seed on the ground" to avoid fulfilling his "levirate" duty[5] to his deceased brother's wife, Tamar, and to prevent her from conceiving a child that would not be his own.[6] He thus deliberately violated God's primal command to "be fruitful and multiply." From the severity of the punishment meted out to Onan, the Talmud and Codes conclude that *hotzaat zera levatalah* is a major sin.[7]

THE JEWISH VIEW OF CONTRACEPTION

Since it is only the man who is commanded to propagate, and it is his seed that may not be "spilled," Jewish law generally does not permit either *coitus interruptus* or the use by males of any contraceptive devices.[8] When a man is obligated to participate in nonprocreative conjugal relations with his wife, i.e., even when conception is not possible, as, for example, when she is sterile or pregnant, this is not considered *hotzaat zera levatalah* or *hash'hatat zera*, so long as the culmination occurs in a natural manner with one's partner and there is a free, natural flow of the seed. The man is not permitted to interfere with or frustrate this process through natural means (e.g., *coitus interruptus*) or artificial impediments (condoms), the latter being considered improper barriers.[9] Under these circumstances, the essence of the act is considered to have been thwarted by the man.

The woman's position, however, is altogether different. The prohibition against *hash'hatat zera* does not apply to her. Additionally, she is excused from the command to propagate.[10] Childbirth has historically represented a potential danger to the woman's health and well-being. Her exemption from the obligation to produce children has provided her with the option to choose whether or not she wishes to conceive if conception poses a hazard to her. The Talmud mentions birth control in referring to three categories of women who may use a *moch,* a kind of contraceptive tampon–one who is under age, one who is pregnant, and one who is nursing–in order to prevent danger to their own lives or to the lives of their offspring.[11]

The principle underlying these laws is the primacy in Judaism of the preservation of life and health and the assumption that these may not be jeopardized in order to fulfill a commandment, even one as vital as that of procreation. The Torah is called *Torat Hayim,* the instruction for living, and it does not require one to give up life in order to keep a Torah precept.[12] Indeed, Jewish law prohibits the endangerment of one's life or health in order to fulfill a *mitzvah.* There is a talmudic discussion about *pikuah nefesh,* the duty of saving one's life. The Sages teach that this supersedes the observance of the Sabbath:

> R. Elazar says, we derive the rule from circumcision, for which the Sabbath may be set aside even though it is for the purpose of but one of the 240 organs in the body; how much more important is it to override the Sabbath when the entire body requires it!
>
> . . . R. Jonathan ben Joseph says, we derive it from the verse, "And you shall keep the Sabbath for it is holy to you."[13] That is to say, the Sabbath is given over to you, but you are not given over to the Sabbath.
>
> R. Simon ben Menasia says, we derive it from the verse, "And the Children of Israel shall keep the Sabbath, to observe the Sabbath through the generations."[14] That is to say, violate one Sabbath if necessary, so that you will consequently be enabled to observe many Sabbaths afterwards.
>
> R. Judah says in the name of Samuel, [the principle of violating commandments of the Torah in order to preserve a life] derives from the verse, "Keep my statutes and ordinances, which if a man do them he will live by them."[15] That is to say, live by them, and do not die because of them.[16]

The divine command to man to procreate is therefore nullified in the face of the greater *mitzvah* of preserving the life or health of the woman.

The talmudic *moch* provides a solution permitting the man to fulfill the *mitzvah* of *onah* while at the same time preventing conception when it may harm the woman. It must be emphasized, however, it is only the woman who is at times permitted to use a contraceptive device; not the man.[17]

STERILIZATION

Similarly, a woman is permitted to have herself sterilized, whereas a man may not do so. The Talmud mentions the use by a woman of a *kos shel ikarin,* a "root rink," i.e., a sterilizing potion, or a kind of oral contraceptive known in the ancient world.[18]

In connection with a sterilizing potion, the Talmud relates that Judith, the wife of the Sage R. Hiyah, had experienced extraordinary pains in giving birth to their children, and sought relief. Aware that a decision of such import could be taken only after consultation with a learned rabbi, she decided that the rabbi whom she would approach with a *she'eilah*, a religious query regarding Jewish law, would be none other than her husband, the great R. Hiyah. Knowing that her husband would like more children, she disguised herself and appeared before R. Hiyah and asked: "Is a woman commanded to observe the precept of *piryah verivyah*, to be 'fruitful and multiply'?" R. Hiyah responded in the negative, whereupon Judith left and took a sterilizing potion.[19]

R. Solomon Luria, the sixteenth-century Polish rabbinic authority and talmudic commentator known as the *MaHarshal*, who produced the important halachic work, *Yam Shel Shlomo*, permits a woman to drink a sterilizing potion under compelling circumstances.[20]

In more recent times, a woman who had experienced extreme pain in childbearing asked R. Moses Sofer, the early nineteenth-century Sage of Pressburg known as the *Hatam Sofer*, if she was permitted to render herself sterile. He answered that she might do so, but should first seek her husband's agreement.[21]

WHEN CONTRACEPTION MAY BE PERMISSIBLE

In the last 200 years there has been considerable discussion in the rabbinic *responsa* literature on the subject of birth control. Due to the gravity of the question, no general rules are provided, but each case is judged on its individual merits, and rabbinic decisions are usually made only after all factors have been taken into consideration, in particular, the appropriate medical opinion. Where the reasons for the request to use contraceptives are based on considerations other than medical (e.g., convenience, economic considerations, good looks, interference with career, profession, life-style, etc.) the Rabbis have generally not permitted such use.

However, in cases where pregnancy and childbirth presented potential danger to the woman's health, the Rabbis have often permitted the use of certain types of contraceptive devices by the woman, especially when the minimal obligation of procreation had already been fulfilled (understood as meaning that they already had a son and a daughter). The devices considered least objectionable are those that interfere least with the act, its quality, and its natural completion. These include an intrauterine device, the diaphragm, and the pill. The issue is highly complex, and the rabbinic literature on the subject, especially in recent years, is voluminous.[22] (Where a question regarding Jewish law exists, one should consult a competent halachic authority.)

ABSTINENCE

Although one way of preventing danger to a woman's health would simply be abstinence, this is not considered a viable option in Judaism. On the contrary, Judaism regards abstinence as a sin. A husband may not deny his wife her conjugal rights; if he does not participate in conjugal relations with his wife he transgresses the *mitzvah* of *onah*. Furthermore, by practicing abstinence, he abrogates two of the prime purposes of marriage–procreation and *onah*–rather than only one.

Judaism permits abstinence only in periods of famine, when abstinence is considered mandatory. Significantly, the reason it is obligatory at such times is not the economic factor, but because it is considered inappropriate to participate in pleasurable experiences during periods of national or personal tribulation. It is not consonant with Judaism's requirement of empathetic concern for others. For the same reason, marital relations are not allowed during Tish'ah B'Av, the fast day commemorating tragic events that befell the Jewish people.[23]

"FAMILY PLANNING"

The Jewish response to the argument that "family planning" should be exercised when the economic situation in the household does not allow for more children may be seen from the thirteenth-century book *Sefer Hasidim* by R. Judah HeHasid. This work relates the story of a man who expressed his apprehension to his rabbi about his ability to support more children because of his economic straits.

He pointed out to the rabbi that he already had a boy and a girl and had therefore fulfilled the minimum requirement of procreation. The rabbi answered him: "Before the child is born, the Holy One provides the milk for him in the mother's breast. Therefore you have no reason to be concerned!"[24] The rabbi's message was faith in God and in His ability to provide. God, Who commanded man to procreate, will provide the sustenance for those who fulfill the command and for their children.

The concept of "family planning" as it is known today is a product of our age; it was a phenomenon virtually unknown among Jews of earlier generations, despite the fact that most Jews throughout history were far from wealthy, and many endured economic difficulties. They brought children into the world to form large families, their children were sustained and grew up to make their contributions to the world–and they in turn produced large families.

The irony of modern times is that those seeking to limit family size for economic reasons are rarely those of the lower-income levels. They are people of middle- or higher-income levels who choose personal comfort and convenience over bringing children into the world. Among Jews with large families who subsist on minimal incomes it is singularly rare to hear complaints of too many mouths to feed. On the contrary, in such situations one finds children thriving on the warmth of the family. They may lack costly toys, but they flourish in the atmosphere of values involving giving and sharing, as they see their parents choosing these values over the more ephemeral ones of contemporary society.

In Judaism procreation is a major *mitzvah*. It is not to be avoided. Judaism recognizes birth control as a legitimate consideration when the health and well-being of the woman are at stake; it does not recognize personal comfort and convenience or economic considerations as legitimate factors. Contraception, when allowed, requires contraceptive means that are themselves acceptable.

BIRTH CONTROL: DISSIMILAR JEWISH AND CATHOLIC POSITIONS

The Jewish approach to contraception differs radically from the Catholic position. Birth control via an oral contraceptive potion was equated by the Roman Catechism of the Council of the Catholic Church of Trent in 1545–1563[25] with homicide.[26] In 1588 Pope Sixtus V threatened anyone who practiced it with the death penalty. The Jesuit theologian Father Laymann referred to such contraception as "quasi-murder" and a mortal sin.[27]

What if conception and pregnancy will endanger the life of the woman? Father Laymann asks that the question this way: "Can a woman take medication to prevent conception, if she has learned from her physician or suspects from her own experience that the birth of a child will bring her death?" The Catholic theologian answers a resounding no. He justifies allowing the woman to die rather than to prevent conception as follows: "If women were to be allowed to prevent conception in such cases, this would be an astonishing abuse and great damage would be done to human reproduction."[28] It remained the Catholic position that procreation may not be thwarted, even if the woman will surely die if she conceives and becomes pregnant. Upon the appearance of the birth control pill in the mid-twentieth century, Pope Pious XII vigorously opposed its use even when pregnancy would mean certain death. On September 2, 1958, he declared: "It is inducing a direct and illicit sterilization when one eliminates ovulation, so as to protect the organism from the consequences of a pregnancy that it cannot endure."[29]

Pope Paul VI in *Humanae vitae* in 1968 equated birth control with abortion, stating that contraception "is to be condemned just as much [*pariter damnandum est*] as abortion."[30] Comments the Catholic theologian Dr. Uta Ranke-Heinemann:

> Thus a certain number of abortions must be credited to the popes, especially since by equating contraception with abortion they helped to trivialize abortion. If, as Paul VI says, contraception counts as much as abortion, we can infer that abortion counts as little as contraception.[31]

ABORTION

The Torah contains an oblique reference to abortion, or the artifical termination of pregnancy through the destruction of the unborn fetus, in a passage describing an injury to a pregnant woman as the incidental result of a quarrel between two people:

> If men fight and hurt a pregnant woman so that her unborn children depart, but no harm [fatality] ensues, he shall be fined in accordance with the demand of the woman's husband, and he shall pay as the judges determine. If, however, harm [fatality] ensues, then you must give life for life.[32]

The Talmud understands the harm or fatality referred to as applying to the woman and not to the fetus.[33] If a person causes a woman to miscarry, only monetary compensation is required, feticide being considered a transgression punishable by a fine and not a capital crime such as homicide. Other talmudic statements substantiate that abortion of a fetus, though prohibited and a serious transgression,[34] was not considered to be murder. This is confirmed as the traditional Jewish interpretation by the historian Josephus, who writes of Torah law on the subject as it was understood in ancient Israel in the first century C.E.:

> He that kicks a woman with child so that the woman miscarries, let him pay a fine in money, as the judges shall determine, as he diminished the multitude by the destruction of what was in her womb . . . but if she die of the stroke, let him also be put to death. . . .[35]

The fetus of a Jewish mother has the legal status of being part of the mother's body (rather than an independent entity in its own right).[36] This is expressed in the Talmudic term *ubar yerech imo* (lit., "the fetus is the thigh of its mother").[37] The fetus is considered to be like a limb of the mother.[38]

The child is not considered a *bar kayama*, a viable human being, in Jewish law, until it is born.[39] This is evident from a talmudic discussion regarding the biblical formulation for the law regarding homicide, *makeh ish umet*, "he who smites a man who dies."[40] Since the Torah employs the word *ish*, man, rather than *nefesh*, a person (lit., a soul), the Sages deduce that the murdered one must be a viable person, i.e., at least a day old.[41] (However, for the purpose of conducting a funeral and for mourning traditions, the infant must be at least 30 days old.)[42] Feticide, therefore, is not homicide, although it is considered a serious criminal transgression, akin to damage to people or things.

THE SEVERITY WITH WHICH ABORTION IS VIEWED

Similarly, abortion, although not murder, is nevertheless viewed with enormous severity in Jewish tradition. The *Zohar* makes the following comment:

> There are three persons who drive away the Divine Presence from the world, making it impossible for the Holy One, Blessed be He, to fix His abode in the universe, and causing prayer to be unanswered. . . . [The third is] the one who causes a fetus to be destroyed in the womb, for he desecrates that which was created by the Holy One and His craftmanship. . . . For these abominations the Spirit of Holiness weeps. . . .[43]

The *Zohar* goes on to declare that the Jewish nation in Egypt was praised because, notwithstanding Pharaoh's merciless decree that "every son that is born shall be cast into the river,"[44] "there was to be found" no one who would kill the fetus in the womb of a woman, much less after its birth. By virtue of this, the Jewish people merited redemption from Egyptian bondage.[45] As much as abortion was considered abhorrent amongst the Jews, it was a common practice of the ancient Egyptians, as indeed it was in almost every society throughout history.

Judaism permits the inducement of abortion where the continuation of pregnancy will result in danger to the woman's life or to her physical or mental well-being. However, rabbinic discussion on the subject of abortion always expresses awe at the enormity of the deed of depriving an embryo of life and condemns abortion without acceptable reason.

R. Jacob Emden, the eighteenth-century German sage, though he was concerned about providing halachic sanction for the termination of pregnancy under certain circumstances, was horrified at the possibility of abortion: "Who could possibly permit killing an embryo without valid reason, even should the crime not be punishable with the death penalty?"[46] This thought is echoed by R. Yehezkel Landau of Prague, the eighteenth-century rabbinic authority known as the *Noda be Yehudah*, who emphasizes how terrible an offense it is to kill a fetus, even if it is not considered murder.[47]

R. Meir Simhah of Dvinsk, the late-nineteenth- early-twentieth-century Russian talmudic authority, writes in his Torah commentary *Meshech Hochmah* that although there is no death penalty for feticide, for it is not an act of murder, someone who kills a fetus needlessly is punishable by *mitah beyedey Shamayim*, "death at the hands of heaven."[48]

These views may be based on a statement in the Talmud by R. Ishmael,[49] who quotes the biblical command–one of the seven universal moral laws of mankind given to the sons of Noah following the flood–regarding the punishing of a murderer by his peers, "He who sheds the blood of a man, by a man shall his blood be shed."[50] The Hebrew text reads literally, "He who sheds the blood of a man *in* a man . . ." (*Shofech dam haadam baadam*). R. Ishmael derives from the peculiarity of the wording that there is a reference here to a human *inside* another human, i.e., a fetus, and that the Torah passage is designed to stringently warn both Jews[51] and gentiles (the "sons of Noah") of the prohibition against abortion.

WHEN ABORTION IS ALLOWED

The Mishnah teaches:

> If a woman is in travail when giving birth [and it is feared that she may die] one may sever the fetus from her womb and remove it, [even, if necessary,] limb by limb, for her life takes precedence over its life. Once most of the fetus has exited, one may not touch it for one may not put aside one life for another.[52]

Comments *Rashi*: "So long as it has not emerged into the air of the world it is not a human being and it is permitted to kill it in order to save the mother's life. However, once the head has come out one must not kill it, for it is considered as if born."[53]

Once the forehead or the greater part of the head has emerged from the womb, birth has taken place, according to *Halachah*. It is then considered to be a viable entity, and the process of birth must be seen through to the end. The life of the child is now viewed as equal to that of the mother, and one may then not kill the child at this stage even in order to save the mother, for the child "is considered as if born,"[54] and, in the words of the Mishnah, "one may not reject one life in favor of another."[55] However, according to some halachic decisors, in these circumstances the mother herself is permitted to kill the fetus if her life is endangered, since she is allowed to protect her own life when threatened.

Most rabbinic authorities understand the Mishnah to not only sanction, but to make *mandatory* the subordination of the life of the fetus to that of the mother when it presents a clear and present danger to the mother's life. The Talmud indicates that in such circumstances the fetus has the status in Jewish law of a *rodef*, a pursuer seeking to kill someone, i.e., its mother. The fetus thereby forfeits its right to life because it is in the process of trying to kill an innocent person, and it may be dealt with as one would a *rodef* in order to save the intended victim.[56]

Maimonides, in his Code, sums up the law as follows:

> It is known to be a negative precept in the Torah not to take pity on the life of a *rodef* [a pursuer seeking to kill someone]. Therefore, the Sages ruled that when a fetus is causing great travail to a woman in childbirth it may be removed from her womb [aborted], either through drugs or by hand [surgery], for the fetus is like a *rodef*, a pursuer trying to kill her. However, once its head has emerged, the fetus may not be harmed, for one does not reject one life for another. This is but the natural course of the world.[57]

Implicit in Maimonides' wording is that the hazard to the woman is clear and present; she is in a life-threatening situation, and this is what justifies so drastic a move as abortion. R. Joseph Karo makes the same ruling in his Code.[58]

In the Jewish understanding, therefore, the "right to life" of a fetus is not absolute; a mother's right to continue living takes precedence. Judaism believes in the *sanctity* of life. The absolute right to life begins after the child is born. Then its sanctity equals the mother's, and its right to life is then unequivocally equal to that of the mother.

When the woman is not in a life-threatening situation, however, abortion is not permitted. Indeed, latter-day rabbinic authorities have discussed the question of whether abortion is permitted if the woman has a serious medical problem and the fetus is not a *rodef*, i.e., the fetus in itself is not a threat to the woman's life.

IF THE FETUS HAS AIDS, TAY-SACHS, OR DOWN'S SYNDROME

In situations where the fetus is expected to be born as a child suffering from a fetal illness or a mental or physical defect or malformation, such as Tay-Sach's disease, Down's syndrome, German measles, or AIDS, etc., by and large the Rabbis have been hesitant to approve abortion.[59] A significant exception appears to be the twentieth-century rabbinical authority R. Eliezer Waldenberg, who permitted performing a therepeutic abortion in the instance of a Tay-Sachs baby. Under certain circumstances R. Waldenberg allowed the termination of pregnancy during the first three months only, providing that the mother had as yet not perceived any fetal movement in the womb.[60]

Where there are grounds to believe that the birth of a malformed or defective child would affect the physical or mental well-being of the mother, the Rabbis have been prone to consider the possibility of allowing early termination of the pregnancy.

The eighteenth-century German rabbinic authority R. Jacob Emden has ruled that abortion is permissible in instances where the fetus was conceived in a situation of rape,[61] but this view is by no means universal. Regarding the possibility of abortion where conception is the result of an adulterous or incestuous relationship, rabbis have been prone to disallow it in such circumstances, on the grounds that the life or health of the woman is not in danger. Some rabbis have expressed the thought that allowing the termination of pregnancy in such instances would remove a necessary deterrence to transgression.[62]

In conclusion, abortion at will, or abortion without valid reason – because a baby is unwanted, or to limit the size of the family, or to avoid the travail of childbirth and child-rearing, or for economic reasons – is condemned in Judaism as a serious transgression. All too often, acts against nature in the name of freedom and liberty end up limiting liberty and freedom and causing death.

Where a mother's life or health is endangered, rabbis allow abortion as an extraordinary procedure on the basis of the Jewish view of the reverence of life and on the principle that everything should be done to save the woman's life. Abortion is a last resort, however, and must be performed only after consultation with a competent halachic authority.

WHERE CATHOLICS AND JEWS DIFFER ON ABORTION

Jewish opposition to abortion has at times been compared, incorrectly, with that of the Catholic Church. They are, in fact, absolutely different, and in most instances, in virtual total opposition. The Jewish view is that abortion should be avoided, but where the woman's life or health is endangered, the fetus may be aborted. Abortion is not murder. In a situation where a woman will definitely die if the fetus is not aborted, and she is allowed to die in order to save the fetus, the person responsible for this decision is guilty of a major transgression. The life of the woman is more important than that of the unborn fetus.

The view of the church is that abortion is never in order. The fetus must be saved at all cost, and if the woman's life is at risk, she should die rather than the fetus be aborted. The Church views aborting a fetus as murder, and allowing the woman to die as a consequence of saving the fetus is regrettable, but acceptable, so long as the fetus lives. The life of the unborn fetus is more important than that of the woman.

The Catholic attitude is based on that of classical Christianity, which has long been concerned with the time of "ensoulment" of the fetus, i.e., the entry of the soul into the body.[63] The reasoning is that even where the mother's life is in danger if the pregnancy is not terminated, the fetus may not be aborted, since as the mother is presumed to have been baptized as a child and lived her life as a Christian, she is entitled to "go to her just reward." This is not the situation of the fetus, which has not been baptized as a Christian. On the basis of the Christian doctrine of original sin, the soul of the fetus suffers from the impure stain of its primordial ancestors and requires baptism for its salvation. The tainted fetus is therefore entitled to be carried to term in its mother's womb and to be baptized as a Christian in order to be purified and saved from eternal perdition.

This is based on the Augustinian belief that the souls of embryos were condemned to eternal perdition if they weren't baptized, which is spelled out in a classical statement by the bishop and theologian Saint Fulgentius of Ruspe (c. 467–533) in his important treatise, *De Vide*:

> It is to be believed beyond doubt that not only men who are come to the use of reason, but infants, whether they die in their mother's womb, or after they are

> born, without baptism . . . are punished with everlasting punishment in eternal fire, because though they have no actual sin of their own, yet they carry along with them the condemnation of original sin from their first conception and birth.[64]

THE CHURCH: THE FETUS IS TO BE FAVORED OVER THE MOTHER

In this, Saint Fulgentius, known as "Abbreviated Augustine" because of his fidelity to the influential Church Father, was echoing Augustine's conviction that the souls of embryos were eternally damned if they died without baptism.[65] In fact, abortion came to be considered as *worse* than murder by the Church.[66] The reasoning of the Church, according to one observer, is that "the death of a baptized mother is only the beginning of an eternity of salvation, while the death of an unbaptized infant is the beginning of an eternity of perdition."[67]

The Christian idea of original sin contrasts absolutely with the Jewish idea than humans are born pure. Every morning the Jew recites a prayer of gratitude of talmudic origin:[68] "My God, the soul that You placed within me is pure."[69] The untainted soul with which each child is born can be sullied only by the person's own deeds.

Practically speaking, the Church's conviction that the fetus must be purified from original sin and saved from eternal perdition by being baptized results in sacrificing the baptized mother when her life is in danger in order to save the unborn, unbaptized fetus, i.e., Church doctrine deems it more important to baptize the fetus than to allow the mother to live.

Where both mother and fetus would die if an unborn fetus with too large a head is not operated on with a craniotomy, but the operation would save the mother but not the fetus, a Church decree in Rome does not allow such an operation to take place.[70] Justification for the Church's decision and approval for its allowing the woman to die rather than harm the fetus is provided by two leading twentieth-century Catholic moral theologians, Joseph Mausbach and Peter Tischleder, in their work *Katholische Moraltheologie* ("Catholic Moral-Theology"), as follows:

> The argument that in sparing the child two lives are generally lost, whereas by sacrificing the child only one is, impresses most people. . . . The violent destruction of an innocent life is simply never permitted; it cannot be allowed at all, without leading people astray into further disastrous and life-destroying steps.[71]

In response to widespread revulsion, especially in the medical profession, at the readiness of the Church to have the woman die in order to save the fetus,

Bernard Haring, Germany's highly influential Catholic moral theologian defends the stance of the Church in his book *Das Gesetz Christi* ("Christian Law"):

> Whatever the judgment of medical science may be, the Church sticks inexorably to the basic principle that under no circumstances can it be permitted directly to assault the life of an innocent child in the mother's womb. See the address of Pope Pius XII given on October 29, 1951.[72]

The basis for the Church's uncompromising position regarding choosing the life of the fetus over that of the mother was laid down by the important Jesuit moral theologian Thomas Sanchez of Cordoba (d. 1610). Sanchez was the supreme authority on marital issues for the Catholic Church in his own century and he set the Church standards on questions of marriage for the following centuries. Sanchez, considered a moderate and progressive, set down a rule that, in the view of the Catholic observer and critic Dr. Uta Ranke-Heinemann, "would prove fatal for many mothers," and "its dreadful implications, in fact, are still being felt to this day."[73] Sanchez declared that a pregnant woman is forbidden to take medication if its side effect can be the abortion of the fetus. If after the mother's death the child would have lived and could have been baptized, then the mother has committed a mortal sin. Sanchez adds that under certain circumstances the mother is expected to lay down her life for the baptism of a "dying" child. Comments Ranke-Heinemann: "She is obliged to prefer the spiritual life of her child to her own bodily life."[74] This is based on the Augustinian belief that the unbaptized child is eternally damned.

Alphonsus Liguori (d. 1787), the most important Catholic moral theologian of the eighteenth century, states that even if only the faintest hope exists that the child will outlive the mother long enough to be baptized and if medication were her only hope of recovering, she is forbidden to take it, since if she does the child would be "in danger of mortal death."[75] She may take the medicine only if otherwise both child and mother will die.[76]

Similarly, Alphonsus Liguori says that a mother must endure possible death under the surgical knife if this will bring about the possible baptism of the child. If her death from surgery is certain and the prospect of getting the child baptized is questionable, however, then she need not accept certain death.[77] In 1967 Catholic ethicist Bernard Haring argued that the mother is obligated to undertake some personal sacrifices for the spiritual well-being of her child: "If there is no hope of securing the child's life and above all its baptism in any other way, then the mother is obliged to submit to one such operation."[78] Operations such as Caesarian section, Haring declares, "primarily aim at saving the child, and no doubt pose certain risks for the mother." He pointed out that "the spiritual health of the mother" must not be valued less "than the mere saving of the mother's corporeal life."[79] In this view, the woman is better off dead, but with spiritually correct thinking, than she is alive, and with spiritually defective thinking.

The Catholic position is expressed succinctly in *Abortion and Law*, a publication issued under the imprimatur of the Archdiocese of St. Louis: "Clearly, when balancing an embryo's life against the health of a woman, the scales of justice – though some find this hard to accept – would tilt in favor of life for the embryo."[80]

THE JEWISH VIEW

Jewish tradition cannot reconcile Christianity's readiness to sacrifice life (the mother's) for the soul of the unborn child with proper ethical behavior. Jewish tradition also cannot reconcile contemporary society's casual readiness to sacrifice life (the unborn child's) for the questionable sake of the body with proper ethical behavior.

THE HIGH ABORTION RATE IN ISRAEL TODAY

In Israel today the law permits legal abortion under the following circumstances: if the woman is under seventeen, the legal marriage age, or over forty; if the pregnancy is the result of relations prohibited by criminal law, or of incestual or adulterous relations; if the fetus is likely to have a physical or mental defect; if the continuation of pregnancy to term is likely to endanger the woman's life or cause her physical or mental harm.[81]

Officially, more than 15,000 legal abortions were performed annually during the 1980s in hospitals in Israel, a ratio of about 15.1 terminations of pregnancy for every 100 live births.[82] The figure rose to about 16,000 in the early 1990s.[83] According to government estimates, two illegal abortions are performed in Israel for every officially sanctioned termination of pregnancy in a hospital.[84] On the basis of these figures, therefore (considered low by nongovernmental observers),[85] for approximately every two live births in Israel there is one abortion.

THE MASSIVE JEWISH POPULATION LOSS AND ITS CAUSES

Jews are rapidly disappearing in the United States. With the notable exception of the Orthodox sector of the population, which is experiencing vigorous growth and vitality, each year sees an acceleration of the population decline. Masses of Jews are lost every year. In 1990 only 4,400,000 Americans considered themselves Jewish–including 185,000 converts and non-Jews who practiced Judaism[86]–compared to the figure of 6 million Jews that has for decades been considered the Jewish population in America. Less than half of the number of Jews in America in 1990 was affiliated with a synagogue.

In their study *Basic Trends in American Jewish Demography*,[87] demographers Professors U. O. Schmelz and Sergio DellaPergola point out that Jewish demographic continuity is dependent on two factors: cultural, i.e., the ability to preserve group identity and transmit it to future generations; and biological, i.e., births and deaths.[88] Based on both, American Jews demonstrate a marked disinclination to perpetuate themselves.

JEWISH EDUCATION TODAY

As for the cultural aspect, the primary educational institutions for Jewish instruction, the afternoon Hebrew school and the weekly Sunday school, have failed to inculcate Jewish group identity. American Jewish children do not emerge as Jewishly knowledgeable adults living identifiably Jewish lives and committed to Jewish continuity. Nevertheless, the Hebrew and Sunday schools continue as the main medium for the transmission of Judaism and Jewish identity.

However, Jewish day schools, the most effective Jewish educational medium, are experiencing a dramatic increase in students.[89] Day-school students are overwhelmingly from the traditional sector of the population, but a growing number are among Conservative and Reform Jews.[90]

THE AMERICAN JEWISH FAMILY TODAY

The Jewish family, which has traditionally served as the central medium for the inculcation of Jewish values and the Jewish way of living, is no longer a vital factor for the preservation of Jewish identity among most American Jews. The high divorce rate and the proliferation of single-parent homes is one reason for the disintegration of the Jewish family.

Another reason is the widespread cessation of Sabbath observance. The Sabbath, with its aura of peace and tranquillity and its opportunity for weekly family togetherness, its weekly feasts, and the special time it provides for religious and moral instruction of the children has been a prime factor in the near legendary cohesion of the Jewish family. When Jews stopped observing the Sabbath the effect on the nuclear Jewish family was disastrous. In the traditional sector, where Sabbath observance continues, the family has generally remained intact. Divorce in these circles remains a small fraction of that of the general population, and the family remains strong and continues to be the primary medium for the transmission of Judaism and Jewish identity to the young.

INTERMARRIAGE

The rate of intermarriage among American Jews has accelerated. In 1900 about 1 percent of American Jews married non-Jews. By 1940, 4 percent of Jews were "marrying out." By 1965 the rate had gone to 10 percent. Between 1965 and 1974 it went up to 25 percent. The 1974–1985 figure was 42 percent. Between 1985 and 1990 the intermarriage rate soared to 52 percent.[91] It is estimated that in the 1990s two out of three Jews were marrying non-Jews. There are thus increasingly fewer Jewish children, and in the future there will be fewer still. Some argue that intermarriage brings accretions, since converts occasionally come into the fold. It has been found, however, that only 10 percent of intermarrying non-Jewish spouses undergo even a minimal conversion to Judaism.[92] It is thought that intermarrying couples also have a lower fertility rate than all-Jewish couples.

A report on children of intermarried couples found that only one out of four were Jews, according to their own definition.[93] Only 27.8 percent of children of mixed marriages are being raised minimally Jewish. The other 72.2 percent are being raised as Christians or as "nothing."[94] A study in Philadelphia found that mixed marriages produced, in turn, increasingly greater percentages of mixed marriages and increasingly smaller percentages of Jewish children in succeeding generations. If the grandparents were mixed, none of the grandchildren remained Jewish.[95] "What do you call the grandchildren of intermarried Jews?" Milton Himmelfarb once asked. "Christians," was the reply.[96] Indicative of the attitude of American Jews toward intermarriage is a survey which finds that only 2 to 9 percent of American Jews would be strongly opposed to their children marrying non-Jews.[97]

Intermarriage leads to a reduction in the Jewish population. While in the short term the Jewish population may appear to expand through mixed marriages, demographers conclude that ultimately the number of Jews inexorably diminishes through intermarriage.

JEWISH DEMOGRAPHIC LOSSES

The contemporary women's movement has contributed significantly to Jewish population decline. In the process of initiating significant change in the status of women, the movement has greatly influenced Jewish women—and has had a disastrous effect on the American-Jewish population.

In the later decades of the twentieth century the women's movement came to the fore of American culture. Marriage and children were discouraged, and the family was derided. Betty Friedan referred to the "comfortable concentration camp" of traditional family life. Women needed to be "liberated" from it—to value themselves for their career achievements, but not for motherhood.[98] The rate of Jewish marriages dropped drastically. The fertility and birth rates of American Jews declined as women remained single or married late and had few or no children. The Jewish nuclear family rapidly eroded.

ASSIMILATION AND PERSONAL STATUS PROBLEMS

Based on demographic data, millions of Jews currently on the Jewish religious periphery will be lost to the Jewish people. The assimilatory process is taking them constantly farther from their heritage; they are not perpetuating themselves, and when they do have children most do not remain within the Jewish fold.

In addition, liberal religious groupings have been gradually severing their relationship to historical Judaism as they reject Judaism's traditional legal norms for marriage, divorce, and conversion. These norms, which many liberal Jews view as not relevant to the times, have served as central elements of Jewish cohesion throughout history. The far-reaching changes in the personal status of many Jews are the direct consequence of their rejection of these norms. These changes bestow on them a unique quasi-Jewish status. Normative Jews—i.e., those who adhere to *Halachah*—are forbidden by Jewish law to marry them.

Most non-Jewish partners in the many intermarriages of the late twentieth century did not convert to Judaism. The few who converted underwent procedures that were often not in accord with the requirements of *Halachah*. In addition, Reform Judaism considers Jewish a child of a mixed marriage as long as either parent is Jewish.[99] Jewish law prohibits marrying them or their descendants.[100]

Most of the many divorces among American Jews do not fulfill Jewish legal requirements. Often they are civil divorces—considered valid by Reform Judaism—or they are performed by rabbis who do not personally observe Jewish law. The Jewish divorce laws are complex and require specialized knowledge and expertise. A rabbi who is not expert, or does not subscribe to *Halachah* himself, cannot perform a credible halachic divorce. A couple who lack a valid Jewish divorce are, under Jewish law, still married.[101] Subsequent marriages are not only illegal, but fall into the category of adulterous relationships. After such a relationship has commenced, even a valid *get*, a legal Jewish divorce terminating the first marriage, will not render the second relationship licit; the couple are forever prohibited to each other.

Jewish law considers the children of the second union to be *mamzerim*, or illegitimate "bastards." The *mamzer* is not to be confused with the "bastard" of the non-Jewish world. A *mamzer* is not, as is often erroneously believed, the issue of an unmarried couple. Although Judaism disapproves of sexual relations between an unmarried couple, a child born from them is fully "legitimate." The parents are permitted to marry each other. A *mamzer* is the issue of a prohibited sexual relationship punishable in the Torah by death. The relationship is either an incestual one[102] or when one partner is validly married to another person according to Jewish law.

Jews are forbidden to marry the sons or daughters of such a union.[103] The Torah says: "A *mamzer* may not enter into the community of Israel, even unto the tenth generation."[104] A *mamzer* may only marry another *mamzer*[105] or a proselyte.[106] Even the descendants of a *mamzer*–children, grandchildren, and great-grandchildren–remain forever proscribed as marital partners to legitimate Jews, "since *mamzerim* are forbidden . . . for all time."[107] Although the *mamzer* is fully Jewish, he or she has, in certain ways, a legal status that is more prohibitive than that of a non-Jew. The non-Jew may become a normative Jew, but a *mamzer* can never do so. Jews are permitted to marry converts,[108] but not *mamzerim* or their descendants.[109] A *mamzer* is conceived in a state of impurity and unholiness[110] through sexual relations prohibited by the Torah. Since Judaism attaches great importance to the moral strength of the family unit, and the *mamzer* is the embodiment of an immoral, antimarriage, antifamily act, the *mamzer* may not marry into the Jewish family and the Jewish community.

During periods of changes in personal status that are not in accordance with Jewish law, groups eventually evolve that fall into a similar legal category as Karaites. The Karaites were a Jewish group originating in the eighth century. They rejected the Talmud and traditional *Halachah* and departed from accepted Jewish legal norms in personal status. Because of their defective status in Jewish law–their method of divorce does not conform with that of Jewish law, and therefore a Karaite woman divorced by the Karaite system is not considered divorced, and the children of subsequent marriages are considered possible *mamzerim*–Karaites are forever forbidden as Jewish marital partners.

Similarly, today, a Jew changing his or her personal status in a manner that does not meet the requirements of Jewish law is not involved in a private process. His or her descendants will never be able to become legitimate Jews by converting to normative Judaism, nor ever marry normative Jews. A Jew undergoing change in status creates reverberations that echo through posterity.

REPLENISHMENT

Massacres and forced conversions have over the ages elicited an instinctive compensatory response among Jews. Jews felt a drive to replace lost "limbs" by replenishing depleted numbers. Procreation in the face of adversity has been a traditional Jewish response of defiance to persecutors and an act of faith in the continuity of the Jewish people.

Curiously, the post-Holocaust generation, in response to what is probably the most significant depletion of Jewish population in history, has manifested a reverse tendency. Rather than defying the hemorrhaging of the Jewish people, they have contributed to it. They produce fewer, rather than more, children.

THE LACK OF CONCERN FOR JEWISH POSTERITY

Modern Western society essentially pampers the self. It is less concerned with community or family. This period has been called the age of narcissistic hedonism. One relates neither to history nor to the future—only to the present. John Lennon said, "My thing is out of sight, out of mind. That's my attitude towards life. . . . I don't believe in yesterday. . . ."[111]

The waning sense of historical time characterizing this age is shared by many young Jews today. Missing basic Jewish knowledge, many lack a connection to their Jewish past and an interest in the future. They know little of the age-old teachings that have made the Jew the spiritual conscience of humanity.

Lacking a concept of Jewish historical continuity, and having absolutely no awareness of their own place in ongoing Jewish history, neither predecessors nor posterity interest today's Jew. Identification with one's generation as a vital link in a long chain of tradition, originating in the past and continuing into the future, is, for most American Jews, a foreign concept. The crisis characterizing many Jews today is reflected not only in ignorance of their Jewish heritage and obliviousness to Judaism's contributions to the moral and spiritual development of humanity, it is distinguished especially by an unconcern with Jewish posterity. In a world that prizes selfism, Jewish time, energies, and resources are increasingly devoted to self. As a result, the Jewish identification of the growing numbers of Jews who identify with modern Western society has decreased dramatically as they have absorbed the values of that society, and simultaneously they and their children have been rapidly disappearing as recognizable Jews.

"THE VANISHING JEW"

The Jewish people lost six million Jews during the Holocaust, one third of the entire Jewish nation. The Jewish population has continued to decrease throughout the world at an alarming rate. When concern is expressed in some quarters about the world's "population explosion," one wonders whether it is appropriate for Jews to give this personal priority at a time when Jewish existence is endangered; Jews are disappearing from the face of the earth.

Demographers speak of "the vanishing Jew." The birth rate of Jews everywhere is below that of their neighbors, falling well below the replacement level. There has been a 50 percent drop in the fertility rate of American Jewish women, from 2.8 children per woman in 1955 to less than 1.5 in the 1990s.[112] To maintain replacement level, a fertility rate of 2.1 for all women, both single and married, is required.[113]

Demographers point out that the fertility rate of American Jewish women has historically been lower than that of other whites.[114] Professors Schmelz and DellaPergola foresee a continued sharp decline in births for American Jews.[115] They project a Jewish population in America of 3.7 million by 2020,[116] a figure that includes many non-Jews in Jewish households. This projection is considerably below the figure of 6 million that had been the accepted American Jewish population figure for many years. It is also highly optimistic.[117]

THE FUTURE: A REVITALIZATION FROM THE CORE

The only significant exception to the American Jewish demographic catastrophe is the traditional sector of the population. Historically, Jews have found their greatest joy to be with large families. For religious reasons and out of an acute feeling of responsibility for Jewish continuity and a corresponding desire to replenish the huge losses being incurred, traditional Jews have been having larger families. Five, six, or seven children is not uncommon, and there are many observant Jewish families with eight, ten, or more children.

These children, in turn, marry earlier, during their peak reproductive years, and have similarly large families. Demographer Schmelz finds them to be deliberately planning their family size above replacement needs, and they aim at increasingly higher targets as their religiosity rises.[118] Professor Schmelz's comments about current population growth in Jerusalem are equally appropriate to the observant Jewish sector in the United States: "This is a large-scale instance of family planning for intergenerational surpluses in a technologically advanced modern population."[119]

The efforts of this core group are focused on creating and sustaining the educational institutions necessary for the preservation of Judaism and its transmission. These include intensive Jewish all-day schools and centers for advanced Jewish study. In the past mostly confined to enclaves in a handful of major urban centers, the numbers in the core group are rapidly growing, and they are revitalizing many Jewish communities. Jewishly knowledgeable and intensely committed to communal causes, the committed core-group Jews are gradually assuming leadership positions in the American Jewish community and are playing an increasingly influential role in redirecting priorities of fund allocations to areas that are geared to Jewish continuity.

Demographer DellaPergola concludes that "the core of the American Jewish community will grow and widen and increase in quality and intensity, while erosion will continue at the periphery."[120] Paradoxically, therefore, as the Jewish population decreases, the continued expansion of the traditional core signals rejuvenation and revitalization. The 1.5 to 2 million or so Jews who will be left in the United States by 2030–2040 will probably be far more Jewishly committed than any generation before them. Jewish children will receive the education necessary to know their heritage and live full Jewish lives, thus maintaining their distinctive Jewish identity in a Christian society.

This committed core group will produce larger numbers of Jewish children than any generation of American Jews before them. The new era of growth will thus assure both Jewish continuity and the perpetuation of Judaism in the United States.

10

Divorce

THE JEWISH DISCOURAGEMENT OF DIVORCE

Behind Jewish divorce laws lies the intent of discouraging divorce. "All things can be replaced," cautions the Talmud, "except the wife of one's youth."[1]

Rabbis have gone to great lengths to make peace between husband and wife and to prevent divorce. The Talmud illustrates the lengths to which the second-century Sage R. Meir went to reconcile a couple. Every Friday evening R. Meir lectured in the synagogue at Hamat near Tiberias. One evening he concluded his discourse later than usual. A woman who had attended his lecture returned home late. Her husband asked her where she had been. When she replied that she had been at R. Meir's lecture, her husband angrily banished her from the house, telling her she could not return until she spat in the great rabbi's eye.

At the next lecture R. Meir, having learned of the husband's demand, asked that the woman come forward. Before the assembled onlookers, he told her that his eye was troubling him. He asked her if she would spit in his eye to relieve it. When she hesitated, R. Meir insisted, saying that if she spat in his eye seven times it would be fully healed. The woman finally did as he asked, after which he told her to tell her husband that she had done even more than he had asked. He had asked that she spit once, and she had done so seven times.

R. Meir's students remonstrated with their teacher, saying "Rabbi, the dignity of the Torah is shamed! If you had informed us of what the husband had done we would have had him brought to the synagogue and forced him to apologize to his wife."

Replied R. Meir: "And is my name greater than that of the Creator? If the Holy Name of God, written in holiness, may be erased in order to bring peace between man and wife,[2] surely R. Meir's honor may be diminished for the sake of this vital task of promoting peace between husband and wife."[3]

WHEN THE TRUTH NEED NOT BE SAID

In a similar vein, the Talmud teaches that one may avoid saying the whole truth in order to maintain *sh'lom bayit,* peace in the home. When God informs Sarah that she is to have a son, she laughs and says, "Now that I am withered, am I to have enjoyment—with my husband so old?"[4] However, when God speaks to Abraham, God says, "Why did Sarah laugh, saying, 'Shall I in truth bear a child, old as I am?' "[5]

The Talmud explains that God deliberately altered Sarah's words in telling them to Abraham so as to conceal from him that his wife had complained of his old age. God thereby maintained harmony between Abraham and Sarah.[6]

The idea of marriage as a permanent union is evident in Scripture.[7] There are no instances in the Bible where divorce is undertaken lightly. Ezra's ruling, in the pre-Second Temple era, that men must give up their non-Jewish wives met with significant opposition.[8] In the fifth century B.C.E. the prophet Malachi denounced the frequency of divorce in Judaea with a cry of moral anguish.[9]

When a man and woman are contemplating divorce, a variety of means are employed to convince them to reconsider a decision that might have been hastily reached. Attempts are made to convince them to remain together for their own sakes and to keep the marriage intact for the benefit of their family. Rabbinical courts will often recommend marriage counseling. They might intentionally procrastinate in dealing with the case and insist on frequent visits by the couple to the court. Many of the special provisions relating to Jewish divorce procedure are designed to provide time for a couple to reconsider the decision to divorce, to encourage reconciliation, and, as will be seen, especially to protect the woman.

"BRINGING PEACE BETWEEN MAN AND WIFE"

Among Jewish communities there have always been powerful motivating factors—economic, social, and communal—that worked to strengthen the sanctity of marriage and to militate against divorce. Under ordinary circumstances, communities held the conviction that there was a permanence to Jewish marriage. Divorce was resorted to rarely, and only when all efforts at mediation and reconciliation had failed. Minor grievances and insignificant differences that are often exaggerated and can trigger divorce proceedings do not tend to cause the dissolution of Jewish marriages, in the face of strong pressure in the Jewish community to preserve the family. Rabbis and members of the community take seriously the dictum of the talmudic Sages: "These are the precepts whose fruits a person enjoys in this world but whose principal remains intact for him to enjoy in the world to come . . . bringing peace between a man and his wife."[10]

Judaism sees tragedy in divorce—the painful disintegration of what was once built with great hopes and aspirations. At the same time, Judaism insists on the necessity for two people who are desperately unhappy to be allowed a way out of their predicament.

The final passage in the talmudic tractate *Gitin*, Divorces,[11] states:

> R. Elazar says: Whoever divorces his first wife, even the altar sheds tears, as it is written: '. . . . you cover the altar with tears, weeping and sighing. . . . Why? Because the Lord has been a witness between you and the wife of your youth with whom you have broken faith, though she is your partner and the wife of your covenant.'[12]

Also, the Sages emphasize the difficulty in which divorce often places the woman: "When a woman is divorced from her husband the resulting cry is heard from one end of the world to the other."[13]

HOW R. ZUSYA SAVED HIS MARRIAGE

A story is told of the eighteenth-century Polish hasidic leader R. Zusya ("Reb Zisha") of Hanipoli (d. 1800), reknowned for his simplicity and humility. It alludes to the talmudic passage that the altar sheds tears for a couple who divorce. Unhappy with their marriage, R. Zusya's wife persistently asked for a divorce.

One night, the hasidic rabbi called to his wife, "Hendel, look here." He showed her that his pillow was wet. "The Talmud tells us," R. Zusya said, "that if a man divorces his wife, the altar itself sheds tears for him. My pillow is wet with those tears. Now, do you still insist that we divorce?" From then on, R. Zusya's wife was at peace.[14]

The Midrash relates a poignant tale about R. Simon bar Yohai, the second-century mishnaic Sage of the Talmud, of the extensive efforts exerted by one woman to avoid divorce:

A couple who had been married more than ten years without having been blessed with children decided to divorce. The husband told his wife, "Take the most precious object in my house and go back to your father's house." They then went to R. Simon ben Yohai, who tried to dissuade them from divorcing. However, the husband persisted. Whereupon R. Simon said to them, "When you wed, you rejoiced and entertained your friends with food and drink. Now, too, let your separation be like your union. Prepare a feast like your wedding feast, and on the following day come and see me."

The couple did as R. Simon instructed and arranged a "separation feast" which was like a wedding. During the feast, the husband became merry with wine and fell into a deep sleep. Whereupon his wife had him carried to her father's house. Upon awakening, the husband was startled to find himself in a strange place. "Where am I?" he asked. His wife replied that he was in her father's house. "Why should I be in your father's house?" he asked. His wife replied, "Didn't you tell me to take the most precious object in your house and go back to my father's house? I have no object more precious than you, and by our promise I am entitled to keep you."

Her words greatly moved her husband, and, overcome with emotion, they went back to R. Simon. He advised them not to part. He said he would pray for them to have children, and he was certain that God would reward such a good wife. The couple heeded his advice and returned home together. The following year, R. Simon participated in the circumcision of their son.[15]

WHEN DIVORCE IS THE ONLY OPTION

There are times, however, when the greatest efforts are of no avail. The marriage is simply unworkable. There are couples who should never have married, whose personalities are deeply, intrinsically incompatible. Where there was once love, compassion, there is only dissonance and quarreling. The community of spirit that they may once have shared has ceased to exist.

If all efforts to achieve reconciliation fail and a marriage is beyond remedy, Judaism recognizes that the union has lost its sanctity and the couple no longer forms a marital superentity. Jewish law regards divorce as a legitimate, realistic possibility. Indeed, the Talmud considers the divorce of an intolerable spouse to be praiseworthy,[16] commenting matter-of-factly that one cannot be expected to live in close quarters with a serpent.[17]

GET: THE JEWISH DIVORCE AND ITS EXECUTION

Essentially the *get piturin* (divorce contract; in short–*get*) is a bill of divorce prepared by the husband–or by his agent, i.e., the scribe–and delivered to the wife, either by the husband or by his agent authorized through a power of attorney. The *get* itself must be written by a communally authorized scribe known to be an observant Jew. It must be written especially for the parties concerned (it may not be a printed or a filled-in form) and it must conform to many detailed and exacting rules.

The laws relating to the *get* are formal and exact and must be stringently observed. The *get* is traditionally written in Aramaic. Numerous rules and regulations concern its writing, signature, and delivery. The slightest deviation in form renders a *get* invalid. Therefore, even rabbis who are knowledgeable in all other areas of Jewish law are ordinarily not qualified to conduct Jewish divorce procedures and usually refrain from doing so.

Unless a rabbi is himself fully observant of Jewish law, he is not considered qualified to carry out all the Jewish legal requirements relating to divorce. Unless he has the requisite specialized qualifications and has sufficient expertise to supervise all aspects of the complex divorce process he cannot properly perform the intricate divorce procedure. The "divorced" couple may actually remain legally married even after they are pronounced divorced. Subsequent remarriages are then illegal, and the couple unwittingly subject themselves and their partners to bigamy and adultery. The woman's subsequent children are *mamzerim* and are forever forbidden to marry normative Jews.

Therefore, the Talmud and the Jewish law codes specifically caution those who are not expert in this highly specialized area of Jewish law to refrain from participating in divorce procedures.[18] It is incumbent upon those seeking to divorce to ascertain that the entire procedure is conducted by an acknowledged specialist who meets all of the required halachic criteria, in order to assure that their divorce and any subsequent remarriages will be universally recognized.

JUDAISM'S LIBERAL ATTITUDE TOWARD DIVORCE

An interesting discussion in the Mishnah deals with grounds for divorce. The School of Shammai maintains that the only grounds for divorce are adultery. The School of Hillel argues that divorce should be easy—"even if he has nothing more against her than that she has spoiled the soup."[19] R. Akiva argues for facilitating divorce and easing the permissible grounds. He contends that a man may divorce his wife for the "sole reason that he has found a woman more attractive than she."[20] These trivial grounds such as the soup being spoiled or that a more attractive woman comes along obviously do not seriously constitute adequate grounds. Rather, Hillel and R. Akiva, by the use of exaggeration, wish to establish an important principle. They oppose the stringent position regarding divorce taken by the School of Shammai, which limits grounds for divorce to adultery. They urge the adoption of a merciful attitude, one that allows divorce on the simple grounds of irreconcilable differences that make living together unbearable.

Judaism has adopted the lenient position, that is, that divorce should be granted on the grounds of incompatibility,[21] and not limited to that extreme of marital dissatisfaction, adultery. Jewish law, therefore, does not see divorce as an admission of a crime and therefore does not seek a guilty party. Rather, divorce is viewed as a frank admission of failure: this marriage was a mistake; it should never have taken place; these two people recognize that they cannot live together happily and peacefully, or even tolerably well. This fact constitutes the strongest argument for a couple to divorce. A more liberal position on divorce is scarcely imaginable.

The basic liberality of the Jewish divorce law reflects an insight into family dynamics: the Sages believe that two people may harm more than just each other by their destructive proximity. The lives and well-being of the offspring of their union are involved. The children's suffering grows progressively more acute as their awareness develops and as their parents' marriage hobbles along and deteriorates. In certain cases early termination of a poor marriage is in the children's best interests.

Though it is difficult for an outsider unaware of the nature of the interaction between husband and wife to apportion blame for the failure of a marriage, there is a tendency to fault the man for the breakup of a marriage, possibly because the initiative to terminate the marriage is often his.

HUSBAND AND WIFE (NOT COURTS) DECIDE ON JEWISH DIVORCE

In most systems of law, the court decides whether a divorce is in order. In Jewish law, divorce is decided by the parties to the marriage agreement. Divorce, like marriage, is a contract in Jewish law and thus is unilaterally executed. For the divorce to be valid, however, both parties must consent to its execution. There must be free will on the part of the husband to give the *get*—unless the *Bet Din*, the rabbinic court, compels him to grant it—and there must be free will on the part of the wife to receive the *get*.[22] Mutual consent, the agreement of both husband and wife, is, in Jewish law, the basis of—and is sufficient for—divorce.[23]

The function of the courts under Jewish jurisprudence is to decide under what conditions a divorce agreement is to be executed and to ensure that the legalities of the divorce procedure are punctiliously maintained. Until the parties concerned complete the transaction of giving and receiving a *get piturin*, however, they remain married to each other. Therefore, should one of the parties decide prior to the divorce on a change of mind, there is an absence of mutual consent, and the other party must perforce go along and remain subject to all the matrimonial obligations. However, the party requesting to withdraw from an agreement to divorce is then subject to all penalty provisions previously agreed upon by the parties for such a violation of an agreement to divorce.

JEWISH DIVORCE IS NOT DEPENDENT ON APPORTIONING BLAME

In many legal systems divorce is conditional upon establishing a "guilty party," i.e., that one of the marital partners is at fault and bears the blame for the breakup of the marriage. In English law, until quite recently, the commission of a matrimonial offense was a *sine qua non* for divorce.[24] Under Jewish law, divorce is not dependent on the establishment of legal responsibility or blame. In Jewish law, if both parties agree, a divorce is granted with no specific cause required. Paradoxically, such an agreement in other legal systems might be considered collusion and could constitute a bar to legal dissolution of the marriage.

In the absence of an agreement between the parties to a divorce, the rabbinic courts are empowered to decide if there is a legal basis to compel the granting of a *get piturin*, a writ of divorce. Under certain conditions, if the parties are unable to arrive at a mutually satisfactory agreement, the courts have the right to use methods of compulsion to terminate a marriage. Such powers have been particularly useful in protecting wives whose welfare was threatened by their husbands' refusal to participate in a divorce. The court is not empowered to arbitrarily issue a divorce, but must base its decision on established legal grounds. (See the following.)

THE POWER OF THE RABBINIC COURTS TO AID THE WOMAN

In the event of a recalcitrant husband refusing to grant a divorce where circumstances require it, Jewish law has empowered rabbinic courts to force him to do so. Thus, if a woman has valid grounds for divorce – and Jewish law provides the woman with considerably more grounds for divorce than it provides the man – she can petition the *Bet Din* to direct the husband to give his wife the *get*, and this court has the jurisdiction to implement its decision. Indeed, the *Bet Din* can even apply physical force where necessary. Maimonides rules:

> If one is obliged by law to divorce his wife and he refuses to do so, a Jewish court in every place and in every period may even cause him to be beaten until he declares "I am willing." He then writes the get, and it is a valid divorce contract.[25]

The use of force to compel a difficult husband to issue a divorce is obviously limited to countries in which Jewish courts have such power. In modern Israel, for example, where the rabbinic courts hold jurisdiction in the areas of marriage and divorce, imprisonment (and even its implicit threat) has been a powerful weapon that the courts have used on occasion to force men to grant divorces to their wives when circumstances have been considered serious enough to warrant such an approach.

As for countries in which Jewish courts have no power to enforce their decision, Maimonides rules that non-Jewish courts may enforce the decisions of the Jewish court:

> If the non-Jewish court beat him and said to him, "Do what the Jewish court told you," and they applied pressure on the Jew until he had no choice but to initiate divorce, the divorce is nonetheless valid.[26]

Maimonides rules, however, that the dissolution of a marriage enforced by non-Jewish courts where the Jewish courts had not previously ruled on the matter is invalid. Even if the woman's claims for divorce are valid, she must first approach Jewish courts.[27]

MALTREATING AND ABUSING A WIFE

The woman can demand a divorce for two primary reasons: incompatibility, based on her husband's mistreatment of her, and her husband's physical defects.

Jewish law views physical maltreatment and abuse of a wife as totally unjustifiable. Judaism treats the wife-beater with the greatest severity. R. Meir of Rothenburg, the great thirteenth-century German halachic authority, emphasizes the magnitude of the crime in his ruling:

> Every son of the covenant is obliged to respect his wife more than he respects himself. . . . She was given to him to live a good life and not to suffer, as it is written in the *ketubah*: "I [the husband] undertake to work for and respect and provide sustenance, etc."
>
> He who beats his wife should be dealt with more stringently than one who strikes his neighbor, since he is not bidden to respect his neighbor – but is bidden to respect his wife. That is the way of the Gentiles; God forbid that a Jew should do such a thing, and he who does it should be excommunicated and whipped and punished, even to the extent of chopping off his hand if he persists and continues to do so. . . .[28] A man who beats his wife . . . is compelled to grant her a divorce. . . .[29]

The codifier R. Joseph Karo does not agree that the husband should be compelled to grant a divorce under these circumstances, but quotes the *Mahzor Vitri* compendium of laws and customs of R. Simhah ben Samuel of Vitri, which states that a man who beats his wife should be treated more severely than one who beats his fellow, since he is obligated by Jewish law to treat his wife better than he treats himself. He rules, therefore, that a wife-beater should be excommunicated and flogged, and if a husband repeats this and beats his wife regularly, he should even have his hand cut off and he should be forced to grant his wife a divorce and pay her *ketubah* sum.[30]

DISRESPECT AS GROUNDS FOR DIVORCE

Mistreatment need not be limited to beating. Improper treatment of a wife based simply on disrespect constitutes a prime basis for her to demand a divorce. If the husband initiates constant quarreling between them and habitually employs disrespectful language toward his wife, this is considered cruel behavior not in accordance with what is expected of a Jewish husband and therefore constitutes grounds for divorce.

A husband's maltreatment of his wife also includes not providing sufficient or proper maintenance when he is able to do so.[31]

The principle that forms a fundamental basis for Jewish married life is stated in the Talmud[32] and enunciated by Maimonides in his Code as follows:

> A man should honor his wife more than he honors himself and love her as he loves himself. And he should seek to provide for her according to his means. And he shall not unduly impose his fear upon her, but should speak to her gently and he should not be overly sad nor angry.[33]

Some of the grounds for which a woman has the right to compel divorce are shared by the husband. However, a husband's rights to demand divorce are more restricted than the wife's. Judaism manifests concern for the protection of the wife's rights to conjugal relations, protecting her rights to a much greater extent than it protects those of the man. A childless woman may be granted a divorce if she wants children but her husband is incapable of fathering them. But the Sages also protect the woman's rights to marital relations for their own sake. If her husband suffers from a contagious and dangerous disease that prevents her from cohabiting with him, she may demand a divorce; similarly, if a physical defect in him arouses in her feelings of revulsion or if she simply finds him repugnant and cannot bring herself to have conjugal relations with him. If he does not agree to divorce she can have the rabbinic court compel a divorce.

If the woman is denied conjugal relations, for whatever reason, she may demand a divorce, and if the husband is not amenable she can have the rabbinic court compel a divorce. She is also entitled to a divorce if her husband is malodorous, or even if his occupation is such that it prevents her from cohabiting with him frequently.

Moral dissolution, adultery, or a change of religion on the part of the husband are instances where the wife can petition the court to compel a divorce.

The woman is also entitled to a divorce if the husband causes her to transgress the dietary laws when she observes them, or if he insists on conjugal relations when she is in her *niddah* (menstrual and seven-day post-menstrual) period.

Should the woman wish to live in *Eretz Yisrael* and her husband refuses, she can compel a divorce, and vice versa.

The following are the gounds for divorce that Jewish law provides men and women.

NINE INSTANCES WHEN THE HUSBAND MAY COMPEL DIVORCE

Under the following conditions, a husband can unilaterally compel divorce:

1. The wife changes her religion or knowingly transgresses "the laws of Moses and Judaism," or knowingly misleads him into doing so, e.g., causes him to transgress the dietary laws or to have conjugal relations when she is a menstruant or during her *niddah* period.[34]
2. The wife commits adultery, or the husband produces two witnesses who provide convincing probability that she has committed adultery.[35]
3. The wife is guilty of habitually indecent behavior, dresses immodestly in public,[36] or so loudly demands conjugal relations of her husband that outsiders hear her discussing the matter,[37] and he is shamed.
4. The wife grossly and publicly insults her husband or her father-in-law by cursing or assaulting either of them.[38]
5. The wife refuses conjugal relations for the course of a whole year.[39]
6. The wife suffers from a disability or illness that precludes marital relations.[40]
7. The wife is barren, after ten years of marriage.[41]
8. The wife unjustifiably refuses to move with him to another domicile in the same country where the standard of living is not lower.[42]
9. The wife refuses to settle with him in *Eretz Yisrael*; this applies even if the move will result in a reduction in their standard of living.[43]

TWENTY INSTANCES WHEN THE WIFE MAY COMPEL DIVORCE

A wife can compel her husband to give her a divorce under any of the following circumstances:

1. The husband changes his religion[44] or forces her to violate the laws of Judaism knowing that she observes them.[45]
2. The husband is morally dissolute or commits adultery.[46]
3. The husband suffers from a major physical defect.[47]
4. The wife finds him repugnant and cannot bear marital relations with him.[48]
5. The husband refuses marital relations with her.[49]
6. The husband insists on having marital relations while clothed.[50]
7. The husband becomes weakened or debilitated to the extent that for a period of more than six months marital relations are not feasible.[51].
8. The wife claims her husband is impotent–even should he deny it.[52]
9. The wife wants children and her husband is incapable of begetting them.[53]
10. The husband is malodorous.[54]
11. The husband is engaged in a disgusting trade.[55]
12. The husband is chronically angry and quarrelsome and habitually turns her out of the house.[56]
13. The husband habitually beats his wife.[57]
14. The husband refuses to support his wife.[58]
15. The husband prevents her from visiting her parents at reasonable intervals.[59]
16. The husband prevents her from attending a wedding or paying a consolation visit to mourners.[60]
17. The husband insists that they live with his parents when she claims they are unpleasant toward her.[61]
18. The husband prevents her from adorning herself.[62]
19. The wife wishes to leave a neighborhood, which has undesirable elements, and wishes to move to another domicile, and her husband unreasonably refuses.[63]
20. The wife wishes to leave the Diaspora and move to Eretz Yisrael, and her husband refuses.[64]

THE PROBLEM OF THE *AGUNAH*

Agunah, "anchored (or tied) woman," is the term for a wife whose husband has left her or is missing, but who is prevented from remarrying, either because she cannot obtain a divorce or an uncertainty exists as to whether her husband is alive.

The problem of the *agunah* is one of the most complex of Jewish law and is one of the most-discussed situations in *Halachah*, especially in recent years. Since Jewish divorce requires the agreement of both parties and is not simply a legal act executed by the court, in the absence of proof of a husband's death or in the instance of a husband's refusal to grant a *get*, the possibility of the woman's becoming free to remarry are limited. Rabbinic sympathy with the plight of an *agunah* is tempered with a hesitancy to be overly permissive in allowing an *agunah* to remarry because of the grave concern that rabbis could thereby validate an adulterous marriage. Children who are the product of the second marriage and are considered the issue of an adulterous relationship and are *mamzerim*, bastards, are forever forbidden to marry normative Jews. The complexity is aggravated because of the stipulation in Jewish law that if the first husband reappears, the woman is compelled to divorce her second husband, but is prevented from rejoining her first spouse as well.

The situation is aggravated further during times of war when soldiers are missing in action or when vast upheavals of population and mass killings occur among civilians (as happened during the Holocaust, for example) and when substantiation of death is difficult to obtain. The overwhelming majority of cases of *agunot* relate to the disappearance and presumed death of the husband.

Jewish law is very lenient in the case of an *agunah*. R. Asher ben Yehiel, the thirteenth- to fourteenth-century codifier known as the *Rosh*, laid down a general guideline for handling this painful human predicament: "One is required to carefully examine all possible procedures in order to release the *agunah*."[65] Accordingly, the stringent rules of evidence required for court attestation are suspended in the situation of an *agunah*, including the acceptance of "hearsay" and documentary evidence, single-witness testimony, and testimony by those who are otherwise considered legally incompetent as witnesses—even overheard conversation among non-Jews—and there is a suspension of the cross-examination of witnesses.[66] Such relaxations of legal restrictions are based on the presumption that witnesses will hesitate to falsely testify to someone's death in the knowledge that he may suddenly appear.[67]

Maimonides says that the reason for the relaxation of the strict rules of legal testimony is "so that there should not be *agunot* among the daughters of Israel."[68]

The testimony of the *agunah* herself about her husband's death is accepted as valid evidence. She is considered a reliable witness to her husband's death even though she is obviously not a disinterested party in the matter. The woman may be allowed to remarry on the strength of her own testimony alone when she is known to have lived harmoniously with her first husband and when he is not a soldier who is missing in action.[69] This is because it is believed that she will ascertain the facts very well before testifying, since she is aware that in the event of her remarriage and her first husband's subsequent return she will be considered an adultress, her children will be *mamzerim*, and she will not be permitted to live with either of her two husbands.[70]

As flexible as *Halachah* is regarding the acceptance of evidence in the instance of an *agunah*, the fear of legimitizing a possible adulterous union remains. This makes it impossible for rabbinic courts to give a woman *carte blanche* to remarry when she lacks even the minimal evidence of her husband's death required by the court.

ALLEVIATING THE SITUATION OF THE *AGUNAH*

There are instances where soldiers going to war have left their wives a conditional *get*, to become effective should they be missing in action. The Talmud teaches:

> Whoever went out to participate in the wars of the House of David would write a Writ of Divorce for his wife.[71]

A number of attempts have been made to alleviate the situation of the *agunah* in recent years. Conditional marriages have been proposed. Another idea has been to have the groom transmit a conditional bill of divorce at the time of the wedding. Possibilities were raised of having the *ketubah*, the Jewish marriage contract, contain a clause incorporating a commitment by the husband and wife to accept the authority of a religious court in the event of a divorce and to authorize the court to impose penalties for failure to comply with the decisions of the religious court to have the husband grant a *get*.

However, none of these propositions have had rabbinic sanction. All were found by rabbinic authorities to be not in conformity with *Halachah*. In order for a marriage to be valid, Jewish law requires an absolutely unconditional commitment by each of the parties to the other at the time of the wedding. Additionally, the *ketubah* proposal was found to be unenforceable in the United States according to American law.[72]

Regarding the recalcitrant husband, the solution in Israel may be for the rabbinic courts to make more frequent use of their powers to threaten imprisonment of those who do not grant a *get* when directed to do so by the courts.

Elsewhere, the solution may well be the enforcement by the secular courts of the decisions of the rabbinic courts. The Jewish husband committed himself in the *ketubah* at the time of the wedding to abide by "the laws of Moses and Israel." His not delivering a *get* when directed by a rabbinic court to do so should be considered by the secular court as a breach of his agreement to abide by "the laws of Moses and Israel." Consequently, the secular court could employ the legal means at their disposal to force the husband to abide by his contractual agreement.

The problem of the *agunah* is one that the rabbis have dealt with sensitively in the past. It is urgent that the problem be confronted sensitively and compassionately today, so that, in Maimonides' words, "there should not be *agunot* among the daughters of Israel."

V

n Civil Law

11

Civil, Criminal, and Inheritance Law

THE WOMAN IN JEWISH CIVIL AND CRIMINAL LAW

In Jewish civil and criminal law there is no fundamental distinction between the rights of the man and those of the woman. A woman may initiate a court case, or she may be sued, just as a man may. If a woman commits a crime she is subject to the same criminal penalties as a man.

A woman who is the victim of a criminal act has the same legal recourse as a man; if, for example, an ox gores a man or a woman, the Torah does not differentiate in the penalty to be paid.[1] The penalties for violation of the Torah laws regarding *arayot*, prohibited incestuous or adulterous relations, are equally incumbent upon both sexes.[2]

The principle of equality under law is spelled out in the Talmud:

> The school of R. Ishmael learned . . . Scripture provides equality of the woman in regard to all of the penalties of the Torah. . . . The school of R. Elazar learned . . . Scripture provides equality of the Torah in regard to all of the laws of the Torah.[3]

Exceptions to the equality principle are usually instances in which a woman is given preference. Because of woman's greater sensitivity she is singled out for more favorable treatment. For example, if a man and a woman are in court together, deference is given the women and she is granted the privilege of being heard first.[4]

WOMEN AS WITNESSES

However, women are excluded from being court witnesses.[5] Consequently, the misconception has arisen that women are considered less reliable or less credible than men. The disqualification of women from giving testimony, like that of certain other categories of people who are equally disqualified from giving testimony, is not based on a lack of credibility, but on what we might today term technical considerations.[6]

In this, the situation of women can be compared to other groups of people, kings for example, who are excluded from giving testimony.[7] In Jewish law, credibility and incontrovertible knowledge are insufficient to qualify an individual to testify in court as a witness. Neither King David nor King Solomon would have been permitted to testify in court. Moreover, a king is not merely relieved from having to testify, but is absolutely *disqualified* as a witness in court.[8] That is not to say they lack credibility, rather the absolute disqualification of the king is a technical one; it is based upon a *Gezerat HaKatuv*, a divine decree,[9] for which no explanation is given.

Similarly, a *kohen gadol* (high priest) is excused from testifying.[10] Should there be many trustworthy witnesses who agree on the facts, but only one who denies them, none of the testimony of the many witnesses is to be accepted, even though all of them may have undergone a thorough investigation and cross-examination, and even though their testimony was shown to be credible. In all these instances the reason for the disqualification is a *Gezerat HaKatuv*, a divine Torah decree.

Relatives, too, are forbidden to testify in court. Here, too, the disqualification is not based on credibility or reliability, but on technical grounds–it is a divine decree. Maimonides explains:

> The disqualification by the Torah of relatives is not because they may be presumed to love one another [and therefore favor their kin in their testimony]. For one is forbidden to give testimony on behalf of or against a relative. It is simply a *Gezerat Hakatuv*, a divine decree of the Torah [for which no explanation is provided]. Therefore, both a friend and an enemy are fit for testimony, even though they are disqualified from judging the case. The Torah did not decree this disqualification except for the relatives.[11]

Similarly, the disqualification of women is also based on a *Gezerat HaKatuv*. While other categories of people are not permitted to testify due to lack of credibility, this is not the case regarding women. The *Tosafot* commentary explains:

> . . . It is not a matter of credibility at all [but a technical disqualification based upon divine decree], for even Moses and Aaron could not give testimony.

Certainly their disqualification is not because they were not credible [but rather due to divine decree.] . . .[12]

In order to understand the reason women are not allowed to give testimony, we must examine the criteria for establishing facts in Jewish law. Two distinct procedures are required for determining facts and for mandating judicial action based on the determined facts. According to Torah law, any single, credible witness, male or female, suffices to determine a fact.[13] For mandating judicial action Jewish law requires two adult unrelated Jewish male witnesses who have no criminal record.[14]

In the private realm determination of fact is sufficient. In any court action, or in cases where marriages are created or dissolved, a mandate of judicial action is involved. Neither of these two categories is considered of greater or of lesser significance. The extraction by someone of even the smallest sum from another in a Jewish court involves a mandate of judicial action and therefore requires two adult male witnesses. But to establish marital status, "determination" (any single credible witness, male or female) is sufficient,[15] even though, according to the Torah, a capital transgression involving life or death could be involved. The disqualification of women in instances of lesser, monetary significance is thus not on the basis of reliability, but on that of legality.

CREDIBILITY IN COURT

In certain cases, the court will accept the evidence of a solitary woman. For instance, when it comes to ascertaining whether a woman's husband is alive or dead so a court can grant a woman permission to remarry, the testimony of one witness, male or female, to the death of the husband is sufficient.[16] The credibility of this witness is not in doubt; if he or she gives false testimony, the result could be the validation of an adulterous union, punishable by death, according to Torah law.

Similarly, if a woman serves as a *shohet*, a ritual slaughterer of animals, she is to be fully trusted as having performed the *shehitah* according to the rigid rules of the *Shulhan Aruch*, the Code of Jewish Law, and her *shehitah* is accepted as being perfectly kosher on the basis of her statement alone. In practice, it is extremely rare for a woman to serve as a *shohet*, although it is permitted, because Jewish tradition is concerned about the sensitive and compassionate nature of the woman and, perhaps, does not consider it a dignified occupation for a woman–but she is fully acceptable in this category.

Similarly, it is the woman whose primary responsibility in the home encompasses the *kashrut* of the home. She supervises the fulfillment and proper observance of a vast array of laws, some of which are highly complex.

The laws regulate the nature of the meat, fish, and poultry that may be brought into the home; the proper salting of meat for the removal of blood; which processed and packaged foods may be purchased for family consumption; the preparation of foods in the home; and the separation of dairy and meat products, dishes, and cutlery–in short, many *mitzvot* in the Torah that are included in the overall category of "*kashrut.*" In Israel, *trumot* and *ma'asrot*, the biblical laws of separating portions of the foods for gift offerings and tithings comprise an additional aspect of the complex laws of *kashrut*. Parts of purchased foods must be put aside and not eaten. In all these adherences the woman is trusted absolutely and unquestioningly on the basis of her statement alone.

If a woman does not scrupulously and knowledgeably carry out all the rules and regulations relating to *Taharat HaMishpahah*, Family Purity, she involves both herself and her husband in grave halachic consequences. Nevertheless, her statement that she has properly observed these laws is unquestioningly accepted.

While some individuals are disqualified from giving testimony due to a lack of credibility, specifically people who have been convicted as criminals, deaf mutes, mentally defective people, and minors, the woman is considered entirely credible in Jewish law. Self-incriminating testimony is also not considered credible. Unlike slaves and non-Jews who are technically disqualified because they do not fulfill the requirement of being fully obligated Jews, the Sages point out that since women are fully obligated Jews, the substantive disqualification of these categories cannot be equated with the technical disqualification of the woman.[17]

In no way, therefore, is the woman viewed as lacking in credibility in Jewish law. The disqualification of women is based on a divine Torah decree. Unlike secular law, where a legal rationale must be presented for arriving at a decree, the Torah contains several divine decrees for which no reason is provided and for which the rationale is not readily determined. The Jew obeys the Torah first and foremost because God commanded him to do so. The Jew knows that if no reason is given for a Torah directive, God, in His infinite wisdom, knows what humans need. However, without presuming that we have arrived at the rationale behind these divine decrees, we may speculate as to some reasons, and assess their possible benefits.

COURT TESTIMONY

One reasonable hypothesis for the disqualification of women as witnesses in court is the thesis enunciated earlier concerning the Torah's division of men and women into public and private roles. The essentially private role of women in Jewish life is not one that is consonant with the public role of the witness in court. The validation of a fact by a witness is an integral part of the public functioning of the court, and such testimony is therefore an intrinsically public affair. This is not the case with status clarification, which is essentially a private matter.

Additionally, giving testimony in court is not only a right, it is a legal obligation.[18] In Jewish law, an individual may not avoid testifying when personally aware of facts that are germane to a case and when summoned to testify. The feminine sensitivity does not lend itself to the stresses of public testimony and the associated rigorous examination, close questioning, and cross-examination that are generally part and parcel of criminal and monetary cases.[19] In accordance with its understanding of the inherent nature of woman and the care it takes to ensure that her role should be in consonance with it, Judaism considered it imperative that the woman not be placed in a position where she would be obligated to perform an act that would be in conflict with her nature.

The Torah specifies that a thorough investigation is required before conviction. "And you shall inquire and shall investigate and shall probe diligently," the Torah states in one instance.[20] This a thorough and intense cross-examination in court, an indignity from which Judaism wishes to excuse women. "It is embarrassingly discomfitting for a woman to go to court," the Talmud teaches.[21] Indeed, this is a reason that might apply both to the disqualification of testimony from women and from kings.

Furthermore, in the instance of capital punishment, the Torah says that "the hand of the witnesses shall be the first upon him to put him to death."[22] Obviously, the Torah was unwilling to put the woman in the position of being the executioner. A woman who is a witness in a trial involving capital punishment could not be excused from testifying on the grounds that she is too sensitive to take personal part in an execution. If a woman would be allowed to give evidence, her testifying would not be optional. In criminal cases, witnesses are obligated to testify on matters of which they have direct knowledge.[23] If a woman was allowed to give testimony in such situations, she would be compelled to fulfill a responsibility that is fundamentally opposed to her inner nature, a contradiction the Torah does not permit.

Similarly, a woman is considered to be more easily embarrassed than a man,[24] which is why, in Jewish law, if a judge is faced with numerous litigants, he is required to hear the woman first. For the same reason she is to be favored over the man in the distribution of charity, food, and clothing.[25]

We see that one of the reasons women are barred from giving testimony in no way reflects lack of credibility. A woman's oath in court is believed unequivocally, the same as that of any other witness. Her reliability in fact-determination is not questioned, as may be deduced from the Torah,[26] and she is believed in matters of immense religious significance.[27] The Talmud mentions a case in which a woman's single-witness testimony was accepted in court while the single testimony of a talmudic Sage was rejected.[28]

A number of halachic authorities maintain that women may be judges, as were the biblical Deborah[29] and Yael,[30] but others disagree, reasoning that only someone who has the legal right to testify may legally judge others.[31]

INHERITANCE LAWS

On the death of the parents, children take precedence in the inheritance of estates in Jewish law and, in theory, sons have priority over daughters. In practice, however, Jewish law provides women with far more benefits than it provides for men. While sons and daughters possess essentially equal claims to maintenance from an estate, the woman is granted precedence in order to guard her privacy and modesty. Once again, a basic instrument for the protection of the woman's position is the *ketubah,* the Jewish marriage contract. In his encompassing study, *Jewish Woman in Jewish Law,* the Jerusalem talmudic authority R. Moshe Meiselman comments that the benefits the *ketubah* provides the wife and daughter after the husband's death "far exceed the wildest imagination of anyone who has ever dealt with dower or its Anglo-American equivalents."[32]

While the wife is not a legal heir to her husband's estate, the Jewish laws of inheritance benefit her by acknowledging and providing for her real needs. For example, the woman is entitled to sustenance from the estate and provision for her needs until her death or remarriage. These include the return of all the property she brought into the marriage and either the *ketubah* sum, the dowry increment listed in the *ketubah* paid to her in a lump sum, or further maintenance until the time of her death or remarriage.

Unlike a male heir, who has no lien on the property of the deceased and takes only what is left after all creditors and those with liens against the property have been satisfied, the wife and daughters function as secured creditors. They are guaranteed support before anyone else may receive any of the proceeds of the estate. They have a prior lien against the property of the deceased that supersedes and precedes that of all male heirs and all creditors of the estate.[33] Neither gift nor sale cancels the lien; the minimum claims of wife and daughters must be satisfied first, and only afterward may bequests decided on by the deceased before his death be carried out. Thus, although sons are the legal heirs of the estate, the wife and daughters must first be provided with maintenance from the estate. So, if the estate is small, the sons could be left with nothing.

On the death of her husband, a widow has two options: she may elect to either take a settlement in one lump sum or she may receive continuous support from the estate, which includes the use of the home and household effects and money for food, clothing, medical expenses, personal needs, and even burial costs, for herself and her unmarried daughters. Such maintenance must be on a level with the standard of living previously enjoyed by the deceased and his widow and must continue until her death or remarriage.

DAUGHTERS PREFERRED IN SUPPORT AND MAINTENANCE

Daughters are also provided with support from the estate, and upon reaching maturity are given a lump sum bequest, in accordance with a Mishnah:

> One who dies and leaves sons and daughters – when the estate is large the sons inherit and the daughters receive maintenance support. When the estate is small, the daughters receive maintenance support and the sons go begging from door to door. Admon says: Should I lose all of my inheritance because I am a male? R. Gamliel says: I can appreciate Admon's objection.[34]

We can see the Torah's concern for the vulnerability of a female orphan from the following *Tosefta:*

> If both a male orphan and a female orphan require support, one is obliged to support the female orphan first and only afterward do we support the male orphan, for the male orphan can beg everywhere [if necessary], while the female cannot do so.
>
> If a male orphan and a female orphan request to marry, the female orphan is to be married off first, and only afterwards is the male orphan to be married, because a woman's shame is greater than that of a man.[35]

If male heirs to the estate exist, daughters receive only maintenance. If, however, there are no sons, the daughters share the estate, even if they are minors.[36] Daughters also receive a sum from the estate for their dowry, in the same manner as the father would provide if he were alive.[37]

We may now better understand the following talmudic passage:

> *Le'inyan yerushah ben adif lei; le'inyan harvahah bito adifa lei.* When it comes to inheritance the son is preferred; when it comes to comfort the daughter is preferred.[38]

Rabenu Gershom interprets this passage to mean that the daughter is given preference when it comes to maintenance ("comfort") because the son can usually more easily maintain himself than can the daughter[39] and go where he wishes in order to find a source of a livelihood.

In practice, a daughter often inherits more than a son. R. Moses Isserles, the halachic codifier, writes: "The reason for the legislation is so that the daughter should receive as much as the son; however, the custom is to give the daughter more than the son, and that is how we conduct ourselves in our countries."[40] In many countries it became customary to give equal inheritances to sons and daughters.[41]

The *Halachah* guaranteed the support of women to ensure that women would not be left destitute in instances where the estate was small, recognizing that men would be able to support themselves more easily than women. The *Halachah* went so far as to provide a legal lien on the estate on women's behalf that took precedence over all other claims of male heirs. In this way, through the inheritance laws Jewish law secured the interest of the woman and thus strengthened the structure of the family.

PROPERTY RIGHTS

According to the Torah, a woman has full property rights; she can buy, sell, retain, or mortgage property. By rabbinic ordinance, her rights are reduced somewhat in marriage–the husband has the use of the earnings of his wife's property for the duration of the marriage.[42] The husband may not sell the property, mortgage it, or encumber it with any lien without his wife's consent, except in certain exceptional circumstances. If such circumstances arise and he does sell the property, he is required to replace it with one of equivalent value.

VI

Women in Religious Law

12

Religious Laws and Customs

This chapter and the ones following it list some of the religious laws and regulations in Judaism that apply specifically to women and that have not been discussed elsewhere in this work.

Women are obligated to fulfill all the *Taryag Mitzvot,* the 613 Torah Precepts, except for a few. The *mitzvot* excepted contain among them the ones that are gender-linked and apply exclusively to men as a result of their biological attributes, such as circumcision. There are also gender-linked *mitzvot* that are associated with women's biological attributes and apply only to women, such as those related to the *niddah,* Family Purity rules, which are treated elsewhere in this book.

The listing in these chapters should be seen as neither definitive nor exhaustive. The information presented is based on *Halachah,* Jewish law. However, this should not be regarded as a substitute for the *Shulhan Aruch,* the Code of Jewish Law. A competent, halachically observant rabbi should be consulted prior to determining *Halachah* pertaining to specific practices.

> And the daughters of Judaea rejoiced,
> Because of Your statutes, O Lord.
> (Psalms 97:8)

WOMEN'S EXEMPTION FROM SOME TORAH PRECEPTS

Of the 248 Positive Commandments in Maimonides' enumeration of the Torah's 613 *mitzvot,* the *Rambam* finds that 60 are incumbent on every adult

Jew at all times and at all places and under all circumstances. Maimonides notes: "Of these 'Unconditional Commandments,' forty-six are binding upon women as well as men, and 14 are not binding upon women."[1]

The fourteen *mitzvot* from which women are exempted are: reading the *Shema* prayer; studying the Torah; donning the *tefillin* (phylactery) on the head; donning the *tefillin* on the arm; wearing *tzitzit*, fringes on four-cornered garments; writing (or acquiring) a Torah scroll; counting the *Omer*; dwelling in a *sukkah* during the Sukkot festival; waving the *lulav* (palm) on Sukkot; hearing the *shofar* on Rosh HaShanah; being "fruitful and multiplying"; marriage; devoting oneself to one's wife during the first year of marriage; and circumcision.

There is no differentiation between men and women in their obligations to observe the 365 Negative Precepts of the Torah.

The reasons that certain *mitzvot* are incumbent on men and not on women are varied: certain *mitzvot* cannot be performed by women simply because of physical inapplicability – for example, causing one's wife to rejoice during the first year of marriage, circumcision, not cutting off the *peyot* at the sides of the beard.

In a like vein, male and female differences in personality and the greater physical vulnerability of women account for differences in the observance of some *mitzvot* by the woman. For instance, according to Jewish law, women who are captive slaves must be redeemed before male captives.[2] Similarly, the exemption of women from the *mitzvot* of marrying and having children are based on Judaism's sensitivity to the physical hazards of pregnancy and childbirth for the woman.[3] Therefore, these are elective *mitzvot* for women that they can optionally accept upon themselves.

WOMEN ARE EXCUSED FROM FULFILLING FOURTEEN POSITIVE PRECEPTS

Of the fourteen Positive Precepts from which women are exempted, most are related to the exemptions from performance of *mitzvot* that are restricted to fixed times. Although there are some exceptions to the rule, there are seven *mitzvot* that are specifically included in this group of time-dependent Positive Precepts: *tefillin*; *tzitzit*; *sukkah*; *lulav*; *shofar*; the recitation of the *Shema*; and the counting of the *Omer*.

Exceptions include eating of *matzah* on the first evening of Passover;[4] rejoicing during the festivals;[5] and *Hakhel*, the public "coming together" gathering ceremony to hear the Torah read at the conclusion of the sabbatical year on Sukkot; all of which are time-dependent Positive Precepts that are nonetheless obligatory upon women. Additional biblical or rabbinically ordained time-dependent Positive Precepts that women are required to observe include *Kiddush* on the Sabbath;[6] hearing the reading of the *Megillah*, the Book of Esther, on Purim;[7] the lighting of the Hanukkah lamp;[8] and drinking four cups of wine at the Passover *seder*.[9]

Concerning the exemption of women from most time-dependent *mitzvot*, the principle is spelled out in the Mishnah:

> Regarding all Positive Precepts that are time-dependent–they are incumbent upon men, but women are exempt. However, regarding all Positive Precepts that are not time-dependent–they are equally incumbent upon men and women. . . .[10]

Adds the *Tosefta*:

> Which are the Positive Precepts that are time-dependent? For example, *sukkah*, *lulav* and *tefillin*. Which are examples of Positive Precepts that are not time-dependent? The return of lost objects, releasing a mother bird from the nest, building a parapet around the roof, and *tzitzit* [wearing fringes on cornered garments]. R. Simon [however] exempts women from the wearing of *tzitzit* because it is a Positive Precept that is time-dependent. . . .[11]

The time-dependent precepts from which women are exempted are ones whose performance may conflict with the essential duties associated with women's role as wife and mother in the conduct of their households and in the education of their children. Such responsibilities often cannot be put off. A woman occupied with caring for her children and with the conduct of her household may find herself caught between religious and familial obligations, both of which make conflicting demands on her limited time. The situation contains elements that could threaten *shalom bayit*, the peaceful Jewish home. A central concept in Judaism is the harmonious functioning of the home and family unit. Since the woman plays the key role in this, Jewish law excuses her from adhering to many of the time-related *mitzvot*.[12]

WOMEN'S SPIRITUALITY

Women function on a different spiritual plane than men, teach the Rabbis. Men need as many precepts as possible. They are corrupted daily in the commercial world "marketplace." They require *mitzvot* laden with symbolic value in order to make them realize where true values lie.

Women were ordinarily not subject to the daily corruptive influences. They retained their spiritual level and did not require periodic reminders. Also, the woman gives birth to the children, raises them, and essentially creates the

Jewish home. She is automatically in touch with the deepest dimensions of life. She has less need than the man for aids to attain higher spiritual levels.

This corresponds with the view of R. Judah Loew, the *MaHaral* of Prague (1525–1609). The rabbinic authority teaches that women are exempt from these *mitzvot* because they are more spiritual by nature than men.

The *MaHaral* teaches that precepts are a means that God has given man to attain spirituality and closeness to God. Man, coarser and more aggressive by nature, must strive harder at spiritual tasks. Woman, by nature a more spiritual person, requires fewer *mitzvot* to attain spiritual perfection. The *MaHaral* understands the talmudic passage, "Greater is the reward the Holy One promises to women than to men,"[13] to refer to the higher spirituality of women.[14]

Yalkut Shimoni, the comprehensive midrashic and halachic anthology attributed to R. Simon of Frankfurt, twelfth to thirteenth century, teaches a similar principle. Women do not have a *yetzer hara*, an impulse to do evil. Their natural impulse is simply to perform God's will.[15]

R. Samson Raphael Hirsch writes:

> [It is] . . . likely that the Torah did not impose these *mitzvot* on women because it did not consider them necessary to be demanded from women. All time-associated precepts are meant to be symbolic procedures, to bring certain facts, principles, ideas and resolutions afresh in our minds from time to time, to spur us on afresh and to fortify us to realize them and to keep them. God's Torah takes it for granted that our women have greater fervor and more faith and enthusiasm for their God-serving calling, and that this calling meets less danger in their case than in that of men from the temptations which occur in the cause of business and professional life.
>
> Acordingly, the Torah does not find it necessary to give women these repeated spurring reminders to remain true to their calling and warnings against weaknesses in their business lives. Thus, at the very origin of the Jewish people, God's foresight did not find it necessary to ensure their bond with Him by giving women some permanent symbol on their body comparable to circumcision for men.[16]

Woman has *binah yeteirah*, additional wisdom,[17] more refined sensitivity and compassion,[18] greater piety and holiness,[19] an inclination to perform *hesed*–acts of loving-kindness for others[20]–and a natural desire to perform God's will and fulfill His *mitzvot*.[21] These exempt her from masculine obligations that men perform in order to attain a level of spirituality that women by their nature already enjoy.

WOMAN'S OPTION TO PERFORM THE EXEMPTED *MITZVOT*

Most authorities maintain that if the woman chooses to fulfill most commandments from which she has been released she is free to do so. If she exercises her option and performs such precepts, they are perceived as meritorious deeds and not as meaningless acts.[22]

However, there is a rabbinic principle, *Gadol hametzuvah veoseh yoter mimi she'eino metzuvah ve'oseh*, "Greater is it when the act is performed by one who is commanded to perform it than when the act is performed by one who is not commanded to perform it,"[23] meaning that the value of performing a *mitzvah*–i.e., "divine command"–lies in discharging a divine command.[24]

Based on this principle, if a woman fulfills an optional *mitzvah*, it is probably considered a meritorious personal *minhag* (custom) or *neder* (religious vow) rather than a precept directly commanded by God. Therefore, the woman's reward for performing the *mitzvah* is reduced because the significance of the performance of the precept is reduced.

In the words of Maimonides:

> Those who perform a precept which they were not commanded to execute [are rewarded, but] are not rewarded to the same degree as those who are commanded to perform the precept, but to a lesser degree.[25]

Authorities are divided over whether one who observes an optional *mitzvah* may recite the benediction that usually accompanies the performance of that precept.[26] *Rama* and others maintain that a woman may recite the blessing when performing optional *mitzvot*,[27] and this is the custom among Ashkenazic Jews.[28]

In practice, women have accepted most of the time-dependent *mitzvot* as if they were obligatory, and Judaism has sanctioned this acceptance. These include the reading of the *Shema*,[29] the counting of the *omer*,[30] the hearing of the sounds of the *shofar* on Rosh HaShanah,[31] taking the Four Species on Sukkot,[32] and eating in the *sukkah*.[33] Women may perform all the time-dependent Positive Precepts except for *tallit* and *tefillin*.

DOING EXEMPTED PRECEPTS THAT ARE NOT OPTIONAL ONES

When considering performing a *mitzvah* that one was not commanded and *that has not been sanctioned as an optional one by Halachah*, one must consider the following Jewish principle: a person's task is to fulfill God's will and to live one's life in accordance with God's will; there is no principle that takes precedence over this. Consequently, performing a *mitzvah* that one is not commanded to perform and that has not been sanctioned as an elective *mitzvah* is, by definition, not meritorious and might possibly fall into the category of "sinful arrogance." (See Chapter 1.)

R. Samson Raphael Hirsch comments about Aaron's sons Nadab and

Avihu, who brought sacrifices that they were not commanded: "Perhaps they were so greatly taken with their own sense of self-worth as individuals that they felt sufficient unto themselves. . . . each followed his own impulse."[34]

Women who follow their own impulses in this regard rather than the directives of *Halachah* might consider whether, fundamentally, their primary motivation is to fulfill God's will or to pride themselves for performing a task given to men.

Similarly, when Saul was commanded to kill all the sheep and cattle of the Amalekites and did not do so but left some alive, Samuel angrily confronts him, asking, "Why did you not hearken to God's voice?" Saul responds that some sheep and cattle were taken from the spoils in order to bring sacrifices to God. Samuel answers: "Does God really want burnt offerings and sacrifices? What He desires is but to listen to the voice of God! Listening is preferable to the fat of rams."[35]

The Jewish idea is that people do not serve God in the optimum manner when they perform "*mitzvot*" that they are not commanded and that are not sanctioned as optional. This holds true no matter how elevated the motivation and no matter how satisfying the experiences to those who perform them. What God wants is to be obeyed. Everyone is required to follow God's will–to do what God wants of him or her.

THE OBLIGATION TO FULFILL ALL THE NEGATIVE PRECEPTS

Women are obligated to observe the Negative Commandments, both precepts ordained in the Torah, *mide'oraita*, and rabbinical precepts, *miderabanan*. The principle is enunciated in the Mishnah:

> All Negative Precepts, both those which are time-dependent, and those which are not time-dependent–men and women alike are obligated to observe them. . . .[36]

THREE PRECEPTS DEVOLVING UPON WOMEN

There are three commandments that, though they may be discharged by men, have primarily devolved on women, are *mitzvot* in which women take precedence over men.

They are: *Hadlakat Ner Shabbat*, the kindling of the Sabbath and festival lights; *Hallah*, the taking of the dough portion; and *Taharat HaMishpahah*, the Family Purity laws. The Talmud associates all three with women,[37] and it is taught that these three create a unique bond between woman and God.

13

The Sabbath and the Festivals

A – The Sabbath

The Sabbath, the Jewish island of time, is a refuge of tranquillity and serenity from the pressures and vicissitudes of everyday life to which Jews retire every seven days to be with their families. It is a precious possession of the Jewish nation and has helped maintain and preserve the Jews as a people for more than three thousand years. Men and women alike are required to observe the Sabbath.

KINDLING THE SABBATH LIGHTS

The distinctive manner in which the Sabbath is observed in the Jewish home is underscored at the very beginning of the holy day, late Friday afternoon when the Sabbath is inaugurated by the kindling of the Sabbath lights by the woman. If there is one *mitzvah* that Jews associate with their tradition more than any other, quite likely it is the woman's candlelighting before the onset of the Sabbath.

First, the woman customarily drops some coins in the charity box.[1] Then, in a simple, moving ceremony, the Jewish wife and mother, dressed in Sabbath finery, stands by the festive Sabbath dinner table with her children around her, kindles the lights at the table, and covers her eyes as she recites the blessing and silently prays for the welfare of her household and for scholarly children.[2] Then she opens her eyes and says "Good Shabbos" or "*Shabbat Shalom*" ("Peaceful Sabbath"). With this act she has ushered the Sabbath into her home.

Lighting the candles before sunset is an important *mitzvah*. The Talmud states that those who assiduously observe the precept of kindling the Sabbath lights will be blessed with scholarly children.[3] *Rashi* explains:

> As it is written, "For the *mitzvah* is a lamp, and the Torah is light."[4] The performance of the *mitzvah* of candlelighting for the Sabbath and Hanukkah causes the light of Torah to shine.[5]

Maimonides teaches:

> The kindling of the Sabbath lights is not optional . . . but obligatory, and both men and women require Sabbath candles in the home . . . for having Sabbath candles burning on the Sabbath is part of the joy of the Sabbath. . . . The kindling of the Sabbath lights should be done while it is still day, before the sun sets. The *mitzvah* falls primarily upon women because they are usually at home at the time.[6]

PRECEDENCE ACCORDED THE WOMAN IN KINDLING THE LIGHTS

A woman takes precedence in kindling the Sabbath lights.[7] Even if a man is present, the woman is accorded the honor of bringing the Sabbath into the Jewish home by carrying out this *mitzvah*, and the man must not kindle the Sabbath lights.[8] This is because the woman is usually in the home more than the man,[9] and it is she who is primarily responsible for *shalom bayit*, bringing peace, serenity, and joy into the Jewish home, a spirit that is symbolized by the Sabbath.

If the woman is not at home or is prevented from lighting or is delayed, the husband or any other member of the family may perform this task. Otherwise, the woman's husband is customarily expected to help her by preparing the candles[10] and by inserting them into the sockets.[11]

The woman lights at least two candles,[12] each representing a different biblical phrasing of the commandment to keep the Sabbath in the Torah, one, *zachor*, to "remember the Sabbath day," and the second, *shamor*, to "observe the Sabbath,"[13] the two candles together representing *shalom bayit*, the peaceful Jewish home.

While two candles are the minimum, traditionally most women kindle more than the minimum, with differing customs calling for 7, 10, and even 36 Sabbath candles.[14] The most widespread custom appears to be for the woman to light as many Sabbath candles as there are members of the household. When away from her home, however, a woman kindles 2 candles.[15]

Generally, the Sabbath candles are kindled about twenty to forty minutes before sunset, although there are slight differences in candlelighting times in different areas.[16] One can bring the Sabbath in earlier by kindling the Sabbath lights earlier; indeed, it is considered praiseworthy to do so.[17]

Once the sun sets, however, it is absolutely prohibited to light the candles.[18] Even if it is dark and there is no other light, it is preferable to sit in the dark rather than to kindle the Sabbath lights late.[19] Lighting candles after the onset of the Sabbath is a serious transgression, and is considered a profanation and mockery of the Sabbath, and should never be done. Men and women alike are obligated to observe all the laws of the Sabbath.

HALLAH

Whenever bread is baked, a portion of the dough, called *hallah*, is burned and set aside, and a blessing is recited. The purpose of taking *hallah* is to remind Jews of the custom in the time of the Temple in Jerusalem of giving a portion of dough to the *kohen* (priest).[20] *Hallah* is one of the twenty-four privileges granted to the priests who were not granted portions of land, in order that they might be able to subsist.[21] There is a separate mishnaic tractate named *Hallah*, which has *Gemara*, talmudic elaboration, in the Jerusalem Talmud.

The name *hallah* is the same as that of the braided loaves of bread that are baked for the Sabbath. The reason for the Sabbath bread being called *hallah* is to provide a constant reminder to separate the *hallah* portion from the dough and to burn it prior to the baking of the Sabbath bread.

Similarly, the custom of the baking of Sabbath *hallot* in the home before Shabbat is so that the ancient rite of sharing with the *kohen* will be remembered through the separation of the *hallah* from the dough before it is placed in the oven.

Like the kindling of the Sabbath lights, the reason for the woman's primary involvement in this *mitzvah* is because she is more likely to be in the home at the time it becomes necessary to separate the *hallah*.

Dr. Tamar Frankiel sees the *mitzvah* of the separation of *hallah* as relating to the psychological and spiritual dimension of food for women and its symbolic significance as a form of feminine expression, and the braided loaf of Sabbath and festival *hallah* bread as a specifically Jewish feminine symbol.[22] She finds braiding to be an archetypal feminine image related to weaving, which symbolically represents the act of containing energy and turning it into a specific form. By making the elaborate chains in the springy dough for the braided *hallah* loaf, Frankiel finds, women establish the channels through which energy will run. The sense of energy that a woman has when she weaves and shapes the dough into graceful and powerful forms represents a significant feminine symbolism—the woman helping to shape and create bread, the staff of life, the vital energy that gives life.[23]

Thus, the act of separating a small *hallah* portion from the dough reminiscent of the portion given to the *kohen* in the Temple, in the words of Tamar Frankiel,

> puts all our nurturing, giving, bonding activities around food in a different perspective . . . [because] we are giving a special kind of *tzedakah*, or charity, from the heart of life. We give it, symbolically now, to nourish the work of the Temple because the Temple . . . represents the womb of our spiritual life . . . which we now give back to the source of life. . . . We [thus] dedicate our bread to the holy work of nourishing our souls as well as our bodies. The rest of the bread will be taken to our table, the extension of the Temple altar and the echo of Sarah's tent, to become the center of holy nourishment in our own families and communities.
>
> By extension, the *mitzvah* of *hallah* refers to the entire area of food: that food should be dedicated to a holy purpose and be prepared in the special way described in the laws of *kashrut*. Further, it reminds us to be mindful of God and of God's purpose for us as women when preparing or eating food. . . . Other forms of *tzedakah* we give as a general sacrifice, reminding ourselves that all comes from God; but in taking the piece of *hallah*, giving it to the fire, to the work of holiness, we are giving a piece of our uniquely feminine life energy, of our womanhood.[24]

KIDDUSH

A woman is required to recite or partake from the *Kiddush*, the Sabbath sanctification ceremony performed over a cup of wine that inaugurates the Sabbath eve and Sabbath day feasts. The Talmud teaches:

> R. Ada bar Ahavah said: Women are required to participate in *Kiddush* on the Sabbath by virtue of the Torah. Why is this so? Is it not a time-dependent Positive Commandment from which women are excused from performing?
>
> . . . Rava explained: Scripture says: *Zachor* and *Shamor*—"Remember the Sabbath day"[25] and "Keep the Sabbath day."[26] "Whoever is enjoined to keep [and not desecrate] the Sabbath is also enjoined to remember it [by participating in its joyous rituals]."[27]

The *Shulhan Aruch*, the Code of Jewish Law, states that women may recite the *Kiddush* on behalf of men, "since the Torah obligates women as it does men."[28]

THE THREE SABBATH MEALS

Similarly, women and men are equally obligated to partake of all the three festive Sabbath meals,[29] as they are to break bread over twin loaves of Sabbath bread at each of the three meals,[30] reminiscent of the double portion of *mannah* that scripture describes as having been provided to the Israelites in the desert for the Sabbath.[31]

HAVDALAH–SEPARATING THE HOLY FROM THE PROFANE

Maimonides teaches:

> One is required to "remember" the Sabbath both at its inauguration and conclusion. At its inauguration with the *Kiddush*, and at its conclusion with the *Havdalah*.[32]

Havdalah, or "separation," is the brief ceremony that formally concludes the Sabbath on Saturday night. It marks the division between the "holy and the profane"–in the words of the *Havdalah* service–between Sabbath bliss and the weekly cycle of creativity.

The *Havdalah* ritual is filled with symbolism. Three principal elements are involved, and a blessing is recited over each. The Talmud teaches:

> Upon entering the home upon the conclusion of the Sabbath, one recites a blessing over the wine, over the light, and over spices.[33]

A cup of wine is filled to overflowing to symbolize the hope that the new week will provide the blessing of abundance in the home[34] and will be brimful of joyous living. Another item for the ceremony is a *Havdalah* candle, a braided taper kept lit throughout the service to signify the pleasure derived from the renewed permission to kindle fire–something forbidden during the preceding twenty-five hours. Lighting this candle also commemorates God's gift of fire at the conclusion of Creation week,[35] as well as the assumption by humans of mastery over nature when, according to the Midrash, God gave Adam two stones to rub together to produce fire.[36]

The third element in the *Havdalah* ceremony is aromatic spices. Since the Sabbath, with its special food, its joy, and its rest and quiet provide the individual with a renewed spiritual strength (*neshamah yeteirah*) that is a source of invigoration and consecration, the pleasure of smelling aromatic spices was considered something of a compensation for the natural letdown at its end.[37]

The *Shulhan Aruch* rules that "women are obligated to participate in *Havdalah* just as they are obligated to participate in *Kiddush*," but adds that "some disagree."[38] The reason some authorities disagree over whether *Havdalah* may be optional is that they question whether Maimonides' and R. Joseph Caro's analogy between *Kiddush* and *Havdalah* is sound–i.e., that *Havdalah* is, like *Kiddush*, of Torah origin, and since men and women alike are duty-bound to observe all the laws of the Sabbath, they are equally obligated to recite *Havdalah*–and they maintain that *Havdalah* is not included in the scriptural Sabbath laws and is therefore not obligatory upon women.[39]

Consequently, *Rama* comments, "Therefore, women should not recite *Havdalah* on their own, but should listen to *Havdalah* recited by men [who are definitely obligated]."[40] *Rama* adds that women should, nevertheless, recite the brief *Havdalah* blessing on Saturday nights, *Baruch HaMavdil Bein Kodesh Lehol*, "Blessed be He who separates the holy and the profane."[41]

However, later authorities maintain that women are free to recite the entire *Havdalah* service if they wish to do so.[42] The *Mishnah Berurah* declares:

> The *Ba"h* writes, that even according to those authorities who maintain that women are exempt from *Havdalah*, women may nevertheless take upon themselves the obligation to recite *Havdalah* [in full] as is the situation with *shofar* and *lulav*, where, although women are exempt from fulfilling these *mitzvot*, nevertheless recite the blessing when they perform them. . . . And the *Magen Avraham* concludes that the *Halachah* is according to the *Ba"h*.[43]

It is customary among many Jews to partake in a festive *Melaveh Malkah*–"Escorting the [Sabbath] Queen"–light repast following *Havdalah*.[44]

B–The Festivals

THE OBLIGATION OF MEN AND WOMEN TO KEEP THE FESTIVALS

Men and Women alike are required to observe and celebrate the festivals. Some laws, however, relate specifically to women. The kindling of the lights before the onset of the festival devolves, as does lighting the Sabbath lights, primarily upon women. Women's obligations to reciting *Kiddush* and *Havdalah* for the festivals are similar to the laws for the Sabbath.

While women are exempt from the fulfillment of scriptural time-dependent commandments, there are three rabbinic time-dependent precepts that women are specifically required to observe: kindling the Hanukkah lights;[45] listening to the reading of the *Megillah* (the Book of Esther) on Purim;[46] and drinking the four cups of wine at the Passover Seder.[47]

These three festivals, Hanukkah, Purim, and Passover, commemorate the three most important redemptions of the Jewish people, and in all three, women were instrumental in bringing about that salvation. The French medieval commentators *Rashi* and R. Samuel ben Meir, known as the *Rashbam*, make this point:[48]

> [Regarding the obligation of women to drink the four cups of wine at the Passover *seder*] it is stated in [the talmudic tractate)]*Sotah*, "In the merit of righteous women were we redeemed."[49] Indeed, it is the same regarding listening to the *Megillah* reading on Purim, for it was because of Esther [that the redemption came about]. And similarly this is the situation regarding Hanukkah as we see in [the talmudic tractate] *Shabbat*.[50]

THE MAN'S *MITZVAH* TO PLEASE HIS WIFE AT THE FESTIVALS

A Jew is required to rejoice during the Pilgrimage Festivals, in fulfillment of the scriptural passage, "And you shall rejoice on your festival."[51] However, it is the husband who is commanded to *cause* his wife to rejoice, in accordance with the talmudic teaching: *Ishah baalah mesamhah*, "A husband must make his wife rejoice."[52]

Rashi explains: "The obligation does not devolve upon her, but upon her husband, who is required to *cause* her to rejoice. Therefore [for these purposes] read not the scriptural passage as '*vesamahta*' [*b'hagecha*], 'and you shall rejoice [in your festival],'[53] but [as if it were written] '*vesimahta*,' 'and you shall *cause her* to rejoice.' "[54]

How should a man make his wife rejoice? By buying her beautiful clothing for the festivals. The Talmud teaches:

> R. Joseph learned: In Babylonia [a man must make his wife rejoice] by purchasing colorful garments for her. In *Eretz Yisrael* he does so by buying her smart linen outfits [for the festivals].[55]

The *Shulhan Aruch* codifies this as law: "Men must buy for their wives clothing and jewelry [for the festivals] in accordance with their means."[56] At the very least, men should buy their wives shoes for the festival.[57]

LISTENING TO THE *SHOFAR*

The *shofar*–usually a ram's horn, but the horn of any kosher animal except a bull is acceptable–is one of the central ceremonial objects in the Jewish tradition. It is sounded to commence the ten-day period of reflection and atonement beginning with Rosh HaShanah, the Jewish New Year. It is also sounded daily during the month preceding Rosh HaShanah and again to mark the end of the ten-day period, Yom Kippur, the Day of Atonement.

In Jewish tradition, the *shofar* was the instrument that, according to scripture, was sounded at Mount Sinai at the giving of the Torah.[58] There is reason to believe that in ancient times the main Rosh HaShanah rituals were the special Temple sacrifices and listening to the sound of the *shofar*. One can readily understand, therefore, why in the time of Philo of Alexandria (20 B.C.E.–40 C.E.) Rosh HaShanah was known as "the *Shofar* Festival." To this day, the key observance of Rosh HaShanah is listening to the sounding of the *shofar*.

Women are excused from listening to the sound of the *shofar* on Rosh HaShanah, as it is one of the time-dependent Positive Commandments[59] from which women are exempted.[60] It is an optional *mitzvah* for women, which a woman may observe[61] either by listening to the *shofar* or by sounding it herself.[62] Although sounding a *shofar* when one is not commanded to do so might ordinarily be considered playing a musical instrument on the festival, which is forbidden, this is not the situation when a woman sounds the *shofar* on Rosh HaShanah. In fact, when she does so, even though it is for her an optional *mitzvah*, she may recite the appropriate blessing.[63]

A woman may not sound the *shofar* for others, however, on the principle that only one who is obligated to perform a precept may perform it for others.[64] Most observant women today have accepted upon themselves the obligation of the *mitzvah* of *shofar*. When a woman has accepted the obligation of fulfilling the *mitzvah* of listening to the *shofar* for several years, she is obligated to continue to do so. If a woman who customarily fulfills the *mitzvah* is prevented by circumstances beyond her control from coming to the synagogue on Rosh HaShanah, the custom is that efforts are made for the *baal tokeya*, the one who sounds the *shofar* in the synagogue, to come to her home to sound the *shofar* for her.[65]

FASTING ON YOM KIPPUR

Yom Kippur, the Day of Atonement, is, after the Sabbath, the most important day in the Jewish year. Like those of the Sabbath, the regulations governing Yom Kippur are equally incumbent upon men and women. Therefore, women are required to fast and afflict themselves in various ways on Yom Kippur and to refrain from doing any work.[66]

It is an obligation to eat before the holy day in order to more easily fast on Yom Kippur. The Talmud declares that "all who eat on the ninth of the month are considered as if they had fasted on the ninth and tenth."[67] Therefore, men and women are equally obligated to fulfil the *mitzvah* of eating during the late afternoon feast just prior to the onset of Yom Kippur.[68]

A pregnant woman fasts on Yom Kippur[69] unless she says she must eat, in which event she eats in small amounts, until she is satisfied that she needs no more.[70] A woman in childbirth, from the time of the start of her labor pains until three full days following the birth of a child, must not fast at all and is required to eat normally.[71] During this period, if a physician says she should eat, even should the woman be silent or state that she does not require it, she must eat normally.[72] If she and the physician agree that she need not eat, the *Halachah* is that she must in any case be given food, but in small quantities.[73] A pregnant woman who has lost children in childbirth in the past and is considered by her physician to be in danger of losing her fetus if she does not eat must not fast; indeed it is considered a *mitzvah* for her to eat under these circumstances.[74]

Upon the completion of seventy-two hours following childbirth and until one week following the event, if she wishes to eat and her physician does not object–or, if she doesn't want to eat, but her physician says that she should eat–she eats normally.[75] Should she desire to eat but her physician or her friends say it is not necessary, she eats nevertheless, but in small quantities until she is satisfied.[76] Thereafter, if she desires to eat on Yom Kippur, she is considered as if she were someone who is ill and who may be fed on Yom Kippur under certain conditions.[77]

DWELLING IN THE *SUKKAH*, AND THE FOUR SPECIES

Four days after Yom Kippur, Sukkot begins. It is an eight-day autumn festival of thanksgiving, during which Jews dwell in outdoor booths roofed with branches as a poignant reminder of human frailty, to manifest confidence in divine providence, and to appreciate God's bounty.

Every morning except for the Sabbath, God is worshipped with "the Four Species," the *lulav* (palm), *etrog* (citron), *hadas* (myrtle), and *aravah* (willow).

Women, being exempted from the time-dependent *mitzvot*, are excused from fulfilling both the *mitzvah* of dwelling and eating in a *sukkah*,[78] and taking the Four Species.[79] These are considered optional *mitzvot*, however, and many women choose to fulfill both precepts.[80]

Women, like men, must not work during *Hol HaMoed*, the intermediate days of Sukkot and Passover.[81]

HAKAFOT: REJOICING WITH THE TORAH ON SIMHAT TORAH

Simhat Torah, which comes at the end of Sukkot, concludes the fall group of Jewish festivals and marks the completion of the annual cycle of the reading of the Torah in the synagogue and the commencement of the new cycle. It is celebrated by rejoicing and thanking God for the Torah. All the Torah scrolls with their splendid adornments are removed from the Torah ark and marched in a circular procession around the synagogue–*hakafot*–and there is joyous dancing with the Torah scrolls.

Dancing with Torah scrolls is an activity that has traditionally been done by men. Under the influence of the women's movement there has in recent years been an effort in some traditional synagogues on the part of some women to conduct *hakafot* with the Torah scrolls on Simhat Torah. While a woman, like a man, is permitted to touch and hold the Torah scroll at all times,[82] the practice of women's *hakafot* has been opposed by all contemporary halachic authorities.[83]

Rabbinic opposition to women's *hakafot* is apparently based not on *Halachah*, but simply because the practice is viewed as an innovation in traditional practice that is advocated by a movement they see as undermining Judaism. Many traditional rabbinic leaders view feminism as linked to antifamilism and the destruction of the Jewish family in America in the last decades, and therefore a movement antagonistic to Jewish continuity–an implacable foe to be firmly resisted. Consequently, these authorities oppose all innovations in traditional Jewish practice that are influenced by feminism.

The situation has been compared to the introduction by early nineteenth-century European Reform rabbis of the custom of conducting weddings in the synagogue. Though an obvious emulation of Christian church weddings, the innovation could not be opposed on the basis of *Halachah*; indeed, what could be more in harmony with the Jewish idea of marriage as *kiddushin*, sanctification, than sanctifying the ceremony of holy matrimony in the synagogue?

However, led by R. Moses Sofer of Frankfurt and Pressburg, known as the *Hatam Sofer* (1762–1839), the practice was universally condemned and opposed by the *Gedolim*, the leading rabbinic authorities of the day. They saw this innovation as a conspicuous emulation by the Reform movement of Christian practice. Their opposition was not based on a determination that the practice contravened *Halachah*, but because Reform was seen by the rabbinic authorities as a clear threat to Jewish viability and continuity–a movement they viewed as undermining Judaism and leading Jews to assimilation and apostasy. Consequently, they deemed it necessary to firmly oppose every proposed innovation of Reform in traditional Jewish practice as a threat to Jewish viability.

The subsequent apostasy of vast numbers of early nineteenth-century German Reform Jews and their descendants and the rapid assimilation into the majority culture of subsequent generations of Reform Jews in the United States and their losses to the Jewish people became, for the traditionalists, an abject lesson. To succeeding generations of rabbinic authorities it demonstrated that the decision of the *Hatam Sofer* was a farsighted one.

THE HANUKKAH LAMP

Hanukkah, the Feast of Lights, whose primary observance is the kindling of the Hanukkah lamp, is an eight-day midwinter celebration in remembrance of Israel's liberation from the Syrio-Greeks by Judah the Maccabee in 165 B.C.E.. The defilement of the Temple by King Antiochus, his introduction of pagan priests and paraphernalia, and the brutally enforced decrees that commanded the Jews to forsake their religion sparked the rebellion led by Mattathias and his sons, the Maccabees.

After the Syrio-Greek priests had been driven out, the Temple had to be cleansed and reconsecrated by the lighting of the *menorah*, the Temple candelabrum. But only one vessel of the pure olive oil—enough for one day—was found, and eight days were required to prepare additional ritually pure sacramental oil. Miraculously, the single day's supply of oil burned for a full eight days. This event is commemorated by the lighting of the eight-branched Hanukkah lamp.

KINDLING THE HANUKKAH LIGHTS

Men and women are both required to light the Hanukkah lamp. The Talmud declares:

> A woman certainly kindles the Hanukkah lamp, as R. Joshua ben Levi says: Women are obligated to kindle the Hanukkah lamp because they, too, were involved in the miracle.[84]

The reference is to Judith of Bethulia who lived in Second Temple times and who became a heroine of Israel when she killed the military commander Holofornes, who laid siege to Bethulia, whereupon Holofornes' army panicked and fled.

Therefore, although it is customary for the man to light the Hanukkah lamp on behalf of the entire household and the *mitzvah* is a (rabbinic) time-dependent precept,[85] a woman may perform this *mitzvah* as well.[86] When a woman kindles the Hanukkah lamp she may do so with a blessing and light not only for herself but also on behalf of the members of her household and others.[87]

When she is unmarried or widowed or is otherwise not living with a husband who would light on her behalf, the woman is duty-bound to perform the *mitzvah* of lighting the *hanukkiyah* and to recite the blessing.[88] Her daughters should also light their own Hanukkah lamps.[89]

When the woman or the members of her household light the Hanukkah lamp on the eve of the Sabbath, the procedure should be completed late Friday afternoon before the Sabbath lights are kindled,[90] since by kindling the Sabbath lights the woman has ushered the Sabbath into her home and she must not light a fire thereafter.

Women are forbidden to perform any work in the home during the period that the Hanukkah lamp is lit.[91] This is in remembrance of Judith's heroic act and is a means of underscoring the centrality of the role played by women in the story of Hanukkah.

THE PURIM FESTIVAL

As winter draws to a close, Jews celebrate the jolliest and most cheerful day of the Jewish calendar, the Purim festival, during the early spring month of Adar. It commemorates a momentous event in Jewish history that took place in Susa (Shushan), capital of Achaemenian Persia, in the fifth century B.C.E. The story is told in the *Megillah*, the "Scroll" of the biblical Book of Esther. The *Megillah* relates how a plot by Haman, vizier of King Ahasueros, is undone by Esther, Ahasueros' queen, who was a concealed Jewess. She is aided by her uncle Mordecai. Revealing her identity as a Jewess and exposing Haman's scheme, Esther appeals to the king. Ahasueros grants the Jews the right to defend themselves and, instead of the predicted day of sorrow, that was, by lot (*pur*), to have fallen on the thirteenth of Adar, there is a day of rejoicing.

The Purim story embodies many of the trials and vicissitudes that the Jewish people have experienced in far-flung lands throughout the ages, in which entire communities subjected to heinous persecutions and threats of total annihilation were saved. It is easy to see why Purim became such a joyous and popular festival, for the story told in the *Megillah* provides a reminder of God's providence and the promise of deliverance from impending doom. With its dominant theme being one of faith, gratitude, and dependence on God, Purim is celebrated with the reading of the *Megillah* in the synagogue, the giving of gifts of food to friends, and the distribution of food packages and charity to the poor.

READING THE *MEGILLAH*, THE SCROLL OF ESTHER

Men and women are required to hear the reading of the *Megillah*.[92] The Talmud in the tractate *Megillah* teaches:

> *R. Joshua ben Levi said: Women are obligated with the mitzvah* of reading the *Megillah*, for they too were involved in the miracle [of Purim].[93]

It is Esther, after whom the *Megillah* is named, who was the key figure in the salvation of the Jewish people and who made the Purim festival possible.[94] Thus, although the *Megillah* reading is a (rabbinic) time-dependent precept, it is inconceivable that women should be excused from listening to the reading of the Book of Esther, which relates the story of Esther's rescue of the Jewish people.[95]

Commenting on the *Halachah* requiring women to hear the reading of the *Megillah*, the *Mishnah Berurah* advises men to read it to their wives and daughters–including, for purposes of education, even younger daughters–at home, since he doubts that women could properly hear the *Megillah* reading in some of the women's galleries extant in Eastern Europe in his day.[96]

One fulfills the obligation either by reading from the *Megillah* or by listening to it being read by another. Therefore, a woman may read the *Megillah* herself from a valid, handwritten parchment *Megillah*. The Talmud teaches:

> All are eligible to read from the *Megillah*. Whom is the word "all" designed to include? It is intended to include women, in accordance with R. Joshua ben Levi, who said: "Women are obligated with the *mitzvah* of reading the *Megillah*."[97]

There is some difference of opinion by the halachic codifiers whether a woman may also discharge this obligation for others,[98] although if a man cannot read the *Megillah* a woman can discharge the obligation for him.[99] However, it is clear that a woman may not read the *Megillah* publicly in the synagogue, on the basis of the same ruling that forbids women from reading the Torah in the synagogue.[100]

It is best for the *Megillah* to be read before at least ten people, and women may be included in the count of ten.[101] Indeed, all ten–or more–who congregate for the reading may be women,[102] and the reading is subject to all the rules of the *Megillah* reading, including the recitation of the blessings.[103]

PURIM GIFTS TO FRIENDS AND TO THE POOR

The Book of Esther relates that Purim is celebrated by "feasting and joy, and the sending of gifts, each to his friend, and gifts to the poor."[104] The *Shulhan Aruch* codifies these obligations into Jewish law, making it obligatory to send two gifts of food to each of at least two friends, adding "whosoever augments this by multiplying the number of people to whom he sends gifts is to be praised."[105] Indeed, the custom is to send gift parcels of food to many people, as it is to give charity to many on Purim.

Men and women are equally obligated to give gifts to friends and to the poor.[106] However, since gifts of friendship are considered indicative of a close relationship, it is customary for men to send gifts to males and women to female friends and for gifts not to be sent to acquaintances of the opposite sex unless they are affianced.

Women are obligated to participate in the Purim feast,[107] but there is a difference of rabbinic opinion whether women are obligated, as are men, to rejoice on Purim by drinking wine until they "do not know the difference between [the expletive] 'Cursed be Haman' and [the invocation] 'Blessed be Mordecai.' "[108]

PASSOVER: *HAMETZ* AND *MATZAH*

The Torah enjoins that Passover be celebrated to commemorate Israel's redemption from Egyptian bondage and the triumphant Exodus that took place in the middle of the second millenium B.C.E. There not having been sufficient time to bake bread as they were fleeing Egypt, the Jews hurriedly baked flat, unleavened bread – *matzah*.

In commemoration of the Exodus, therefore, Jews must not eat ordinary, leavened bread (*hametz*) during the entire festival and are required to eat *matzah*, at least during the first day of Passover (the eating of *matzah* is optional during the balance of the festival).

The Talmud teaches:

> R. Elazar said: Women are obligated by the Torah to eat *matzah*, as it is written, "You shall not eat leaven [*hametz*] with it [the Passover sacrifice]; for seven days you shall eat *matzah* with it."[109] Whoever is obligated by the command not to eat *hametz* is obligated as well in the eating of *matzah*. And since women are included in the prohibition against eating *hametz* they are included as well in the command to eat *matzah*.[110]

THE FOUR CUPS OF WINE

The *seder*, a joyous and elegant ritual feast, observed for two evenings outside Israel and one evening in Israel, inaugurates the eight-day Passover celebrations. It is highlighted by the drinking of four cups of wine by *seder* participants and the eating of symbolic foods such as *maror*, bitter herbs, that serve as mnemonic reminders of Egyptian bondage and the redemption from slavery.

The focal point of the Passover *seder* is the reading of the *Haggadah*. The *Haggadah* is a *seder* handbook, written to fulfill the scriptural injunction to the Jews to relate the story of the Exodus and the accompanying miracles to their children. Read aloud during the festive feast with the participation of family and guests, it has become a storybook of unceasing popularity, containing scriptural and talmudic quotations, narratives, songs, prayers, and even riddles.

While the *seder* eve *mitzvot,* such as drinking the four cups of wine, eating the bitter herbs, and reciting the *Haggadah,* are time-dependent Positive Commandments that women would ordinarily be excused from fulfilling, women are obligated to fully discharge them all.[111] Women, like men, are commanded not to eat *hametz,* and must search the home for *hametz.* They are also obligated to eat *matzah* and bitter herbs at the *seder,* to read–or listen to–the *Haggadah* in a language they understand, and to participate in the *seder*[112] because of the central role women played in the redemption from Egypt.[113] The Talmud relates:[114]

> R. Avira explained: It is in the merit of the righteous Jewish women of that generation that Israel was redeemed from Egypt. At the time that they would go to draw water, the Holy One would arrange for there to be small fish in their pails–they would draw half a pail of water and half a pail of fish.
>
> They would then take two pails to their husbands in the fields, one with warm water and the other with fish. They would wash and feed them, and when their husbands would desire them they would go between the banks of the fields together, as it is written, "When you lie between the banks. . . ."[115] . . . And the women would conceive, and when the time came to give birth they would go to the field and give birth under the apple tree, as it is written, "I woke you under the apple tree."[116]

In a similar vein *Rashi* cites a Midrash regarding the copper basin in the Tabernacle, made "from the mirrors of women who had gathered at the entrance of the Tent of Appointed Times":[117]

> The daughters of Israel had mirrors into which they would look when adorning themselves [which they wished to present to the Tabernacle]. But Moses was repelled by them, because they were employed as a medium to incite sexual desire.
>
> Whereupon the Holy One rebuked Moses, saying: Accept them [for the Tabernacle], for these mirrors are more cherished by me than any other offering! Through these mirrors the women created great hosts of Jews in Egypt.
>
> For when their husbands would return home in the evening bone-weary with exhaustion from their day-long crushing labors in servitude, each would bring her husband food and drink, and then take out the mirror and hold it so that both their images are reflected in it, would say provocatively, "Are I not more beautiful than you?" They would in this way incite desire in their husbands, and would conceive and bear children. . . . And the laver [for the holy Tabernacle] was therefore made from these copper mirrors for the laver was designed as a means of establishing peace between a man and his wife.[118]

It was in the merit of the Jewish women and their indomitable spirit, the Sages teach, that the Jewish people were redeemed from Egypt.

COUNTING THE *OMER*

The Torah declares: "And you shall count for yourselves from the day after that Sabbath, from the day of your bringing the wave offering of the *Omer*; it shall be seven complete Sabbaths."[119]

The counting of the *Omer* during the seven weeks between the second evening of Passover and Shavuot is a duty incumbent on Jewish men, but one from which women are excused, as it is a time-dependent Positive Commandment, Maimonides maintains.[120] Nahmanides, however, disagrees, maintaining that it is a precept that is not time-dependent and is thus equally obligatory on women.[121] The *Shulhan Aruch* merely states that "it is a *mitzvah* for everyone" to count the *Omer*.[122]

The operative *Halachah* is that counting the *Omer* is not obligatory for women but is considered an elective *mitzvah* they can choose to observe.

C–The Fast Days

Men and women alike are obligated to abstain from eating on the fasts of the Ninth of Av (Tish'ah B'av), the seventeenth of Tamuz, the Third of Tishre (Tzom Gedaliah), the tenth of Tevet, and the thirteenth of Adar (the Fast of Esther).[123] Additionally, on Tishah B'Av, men and women are also required to refrain from drinking, washing, wearing leather shoes, immersing in a *mikveh*, and sexual relations.[124]

Pregnant and nursing women may be exempted if they find fasting difficult.[125] New mothers during the first thirty days after childbirth are excused from fasting, whether they are in pain or not,[126] and even if they do not indicate that they are hungry.[127] New mothers are *forbidden* to fast on these days during the first week after childbirth.[128]

D–Rosh Hodesh, the Women's Festival

Rosh Hodesh, the festival marking the start of each month, is a holiday more applicable to women than to men. In the past, it was customarily observed as a one- or two-day festival each month by the abstention from work.[129] However, while men's abstention from work is not considered obligatory,[130] the custom of women abstaining from work on Rosh Hodesh has been given halachic sanction.

The Code of Jewish Law rules that it is permissible to work on Rosh Hodesh, but lauds those Jewish women who customarily refrain from work on Rosh Hodesh, terming it "a good custom."[131]

Halichot Betah, the compendium of laws regarding women, declares:

> The custom of women who refrain from working on Rosh Hodesh is a good one, because Rosh Hodesh was given to women as a festival, and it must not be nullified, for it was established as a law from the time of our teacher Moses. However, men may work on Rosh Hodesh.[132] Even if men are accustomed not to work on Rosh Hodesh, this is not considered a valid Jewish custom but is a mistaken one.[133]
>
> This custom of women refraining from work on Rosh Hodesh is one that is obligatory on every woman and daughter of Israel in every generation, based upon the law of "Do not forsake the Torah of your mother," for women are commanded to observe it by their mothers and foremothers from the earliest generations.
>
> Therefore, it is forbidden for women to make this day like an ordinary, profane day and to perform on it their usual labors, but, at the very least, to separate themselves from some of their routine labors, so that there be a real difference between this day and the other days of the year.[134]

The *Pri Hadash* comments:

> For men, Rosh Hodesh is like any other day of the week. Indeed, for them to refrain from work on Rosh Hodesh is a custom based on ignorance. Men should abandon this custom without requiring any special vow dispensation.
>
> In this area, women are superior to men. Their custom not to work on Rosh Hodesh is praiseworthy and should, therefore, not be dropped.[135]

It is the custom in many Jewish households for women who are not employed outside the home to observe Rosh Hodesh as a holiday from work in the home. Young girls should also be taught about the rules of women abstaining from work on Rosh Hodesh so that they can properly observe them when they mature.[136]

Women are, however, exempted from the obligation to bless the New Moon on its appearance, as it is a time-dependent Positive Precept.[137]

Rosh Hodesh is a day on which it is forbidden for women to fast.[138] The law codes rule that it is a *mitzvah* for women to feast on Rosh Hodesh.[139]

A FESTIVAL PRESENTED AS A REWARD

The reason for Rosh Hodesh being a "woman's festival," one that is more marked by women's observance than by men's, is that it was given to women as a reward for their not having participated in the sin of the golden calf, unlike the men, who were involved in this major transgression.

The Midrash explains:

> The women were unwilling[140] to give their golden earrings to their husbands [to be melted down in order to create the golden calf]. They said to them: "You desire to make a graven image and a molten image without any power in it to deliver."
>
> The Holy One Blessed be He gave the women their reward in this world and in the world to come. What reward did He give them in this world? That they should observe the New Moons more stringently than the men. And what reward did He give them in the world to come? The women are destined to be renewed like the New Moons.[141]

R. David HaLevi (1586–1667), the Polish author of the *Turei Zahav* (*Taz*) commentary on the Code of Jewish Law, comments:

> The Holy One Blessed be He gave the woman as their reward for not having contributed to the sin of the golden calf the observance of Rosh Hodesh. . . . The three pilgrimage festivals of the Jewish year were instituted by virtue of the three Patriarchs [Passover by virtue of Abraham, Shavuot by virtue of Isaac, Sukkot by virtue of Jacob][142] and the twelve Rosh Hodesh festivals of the Jewish year were originally instituted by virtue of the twelve tribes.
>
> However, when they sinned with the golden calf the festival was taken from the men and given over to their wives, to commemorate the fact that the women did not participate in that sin.[143]

While the women refused to help make the golden calf by contributing their jewelry, when it came to contributing toward the construction of the Sanctuary, the Torah emphasizes the prominent role played by the women:

> And the men came after the women, every beneficent heart . . . brought every golden jewel . . . and every woman of wise heart spun with her hands. . . . And all the women whose hearts prompted them in wisdom spun the goats' hair. . . . Every man and woman whose hearts moved them to bring work in accordance with God's command. . . .[144]

Nahmanides, in his commentary on the Torah, interprets the words "after the women" to indicate that the women demonstrated greater enthusiasm in contributing quickly and wholeheartedly to the Sanctuary.[145]

Jewish women showed more righteousness than men did by not participating in the sin of the golden calf. So did they do so, too, in giving wholeheartedly to the building of the Sanctuary. The Sages declare that it was in the merit of the righteous women of Israel that the Jewish people were redeemed from Egypt.[146] Unlike the men who contributed indiscriminately, both to the golden calf and to the Sanctuary,[147] the women's generosity was tempered by greater wisdom and keener insight, as well by as the strength and fortitude with which to resist their husbands' pressure. Demonstrating superiority on both occasions–a negative reaction in the matter of the golden calf and a positive one regarding the Sanctuary–women were granted a festival of their own.

In determining why the women were rewarded with Rosh Hodesh, the Sages point out that the Sanctuary to which the women contributed so liberally was established on Rosh Hodesh *Nisan*, the first day of the month of *Nisan*. As a result, Rosh Hodesh became festival days for Jewish women.[148]

On the occasion of the appearance of a new moon, Jews recite the following blessing:

> And to the moon He said that she should be reborn as a crown of glory to those carried in the womb, for they are destined to be reborn like her and to glorify their Creator for the splendor of His kingdom.[149]

14

Women and Prayer

A–Women and Prayer

THE PLACE OF PRAYER IN JUDAISM

Prayer is an expression of a fundamental human aspiration for an intimate relationship with the transcendent God. On the most basic level, prayer is both a manifestation of human inadequacy and a response to an elemental human longing to open oneself up and express true emotions and feelings before God.

On a higher level prayer represents human striving for nearness to the ideal–to reduce the vast gulf separating mortal man from the Creator. Prayer is thus the manifestation of a compelling natural need by humans for a connection between earth and heaven.

In Jewish thought a prerequisite of prayer is comprehension of the existence of a Creator of the universe and His omniscience and of His interest in human beings. Prayer manifests an awareness by humans of their duty to live in accordance with God's will. It also reflects a simultaneous awareness of human deficiency and a striving to attain a bonding with the eternal Good.

One prays to an Almighty God in periods of distress and need. On a higher level, prayer serves as a means for the Jew to liberate himself from the confines of his finite world and to enter into the spiritual realm of infinity through communication with the Sovereign of the Universe.

The Jewish liturgy includes prayers of petition and prayers for the forgiveness of sins. There are prayers praising God and prayers of thanksgiving. The Jew also prays out of a sense of wonder at what God has wrought in the universe and at the miracles that daily bear witness to His presence.

In Jewish thought, prayer is "service of the heart." The Talmud teaches:

> [The Torah states that one is required] "to love the Lord your God with all your heart."[1] What kind of service is with the heart? Say that this is prayer.[2]

One thanks God for His munificence, for His many beneficent deeds, and for granting us life and sustaining us. One expresses gratitude to "the Compassionate One whose acts of loving-kindness are unceasing" (from the *Amidah*). In the words of the Psalmist: *Hodu laShem ki tov*–"Praise God for He is good."[3]

Judaism has given humanity the idea of congregational prayer. While Jews can pray privately, the Sages regarded communal prayer as being on an exalted level[4] and therefore more acceptable to God.[5] In the words of Scripture, "God stands in the congregation of God."[6] By praying with a congregation, a Jew merges with other Jews at prayer, united before God. Consequently, most prayers are phrased in the plural.

Maimonides teaches:

> The prayer of a community is always heard by God. Even should there be sinners among them, the Holy One Blessed be He does not reject the prayers of the many. One should therefore associate himself with the community and not pray privately, whenever it is possible to pray with the community.[7]

In the synagogue, an ancient institution that existed even alongside the Temple in Jerusalem, Jewish prayer attains its finest form of expression. In the words of the Sages, "prayer is heard best in the synagogue."[8] The Talmud teaches:

> See how exalted He is! Yet, let a person enter the synagogue and but whisper a prayer, and the Holy One Blessed be He hearkens to that prayer.[9]

PRAYER: A DUTY OF MEN AND WOMEN

Prayer is an essential Jewish duty, something Jews are required to do every day of their lives.[10] Prayer for the Jew is a central activity; it accompanies waking, eating, going to sleep, and many acts in between.[11]

Prayer in Judaism is incumbent on both men and women.[12] The biblical archetype of powerful prayer is of a woman. Hanah "prayed to God" for a child, "speaking with her heart, her lips moving but her voice not being heard."[13] She is cited in the Talmud as the paradigm of one who prays to heaven.[14] The prescribed recitation of the *Amidah,* the central prayer in each of the three daily services of the Jew,[15] is based on Hanah's silent prayer. Also, the Midrash derives from Hanah's prayer the obligation of women to pray.[16]

Judaism requires man and woman equally to pray twice daily, in the morning and in the afternoon, the evening prayer being optional.[17] However, men have accepted the evening prayer as an obligation, and it has become obligatory for them. Women have not accepted it as obligatory and are excused from it,[18] but many women nevertheless recite it.[19]

The obligation to recite Grace after all meals[20] is shared by men and women.[21] Women are excused from reciting the *Shema* ("Hear O Israel, the Lord Our God is One God") and the accompanying biblical passages because it is time-dependent[22] (see below), but they are encouraged to recite it.[23] This also applies to the *Hallel* prayer recited during the festivals.[24]

While it is best to recite the prayers in *Lashon HaKodesh,* the Holy Tongue – i.e., Hebrew – those who do not understand Hebrew may recite the prayers in the vernacular.[25]

Although all the fixed daily prayers in Judaism constitute Positive Precepts that are time-dependent, precepts from which women are usually exempted, prayer is nevertheless incumbent on women because of its special nature. Maimonides differs regarding the Torah origin of the fixed daily prayers[26] and maintains that the Torah obligates one to pray. He maintains that it is only the thrice daily prayers at specific times that are of rabbinic origin. Maimonides therefore obligates women to pray because he does not consider daily prayer to be time-dependent:

> It is a Positive Precept to pray every day, as it is written in the Torah, "And you shall serve the Lord your God."[27] We have a tradition that "service" refers to prayer . . . but the fixed number of daily prayers are not of Torah origin, and the Torah does not specify fixed times of prayer. Therefore, women and bondsmen are obligated to pray, for prayer is a Positive Precept that is not time-dependent. . . .[28]

PRAYING WITH A CONGREGATION IS PREFERABLE

Praying with a *minyan,* the quorum of ten that makes up a minimal public "assembly" or "congregation" for communal prayer, is preferable to praying privately, and a man should seek out a *minyan* with which to pray. A *minyan* prays publicly, meaning that the ten-plus participants pray together as a congregation rather than as individuals.

Public prayer is an act that conflicts with the Jewish view of the essentially private personality of the woman. Women are not counted in a *minyan,* and ten women on their own cannot constitute a *minyan* for public prayer either.[29] A woman's participation in prayer is legitimate; indeed, as mentioned, it is obligatory. However, since a woman is exempt from time-dependent Positive Precepts, and since fixed-time congregational prayer might interfere with more important duties, her obligation may be fulfilled privately, independent of a *minyan.* Because she is not equally obligated with men she cannot be included in a *minyan* of those who share the obligation of time-dependent prayer.

In keeping with the private nature of women, woman's prayer is expressed in a private manner.[30] Communal prayer is more in keeping with the essentially public personality of the male and, consequently, his more public role. Public prayer is an expression of the public functioning of the community, and hence the responsibility for public prayer is limited to males.

B – Women's Congregations

The women's movement has engendered an increased interest among women in more active participation in Jewish communal and religious affairs, resulting in the introduction in the United States of the phenomenon of women's prayer groups in recent years.

The women who take part in women's congregations are moved by an increased women's consciousness. Many desire a "hands on" participation in the active conduct of traditional Jewish prayer rituals; rituals they had previously observed only as "passive participants" from the women's sections in traditional synagogues. There is frequently a genuine expression of fervent desire for a meaningful, elevated spiritual experience they feel has been denied them as women.

Congregational prayer is a public, communal function. When ten or more women pray together, their prayers take on a private character, but not a public one, i.e., they do not form a *minyan.* A *minyan,* a congregational quorum of at least ten males, is required for the recitation of a number of portions of the prayer service. The Code of Jewish Law states:

> The *Kaddish* prayer may be recited only in the presence of at least ten free, adult male Jews. The same rule is applicable to the *Kedushah* and *Borechu* prayers[31] [and to everything else that requires ten].[32]

A women's prayer group may not perform *Hazarat HaShatz,* the public reading of the *Amidah,* or the public reading of the Torah. If they recite the blessings, their utterance of God's name is considered in vain and thus a transgression. The more traditional women's prayer groups limit their prayers to the private portions of the service and exclude all parts of the service that require a *minyan,* including the precentor's repetition of the *Amidah* (the *Shmoneh Esrei*) prayer.

HALACHAH AND WOMEN'S *MINYANIM*

The Gedolim, or major rabbinic and halachic authorities of this generation, have not approved women's *minyanim* as conforming to Jewish law. R. J. David Bleich, a contemporary rabbinic scholar, states: "No rabbinic authority of stature has been willing to endorse this innovation" in Jewish religious life. He adds that while there have been some rabbis who have been, at best, "unenthusiastic" about the idea, among others "the reaction is outright condemnation as violation of the halachic norm."[33]

Moreover, R. Bleich points out, a heretofore unknown exclusionary sexism has been introduced into the realm of prayer with the inauguration of the concept of women's prayer groups. He underscores that *tefillah betzibbur* prayer with a *minyan,* while conducted by males, does not exclude females. Women, seated behind a *mehitzah,* or partition, form part of the *tzibbur,* or congregation that prays together. The reverse, however, is not the case. Since female prayer groups led by female officiants do not constitute a *tefillah betzibbur, Halachah* prohibits a man to participate in women's prayer groups even from behind a *mehitzah.*

A woman is obligated to pray at least twice daily. She is not obligated to pray with a *tzibbur.* If she does pray with a *minyan* she enjoys the *kiyum,* or fulfillment, of *tefillah betzibbur,* and the reward for it as one who has performed an optional *mitzvah.* A woman may be spiritually motivated and may derive great satisfaction from participating in a women's congregation. This experience, however, does not afford *kiyum* of *tefillah betzibbur* and the reward of the optional *mitzvah* of prayer with a *minyan.*[34]

RELIGIOUS SCHOOL PRAYER GROUPS FOR GIRLS

Women's *minyanim* have been found by the leading rabbinic authorities to not conform to *Halachah.* However, religious schools for young girls regularly conduct prayer groups for educational purposes. Older students in seminaries pray either with an existing *minyan* comprising at least ten adult males, with the services conducted in a normative fashion, or with women only, in accordance with the all the norms of private prayer.

C–Aliyot to the Torah for Women

The Torah is read in the synagogue on Monday, Thursday, and Saturday mornings, on Saturday afternoons, and on all the festivals of the Jewish year, in order to enable the community to be familiar with its teachings. Congregants are called up to read portions of the Scripture, although the custom has been that those receiving an *aliyah* ("calling up") recite the benedictions for the reading and a reader chants the Torah portion.

"KEVOD HATZIBBUR"

Women may perform the public reading of the Torah–and therefore receive *aliyot*–according to the Talmud. However, the Talmud rules that women should not be called up to the Torah for *aliyot* because it is not considered "in consonance with the dignity of the congregation"–*kevod hatzibbur*:

> All may be counted among the seven who are called up to the Torah, even a minor and even a woman. However, the Sages said, a woman may not be called up for an *aliyah* because of *kevod hatzibbur*.[35]

Kevod hatzibbur (lit. the honor of the community) here is not meant as a demeaning reflection on the woman. The congregational reading of the Torah is a public act that a woman, because of her private role, would ordinarily not fulfill. Calling a woman to publicly read the Torah proclaims publicly that the standards of that community are quite low, i.e., that it does not have enough males who know how to read the Torah, who can fulfill public functions properly–and this would result in the shaming of the congregation.

The *Halachah*, therefore, is that women do not have *aliyot* to the Torah. Thus they must not recite the blessings which include the phrase "Who has selected us . . ."

Some women's prayer groups have adopted the practice of calling women up to the Torah without reciting the blessings, reasoning that such Torah reading does not constitute an *aliyah*. While technically correct, the practice is opposed by most rabbinic authorities[36] because it resembles a halachically forbidden activity and might confuse and mislead people who do not understand the subtle halachic nuances separating the permissible from the forbidden.

The impression that will be left on participants and observers alike is that these *"aliyot,"* while only technically within the law, are in full accordance with all aspects of *Halachah*, i.e., full *aliyot* in no way differentiated from those conducted in accordance with *Halachah* in a halachic *minyan*. People who have witnessed such *"aliyot"* confirm that their perception is that these are normative *aliyot*. However, it is forbidden to perform an activity that resembles one that is forbidden.[37]

Men and women alike have an obligation to listen to the reading of the Torah and the *Haftarah* readings from the Prophets,[38] and the practice in some synagogues where some men and/or women converse—or leave the sanctuary to converse outside the synagogue—during the Torah reading is severely condemned by rabbinic authorities.[39]

D—Separation of the Sexes in the Synagogue

AN ALTERNATIVE FOCUS

The term *kevod hatzibbur* may contain the additional motif of avoiding distraction. Distraction is one of the reasons that man and woman are segregated in the traditional synagogue during prayer. Prayer requires total absorption and concentration. The separation of men and women during prayer is an aid to such concentration.

Judaism is acutely aware of the power of the sexual drive in the male and the subtle factors that activate this drive. The strong focus and intense concentration required during prayer in Judaism, which involves a veritable divorce of the individual from his surroundings in order to attain the requisite unity with God, is incompatible with the presence of women. No matter how lofty a man's intentions, women will provide an alternative focus for his attention and serve to distract his concentration.

In the synagogue, there is one love and one locus. For this reason it is even forbidden to kiss one's child in the synagogue! When standing before God one is required to concentrate exclusively on God. Anything that might distract one or remove one's focus from the intense prayerful concentration required for immersing oneself in prayers is to be avoided.

It is no easy matter to do this when one is surrounded by members of the same sex. It is virtually impossible for most people to focus on God alone when there are members of the opposite sex around.

It is especially difficult for men to separate themselves sufficiently from their immediate surroundings and concentrate totally on prayer when there are women present. Most men, who possess a more easily awakened sexual drive than most women, are fully aware of this reality of life. The Sages, who instituted the separation of men and women during prayer, intended to enable both men and women to attain a true inner concentration when communing with God.

KADDISH

Kaddish, the memorial prayer for the dead, may be recited only before a *minyan*, a quorum of at least ten males.[40] In response to the recent practice of some women to recite the *Kaddish*, most rabbinic authorities have ruled that a woman may not recite the *Kaddish* for a parent in the synagogue.[41] Others permit the recitation of *Kaddish* by a daughter under certain circumstances when there is no son who can recite it.[42]

E – Women and *Tefillin*

THE NATURE OF *TEFILLIN*

Tefillin, possibly from the word *tefillah*, prayer, are two leather cubelike boxes containing scriptural passages handwritten on parchment by a Torah scribe. One box is bound on the left arm[43] with a long leather strip and the other is placed on the head. They are worn during morning prayers every day during the year except on Sabbaths and festivals. In ancient times they were worn throughout the day, and to this day there are Torah scholars who wear *tefillin* all day long.

The commandment to wear *tefillin* is founded on four passages in the Torah, in which the Jew is bid to "put these words as a sign upon thy hand and as frontlets between your eyes." These passages are inserted in the *tefillin*.[44]

While there are no explicit references in the Torah as to how those "signs" and "frontlets" are to be made, the form of the *tefillin* derives from the oral tradition received at Sinai. The oral tradition serves to supplement and elaborate on a tersely written precept given in the Written Torah and to provide the method of performing it. *Tefillin* is frequently cited as the quintessential example of the role of the Oral Torah as the Iluminator of the Written Torah, and of the total unity between the two.

Tefillin, along with *tallit*, are two precepts associated specifically with men. Nevertheless, a passage in the Babylonian Talmud states that Michal, daughter of King Saul and wife of King David, donned *tefillin*,[45] and the Sages did not protest that she was transgressing the precept of *Lo tosifu*, "You shall not add" to the Torah.[46] However, the text, as it appears in somewhat fuller form in the Jerusalem Talmud, reads as follows:

> Women and bondsmen are exempted from the obligations of reading the *Shema* and donning *tefillin*. How do we derive this? It is written, "And you shall teach them to your sons."[47] [Your sons, that is,] and not your daughters. One who is obligated to study Torah is obligated to don *tefillin*. Women, who are not obligated to study Torah, are exempted from the obligation to don *tefillin*.
>
> Question: But did not Michal the daughter of Saul of Kish don *tefillin* . . . and the Sages did not protest? R. Hezekiah said in the name of R. Abahu . . . The Sages did indeed protest.[48]

The Targum Jonathan ben Uziel translation and commentary to the Torah cites the biblical prohibition against one gender donning another's garments and accoutrements as the rationale for women not wearing *tallit* and *tefillin*.[49]

The medieval authorities did, however, permit the wearing of *tefillin* by women. These include R. Solomon ben Adret, known as the *Rashba*,[50] and *Rabbeinu Tam*, one of the *Baalei HaTosafot*,[51] the medieval German and French commentaries on the Talmud. But R. Meir of Rothenburg, the leading European rabbinic authority of the thirteenth century, held that the wearing of *tefillin* is not an option for women, and they may under no circumstances don them.[52]

TEFILLIN: SANCTITY AND *KAVANAH*

Tefillin have great sanctity. The *Halachah* expresses concern about the treatment of *tefillin* and the places where one may go when wearing *tefillin*. The eleventh-century halachic authority R. Abraham ben David, known as the *Ravad*, maintains that a pair of *tefillin* has greater sanctity than the *tzitz*, the ceremonial gold diadem inscribed with the words "Holy unto God" worn by the *kohen gadol* in the Temple in Jerusalem. When wearing the *tzitz*, the *Ravad* points out, the *kohen gadol* had to be conscious at all times of the fact that the sacred *tzitz* was on his head.[53] Correspondingly, when one wears the more sacred *tefillin*, one must be concerned in this respect.

Those wearing *tefillin* are required to maintain bodily cleanliness, they must be humble and God-fearing, and they may not be involved in mirth or idle talk or have improper thoughts. The mind must be dedicated to true and correct matters.[54] As a result of their great sanctity, few people wear *tefillin* all day long as Jews did in ancient times; today *tefillin* are generally donned for the minimum period only, during the daily morning prayers. Boys may not don *tefillin* until just before their bar mitzvah.

The sanctity of *tefillin* in Jewish tradition is such that one does not simply decide to don them; wearing *tefillin* as an option is not considered praiseworthy by the large majority of Sages. They hold that unlike other optional *mitzvot* such as *shofar*, *sukkah*, *lulav*, and *tzitzit*, which women may, if they so desire, perform, the *mitzvah* of *tefillin* is one that women are not to perform under any circumstances.

The *Shulhan Aruch*, the Code of Jewish Law, determines:

> Women and bondsmen are excused from *tefillin* because it is a Positive Precept that is time-dependent.[55] If, however, women wish to be more stringent in their observance [and don *tefillin*], people must object.[56]

F – Women and the *Tallit*

THE *MITZVAH* OF *TZITZIT*

The Torah enjoins Jews to wear *tzitzit*, fringes, on the four corners of their garments as a sign of obedience to God – a mnemonic device to remind them constantly that they are Jews and that they are duty-bound to fulfill God's precepts:

> And the Lord spoke to Moses, saying: Speak to the children of Israel and bid them to make *tzitzit* on the corners of their garments throughout their generations, and they shall place on the *tzitzit* a cord of blue. And it shall be for you *tzitzit* so that when you look upon it you will remember all the *mitzvot* of the Lord and do them; and you shall not go after your heart and after your eyes after which you go astray. So that you may remember and perform all of My commandments and you shall be holy to your God.[57]

The *gematria*, numerical value, of *tzitzit* is 600, and with the eight threads bearing five knots added to this figure, the total comes to 613, corresponding exactly to the number of the commandments in the Torah. When a Jew looks at *tzitzit*, therefore, he is reminded of the commandments of the Torah and of his obligation to fulfill them.

Tallit is Hebrew for "garment"; in ancient times it was a loose, rectangular, cloaklike men's outer garment, which was usually four-cornered, and it was to this type of garment, if it was four-cornered, that *tzitzit* were to be affixed.

WEARING A *TALLIT* AS AN OPTIONAL PRECEPT

According to the Torah, the *mitzvah* of *tzitzit* is an optional one. If a Jew wears a four-cornered garment he is enjoined to have *tzitzit* on the corners; but if he does not wear one, he is not obliged to fulfill this *mitzvah*.

By rabbinical enactment, however, the Jew is required to wear a four-cornered *tallit* to enable him to fulfill the biblical obligation to wear *tzitzit*. Accordingly, a fringed four-cornered garment that slips over the head and rests on the shoulders is worn by traditional Jewish men and boys, usually under the shirt, at times with the *tzitzit* hanging loose outside the garments so that they will fulfill their designated mnemonic function. In addition, during the morning prayers the married Jewish male wears a full-length *tzitzited* *tallit* over his clothing, usually made of wool. Maimonides provides the rationale:

> Even though an individual is not obligated to purchase a *tallit* and to wrap himself in it in order to make *tzitzit* for it, it is not proper for a pious person to exempt himself from fulfilling this precept. Therefore, a person should always endeavor to wear a garment that requires *tzitzit* (a four-cornered garment) so as to be able to fulfill this *mitzvah*. And he should be especially careful to have such a garment on during [morning] prayer, for it is exceedingly shameful for scholars to pray when they are not clothed in a *tallit*.[58]

WOMEN'S EXEMPTION FROM *TALLIT* AND *TZITZIT*

Women are exempted from the commandments of *tallit* and *tzitzit* since the *mitzvah* of *tzitzit* is a Positive Precept that is time-dependent. The Talmud teaches:

> All are obligated to wear *tzitzit*–*Kohanim*, Levites and Israelites, proselytes, women and bondsmen. R. Simon exempts women because it is a Positive Precept that is time-dependent, and women are exempted from all Positive Precepts that are time-dependent.[59]

This is confirmed by the codifiers of Jewish law.[60] There is some discussion among the Sages regarding whether or not women could observe the precept as an optional *mitzvah*, possibly without making the benediction. (Women could not easily recite the words "Who has commanded us . . . ," which form the central part of the *berachah* [benediction], since women are not commanded.) Maimonides declares:

> Women, bondsmen and minors are exempted by the Torah. . . . However, women and bondsmen who wish to wrap themselves in a *tallit* with *tzitzit* may do so without a *berachah*. Similarly, the other Positive Precepts that women are

> exempted from—if they wish to perform them without reciting the *berachah* we do not oppose them.[61]

In his glosses to the *Shulhan Aruch*, the Code of Jewish Law, R. Moses Isserles, the sixteenth-century Polish codifier known as *Rama*, agrees with Maimonides that although women are exempted from *tzitzit* they may don a *tallit*. He maintains that women may recite the appropriate blessing as they may if they perform the other time-dependent Positive Precepts from which they are exempted.[62]

However, Rama adds:

> This would be an act of *yoharah* [excessive pride or exhibitionism]. Therefore, women should not wear *tzitzit*, since it is not an obligation upon the individual. That is, [a woman] is not required to purchase a [four-cornered] garment so as to become subject to the obligation of wearing *tzitzit*.[63]

R. Jacob Molin, the fourteenth-century halachist known as *MaHaril*, writes that "women who wear *tzitzit* are behaving foolishly; it appears as if they are publicly flaunting their piety." Moroever, adds the *MaHaril*, there is a nuance of sin on the part of women who transgress by donning a *tallit*.[64] As a *tallit*—unlike *tefillin*—is a garment, it is likely that, since the *tallit* is identified as purely a male garment, a woman would be transgressing the precept prohibiting women from wearing men's garments and vice versa.[65] This is in accordance with the *Targum Jonathan ben Uziel*, who views the wearing of both *tefillin* and *tallit* as violating this prohibition.[66]

The *Halachah* is that "even a woman who is accustomed to fulfill the other time-dependent Positive Commandments, although she is exempted from them, must nevertheless not don *tzitzit* because it appears as *yoharah* [excessively prideful or exhibitionistic]."[67]

On the wearing of the *tallit* by some traditionalist Jewish women, R. Moshe Meiselman, author of the study, *Jewish Women in Jewish Law*, comments:

> The law of *yoharah* warns us and limits us. . . . The wearing of a *tallit* by a woman, a doubly optional activity [because it is scripturally not obligatory even upon the man], may be a *mitzvah* but it is certainly a marginal one.
>
> A woman who is truly motivated by a desire to adhere to the Divine command will first make herself absolutely proficient in more basic areas before moving into the more esoteric and optional ones. The value of *mitzvot* to a person should be determined by their intrinsic value rather than by their extrinsic appeal.[68]

G—Blessings and Benedictions

The Talmud teaches that one may not enjoy the divinely given pleasures of this world without praising God for them.[69] Accordingly, Jews are required to "sanctify the mundane" in life by expressing gratitude to God when enjoying God's bounty.

Observant Jews bless God, therefore, when they eat and drink, upon donning new garments or items of jewelry, upon eating a new fruit or enjoying a pleasant aroma, upon completing a lengthy journey or recovering from an operation, upon giving birth, and when enjoying an array of the "natural" wonders of nature, such as experiencing thunder or lightning or seeing a rainbow, when coming upon a beautiful tree or field, or, indeed, even when seeing a beautiful person or a Torah scholar or, in fact, any brilliant man or woman.

The obligation to recite blessings falls on whoever experiences these, man or woman.[70]

H–*Birkat HaMazon*–Grace after Meals

THE DUTY TO EXPRESS GRATITUDE

Torah declares: "And when you have eaten and you are satisfied, then you shall bless the Lord your God for the good land that He has given you."[71]

Both men and women are obligated to say Grace following meals, *Birkat HaMazon*, but there is a discussion in the Talmud as to whether the duty of women to say Grace is a scriptural or a rabbinic obligation.[72] If their duty to recite Grace is a scriptural one, women are able to also discharge the obligation on behalf of men.

The *Shulhan Aruch* declares:

> Women are obligated to recite *Birkat HaMazon*. However, it is uncertain whether women's obligation is *mid'oraita* [scriptural], and they can therefore discharge the obligation for men, or their obligation is only *miderabanan* [rabbinic], in which case they can discharge the obligation only for those who are equally rabbinically obligated [women].[73]

As for *Birkat HaZimun*, group recitation of *Birkat HaMazon*, a minimum of three men who have eaten together are required, since, if a woman is included in the *zimun*, the mixed association is considered improper.[74] Once there is a minimum of three men present, a woman who is also present should answer the call of the one who is leading the *zimun*, participate in the *zimun*, and recite the Grace.[75]

Women may participate in their own *zimun*, in accordance with the talmudic statement, *Hakol hayavin bezimun. . . . Nashim mezamnot leatzman*, "All are obligated to participate in *Birkat HaZimun*. . . . Women conduct their own *zimun*."[76] *Tosafot* maintains that women participating in a *zimun* among themselves do so as an elective option, but are not obligated to do so.[77] However, in the view of R. Asher ben Jehiel, the thirteenth–fourteenth century rabbinic authority known as the *Rosh*, women who dine among only other women are *duty-bound* to precede the recitation of Grace with *Birkat HaZimun*, citing the preceding statement in the Talmud that "all are *obligated* to participate in *Birkat HaZimun*."[78]

I—"That He Has Not Made Me a Woman"

THE SEPARATE BENEDICTIONS FOR MEN AND WOMEN

The fact that women are excused from a number of precepts is alluded to in the much-maligned morning benediction in which the man praises God for not having made him a woman.[79] This is commonly understood as derogatory toward women and an indication of her inferiority. In fact, however, man thanks God since, due to the nature of the role assigned to him, he has more opportunities than women to carry out divine precepts.[80] In this way he acknowledges that he accepts the burden of duty involved in the fulfillment of God's commandments.[81]

This is indicated in the *Tosefta*:

> R. Judah said: A man is required to recite daily the benediction . . . Blessed are you O Lord, King of the Universe, who has not made me a woman . . . because women have not been charged with the performance of [all of the] *mitzvot*.[82]

R. Samson Raphael Hirsch comments that it is not a prayer by men thanking God for not having made them female but rather a joyous affirmation of the acceptance of the greater burden placed upon them and a charge to men to contemplate the many duties imposed on them and to properly fulfill the mission they have been given.

As for the women, R. Hirsch remarks:

> And if women have a smaller number of *mitzvot* to fulfill than men, they know that the tasks which they must discharge as free Jewish women are no less in accordance with the will and desire of God than are those of their brothers.[83]

As for the benediction in which the woman thanks God for creating her according to His will, this expresses her gratitude to God for having created her *kiretzono*, with a Godlike will, i.e., with a *binah yeteirah*, a greater discernment and understanding than man and thus a greater similarity to God. This enables her to more easily attain an exalted spiritual level—something man must strive much harder to achieve. She need not take time off from her vital tasks as a woman in order to attain that level. Men, lacking the woman's *binah yeteirah,* must strive harder to achieve the spiritual level of the woman by performing additional *mitzvot.*

R. Moshe Meiselman reasons that, in the blessing, the woman thanks God for having created her with a nature similar to God's will, *kiretzono*:

> We relate to God in His role of enabler and as the archetype of the performer of *hesed* (acts of lovingkindness). These are presented by the creation of woman in a greater sense than the creation of man. Thus women say: "Who has made me similar to His will."[84]

Both the men's and the women's benedictions are acknowledgments of individuals' acceptance of the divine roles accorded them—in the instance of the man, more duties, and in that of the woman, fewer ones—as part of God's plan and of their willingness to fulfill them to the best of their abilities.

15

Torah Study and Bat Mitzvah

A–Torah Study and the Woman

THE IMPORTANCE OF STUDYING THE TORAH

The study of Torah is considered the noblest pursuit of the Jew. The Torah in its entirety, including all of the works of exegesis, occupies such a central place in Judaism that its study takes exalted precedence in the duties of the Jew.

Traditionally, not wealth or success in business or career or profession has been the desired goal of the young Jew, but to be a *talmid hacham*, a Torah scholar. So essential to Jewish life is the study of Torah and so preeminent a task is it, the Talmud teaches, that Torah study may not be interrupted even for the building of the holy Temple. In a listing of the vital duties incumbent on the Jew, the Mishnah concludes, "but the study of Torah surpasses them all."[1]

The reason for learning the Torah is twofold. First, Torah, signifying guidance and instruction, contains God's directives to the Jew. It is the Jew's first duty to learn the laws, principles, and obligations toward God and toward his fellow in order to know how to behave–how to live in accordance with God's will. In brief, the Torah is the Jew's practical guide for life.

Second, Torah study is vital for its own sake, for it contains–in the Bible, the Talmud, and the whole body of Jewish religious-ethical literature—the aggregate of Jewish knowledge, the entirety of Jewish wisdom and culture. The Jew is directed to "study the Torah again and again, for everything is contained in it . . . and there is no better pursuit for you than its study."[2]

True liberation, the Sages teach, comes from the study of Torah: "There is no person who is truly free except for the one who is involved with the study of Torah, for such a one is elevated."[3] One of the three things the Jew will be asked upon coming before the final Tribunal on High is this question: "Did you set aside regular periods of time for Torah study?"[4]

It therefore comes as a surprise to many to learn that Judaism does not require women to study Torah; only the man is commanded to study,[5] although Torah study is not considered to be a time-dependent *mitzvah*.

TEACHING TORAH TO DAUGHTERS

A man is also enjoined to teach Torah to his sons.[6] This is based on the biblical command, *Velimadetem otam et beneichem*, "And you shall teach them diligently to your sons."[7] The Talmud declares, *et beneichem, velo et benoteichem*, "your sons, but not your daughters." The Talmud states that only those to whom it is commanded to teach Torah may study Torah. Therefore, should a son fail to receive a Torah education, he is obliged to study Torah on his own; however, a woman is not, because she is not in the category of *beneichem*, "your sons."[8]

The Sages of the Mishnah differ, however, regarding whether a daughter should be taught Torah:

> . . . Ben Azai says: A man is obligated to teach his daughter Torah. . . . R. Eliezer says: Whoever teaches his daughter Torah is considered as if he teaches her frivolity [*tiflut*]. . . .[9]

The difference of opinion is a significant one. However, the final halachic decision is according to R. Eliezer's opinion.[10] But, since the Sages defined his statement as referring only to specific areas of Torah knowledge, there has been a wide latitude of practice in the area of Torah education for girls over the ages.

The issue of Torah study by women is a complex one. Knowledge of Torah is the key to living the rich Jewish way of life. As mentioned, the first level for learning Torah is the practical one—knowing what to do and how to do it. This is in accordance with the verse, "learn them (the *mitzvot*) and you will take care to observe them."[11]

Since the observance of Judaism is predicated on the knowledge of Torah, it follows that boys and girls, men and women should be taught Torah so as to have within their reach the required information for the proper conduct of their lives. A phrase in the daily liturgy states: *lilmod ulelamed, lishmor velaasot,* "to learn and to teach, to observe and to do";[12] learning is an essential prerequisite to doing.

Sefer Hasidim, the ethical work by the twelfth-century sage R. Judah HeHasid, illustrates this point:

> One is obligated to teach daughters the *mitzvot,* as for example, the legal rulings of the *Halachah.* As to the statement that everyone who teaches a woman Torah is as if they are teaching her frivolity, this refers only to studying in depth and studying the rationale and mysteries of the Torah; these are not to be taught to a woman or a minor.
>
> However, a woman should be taught the laws of the *mitzvot,* for if a woman does not know the laws of the Sabbath how will she be able to observe the Sabbath? And the same applies to all the *mitzvot,* so that she should be able to perform them and to observe them.[13]

A similar thought is expressed by the thirteenth-century rabbinic authority, R. Yitzhak of Corbeil (d. 1280), in his compendium of Jewish laws *Sefer Mitzvot Katan,* which recommends that women peruse the precepts in detail, especially those applying to them, as such perusal will profit them in the same way "as studying Talmud profits the men."[14]

In the nineteenth century, R. Samson Raphael Hirsch wrote:

> No less [than men] should Israel's daughters learn the content of the Written Torah and the duties which they have to perform in their lifetimes as daughter and young woman, as mother and housewife. Many times have Israel's daughters saved the purity of the Jewish life and spirit. The deliverance from Egypt itself was won by the women; and it is by the pious maidens and mothers of Israel that the Jewish spirit and Jewish life can and will again be revived.[15]
>
> . . . While women are not exposed to specialized Torah study or theoretical knowledge of the Torah, which are reserved for the Jewish man, such understanding of our sacred literature as can teach the fear of the Lord and the conscientious fulfillment of our duty, and all such knowledge as is essential to the adequate execution of our tasks should indeed form part of the mental and spiritual training not only of our sons, but of our daughters as well.[16]

Examples abound of leading rabbis who taught their wives and daughters the practical *Halachot.* R. Joshua Neuwirth, a contemporary Jerusalem halachic authority, writes in his monumental treatise of the laws of the Sabbath, *Shemirat Shabbat Kehilchata:*

> The study of Torah is both a goal and a medium. The goal – the actual study and knowledge of it. The medium – to know in order to perform the *mitzvot.* Women

> are obligated only to study in order to perform the *mitzvot*. People are obligated to teach their daughter the laws of the *mitzvot* that relate to her, for if she will not know the laws of the Sabbath how will she observe the Sabbath? And the same goes for all the other *mitzvot*. . . .
>
> It is told about the Rabbi of Jerusalem, R. Joseph Hayim Sonenfeld (1849–1932), that he taught his wife *Shulhan Aruch, Orah Hayim* (the section of the Code of Jewish Law dealing with day-to-day living) half an hour each day. . . . It is told of the Gaon of Vilna (1720–1797) that when he was en route to *Eretz Yisrael* he wrote to his mother and his daughter to study the ethical works of the Sages. . . . Similarly it is told of the *Hatam Sofer* (1762–1839) that he taught his daughters the teachings of the Sages. . . .[17]

The *Halachah* is clear: "Just as it is obligatory to educate a son in the *mitzvot* he is required to follow, so is it obligatory to educate a daughter in the *mitzvot* she is required to follow."[18]

WOMEN AND IN-DEPTH TORAH STUDY

The second level of Torah learning, however, involves intensive study on a deeper, more esoteric level than that required for the acquisition of knowledge for practical use. Ben Azai appears to be unconcerned about woman's capacity to cope with this kind of study to the same degree as the man. Maimonides apparently agrees with him.

Maimonides says that knowledge of Torah "is available to all, young and old, man and woman, those with considerable ability and those with limited ability."[19] In essence, his message is: have a go at it. Everyone will be able to get something out of Torah study no matter what his–or her–capacity.

As no one knew better than Maimonides, however, Torah study that is on a level of genuine attainment is difficult; its pursuit requires a mind characterized by a special orientation, and its study demands a deep, intense concentration of the mind and virtually total dedication in order for the knowledge gained from it not to be shallow. Indeed, Maimonides mentions elsewhere[20] that most women's thought is oriented in a different direction, and not toward study (*"sherov hanashim ein daatan mechuvanot lehitlamed"*).

Casual study of an intensely complex subject by a student who is preoccupied elsewhere is not a desirable thing. One whose concentration is demanded on multiple levels and at all times will not focus all the requisite energy on one exacting and demanding philosophical question. To dabble in the Talmud is to risk drawing superficial, and even erroneous, conclusions. Such conclusions could well be trivial ones and could at times be even worse than no knowledge.

In his Code Maimonides says:

> A woman who studies Torah is rewarded, but not on the same level as a man, because she was not commanded to do so, and anyone who performs a precept that he is not commanded does not have the reward of someone who is commanded to do so, but a lesser one. Therefore, even though she has a reward, the Sages commanded that a man should not teach his daughter Torah because most women's thought is oriented in a different direction, and not toward the study of Torah, and as a result they will turn the words of Torah into frivolity. Our Sages said: Whoever teaches his daughter Torah is as if he taught her frivolity.
>
> This all refers to the Oral Torah. However, regarding the Written Torah he should not set out to teach her, but if he does teach her, it is not considered as if he taught her frivolity.[21]

Maimonides' dual approach on the issue is reflective of the general caution of the Sages who formulated halachic guidelines for Torah study for women.

THE EXAMPLE OF BRURIAH

A number of Sages use the example of the brilliant Bruriah, whose erudition and exceptional knowledge of Torah is referred to on several occasions in the Talmud to show that, if a woman is capable and motivated, the prohibition against Torah study might not apply. The eighteenth-century *Eretz Yisrael* rabbinic authority R. Hayim Yosef David Azulai, known by the accronym *Hida*, writes: "Bruriah was taught because it was recognized that her heart was firmly set on the study of Torah and because of her extraordinary intelligence."[22]

The *Hida* takes Maimonides' statement about the Sages' injunction not to teach one's daughter Torah to be a guideline rather than a strict legal prohibition. Had it been a legal prohibition, the *Hida* reasons, it would apply equally to all women without exception, even in the case of one gifted with the superior motivation and rare erudition of Bruriah.[23] The purpose of the guideline is to ensure that, unless there is sufficient motivation, one should not teach a daughter Torah in depth. However, if one's daughter possesses sufficient motivation and ability, then one has a *responsibility* to teach her Torah.

Where the motivation of women is strong and clear, and this motivation is demonstrated by their actually studying Torah on their own, R. Joshua Falk, the Polish halachic authority known as the *Perishah* (c. 1555–1614), teaches that Maimonides' cautionary prohibition against a woman studying Torah is no longer valid. R. Falk declares:

> Most women lack the requisite concentration necessary for the study of Torah. However, if she does study on her own we see that she is exceptional, and under those circumstances she receives a reward. . . .[24]

Concludes R. Moshe Meiselman, the Jerusalem *rosh yeshivah,* in his work *Jewish Woman in Jewish Law*:

> One does not impose Torah knowledge upon women, as one does upon men, for they are not required to study. But one may teach Torah to a woman who demonstrates the proper motivation. . . . At all times . . . the study of Torah by women remains an optional activity.
>
> [But] a totally different direction has been taken by scholars of the twentieth century. Its effect has been to make Torah study *mandatory* for women.[25]

B – Torah Study for Women in Modern Times

Leading rabbis have held that in modern times, where women are less confined to their homes than they used to be and where they have generally received a varied secular education, they require an advanced Torah education. R. Israel Meir HaCohen, the rabbinic authority and ethical teacher known as the *Hafetz Hayim* (1838–1933), referring to changes in society, urges Torah study for girls in order to strengthen their religious convictions, "lest they stray from the path of God and violate the principles of the Torah."[26]

R. Zalman Sorotzkin (1881–1966), a leading Jerusalem rabbi and educator, declares:

> Not only is it *permitted* to teach torah and piety to girls in our generation, *it is an absolute duty*; it is a great *mitzvah* to establish such schools for girls and to inculcate in their hearts pure faith and love for Torah and *mitzvot*.[27]

He goes so far as to declare that today it is not the teaching of Torah to one's daughter that leaves her prey to *tiflut* (frivolity) but rather neglecting to do so.[28] This is the prevailing view of the majority of contemporary halachic authorities, and, in fact, women's seminaries for Torah study exist in virtually all streams of traditional Judaism.

It is interesting to note here a comment by R. Isaac Arama (c. 1420–1494), the Spanish rabbinic authority and exegete known as the *Akedat Yitzhak*. In the Book of Genesis, Rachel cries out, "Give me children, else I die."[29] The *Akedat Yitzhak* states that, apart from the woman's obvious design for childbearing and nurturation, she shares with the man the capacity to develop her intellectual faculties and those related to the performance of acts of loving-kindness. This is evident in the activities of the Matriarchs and the righteous women and prophetesses, as is indicated in the biblical *Eishet Hayil* (The Woman of Valor) in Proverbs 31.[30] A woman who does not have children does not fulfill her secondary purpose (*hatachlit hakatan*), in the view of the *Akedat Yitzhak*, just as a man who does not father children does not. They can both fulfill their primary purposes in life whether or not they produce children. In the words of R. Isaaac Arama:

> Indubitably, the central aspect of the life-stories of the righteous is the performance of good deeds. . . .[31] Therefore, Jacob was angered when Rachel said "Give me children, else I'll die," rebuking her by pointing out [that she was completely overlooking] the more significant aspect [of life], i.e. . . . the joint purpose of men and women [intellectual attainment and the performance of deeds of loving-kindness] . . . even should there not be children.[32]

"JEWS SHOULD STRIVE TO EMULATE THEIR FOREBEARS"

The ultimate purpose of life for Jews, men and women, the *Akedat Yitzhak* teaches, transcends by far their gender differences. Jews should strive to emulate their forebears, the Patriarchs and Matriarchs, by striving to understand, to gain intellectual attainment, and to devote their lives to the performance of *hesed*.

In summary, it is inconceivable that the woman, who is the prime conveyor of the Jewish tradition in the family, should not be well equipped for this task. It is obligatory for the Torah to be taught to girls as it is to boys, so that as women they will be able to properly fulfill their duties as Jews and perform the precepts of the Torah and to transmit the tradition to their children.

Advanced Torah study– including the study of the Talmud–is optional for women. If a woman demonstrates serious motivation and ability in Torah study on an advanced level, such study is permissable. She may study on her own, and it is permitted to teach her.[33]

R. Meiselman goes further, stating that in contemporary society, where education is a prerequisite for proper motivation, such education is not only permitted, but is also required. R. Meiselman adds: "Very few people with a college education in Western culture and a grade-school education in Judaism can be properly observant. For a college-educated woman, a college-level education in Judaism is not optional, it is absolutely required."[34]

JEWISH INSIGHTS AND MODERN DISCOVERIES

Neither the Sages of the Talmud living nearly 2,000 years ago nor Maimonides living nearly a millenium ago knew of the results of scientific studies made toward the end of the twentieth century confirming the existence of small but significant differences in the brain structures of men and women,[35] the effects of male and female hormones on the disparate abilities of men and women in different areas.[36] There are recognizable differences in intellectual aptitude of the sexes, specifically in the components of cognition.[37]

Studies confirm that females, for example, demonstrate decisive superiority over males in such spheres as verbal,[38] language and articulation ability,[39] and in coordination skills[40] and interpersonal relationships.[41] Males, on the other hand, excel in areas such as visual-spatial ability, mathematics,[42] and analytical reasoning,[43] and consequently the world's engineers, technicians, inventors,[44] and chess grand masters are almost all men.[45]

These determinations, arrived at in hundreds of studies by scientists in every relevant discipline,[46] would not have surprised the Jewish Sages, who perceived keenly that the inherently different physiological and psychological characteristics of men and women enable them to function best in the complementary roles God provided for them. They taught that it is only logical that men and women complement each other mentally and psychologically as they do physiologically.

The mathematical minds of men are considered to be more suited to Torah study than are those of women. This does not make them superior, any more than women's minds are superior because women excel in interpersonal relationships and morality,[47] and therefore in *hesed*, performing altruistic acts of loving-kindness[48]–which Judaism maintains is a central pillar upholding the world. The brains of men and women and their inherent inclinations are different, enabling men and women to truly complement one another by excelling in different spheres of life.

It would be incorrect to say that no women have excelled in Torah scholarship–or, for that matter, in mathematics, engineering, and chess–as it would be to state that no men have been outstanding in language, articulation, interpersonal relationships, and *hesed*. The exceptions, however, do not disprove the rule.

While Jewish tradition expresses an acute awareness of the innate cognitive differences in men and women as they relate to Torah study, it accepts that some women do not fall into this category, and indeed there are Jewish women who pursue intensive Torah study today.

C–*Bat Mitzvah*

Bar mitzvah and *bat mitzvah* (lit. "subject to the commandment") refer to a boy and girl who reach the age of full responsibility to perform all the commandments of the Torah.

A boy attains his religious and legal majority–i.e., he becomes obligated to perform the *mitzvot* and is considered to be no longer a minor but legally an adult for most matters–at age thirteen. A girl attains her religious and legal majority at twelve. *Bar mitzvah* and *bat mitzvah,* therefore, are religious/legal terms meaning the coming of age. Thirteen and twelve are considered to be the approximate ages at which boys and girls attain physical maturity.

To mark this significant milestone and turning point in his life, whereby he is considered to leave his childhood and enter the age of adult responsibility, a boy participates in a public demonstration of his new role as a full adult member of the community by performing a *mitzvah* associated with adulthood: an *aliyah*–being called up–to the reading of the Torah. On the Sabbath of his *bar mitzvah,* he usually receives the last *aliyah* and reads the *Maftir* and the *Haftarah,* a portion from the Prophets that is read in the synagogue following the Torah reading. At times the *bar mitzvah* reads the entire Torah reading and conducts part or all of the synagogue service.

In addition, to demonstrate his knowledge of Torah, he might deliver a *derashah,* a learned discourse on the Talmud and on *Halachah.* In recent years it has become customary to celebrate the occasion with a festive *Kiddush,* a light repast following the synagogue services on the Sabbath, and a separate festive gathering for friends and relatives.

Since women do not participate in the conduct of the synagogue services, a formal synagogue ceremony has not developed to mark the transition of a girl to adulthood in Orthodox Judaism as there has for the boy. Thus, while a *bar mitzvah* celebration is an integral part of the usual synagogue service, this is not the situation with a *bat mitzvah.*

CELEBRATING *BAT MITZVAH* TODAY

The twentieth-century halachic authority R. Moses Feinstein of New York (1895–1986) points out that *Halachah* does not allow the use of a synagogue sanctuary for the purpose of a *bat mitzvah.* Since the sanctuary may be used only for sacred functions associated with the synagogue, R. Feinstein does not allow the synagogue sanctuary to be used for this purpose even at times when it is not used for formal prayer.[49]

However, this does not preclude home or other nonsynagogue observance of the occasion of a girl's reaching her religious majority. Although R. Feinstein has some reservations about nonsynagogue celebrations of *bat mitzvah*[50] on the grounds that such celebrations, instituted by Reform and Conservative congregations, have their origins in Christian confirmation ceremonies, he does not proscribe them, and most twentieth-century halachic authorities permit them.[51]

The talmudic authority and educator R. Jehiel Jacob Weinberg of Montreux (1885–1966) writes in *Seridei Eish:*

> Sound pedagogical principles require that we celebrate a girl's reaching the age of obligation to fulfill *mitzvot*. Discrimination against girls in celebrating the attainment of maturity has an adverse effect upon the self-respect of the maturing girl who in other respects already enjoys the privileges of so-called women's liberation.
>
> Though I am inclined to permit the celebration of a *Bat Mitzvah*, I agree with Rabbi Moses Feinstein that it should not be held in the synagogue, even at night when unoccupied. Let it be held in a private home or in a hall adjacent to the synagogue, provided the rabbi delivers a discourse exhorting the celebrant to properly discharge her religious obligations. . . .
>
> Under such conditions there is ample reason to permit the celebration. . . . Since . . . most . . . in the community are in favor of such a celebration . . . ensure that it truly fortifies the spirit of Torah and *mitzvot* in the hearts of Jewish daughters.[52]

There is some diversity of practice regarding *bat mitzvah* customs among Jews today. In the United States, *bat mitzvah* is celebrated primarily among the more modern elements of the Orthodox sector and among Reform and Conservative Jews. In Israel, most secular and nonobservant Jews do not have *bat mitzvah* celebrations. Such celebrations, however, conducted mostly in the home, are common among observant Jews.

On the day that she attains her majority, it is customary for the *bat mitzvah* to don a new dress and recite a *Sheheheyanu*,[53] the blessing recited on special occasions.

Notes

INTRODUCTION

1. R. Samson Raphael Hirsch, *Judaism Eternal*, vol. 1 (London: Soncino, 1959), 50.
2. Charles-Louis de Montesquieu, *The Spirit of Laws* (London, 1750).
3. Aristotle, *Generation of Animals*, trans. A. L. Peck (Cambridge: Harvard University Press, 1943), 406.
4. Aristotle, *Politics and Poetics*, trans. B. Jowett and T. Twining, Book 7 (New York: Viking Press, 1957), 203.
5. Aristotle, *Generation of Animals*, 133.
6. I Timothy 2:11–12; I Corinthians 14:34–35.
7. I Timothy 2:15.
8. I Corinthians 11:3, 7:9.
9. Genesis 1:27.
10. Gospel of the Egyptians, Strom III, 963.
11. The Gospel of Thomas.
12. Augustine, *On the Sermon on the Mount* 1:15 and 1:41.
13. George H. Tavard, *Women in Christian Tradition* (Notre Dame and London: University of Notre Dame Press, 1973), 68.
14. Q. in Mary Daly, *The Church and the Second Sex* (New York: Harper and Row, 1975), 87.
15. Q. in Julia O'Faolain and Lauro Martines, *Not in God's Image* (New York: Harper, 1973), 130.
16. *Summa Theologiae* I.
17. Ibid., I, 92.
18. Martin Luther, "The Table Talk," trans. and ed. T. G. Tappart, in *Luther's Works*, vol. 54 (Philadelphia, 1967), 8, 25, 171.

19. George Foot Moore, *Judaism in the First Centuries of the Christian Era*, vol. 2 (New York: Schocken Books, 1971), 126.

20. Ibid., 131 and n. 3 ad loc.

21. Simone de Beauvoir, *The Second Sex*, trans. and ed. H. M. Parshley (New York: Alfred Knopf, 1972), 16.

22. Leviticus 19:18.

23. *Avot* 3:13.

24. *Yevamot* 79a; *Numbers Rabbah* 8; see *Yalkut* 889.

25. *Avot* 1:2.

26. Micah 6:8.

27. Micah 7:18.

28. See *Yalkut* 874.

29. See *Avot d'Rabbi Nathan* 4.

30. *Genesis Rabbah* 8.

31. *Sotah* 14a.

32. *JT Nedarim* 9:4.

33. *Tosefta, Pe'ah* 4; *Yalkut* 859.

34. See Proverbs 21:21; *Shabbat* 104a.

35. In the most authoritative study identifying biology as the predominant source for behavioral differences, Stanford University psychologists Eleanor Maccoby and Carol Jacklin, in their book *The Psychology of Sex Differences* (Stanford: Stanford University Press, 1974), analyze more than 1,400 studies relating to the differences between the sexes and determine that biological factors underlie the main behavioral differences between men and women.

36. See Anne Moir and David Jessel, *Brain Sex: The Real Difference between Men and Women* (London: Michael Joseph, 1989), 14.

37. See R. Restak, *The Brain: The Last Frontier* (New York: Doubleday, 1979), 204; N. Geschwind and A. M. Galaburda, "Celebral Lateralization: Biological Mechanisms, Associations and Pathology," *Archives of Neurology*, No. 42, 428–459, 521–552, 634–654; Jeanette McGlone, "Sex Differences in Human Brain Assymetry: A Critical Survey," in *The Behavioral and Brain Sciences* 3 (1980): 215–263; Ralph Holloway and Christine de Lacoste-Utamsing, "Sexual Dimorphism in the Human *Corpus allosum*," in *Science* 216 (June 25, 1982): 1431.

38. See Carl Degler, *In Search of Human Nature* (New York and Oxford: Oxford University Press, 1991), viii, 296.

39. See Doreen Kimura, "Are men's and women's brains really different?" in *Canadian Psychology* 28:2 (1987): 133–147.

40. Carol Gilligan, *In a Different Voice: Psychological Theory and Women's Development* (Cambridge: Harvard University Press, 1982).

41. Ibid., 100.

42. Immanuel Kant, Q. in Carol McMillan, *Women, Reason and Nature* (Princeton: Princeton University Press: 1982), 23.

43. Melford E. Spiro, *Gender and Culture: Kibbutz Women Revisited* (New York and London: Harcourt, Brace, Jovanovich, 1975), 57.

44. Alexis de Tocqueville, *Democracy in America*, vol. II (New York: Vintage Press, 1945), 209, 219.

45. Sylvia Ann Hewlett, *When the Bough Breaks* (New York: Basic Books, 1991), 279.

46. Emma Goldman, "The Tragedy of Women's Emancipation," in Alex Kates Shulman, ed., *Red Emma Speaks: Selected Writings and Speeches by Emma Goldman* (New York: Vintage, 1972), in Alice S. Rossi, *The Feminist Papers* (New York and London: Columbia University Press, 1973), 508–516.

47. Tamar Frankiel, *The Voice of Sarah* (San Francisco: HarperCollins, 1990), xi–xii.

CHAPTER 1

1. I am indebted to R. Moshe Meiselman's celebrated study, *Jewish Woman in Jewish Law* (New York: Ktav, 1978), for some of the concepts in this chapter.
2. *Midrash Tanhuma, Tazria* 5.
3. Psalms 111:10.
4. See R. Samson Raphael Hirsch, *Commentary*, Exodus 20:2.
5. Leviticus 26:12.
6. Deuteronomy 6:4.
7. Deuteronomy 13:5. See *Rashi*.
8. The Midrash states: With reference to the verse, "You should walk after the Lord your God"–is it then possible for a man to walk after the Holy Presence? Is it not written that God is a consuming fire? However, what is meant is that one must emulate the attributes of the Holy One. Just as He clothes the naked . . . so should you do as well; just as He consoles the mourners . . . so should you do as well; just as He buries the dead . . . so should you do as well . . . His ways are acts of love, truth and charity, as it is written, "All the paths of the Lord are mercy and truth" . . . So should you follow after the qualities of God" (*Song of Songs Zutah* 1:25).
9. Micah 6:8.
10. Psalms 14:1.
11. *Tosefta, Shavuot* 3:5.
12. *Avot* 1:1
13. Jeremiah 7: 22–23.
14. Leviticus 10:1.
15. See S. R. Hirsch, *Commentary*, ad loc.
16. Ibid.
17. Ibid.
18. Isaiah 42:6, 49:6.
19. Genesis 1:27.

CHAPTER 2

1. For a fuller discussion of the ideas discussed here, see the author's book, *Love, Marriage and Family in Jewish Law and Tradition*, chap. 4, "The Jewish Idea of Love" (Northvale, NJ: Jason Aronson, 1992).
2. Grace Aguilar, *Vale of Cedars* (1850), chap. 34.
3. Leviticus 19:18.
4. *Sifra*, Leviticus 19:18; *Leviticus Rabbah* 24:7.

5. Deuteronomy 4:5, 6.
6. Deuteronomy 7:9; Daniel 9:4; Nehemiah 1:5.
7. Genesis 1:27 (twice), 9:6.
8. Leviticus 19:2.
9. Deuteronomy 13:5.
10. Genesis 3:21.
11. Deuteronomy 34:6.
12. Maimonides, *Moreh Nevuchim – The Guide for the Perplexed*, pt. 1, chap. 69 (London: Dover Publications, 1956), 104.
13. Q. in B. D. Boxer, *From the World of the Cabbalah* (New York: Philosophical Library, 1954), 79.
14. Q. in Martin Buber, *Tales of the Hasidim* (New York: Schocken, 1974), 227.
15. Genesis 5:2.
16. Genesis 2:18.
17. *Yevamot* 63a.
18. Genesis 5:2.
19. *Zohar*, ad loc.
20. *Genesis Rabbah* 11:6.
21. *Zohar, Kedoshim.*
22. *Zohar, Mishpatim.*
23. *Shevet Musar*, chap. 24.
24. *Igeret HaKodesh.*
25. *Genesis Rabbah* 17:1–2.
26. Genesis 2:18.
27. Ibid.
28. Deuteronomy 14:26.
29. Ezekiel 44:30.
30. Leviticus 17:11.
31. Isaiah 25:6.
32. Ecclesiastes 9:9.
33. Genesis 5:2.
34. Genesis 9:6.
35. Genesis 9:7.
36. Ruth 3:1.
37. *Sanhedrin* 22b, *Yevamot* 56b; see *Shabbat* 111a; *Gittin* 43b, *Kiddushin* 35a.
38. *Shulhan Aruch, Even HaEzer* 1:13.
39. Genesis 2:24.
40. Deuteronomy 22:13.
41. *Kiddushin* 2b.
42. Proverbs 3:17.
43. R. Meir Simha HaKohen, *Meshech Hochmah* to Genesis 9:7.
44. See *Shabbat* 111a.
45. Genesis 1:27–28.
46. *Gittin* 41b.
47. Isaiah 45:18.
48. *JT Yevamot*, end of chap. 6.
49. *Tosafot* to *Gittin* 41b.
50. Maimonides, *Yad, Isurei Be'ah* 21:26; Maimonides, *Yad, Ishut* 15:2.

51. *Shulhan Aruch, Even HaEzer* 1:13.
52. *Yad, Isurei Be'ah* 21:25; *Shulhan Aruch, Even HaEzer* 1:13 and *Rama.*
53. *Yevamot* 113a.
54. Genesis 30:1.
55. *Yevamot* 65b; Maimonides, *Yad, Ishut* 15:10.
56. Maimonides, *Yad, Ishut* 15:10.
57. David S. Shapiro, "Be Fruitful and Multiply," in *Studies in Jewish Thought* (New York: Yeshiva University Press, 1975), 384.
58. The principle usually relates to the giving and raising of moneys for charity.
59. *Bava Batra* 9a.
60. *Hiddushei HaRan, Kiddushin* 41a; see *Teshuvot HaRan* 32.
61. *Hagigah* 2b.
62. *Nedarim* 64b; *Genesis Rabbah* 20.
63. *Shabbat* 31a.
64. *Yevamot* 61b–62a; Maimonides, *Yad, Ishut* 15:4; *Shulhan Aruch, Even HaEzer* 1:5.
65. See *Avot* 1:2.
66. *Yevamot* 61b–62a.
67. *Zohar III*, 7a.
68. See Psalms 30:11, 89:20, 121:2.
69. Genesis 2:1.
70. *Niddah* 45b.
71. Genesis 2:23.
72. Genesis 2:24.
73. *Sforno* to Genesis 2:24.
74. *Ecclesiastes Rabbah* 4.

CHAPTER 3

1. *Shabbat* 62a.
2. See *Akedat Yitzhak* to Genesis 30:1.
3. Although it is impossible to arrange for a pure, culture-free environment where the behavior of men and women can be studied under optimal, scientifically controlled conditions, the Israel kibbutz is probably the best such model available, recognized as the most rigorously egalitarian social experiment undertaken anywhere. This experiment has been examined in a number of studies, most notably by sociologist Melford E. Spiro in *Kibbutz: Venture in Utopia* (Cambridge: Harvard University Press, 1955 and 1971), *Children of the Kibbutz* (Cambridge: Harvard University Press, 1958 and 1965), and *Gender and Culture: Kibbutz Women Revisited* (New York: Shocken Books, 1980); and by Lion Tiger and Joseph Shepfer in *Women in the Kibbutz* (New York and London: Harcourt, Brace, Jovanovich, 1975). The ultimate goal of the kibbutz movement was to create a radically new socialistic, moral society of total equality, where communal commitment was to be the dominant mode of social relations, and radical egalitarianism, both social and economic, was to be practiced.

The men and women founders of the new kibbutz society rejected any notions of biological differentiation between males and females and decided to set up a new system of genuine equality between the sexes. Women were to be fully emancipated, through a sweeping transformation of some of the major institutions and practices of society–education, marriage, economic dependence on a husband, ties to home and housework, the care and rearing of children, the education of women–and a radical transformation in the traditional system of relationships between the sexes, marriage, the family, and sex-role differentiation.

Men and women could choose to work in the fields, with animals, with machinery, in administrative positions, or in the kitchen, laundry, or nursery–all these communal responsibilities being equally incumbent upon men and women.

The family, as the major obstacle to female emancipation, was to be destroyed. Kibbutz members reared their children communally in a totally egalitarian manner specifically designed to minimize sexual differences in behavior and experiences. The children lived and socialized with one another, though they could visit with or be visited by their parents. Boys and girls ate, slept, and showered together, played with the same toys and games, sang the same songs, participated in the same activities in age-graded children's houses, and were totally sexually integrated and undifferentiated. The children were reared in a unified environment by modern child-education experts who were trained in rigorous, kibbutz-sponsored teacher-education courses. They were taught egalitarian values from infancy. Considerable care was taken not to inculcate any sexual differences, and kibbutz children grew up with virtually interchangeable roles.

It was expected that after several generations all sexual differentiation would disappear and a new society would arise that would be sexually neutral and totally egalitarian, in which the woman would be truly emancipated from the sexual, economic, social, and intellectual shackles of modern society.

After four generations, women on the kibbutz have effected a counterrevolution. In opposition to the men on the kibbutz, women choose stereotypically women's occupations and professions, finding this to be most natural for them as women. Moreover, it is the younger women, who were reared on socialist and egalitarian ideology and exposed to the winds of the feminist movement, who do not view sex-role differentiation as a mark of sexual inequality, who are pressing for the return of kibbutz women to traditional "woman's work." Almost all kibbutzim have become "familized," with children taken out of the kibbutz children's houses and placed back in their homes, where they eat and sleep.

Concludes Melford Spiro:

"If, according to received cultural interpretations, sexual differences in behavior are determined by culture, how are we to explain these important differences between . . . boys and girls who . . . were raised in the same learning environment, whose socialization had been uniform, who had been taught the same play and games, and whose socializers (parents and nursery teachers) were committed to the abolition of sex differences in behavior? Since, in this kind of cultural regime, it would be unlikely for these differences to have been culturally determined, it is much more likely that they were determined by precultural motivational differences between the sexes. The kibbutz experience lends support to the thesis that . . . many of the sex differences that are universally found in human societies are a consequence not so much of cultural predetermination as of precultural motivational differences between the sexes" [*Kibbutz Women Revisited*, 76].

The kibbutz experiment has shown that women, provided with free choice, usually select work, education, careers, and places in society in areas traditionally associated with females. The female counterrevolution has been accomplished by kibbutz women in spite of, and in opposition to, an egalitarian culture, and an environment totally committed to egalitarian values and life-style, in which feminist values were inculcated since childhood. It came about as a result of the conclusion by women that such an ideology is fundamentally contrary to the innate nature of women and is harmful to them.

The younger kibbutz women decided that they wanted to be liberated from what they found to be a restricting, socially imposed straitjacket that insisted that their natural feminine nature can be artificially altered by education and an externally imposed cultural determinism, and that in order to have sexual equality they must behave like men. They decided that in order to attain their human potential and to live fulfilling lives in dignity as women they must live in accordance with their inherent feminine nature. As a direct result of the kibbutz experiment, gender polarization and differentiation are even more pronounced in the kibbutz than they are in general Israeli society.

4. Tamar Frankiel, *The Voice of Sarah* (San Francisco: HarperCollins, 1990).

5. R. Samson Raphael Hirsch, *Judaism Eternal*, vol. 2 (London: Soncino, 1959), 53–55.

6. S. R. Hirsch, *Collected Works* (German) (Frankfurt: I. Kaufmann, 1902), 297, q. in Leo Levi, *Man and Woman, The Torah Perspective* (Jerusalem: Ezer Layeled, 1980), 28–29.

7. *Pesikta Rabbati* 45.

8. Micah 6:8.

9. *Ketubot* 67b; *JT Sotah* 3.

10. Psalms 45:14.

11. *Rashi*, ad loc.

12. *Bava Metzia* 87a.

13. Genesis 18:9.

14. *Rashi*, ad loc.

15. *Rashi* to Genesis 21:12.

16. *Genesis Rabbah* 18:3.

17. Ibid.

18. *Sanhedrin* 39a.

19. Ibid. 18:1.

20. *Niddah* 45b.; ibid.

21. *Bava Metzia* 59a.

22. See *Pirkei d'Rabbi Eliezer* 40.

23. The name Kartigna is made up of the Aramaic *karta* and the Greek *gyne*, woman.

24. *Pesikta d'Rav Kahana, Piksa* 9:1.

25. Ibid.

26. II Kings 4:9.

27. *Berachot* 10b.

28. *Zohar*, Leviticus 52.

29. *Bava Metzia* 87a.

30. *JT Ketubot* 5:6.

31. *Genesis Rabbah* 17:8.

32. *Ketubot* 67b.

33. *Eruvin* 21b.

34. *Sotah* 11b.

35. *Yevamot* 63a.
36. *Sifra, Ki Teitzei.*
37. *Exodus Rabbah* 28:2.
38. Numbers 14:4.
39. Numbers 27:4.
40. *Exodus Rabbah op. cit.*
41. *JT Pesahim* 4:1; *Pirkei d'Rabbi Eliezer* 45; *Menorat HaMaor* 131.
42. See *Leviticus Rabbah* 2:1, *Song of Songs Rabbah* 4:20.
43. *Rashi,* Numbers 26:64.
44. *Rashi,* II Kings 22:14.
45. *Megillah* 14b.
46. *Rashi,* II Kings 22:14.
47. *Taanit* 23a.
48. Proverbs 31:20.
49. *Taanit* 23b.
50. *Ketubot* 67b.
51. *Berachot* 10b.
52. *Mishnah, Makkot* 2:6.
53. *Sanhedrin* 43a.
54. *Midrash Mishlei,* Proverbs 31:1.
55. *JT Yevamot* 1:6, 3a.
56. *Genesis Rabbah* 17:7.
57. *Yevamot* 63a.
58. *Genesis Rabbah* 17; *Pirkei d'Rabbi Eliezer* 41.
59. See *Esther Rabbati* 3:10.
60. *Ketubot* 59b.
61. *Ketubot* 65a.
62. Ibid.
63. *Niddah* 45b.
64. Exodus 19:3.
65. *Exodus Rabbah* 28:2.
66. *Berachot* 17a.
67. *Reshit Hochmah, Perek Derech Eretz.*
68. Proverbs 1:8.
69. *Ibn Ezra,* ad loc.
70. Leviticus 19:3.
71. *Kiddushin* 29b.
72. *Niddah* 45b.
73. Exodus 19:3, see *Rashi*; *Exodus Rabbah* 28.
74. Exodus 32:1; see *Megillah* 25a.
75. *Pirkei d'Rabbi Eliezer* 45.
76. Exodus 32:2.
77. *Numbers Rabbah* 21.
78. Ibid.
79. Ibid.
80. S. R. Hirsch, *Judaism Eternal,* vol. 2 (London: Soncino, 1959), 92.
81. *Kiddushin* 82a.
82. *Bava Metzia* 59a.

83. *JT Shabbat* 6a.
84. *Kiddushin* 49b; *Berachot* 48b; *Genesis Rabbah* 70:10.
85. *Tohorot* 7:9.
86. *JT Pesahim* 1:4.
87. *Tohorot* 7:9.
88. *Ecclesiastes Rabbah* 7:46.
89. *Shabbat* 33b; *Kiddushin* 80b; *Rashi*, Genesis 3:15.
90. *Pesahim* 100b; *Sanhedrin* 67a; *JT Shabbat* 15:3; *Zohar* 1:126b; see *Avot* 2:7.
91. *Shabbat* 152a.
92. *Shabbat* 62a.
93. *Berachot* 31b.
94. *Shabbat* 117b, 153a; *Pesahim* 11a.
95. See *Ecclesiastes Rabbah* 5.
96. See *Shabbat* 117b, 153a; *Pesahim* 11a; *Midrash Tanhuma, Naso* 28.
97. *Genesis Rabbah* 8:5.
98. See *Berachot* 10b.
99. See *Bava Metzia* 87a.
100. See *Exodus Rabbah* 28:2.
101. See *Shabbat* 46b.
102. *Genesis Rabbah* 17; see *Nidah* 45b.
103. See *Numbers Rabbah* 21:11; *Pirkei d'Rabbi Eliezer* 45; *Pesikta Rabbati*, *"Ki Pakad HaShem et Hanah-Parah."*
104. See *Ketubot* 67b; *Eruvin* 21b.
105. *Rashi*, II Kings 22:14.
106. *Genesis Rabbah* 17.
107. *Shabbat* 151a.
108. *Menahot* 99b.
109. *Berachot* 24a.
110. See *Kiddushin* 35a.
111. *Sanhedrin* 28a, b.
112. See *JT Berachot* 9; *Yevamot* 62b, 63a; *Nedarim* 41a.
113. Genesis 5:1, 2.
114. Genesis 3:16, 17.
115. *Nedarim* 66b.
116. *Tana d'bei Eliyahu* 9; *Rama, Shulhan Aruch, Orah Hayim* 69:7.
117. Maimonides, *Yad, Ishut* 15:20. The *Shulhan Aruch* doesn't mention them, but *Rama, Shulhan Aruch, Orah Hayim* 69:7 refers to the statements in an appendix.
118. *Sanhedrin* 76a; Maimonides, *Yad, Ishut* 15:20.
119. *Mishnah, Ketubot* 13:10; *Ketubot* 110a–b; *Shulhan Aruch, Orah Hayim* 75:1–5.
120. Ibid.
121. I Peter 3:1.
122. Ephesians 5:22.
123. Ibid.
124. I Peter 3:1; I Timothy 2:12.
125. Genesis 2:18.
126. See I Timothy 2:11–15; 5:3–16.
127. A. E. Kitov, *The Jew and His Home*, trans. Nathan Bulman (New York: Shengold, 1963), 70.

128. *Bava Batra* 9a.
129. Ibid.
130. Isaiah 32:9.
131. *Berachot* 17a.
132. *Menorat HaMaor, Derech Eretz*, 4th Gate; see *Reshit Hochmah*, end.
133. From the daily morning blessings: *"Hanoten la-ya'ef ko'ah."*
134. *Sifra*, Leviticus 19:18; *Genesis Rabbah* 24:7.
135. Deuteronomy 6:5.
136. *Midrash Tanhuma, Shelah* 1.
137. *JT Yevamot* 1.
138. *Ketubot* 62b, 63a; *Nedarim* 50a.
139. Judges 4:4.
140. See *Rashi*, ad loc.
141. *The Hirsch Siddur* (Jerusalem and New York: Feldheim, 1978), 290.
142. George Foot Moore, *Judaism in the First Centuries of the Common Era*, vol. 2 (New York: Schocken Books, 1971), 126, 131 and n. 3.
143. Proverbs 31:10–31.

CHAPTER 4

1. Ruth 3:11.
2. Psalms 128:3.
3. Psalms 113:9.
4. Exodus 23:26; Deuteronomy 7:14.
5. Exodus 20:12.
6. Leviticus 19:3.
7. I Kings 2:19.
8. For a keen analysis of Sarah's spirituality, see Tamar Frankiel, *The Voice of Sarah* (New York and San Francisco: HarperCollins, 1990).
9. Genesis 21:12.
10. R. Samson Raphael Hirsch, *The Pentateuch* (Gateshead: Judaica Press, 1976), ad loc.
11. Genesis 16:2.
12. *Rashi*, ad loc.; see *Targum Jonathan ben Uziel*, ad loc.
13. See *Rashi*, Genesis 16:2.
14. Genesis 12:16.
15. *Genesis Rabbah* 41:2.
16. Ibid.
17. See Genesis 18:9 and *Rashi*.
18. See *Genesis Rabbah* 39:15.
19. Ibid.
20. Genesis 21:12.
21. *Niddah* 45b.
22. R. Samson Raphael Hirsch, *Judaism Eternal*, vol. 2 (London: Soncino, 1959), 68.
23. Genesis 24:67.
24. *Rashi*, ad loc.

25. *Judaism Eternal*, vol. 2, 75.
26. Genesis 30:22.
27. *Rashi*, ad loc.
28. Genesis 31:3–16.
29. *Genesis Rabbah* 85:2.
30. Genesis 38:25.
31. Ruth 4:18–21.
32. Ruth 4:22.
33. *Rashi*, Genesis 38:26.
34. Exodus 15:20; Numbers 12:6; Micah 6:4.
35. Judges 4:4.
36. Isaiah 8:3.
37. II Kings 22:14.
38. Nehemiah 6:14.
39. *Megillah* 14a.
40. Ibid.
41. Ibid.
42. Ibid.
43. *Midrash Tadsheh* 21.
44. Joel 3:1.
45. *Midrash Tanhuma*, Exodus 1; *Song of Songs Rabbah* 4:11.
46. Micah 6:4.
47. Ezekiel 13:17.
48. Judges 4:6–14.
49. See *Pesahim* 9b.
50. See II Kings 22:14–26; compare to Jeremiah 2:2, 5; 4:3; 6:9.
51. *Pesikta Rabbati*, 26:129.
52. See *Targum Jonathan*, II Kings 22:14, and *Ralbag* ad loc. *Rashi* adds that Huldah taught *Torah Shebaal Peh*, the Oral Torah, to the elders of the generation in a building on the Temple grounds to which the Huldah Gate to the Temple Mount led.
53. *Megillah* 14b.
54. II Kings 22:14–20.
55. Judges 4:4–15.
56. I Samuel 25:3; II Samuel 14:2, 20:21–2.
57. Exodus 1:22.
58. *Sotah* 12a-13a; see *Bava Batra* 120a.
59. Exodus 1:15–17.
60. *Sotah* 11b.
61. Exodus 2:2–8.
62. *Sotah* 11b.
63. Exodus 15:20–21.
64. *Avot* 5:6.
65. *Taanit* 9a.
66. *Bava Batra* 17a.
67. *Sanhedrin* 109b.
68. See Exodus 37:2, 8.
69. *Numbers Rabbah* 21:10.
70. Ibid.

71. Joshua 15:19; Judges 1:15.
72. Judges 4:17–24.
73. Judges 5:24.
74. *Rashi*, ad loc.
75. *Midrash Tehillim.*
76. Judges 5:1–31.
77. *Zohar*, Leviticus 19b.
78. I Samuel 1:13.
79. I Samuel 2:1–10.
80. Ruth 1:16.
81. See *Igeret Shmuel.*
82. Ruth explained that she and her mother-in-law are forced to sell the property they inherited from her husband Elimelech, and as their kinsman and redeemer it is Boaz's obligation, in accordance with Jewish tradition deriving from Leviticus 25, to buy the property to assure that it will remain in the family.
83. Since children are the prime means for a person to perpetuate himself, when a married man dies childless and there is no one who will perpetuate his memory, it is a duty of his brother, in accordance with Deuteronomy 25:5–6, to marry the widow and raise up children in her late husband's name, so that through this marriage the brother's name and memory will live on. When there are circumstances that make such a marriage impractical, the Torah provides the means, through a ceremony called *halitzah*, to nullify levirate marriage.
84. Ruth 3:10.
85. Esther 4:14.
86. The Book of Judith 15:10.
87. *Shabbat* 23a.
88. Frankiel, 34–36.
89. Judith 10:19.
90. Judith 9:1–14.
91. Frankiel, 35. Frankiel refers to R. Meir Zlotowitz in *ArtScroll Tanach Series, Genesis* (New York: ArtScroll, 1978), 835, who, citing the *Ramban*, says that the *Mishkan*, the holy Tabernacle, "was meant to be a replica of the Jewish home–not *vice-versa*. Sarah's tent was the Temple upon which God placed His Presence. The *Mishkan* was built to recapture that eminence."

The analogy between the Jewish home and the Temple is not, however, the same as that of the woman's body to the Temple. Nevertheless, Jewish tradition does refer to the necessity of the Jew to keep his body holy, and the *Baal Shem Tov* said that a Jew should strive to become as holy as a Torah.

92. Frankiel, 36.
93. *Taanit* 23a.
94. See *Megillat Taanit* 11, "King Yannai had a good wife. . . ."
95. *Kiddushin* 66a.
96. See *Berachot* 48a; *Genesis Rabbah* 91:3.
97. See *Kiddushin* 66a.
98. *Mishnah, Nazir* 3:6.
99. *Sukkah* 2b.
100. *Tosefta, Sukkah* 1:1.
101. See *Bava Batra* 11a; *JT Pe'ah* 1:1.

102. *Bava Batra*, ibid.; see also *Tosefta, Pe'ah* 4:18.
103. Josephus, *Antiquities of the Jews* 20:49, ff.
104. See also Josephus, ibid., 20:95, *Wars of the Jews* 5:55, 119, 147.
105. *Ketubot* 53a; *Nedarim* 50a.
106. *JT Shabbat* 6:1; *JT Sotah* 9:16.
107. *Shabbat* 25b.
108. *Pesahim* 49b.
109. *Nedarim* 50a.
110. *Avot d'Rabbi Nathan*, chap. 6.
111. *Nedarim*, ibid.
112. *Ran*, ad loc.
113. *JT Shabbat* 6:1; *JT Sotah* 9:16.
114. *Avot d'Rabbi Nathan*, Chap. 6, 15a.
115. *Ketubot* 62b–63a; *Nedarim* 50a.
116. *Pesahim* 62b.
117. "Correctly did Bruria rule." *Tosefta, Kelim* 1:6.
118. *Berachot* 10a.
119. *Eruvin* 53b.
120. *Rashi, Avodah Zarah* 18b, *"Ve'ika de'amri mishum maaseh deBruriah."*
121. Psalms 104:35.
122. *Berachot* 10a.
123. *Yoma* 47a; *JT Megillah* 1:12, 72a; *Midrash Rabbah, Vayikra* 20:11.
124. *Bava Metzia* 59b.
125. *Shabbat* 116a–b; see *Rashi*.
126. *Kiddushin* 70a–b; *Niddah* 20b; *Hullin* 109b; *Berachot* 51b.
127. *Taanit* 23b.

CHAPTER 5

1. Hersh Goldwurm, ed., *The Rishonim* (New York: Mesorah Publications, 1982); *Encyclopaedia Judaica* (Jerusalem: Keter, 1972), 13:1559.
2. As related in *Sivuv*, the twelfth-century travelogue of R. Petahiah of Regensburg.
3. Genesis 35:8.
4. *Meneket Rivkah* (Prague, 1609), introduction.
5. Cecil Roth, in *Oxford Slavonic Papers* 9 (1960): 8–20; C. Roth, *History of the Jews in Venice* (Philadelphia: Jewish Publication Society, 1930), 94; *Encyclopaedia Judaica* (1970), 3:732.
6. Introduction to *Derishah Uperishah*.
7. *Magen Avraham* to *Tur, Yoreh De'ah* 263:12.
8. *Dagul MeRevavah* to *Tur, Yoreh De'ah* 263:12.
9. Numbers 32:41.
10. *Encyclopaedia Judaica* (Jerusalem: Keter, 1972), 4:204.
11. See *Yoreh De'ah* 326:4.
12. Deuteronomy 33:2.
13. Isaac Alfasi, *HaHasidut* (Tel Aviv: Maariv, 1974), 31.
14. Ibid.

15. Ibid.

16. Ibid., 241.

17. Ibid.; Menachem M. Brayer, *The Jewish Woman in Rabbinic Literature: A Psycho-historical Perspective*, vol. 2 (Hoboken, NJ: Ktav Publishing House, 1986), 45–46.

18. Alfasi, 241.

19. Ibid.

20. Ibid.

21. Ibid.

22. Ibid.

23. Ibid.

24. Ibid.

25. Ibid.

26. Ibid.; *Encyclopaedia Judaica* (1972), 11:553.

27. H. Graetz, *History of the Jews*, vol. 4 (Philadelphia: The Jewish Publication Society of America, 1894), 409.

28. C. Roth, *The Jews in the Renaissance* (Philadelphia: The Jewish Publication Society of America, 1959), 54.

29. Ibid.

30. Ibid.

31. Ibid.

32. Ibid.

33. Oded Avissar, *Sefer Teveriah* (Jerusalem: Keter, 1973), 316.

34. Ibid.

35. Graetz, 4:576.

36. Ibid.

37. Ibid. 4:318

38. Ibid.

39. Ibid., 4:596, 610.

40. Ibid., 4:571.

41. Cecil Roth, *House of Nasi: Dona Gracia* (London, 1947), 105–106, 202.

42. Cecil Roth, *The Jews in the Renaissance* (Philadelphia: The Jewish Publication Society of America, 1959), 50.

43. Ibid.

44. Ibid.

45. Ibid., 51.

46. Ibid.

47. Ibid.

48. Ibid.

49. Graetz, 5:69.

50. Graetz, 5:70.

51. Franz Kobler, *A Treasury of Jewish Letters*, vol. 2 (New York: Farrar, Straus and Young, 1952), 442–447.

52. *The Life of Gluckel of Hameln, 1646–1724, Written by Herself*, trans. from the original Yiddish and ed. Beth-Zion Abrahams (New York: Thomas Yoseloff, 1963), 2–3.

53. Deuteronomy 30:19.

54. Deuteronomy 30:20.

55. Leviticus 19:18.

56. Sonia L. Lipman, "Judith Montefiore – First Lady of Anglo-Jewry," in *The Jewish Historical Society of England, Transactions* 21 (1962–1967): 302.

57. Nahum Slouschz, *The Renaissance of Hebrew Literature*, trans. Henrietta Szold, from the French (Philadelphia: Jewish Publication Society, 1909), 82–84.

58. Ibid., 84.

59. Vittorio Castiglione, *Ugav Rachel*, Rachel (1890).

60. David Philipson, *Letters of Rebecca Gratz* (Philadelphia: Jewish Publication Society, 1929), xxiv.

61. Deuteronomy 6:4.

62. See F. Modder, *The Jew in the Literature of England* (1939); A. S. Isaacs, *Young Champion, One Year in Grace Aguilar's Girlhood* (1933).

63. Grace Aguilar, *The Spirit of Judaism* (Cincinnati: Bloch Publishing, 1842), 10–11.

64. Ibid., Preface.

65. Grace Aguilar, *Women of Israel* (New York: D. Appleton and Co., 1854), Preface.

66. Grace Aguilar, *Amete and Yafe.*

67. Gustav Karpeles, "Women in Jewish Literature," in *Jewish Literature and Other Essays* (Philadelphia: Jewish Publication Society of America, 1895).

68. H. E. Jacob, *The World of Emma Lazarus* (New York: Schocken Books, 1949), 178–179.

69. Ibid., 94–96.

70. Karpeles, "Women in Jewish Literature."

71. Jacob, *The World of Emma Lazarus*, 89–90.

72. Ibid., 92–93.

73. Ibid., 89.

74. Ibid., 124.

75. Emma Lazarus, *The Valley of Baca.*

76. Emma Lazarus, *Songs of a Semite* (New York, 1882).

77. Jacob, *The World of Emma Lazarus*, 204.

78. Brayer, *The Jewish Woman in Rabbinic Literature*, 2:172.

CHAPTER 6

1. Exodus 15:16.

2. *Avot* 6:10.

3. *Kiddushin* 2a.

4. See *Kiddushin* 2b.

5. *Kiddushin* 2b; Maimonides, *Yad, Ishut* 4:1; *Shulhan Aruch, Even HaEzer* 42:1.

6. Maimonides, *Yad, Ishut* 3:19; see *Kiddushin* 41a, 81a.

7. *Yevamot* 62b.

8. Maimonides, *Yad, Ishut* 15:19.

9. Maimonides, *Yad, Ishut* 12:1.

10. Maimonides, *Yad, Ishut* 12:2.

11. Maimonides, *Yad, Ishut* 12:2 see *Shulhan Aruch, Even HaEzer* 69:1.

12. *Shulhan Aruch, Even HaEzer* 15:3, based on *Ketubot* 80b.

13. Maimonides, *Yad, Ishut*, 2:3; see *Shulhan Aruch, Even HaEzer* 69:1.

14. *Ketubot* 58b; Maimonides, *Yad, Ishut*, 12:4; *Shulhan Aruch, Even HaEzer* 69:4.

15. Maimonides, *Yad, Ishut* 12:4.

16. See *Ketubot* 58b.
17. *Pesahim* 50b.
18. See Maimonides, *Yad, Ishut* 10:7.
19. *Bava Kama* 89a; Maimonides, *Yad, Ishut* 10:10.
20. See *Shabbat* 14b; see *Ketubot* 82b.
21. *Ketubot* 10a.
22. See R. Samson Raphael Hirsch, *The Pentateuch*, trans. Isaac Levy (Gateshead: Judaica Press, 1976), Exodus 22:16.
23. *Ketubot* 82b.
24. From the text of the *ketubah*.
25. See *Ketubot* 11a, 39b, 54a; see *Yevamot* 89a.
26. *Ketubot*, ibid: *Yevamot*, ibid.
27. *Ketubot* 57a.
28. In the Greek form of Tobit (only several fragments of the original Hebrew or Aramaic versions of Tobit were found among the Dead Sea Scrolls at Qumran) the word "paper" is *biblion*, which means scroll or letter, and the word for "contract" is *syggraphon*, or "that which is written," a literal translation of "*ketubah*."
29. Tobit 7:13–15.
30. Known as Aswan Papyrus G.
31. See Yigael Yadin, *Bar Kokhba* (New York: Randon House, 1971), 222–223.
32. Ibid.
33. *Ketubot* 10a, R. Simon ben Gamliel; *Ketubot* 56b, R. Meir; see *Ketubot* 110b; *Rashi, Ketubot* 10a, "*Hachamim*"; *Tosafot, Ketubot* 10a, "*Amar*"; *Tosafot, Yevamot* 89a, "*Tamah*"; *Sefer Mitzvot Gadol, Asin* 48. The predominant view, however, is that the *ketubah* is ordained by rabbinic legislation. This is the opinion of R. Nahum, R. Samuel, R. Simon ben Elazar, and others (*Ketubot* 10a, 56b). See *Hidushei HaRan, Sanhedrin* 31b; Maimonides, *Yad, Ishut* 10:7; *Helkat Mehokek* 66:26.
34. Exodus 21:10.
35. See Isaiah 36:11; II Kings 18:26.
36. *Ketubot* 82b.
37. *Shabbat* 14b; *Ketubot* 82b.
38. *Ketubot* 11a, 39b, 54a; *Yevamot* 89a.
39. *Rama, Shulhan Aruch, Even HaEzer* 119:6.
40. See I Peter 3:1; I Timothy 2:12; I Corinthians 11:3, 7, 9; 14:34; Ephesians 5:22.

CHAPTER 7

1. For a more extensive treatment of Judaism and sexuality, see the author's book, *Love, Marriage, and Family in Jewish Law and Tradition* (Northvale, NJ: Jason Aronson, 1992), chaps. 5, 6, 10.
2. See *Ketubot* 8a, 48a; *Genesis Rabbah* 49:7.
3. *Kiddushin* 2b.
4. Genesis 38:21–22; Deuteronomy 23:18; Hosea 4:14.
5. R. Samson Raphael Hirsch, *The Pentateuch*, trans. Isaac Levy (Gateshead: Judaica Press, 1976), Leviticus 19:2.
6. Ibid., Genesis 4:7.

7. Leviticus 18:22.
8. Leviticus 20:13.
9. *Sifra* 19:18; Maimonides, *Yad, Isurei Be'ah* 22:2.
10. Leviticus 18:3.
11. Ibid.
12. Ibid.
13. Maimonides, *Yad, Isurei Be'ah,* 22:2.
14. *Bava Metzia* 84a; see *Sanhedrin* 7a.
15. *Yevamot* 61a.
16. *Pesahim* 72b; see *Tosafot, Yevamot* 65a, *"Shebeino"*; see Nahmanides to Exodus 21:10; see also Maimonides, *Yad, Ishut* 12:2, 15:1; *Tur, Even HaEzer* 77:5.
17. *Magid Mishneh* to Maimonides, *Yad, Ishut* 15:1.
18. *Exodus* 21:10; see *Ketubot* 47b, 48a, 59b, 61a, 66b; *Bava Metzia* 59a; *Hullin* 84a; *Yevamot* 62b; *Nedarim* 15b; *Sefer HaMitzvot, Lo Taaseh* 262; *Sefer Mitzvot Gadol* 81; *Sefer Mitzvot Katan* 277–278; *Sefer HaHinuch* 246; Maimonides, *Yad, Ishut* 12:25; *Shulhan Aruch, Even HaEzer* 70, 73, 76.
19. *Igeret HaKodesh.*
20. *Shulhan Aruch, Orah Hayim* 240:1.
21. Deuteronomy 24:5.
22. Exodus 21:10.
23. *Yevamot* 62a.
24. *Baalei HaNefesh, Shaar HaKedushah* (Jerusalem: Masorah, 1955), 139.
25. Maimonides, *Yad, Ishut* 15:18.
26. *Nedarim* 20b; Maimonides, *Yad, Ishut* 15:18; *Isurei Be'ah* 21:9.
27. *Eruvin* 100b; Maimonides, *Yad, Ishut* 15:17; *De'ot* 5:4; *Isurei Be'ah* 21:11; *Shulhan Aruch, Even HaEzer* 25:2; *Orah Hayim* 240.
28. Maimonides, *Yad, Ishut* 15:17.
29. *Eruvin* 100b; Maimonides, *Yad, Ishut* 15:17.
30. See *Magen Avraham* to *Shulhan Aruch, Orah Hayim* 240:7; *Shitah Mekubetzet, Nedarim* 20b.
31. Deuteronomy 24:5.
32. *Pesahim* 72b; see R. S. R. Hirsch, *The Pentateuch,* Deuteronomy 24:5; *Sefer HaHinuch* 582.
33. Exodus 21:10.
34. Deuteronomy 24:5.
35. See *Pesahim* 72b.
36. Deuteronomy 24:5.
37. Exodus 21:10.
38. *Semak* in *Amudei Golah, Mitzvah* 285, ed. Ralberg (New York, 1959), 316.
39. See *Sotah* 22b; *Bava Metzia* 84a; *Sanhedrin* 7a; *JT Sotah* 3:4.
40. David M. Feldman, *Health and Medicine in the Jewish Tradition* (New York: Crossroad, 1987), 62.
41. Ibid.
42. *Ketubot* 62a; *Shulhan Aruch, Orah Hayim* 240:1; Maimonides, *Yad, Ishut* 14:1; see also *Shulhan Aruch, Even HaEzer* 76:1.
43. Maimonides, *Yad, Ishut* 14:1; *Shulhan Aruch, Even HaEzer* 76:1.
44. Maimonides, ibid.; *Shulhan Aruch,* ibid.; see *Igrot Moshe, Even HaEzer* 3:28.
45. Maimonides, *Yad, Ishut* 14:7; *Shulhan Aruch, Even HaEzer* 76:16.

46. *Ketubot* 62b; Maimonides, *Yad Ishut*, 14:7; *Shulhan Aruch, Even HaEzer* 76:16.
47. Maimonides, *Yad, Ishut* 14:7; *Shulhan Aruch, Even HaEzer* 76:5.
48. See *Ketubot* 61b; *Shulhan Aruch, Even HaEzer* 76:5, 76:7 and commentaries.
49. Maimonides, *Yad, Ishut* 14:2; *Shulhan Aruch, Even HaEzer* 76:5.
50. Maimonides, ibid; *Shulhan Aruch*, ibid.
51. *Rama, Shulhan Aruch, Even HaEzer* 76:5.
52. *Eruvin*, 100b; *Shulhan Aruch, Even HaEzer* 76:4.
53. *Ketubot* 62b; Maimonides, *Yad, Ishut* 14:2 *Tur, Even HaEzer* 76:5.
54. Maimonides, *Yad, Ishut* 15:10.
55. Ibid.
56. *Ketubot* 63a; Maimonides, *Yad, Ishut* 14:15, and *Magid Mishneh* thereto; *Shulhan Aruch, Even HaEzer* 77:1.
57. *Ketubot*, ibid.; Maimonides and *Magid Mishneh*, ibid.; *Shulhan Aruch*, ibid.
58. Ibid.
59. Maimonides, *Yad, Ishut* 14:8.
60. *Kiddushin* 19b; *Ketubot* 36a; Maimonides, *Yad, Ishut*, 12:7; *Shulhan Aruch, Even HaEzer* 38:5.
61. *Ketubot* 61b; Maimonides, *Yad, Ishut* 14:6.
62. Maimonides, *Yad, Ishut* 14:7.
63. *Nedarim* 20b; *Shulhan Aruch, Orah Hayim* 240:2.
64. Maimonides, *Yad, Isurei Be'ah* 21:12; *Shulhan Aruch, Even HaEzer* 25:10.
65. *Gittin* 90a; Maimonides, *Yad, Isurei Be'ah* 21:12; *Gerushin* 10:21; *Shulhan Aruch, Even HaEzer* 25:8.
66. Maimonides, *Yad, Isurei Be'ah* 21:12; *Shulhan Aruch, Even HaEzer* 25:8.
67. *Nedarim* 20b; *Shulhan Aruch, Orah Hayim* 240:10.
68. R. Jacob Emden, *Siddur Bet Yaakov* (Lemberg: Balaban Press, 1904), 159a.
69. See *Baalei HaNefesh*.
70. *Pesahim* 72b.
71. Maimonides, *Yad, De'ot* 5:4.
72. See *Orhot Tzadikim, Shaar HaSimhah*; Maimonides, *Yad, Ishut* 14:7.
73. *Eruvin* 100b; *Nedarim* 20b; Maimonides, *Yad, De'ot* 5:4.
74. Maimonides, *Yad, Isurei Be'ah* 21:12; *De'ot* 5:4; *Shulhan Aruch, Even HaEzer* 25:9.
75. Maimonides, *Yad, De'ot* 5:4.
76. Ibid.
77. *Yevamot* 62b; *Rashi, Pesahim* 72b, "*Lesameah*"; *Shulhan Aruch, Orah Hayim* 240:1.
78. *Pesahim* 72b.
79. *Rashi, Pesahim* 72b, "*Lesameah*"; see *Shulhan Aruch, Even HaEzer* 25.
80. Maimonides, *Yad; Isurei Be'ah* 21:9; see also *Rama, Even HaEzer* 25:7.
81. *Teshuvot MaHarit* and *Mitzvot HaBayit*, q. by R. Joseph Epstein, *Mitzvot Habayit* vol. 2 (New York: Torat HaAdam, 1981), *Kuntres Mishpat HaIshut*, 28.
82. *Eruvin* 100b.
83. Ibid.
84. Ibid.
85. Ibid.
86. Maimonides, *Yad, Isurei Be'ah* 21:13.
87. See *Genesis Rabbah* 17:8.
88. *Eruvin* 100b.

89. *Tur, Orah Hayim* 240; Maimonides, *Yad, Ishut* 15:17.
90. Based on *Pesahim* 72b; see *Shulhan Aruch, Orah Hayim* 240:1; see *Mishnah Berurah*; see R. Shlomo Wolbe, *Hoveret Hadrachah Lehatanim*, 26.
91. *Nedarim* 20b and *Ran* thereto; Maimonides, *Yad, De'ot* 5:4.
92. *Igeret Hakodesh, Baalei HaNefesh, Siddur Bet Yaakov*, 159.
93. *MaHaram* of Lublin, *Responsum* #53; see *Eruvin* 100b.
94. *Pesahim* 49b.
95. *Igeret HaKodesh*, chap. 6.
96. See *Zohar, Kedoshim* 24.
97. *Siddur Bet Yaakov* 158a–159a.
98. *Be'er Yehudah* to Maimonides, *Yad, De'ot* 5:4.
99. *Ramban* to Deuteronomy 22:24.
100. See *Ezer Mekudash* to *Shulhan Aruch, Even HaEzer* 25:7.
101. See *Nedarim* 20a and *Rosh* thereto and *Shitah Mekubetzet* thereto; see also *Tur, Orah Hayim* 240 and commentaries.
102. See Shabbat 140b; see *Rashi* and *Meiri* thereto; see *Lehem Mishneh* to Maimonides, *Yad, Ishut* 15:18.
103. *Ketubot* 48a; see *Ritvah, Ketubot* 47b; *Shulhan Aruch, Even HaEzer* 76:13, and *Rama, Bet Shmuel*, and *Helkat Mehokek*.
104. Exodus 21:10.
105. *Ramban*, Exodus 21:10.
106. *Masechet Kalah* 1; *Shitah Mekubetzet, Nedarim* 20b.
107. See *Menorat HaMaor, Ner III*, rule 6, pt. 5, chap. 2, 178.
108. *Temurah* 17a.
109. *Bava Batra* 10b.
110. *Berachot* 60a; *Niddah* 31a.
111. *Igeret HaKodesh*.
112. *Menorat HaMaor*, pt. 6.
113. *Shulhan Aruch, Orah Hayim* 240:1.
114. R. Moses Frankfurt, *Nefesh Yehudah* to *Me'norat HaMaor, Ner III*, rule 6, pt. 5, chap. 3, 179; the *Igeret HaKodesh* explains: "His intention was not only for the pleasure of the act . . . for he perceived his motivation as fulfilling an obligation to her . . . that of the *mitzvah* of *onah* commanded in the Torah . . . and the intention and behavior of this pious man were elevated, and for the sake of Heaven and the *mitzvah*."
115. *Nedarim* 20b; *Masechet Kalah* 1.
116. *Megillah* 13a; see *Rashi*.
117. *Mor U-K'tzia, Shulhan Aruch, Orah Hayim* 240.
118. Maimonides, *Commentary to the Mishnah, Sanhedrin* 7.
119. *Sefer Hasidim*, 509.
120. *Tosafot Rid, Yevamot* 12b.
121. Maimonides, *Yad, De'ot* 3:2, 4:9; Ibn Ezra, Leviticus 18:20; R. Jacob Emden, *Siddur Bet Yaakov*, 135–161.
122. *Siddur Bet Yaakov*, 159.
123. Maimonides, *Yad, De'ot* 4:19, 5:4.
124. *Sanhedrin* 107a; see also *Rashi*; see *Sukkah* 42b, 52b and *Rashi*; *Shulhan Aruch, Even HaEzer* 240:1.
125. *Yad, De'ot* 4:19, 5:4.
126. See *Shulhan Aruch, Even HaEzer* 25:2.

127. *Berachot* 22a; Maimonides, *Yad, De'ot* 5:4; *Isurei Be'ah* 21:11.

128. *Taanit* 11a; Maimonides, *Yad, Taaniyot* 3:8; *Tur, Even HaEzer* 25:7.

129. Maimonides, *Yad, Taaniyot* 3:8; see also *Shulhan Aruch, Even HaEzer* 25:6.

130. *Rashi* to *Taanit* 11a; see also *Rashi* to Genesis 7:7.

131. W. H. Masters and V. H. Johnson, *McCall's* (November 1966), 173, q. David Feldman, *Marital Relations, Birth Control and Abortion in Jewish Law* (New York: Schocken, 1974), 64 n. 36.

132. *Menorat HaMaor* 1:171.

133. See Genesis 2:24.

134. *Igeret Hakodesh.*

CHAPTER 8

1. Genesis 1:10; Exodus 7:10.

2. Isaiah 22:11.

3. See Y. Yadin, *Masada* (New York: Random House, 1966).

4. Ibid., 164–167.

5. Leviticus 20:18.

6. Leviticus 19:1–2.

7. Leviticus 20:7.

8. See *Reshit Hochmah, Shaar HaAhavah* 11. For discussion of the concept of immersion in the *mikveh* as a spiritual rebirth, see R. Aryeh Kaplan, *Waters of Eden* (New York: NCSY/Orthodox Union, 1976).

9. Exodus 29:4, and *Rashi* and *Targum Jonathan*, ad loc.; R. Samson Raphael Hirsch, *The Penteteuch* (Gateshead: The Judaica Press, 1976), ad loc; see Exodus 40:12; Leviticus 8:6.

10. *Tana D'bey Eliyahu Rabbah*, 7.

11. See *Rashi, Shabbat* 68a; *Sifra*, Leviticus 2:26; Maimonides, *Shemonah Perakim*, 6; *Haye Adam* 86:18; see *MaHaritz Hayot, Rosh Hashanah* 16a; Maimonides, *Commentary* to *Mishnah, Makot* 3:1; *Hovot HaLevavot* 3:3.

12. A. Kaplan, *Waters of Eden*, 9–10.

13. See Maimonides, *Yad, Mikvaot* 11:12; *Temurah* 4:13; *Teshuvah* 3:14; *Moreh Nevuchim* 3:24, 31; see *Ramban*, Leviticus 19:19, Deuteronomy 2:6; see *Sefer HaHinuch* 545; see Ibn Ezra, *Exodus* 20:1; see *Tosafot Yom Tov, Berachot* 5:3; see *Etz Yosef, Leviticus Rabbah* 27:10, *Deuteronomy Rabbah* 6:1; see *MaHaritz Hayot, Sotah* 14a; see *Tosafot, Sotah* 14a, *Hullin* 5a, *"Keday," Gittin* 49b, *"R. Shimon"*; see *MaHaram*; see *Tosafot Yom Tov* to *Sanhedrin* 8:6; see also *Bava Kamma* 79b, *Bava Metzia* 31.

14. Aron Barth, *The Jew Faces Eternal Problems* (Jerusalem: The Jewish Agency, 1965), 210.

15. R. Samson Raphael Hirsch, *The Pentateuch*, Leviticus 20:18.

16. See *Tosafot, Yevamot* 62b.

17. *Responsa of MaHaram of Lublin*, 53.

18. R. Shlomo Wolbe, *Binyan Adei Ad* (Jerusalem: D'var Yerushalayim, 1979), 52.

19. *Shabbat* 64b; *JT Gittin*, end; *Sifra, Metzora* 9:12.

20. Maimonides, *Yad, Isurei Be'ah* 11:19; *Sefer Mitzvot Gadol, Lavin*, 111. See also *Shulhan Aruch, Yoreh De'ah* 195:9, where the *Bet Yosef* writes *"bekoshi hitiru lah lehitkashet,"* indicating that while the Sages permit women to make themselves physically attrac-

tive during the *niddah* period, it is an instance of rabbinic acquiescence in order that women remain attractive to their husbands. But the reluctance implied in the words "*bekoshi hitiru*" implies concern at the possibility that such adornment could result in improper consequences.

21. *Niddah* 31b.

22. Proverbs 9:17.

23. Susan Weidman Schneider, *Jewish and Female* (New York: Simon & Schuster, 1984/5), 206.

24. Ibid., 206–207.

25. *Song of Songs Rabbah*, 7; see Midrash to Psalms 2:15; see also *Sanhedrin* 37a and *Tosafot*, "*HaTorah he'idah.*"

26. Deuteronomy 4:2, 13:1; Proverbs 3:6.

27. *Bet Yosef, Tur, Yoreh De'ah* 193.

28. Gila Berkowitz in Schneider, 205–206.

29. Norman Lamm, *A Hedge of Roses* (New York: Feldheim, 1966), 68–70.

30. Genesis 2:3.

31. Lamm, 76–78.

32. David M. Serr, *Israel Magazine* (Tel Aviv, February 1972).

33. Moses D. Tendler, *Pardes Rimonim* (New York: The Judaica Press, 1979), 14.

34. Ibid., 13–14.

35. M. Coppelson, *British Journal of Hospital Medicine* (1969): 961–980, q. in M.D. Tendler, *Pardes Rimonim*, 153–155.

36. *Maariv* (Tel Aviv, March 3, 1984).

37. See *Pardes Rimonim* 15.

38. "During the Middle Ages, the Jewish communities were surprisingly free of disease and plague in comparison to their non-Jewish neighbors, notwithstanding the very limited living space they had. This fact often led to pogroms, as the Jews were suspected of magical practices. There can be no doubt that the strict observance of the *Halachah* contributed in no small measure to their immunity" (*Encyclopaedia Judaica* [Jerusalem: Keter, 1972], 8:1141).

39. A. E. Kitov, *The Jew and His Home*, trans. Nathan Bulman (New York: Shengold, 1963), 153–155.

40. Maimonides, *Yad, Mikvaot* 11:2; *Sefer HaHinuch*, 175.

41. *Yoma* 85b.

42. Genesis 1:2.

43. S. R. Hirsch, *The Pentateuch*, Exodus 29:4.

44. Maimonides, *Yad, Mikvaot* 11:12.

45. Ezekiel 36:25.

46. Maimonides, *Yad, Tumat Ochlin* 16:12; See *JT Shekalim* 3: 5; *Sotah* 49a; *Avodah Zarah* 20b.

47. Leviticus 20:18.

48. Leviticus 20:17.

49. Leviticus 23:29.

50. Ezekiel 18:5, 6.

51. R. Naftali Zvi Yehudah Berlin, *Meshiv Davar*, 1:45.

52. *JT Hagigah* 1:8.

53. See Berlin, op. cit.

54. J. H. Hertz, *The Pentateuch and Haftorahs* (London: Soncino, 1981), 592.

CHAPTER 9

1. Genesis 1:28.

2. For a specialized work discussing the halachic approach to birth control and abortion, see David M. Feldman's fine study, *Marital Relations, Birth Control and Abortion in Jewish Law* (New York: Schocken Books, 1974), which served as a source for much of the information in this chapter. R. Feldman's approach is usually somewhat on the liberal side, and for a full understanding of the *Halachah*, his book should be used in conjunction with the *Shulhan Aruch*, The Code of Jewish Law, and the other halachic codes and commentaries, and the latter-day responsa literature on the subjects, especially the *Igrot Moshe* of R. Moses Feinstein. For all halachic questions, a knowledgeable, observant rabbi should be consulted.

3. *Baalei HaNefesh, Shaar HaKedushah.*

4. *Menorat HaMaor, Ner III, Klal VI*, pt. 5.

5. Levirate marriage is that between a widow whose husband died without children and the brother of the deceased, in order to raise up children on behalf of the deceased, in accordance with Deuteronomy 25:5–6. It is not practiced today.

6. Genesis 38:9–10.

7. *Niddah* 13a; *Shulhan Aruch, Even HaEzer* 23:1.

8. *Shulhan Aruch, Even HaEzer* 23:1.

9. Ibid.

10. See *Rashi, Ketubot* 39a, *"Meshamshot"*; *Tosafot, "Shalosh"*; *Tosafot, Yevamot* 12b, *"Shalosh."*

11. *Yevamot* 12b, 100b; *Ketubot* 39a.

12. There are three exceptions to this rule. Judaism requires a Jew to give his life rather than transgress the commandments regarding murder, incest, or idol worship.

13. Exodus 31:14.

14. Exodus 31:16.

15. Leviticus 18:5.

16. *Yoma* 85b.

17. The sole exception where a man is halachically permitted the use of a contraceptive device is the instance of *pikuah nefesh*–where there exists a life-threatening situation.

18. *Tosefta, Yevamot* 8:4.

19. *Yevamot* 65b.

20. *Yam Shel Shlomo, Yevamot* 6:44.

21. *Teshuvot Hatam Sofer, Shulhan Aruch, Even HaEzer* 1:20.

22. See Avraham Sofer Avraham, *Nishmat Avraham* (Jerusalem), *Even HaEzer* 5:13, 59–72.

23. Marital relations are also forbidden on Yom Kippur, the Day of Atonement.

24. *Sefer Hasidim*, 520.

25. In view of the challenge of Protestantism, the Council of Trent clarified many points of Church doctrine and practice.

26. Uta Ranke-Heinemann, *Eunuchs for the Kingdom of Heaven*, trans. (from the German) Peter Heynegg (New York: Doubleday, 1990), 273.

27. Ibid.

28. Ibid.

29. Q. in Ranke-Heinemann, 295.

30. Ibid., 298.
31. Ibid.
32. Exodus 21:22–23.
33. *Bava Kamma* 42a.
34. See *Yevamot* 62b; *Niddah* 13a, 31a.
35. Josephus, *Antiquities of the Jews*, IV, 8:33.
36. See *Bava Kamma* 78a; *Bava Kamma* 47a, *Tosafot*, *"Mai taama gufah hi"*; *Sanhedrin* 80b, *Tosafot*, *"Ubar yerech imo."*
37. *Hullin* 58a; *Sanhedrin* 80b; *Gittin* 23b.
38. *Gittin* 23b; see *Rashi*, *"Kasavar."*
39. See *Sanhedrin* 84b, *Niddah* 44b, and *Rashi*.
40. See *Niddah* 44b.
41. *Sanhedrin* 84b; *Niddah* 44b;
42. *Shulhan Aruch, Yoreh De'ah* 344:8.
43. *Zohar*, Exodus 3b.
44. Exodus 1:22.
45. *Zohar*, 3b.
46. *Hagahot Yaavetz*, *Niddah* 44b.
47. *Noda BeYehudah, Mahadurah Tinyana, Hoshen Mishpat* 59.
48. *Meshech Hochmah*, Exodus 35:2.
49. *Sanhedrin* 57b.
50. Genesis 9:6.
51. See *Tosafot*, *Sanhedrin* 59a, *"Leka."*
52. *Oholot* 7:6.
53. *Rashi*, *Sanhedrin* 72b, *"Yatza Rosho."* The text in the Mishnah in *Oholot* reads *"Yatsa rubo,"* "Once most of the fetus has exited," while a variant version in *Sanhedrin* reads *"Yatza Rosho,"* "Once the head has exited." *Rabbeinu Shimshon* comments on the differing versions (*Oholot* 7:6) that the head is considered to be the equivalent of most of the other organs of the body.
54. *Rashi*, *Sanhedrin* 72b, *"Yatza Rosho."*
55. *Oholot*, 7:6; *Shulhan Aruch, Yoreh De'ah* 194:10.
56. *Sanhedrin* 72b.
57. Maimonides, *Yad, Hilchot Rotse'ah UShemirat HaNefesh*, 1:9. Maimonides bases his decision to allow abortion on the consideration that the fetus is regarded legally as a *rodef*, a pursuer who is seeking to kill the woman, and not as is implicit in the preceding Mishnah and in *Rashi*'s commentary, on the basis of the fetus not being considered a viable human until the head or most of the body of the fetus has exited.

Many rabbinic authorities have attempted to reconcile what appears to be a deviation, at least theoretically, from the sense of the Mishnah on the part of Maimonides. R. Hayim Soloveitchik in his commentary, *Hidushei R. Hayim HaLevi* to the *Mishneh Torah*, explains that the laws of *pikuah nefesh*, saving a human life, apply to the near-human fetus—which is a potential person and therefore a *nefesh*—as well as they do to the woman. Consequently, he determines, if the *Halachah* was to be based on the woman's right to destroy the fetus because of *pikuah nefesh*, the unborn fetus would enjoy a similar legal consideration, and since one *nefesh* must not be saved by killing another, the fetus could not be aborted in order to save the mother's life. Therefore, R. Hayim maintains, the *Halachah* is based on saving the mother from a pursuer and the unassailable biblical prerogative of an individual to protect himself or herself from a murderous pursuer.

58. *Shulhan Aruch, Hoshen Mishpat* 425:2.

59. See *Igrot Moshe, Hoshen Mishpat* 71; see also *Hoshen Mishpat* 425:1.

60. *Tzitz Eliezer*, pt. 13, no. 102.

61. See R. Jacob Emden, *She'elot Yaavetz, Responsum* 43.

62. David Feldman in *Marital Relations, Birth Control and Abortion in Jewish Law* (New York: Schocken, 1974), 294, cites R. Immanuel Jakobovitz, in "Jewish Views on Abortion," in David T. Smith, ed., *Abortion and the Law* (Cleveland: Western Reserve University, 1967), who presents the stringent position.

63. There is talmudic treatment of the subject as well. See *Sanhedrin* 91b, the discussion between Rabbi (R. Judah HaNasi) and the Roman Emperor Antoninus.

64. *De Fide*, 27, q. by Feldman, *Marital Relations*, 269.

65. *The Catholic Encyclopaedia*, Vol. 2, 266, cited by Feldman, 270.

66. Feldman, 270.

67. Ibid.

68. *Berachot* 60b.

69. The Daily Prayer Book, morning blessings.

70. Ranke-Heinemann, 301.

71. J. Mausbach and P. Tischleder, *Katholische Moraltheologie*, q. in Ranke-Heinemann, 302.

72. Bernard Haring, *Das Gesetz Christi*, q. in Ranke-Heinemann, 302.

73. Ranke-Heinemann, 307.

74. Ibid.

75. Ibid.

76. Ibid.

77. Ibid.

78. Ibid., 309.

79. Ibid.

80. Paul Gastonguay, *Abortion and Law* (St. Louis: Liguori Publications, 1983), 13.

81. Israel Government, "Penal Law–1977, Termination of Pregnancy."

82. *Statistical Abstract of Israel, 1990* (Jerusalem: Government Central Bureau of Statistics, 1990), 140.

83. In a report in the *Jerusalem Post* (November 3, 1992), 3, the number of official abortions performed in 1991 was given as 15,800.

84. Minister of Health Shoshana Arbelli-Almosnino, in reply to a parliamentary query in the Knesset on July 14, 1987.

85. Dr. Eli Joseph Schusheim of Jerusalem, chairman of *Agudat Efrat*, an organization that provides information for women contemplating abortion, informed the author that the government's estimates are low.

86. *National Jewish Population Survey* (New York: Council of Jewish Federations, 1991).

87. U. O. Schmelz and Sergio DellaPergola, *Basic Trends in American Jewish Demography* (New York: The American Jewish Committee, 1988).

88. Ibid., 1.

89. The increase in the six-year period 1981–1983 and 1987–1989 was 75 percent, according to demographer Professor Sergio DellaPergola of the Hebrew University, Jerusalem, as reported in *The Jerusalem Post* (July 8, 1991).

90. Ibid. About 80 percent of American Jewish day schools are Orthodox, 10 percent Conservative, and about 2 percent Reform.

91. *National Jewish Population Survey*, 1991.

92. Ibid.

93. Schmelz and DellaPergola, *Basic Trends*, 23.

94. *National Jewish Population Survey*, 16.

95. Schmelz and DellaPergola, *Basic Trends*, 23.

96. Edward Noren, in "Counting the Jews," *Commentary* 93 (October, 1991): 42.

97. *National Jewish Population Survey*, 29.

98. Q. in *Fortune* (August 10, 1992), 59.

99. Reported in *The Jerusalem Post* (July 18, 1983).

100. *Halachah* requires that the mother be Jewish in order that the child be Jewish.

101. See *Kiddushin* 6a, 13a; *Shulhan Aruch, Even HaEzer* 44:93.

102. Maimonides, *Yad, Isurei Be'ah* 15:1; *Shulhan Aruch, Even HaEzer* 4:13.

103. *Yevamot* 78b; Maimonides, *Yad, Isurei Be'ah* 15:33; *Shulhan Aruch, Even HaEzer* 4:24.

104. Deuteronomy 23:3.

105. *Yevamot* 45b; *Kiddushin* 69a; Maimonides, *Yad, Isurei Be'ah* 15:33; *Shulhan Aruch, Even HaEzer* 4:24.

106. *Yevamot* 79b; *Kiddushin* 67a and *Rashi*; Maimonides, *Yad, Isurei Be'ah* 15:7, 33; *Shulhan Aruch, Even HaEzer* 4:22.

107. *Yevamot* 78b.

108. Maimonides, *Yad, Isurei Be'ah* 12:17; *Shulhan Aruch, Even HaEzer* 4:9. The exception is a *kohen*, who may not marry a convert.

109. Deuteronomy 23:3; *Yevamot* 78a; *Shulhan Aruch, Even HaEzer* 4:1.

110. See *Targum Jonathan Ben Uziel* to Deuteronomy 23:3.

111. Q. in *The New York Times Book Review* (Nov. 29, 1981), 7.

112. *National Jewish Population Survey*, 15.

113. In comparison, in Israel there is a not insignificant natural increase in the Jewish population. The Jewish fertility rate was 2.6 in 1991 (compared to a Moslem fertility rate in Israel of 4.7), down 23 percent since the 3.56 rate of 1965–1969, but well above the 2.1 replacement rate. Since the general fertility rate of secular Jewish women in Israel is thought not to be substantively different from that of their American Jewish counterparts, the considerably higher average fertility rates of Israeli Jewish women can be largely attributed to the substantially higher proportion of religiously observant Jews in the Jewish population in Israel.

In a study by Professor Uziel Schmelz of Jerusalem, the fertility rate of the rapidly growing *haredi* (stringently Orthodox) segment of the population of Ashkenazic, or European origin, Jews is found to range from 7.2 to 7.6, and the fertility rate of the general (non-*haredi*) Orthodox population in Israel is estimated at 4.0. As the percentage of Orthodox Jews in Israel continues to grow, the differential between the fertility rates of Israel's Jewish and Moslem populations is diminishing. In Jerusalem, where the overall Jewish fertility rate, 3.8, is considerably higher than that of all Israel because of the city's substantial religious Jewish population, in 1992 the rate already exceeded the 3.6 rate for all Jerusalem non-Jews, the overwhelming majority of whom are Moslem (Schmelz, 176–177).

114. *Basic Trends*, 13–14.

115. Ibid., 14.

116. Ibid., 32.

117. The estimated figure of 5,515,000 "core Jews" cited in the "National Jewish Population Survey" includes an estimated 1,120,000 individuals who identify themselves as having been born to Jewish parents but do not consider themselves as having any religion. If this group is deducted from the total, the estimated U.S. Jewish population in 1990 was 4,395,000, which included 185,000 converts to Judaism.

118. U. O. Schmeltz, "Relgiosity and Fertility among the Jews of Jerusalem," in U. O. Schmeltz and S. DellaPergola, *Papers in Jewish Demography* (Jerusalem: The Institute of Contemporary Jewry and The Hebrew University of Jerusalem, 1989), 166.

119. Ibid.

120. In conversation with the author.

CHAPTER 10

1. *Sanhedrin* 22a.

2. In accordance with Numbers 5:11–31, where a suspected adulteress is given "bitter waters" into which a piece of paper bearing a curse with the name of God was dipped until erased.

3. *JT Sotah* 1:4.

4. Genesis 18:12.

5. *Genesis* 18:13.

6. *Yevamot* 65b.

7. See Genesis 2:24; II Samuel 3:11–16.

8. Ezra 10.

9. Malachi 2:14–16.

10. *Shabbat* 127a.

11. *Gittin* 90b.

12. Malachi 2:13–14.

13. *Yalkut*, Psalms, 743.

14. Louis I. Newman, *The Hasidic Anthology* (New York: Schocken Books, 1963), 240.

15. *Song of Songs Rabbah* 1:31; *Pesikta d'Rav Kahana*, 22.

16. See *Yevamot* 63b; *Gittin* 90a.

17. *Yevamot* 112b.

18. *Kiddushin* 13a.

19. *Gittin* 90a.

20. Ibid.

21. *Rama, Shulhan Aruch, Even HaEzer* 119:2; see *Helkat Mehokek* and *Bet Shmuel*.

22. Under unusual and compelling circumstances a man may unilaterally give a *get* without his wife's consent, but such an act requires the consensus of no fewer than 100 rabbis, all of whom must be aware of the compelling reason for such a *get* and all of whom must sign the consent authorization. In practice it has been almost impossible to secure such a consent authorization by 100 rabbis, and consequently such a *get* has rarely been granted.

23. *Rama, Shulhan Aruch, Even HaEzer* 134:1–3.

24. See Aaron Owen, "Legal Aspects of Marriage," in Peter Elman, ed. *Jewish Marriage* (London: Soncino, 1967), 126.

25. Maimonides, *Yad, Gerushin* 2:20.

26. Ibid.

27. Ibid.

28. *Responsa of MaHaram* (R. Meir of Rothenburg) (Prague, 1608), *Responsum* no. 81.

29. Q. in *Darchei Moshe, Tur, Even HaEzer* 154:11.

30. *Bet Yosef, Tur, Even HaEzer* 154:15.

31. See *Shulhan Aruch, Even HaEzer* 70:3.

32. *Yevamot* 62b.

33. Maimonides, *Yad, Ishut* 15:19.

34. *Ketubot* 72a,b; Maimonides, *Yad, Ishut* 24:10, 11, 12; *Tur, Even HaEzer* 115:1–4; *Sefer Mitzvot Gadol, Taaseh*, 48. See chap. 8, "Family Purity."

35. *Yevamot* 24b, 25a; Maimonides, *Yad, Ishut* 24:6, 10, 15; *Yad, Sotah* 2:13; *Shulhan Aruch, Even HaEzer* 11:1.

36. *Ketubot*, 72a, b; Maimonides, *Yad, Ishut* 24:6, 10, 15; *Sotah* 2:13; *Shulhan Aruch, Even HaEzer* 11:1, 115:4, 119:4.

37. *Ketubot, 72a, b; Sotah 25a; Shulhan Aruch, Even HaEzer* 11:1, 115:4, 119:4.

38. *Ketubot*, ibid.; *Sotah*, ibid.; *Shulhan Aruch* and *Rama*, ibid.

39. *Ketubot* 100b; Maimonides, *Yad, Ishut* 14:8–14, 24:5, 9; *Tur, Even HaEzer* 115; *Sefer Mitzvot Gadol, Taaseh*, 48.

40. *Niddah* 12b; Maimonides, *Yad, Ishut* 25:7–9; *Shulhan Aruch, Even HaEzer* 39:4, 117:1, 2, 4.

41. *Yevamot* 64a,b, 65a,b; *Ketubot* 100b; Maimonides, *Yad, Ishut* 15:8, 24:1; *Shulhan Aruch, Even HaEzer* 154:10; see *Rama, Shulhan Aruch, Even HaEzer* 1:3.

42. *Ketubot* 100a, b; Maimonides, *Yad, Ishut* 13:17; *Shulhan Aruch, Even HaEzer* 25:1.

43. *Ketubot* 110b; Maimonides, *Yad, Ishut* 13:19; *Shulhan Aruch, Even HaEzer* 75:3, 4. The Talmud (*Ketubot* 110b) adds: "One should, under all circumstances, reside in *Eretz Yisrael* even if in order to do so one must live in a city that is populated in the main with idol worshippers. A person should not live outside *Eretz Yisrael* even if he does so in a city populated mainly by Jews. For he who resides in *Eretz Yisrael* is likened to one who has a God, while he who resides outside *Eretz Yisrael* is likened to someone who has no God. As it is written, 'To give you the land of Canaan and to be a God unto you' (Leviticus 25:38). Therefore, he who does not reside in *Eretz Yisrael* has no God." The passage adds that he who resides outside *Eretz Yisrael* is as if he worships idols.

44. *Rama, Shulhan Aruch, Even HaEzer* 154:1.

45. *Shulhan Aruch, Even HaEzer* 154:3; see *Rama* and *Ba'er Hetev*.

46. *Shulhan Aruch, Even HaEzer* 154:4.

47. *Ketubot* 77a; Maimonides, *Yad, Ishut* 25:12; *Shulhan Aruch, Even HaEzer* 154:4.

48. *Ketubot* 110b; Maimonides, *Yad, Ishut* 25:11; *Sefer Mitzvot Gadol, Ta'aseh*, 48; *Shulhan Aruch, Even HaEzer* 154:4.

49. *Ketubot* 63b; Maimonides, *Yad, Ishut* 14:8; *Sefer Mitzvot Gadol, Lo Ta'aseh*, 81; *Shulhan Aruch, Even HaEzer* 77:2.

50. *Ketubot* 61b; Maimonides, *Yad, Ishut* 14:6, 7, 15; *Sefer Mitzvot Gadol, Lo Ta'aseh* 81; *Shulhan Aruch, Even HaEzer* 77:1.

51. *Shulhan Aruch, Even HaEzer* 76:19; *Rama* adds that if the wife insists on such an arrangement the husband may also compel a divorce.

52. *Shulhan Aruch, Even HaEzer* 154:7.

53. *Yevamot* 65a; Maimonides, *Yad, Ishut* 15:10.
54. *Ketubot* 77a; Maimonides, *Yad, Ishut* 25:13; *Sefer Mitzvot Gadol, Ta'aseh*, 48.
55. *Rama, Shulhan Aruch, Even HaEzer* 154:3.
56. *Rama* and *HaGra, Shulhan Aruch, Even HaEzer* 154:3.
57. *Ketubot* 63a, 77a; Maimonides, *Yad, Ishut* 12:4; *Shulhan Aruch, Even HaEzer* 154:3.
58. *Ketubot* 71b; Maimonides, *Yad, Ishut* 13:12.
59. *Ketubot* 71b; Maimonides, *Yad, Ishut* 13:13.
60. *Ketubot* 71b; Maimonides, *Yad, Ishut* 14:12, 13.
61. *Ketubot* 70a; Maimonides, *Yad, Ishut* 13:8; *Shulhan Aruch, Even HaEzer* 74:1.
62. Maimonides, *Yad, Ishut* 13:15. Maimonides grants the husband a similar privilege.
63. *Ketubot* 102b; Maimonides, *Yad, Ishut* 13:19, 20; *Shulhan Aruch, Even HaEzer* 75:3, 4.
64. *Ketubot* 110b; Maimonides, *Yad, Ishut* 13:19; *Shulhan Aruch, Even HaEzer* 75:4.
65. *Piskei HaRosh* 51:2.
66. See *Yevamot* 93b, 114b–116; Maimonides, *Yad, Gerushin* 12:15, 29.
67. *Yevamot*, ibid.; Maimonides, ibid.
68. *Maimonides, Yad, Gerushin* 13:29.
69. *Yevamot* 93b, 114b–116; Maimonides, *Yad, Gerushin* 13.
70. *Yevamot* 87b; *Shulhan Aruch, Even HaEzer* 17:3, 56.
71. *Shabbat* 56a; *Ketubot* 9b, and *Rashi* and *Tosafot*.
72. For a discussion of various attempts at solving the problem of the *agunah* through premarital conditions in the *ketubah*, see Moshe Meiselman, *Jewish Woman in Jewish Law* (New York: Ktav, 1978), 103–115.

CHAPTER 11

1. Exodus 21: 28–31.
2. Leviticus 20:10.
3. *Bava Kamma* 15a.
4. *Yevamot* 100a; Maimonides, *Yad, Sanhedrin* 21:6; *Shulhan Aruch, Hoshen Mishpat* 15:2.
5. *Bava Kamma* 88a; *Shulhan Aruch, Hoshen Mishpat* 35:14.
6. *Bava Batra* 159a.
7. Maimonides, *Yad, Melachim* 3:7.
8. Ibid.
9. See *Sanhedrin* 19b; *Bava Kamma* 88a; *Shevuot* 30a; Maimonides, *Yad, Sanhedrin* 2:5; *Melachim* 3:7, and *Kesef Mishneh*; *Edut* 9:2 and *Kesef Mishneh* and *Radvaz*.
10. Maimonides, *Yad, Edut* 1:3.
11. Maimonides, *Yad, Edut* 13:15.
12. *Tosafot, Zevahim* 103a, "*Ain.*"
13. *Gittin* 2b; *Shulhan Aruch, Yoreh De'ah* 1273.
14. Deuteronomy 19:15; *Shulhan Aruch, Hoshen Mishpat* 33, 34.
15. To determine whether a husband has died. See below.

16. *Shulhan Aruch, Even HaEzer* 17:3; see *She'elot U-Teshuvot HaRashba HaMeyuhasot LeHaRamban*, no. 74.
17. Maimonides, *Yad, Edut* 9:2; *Tosafot, Zevahim* 103a, *"Ain."*
18. Maimonides, *Yad, Edut* 1:1.
19. Maimonides, *Yad, Edut* 1:4.
20. Deuteronomy 13:15.
21. *Yevamot* 42b.
22. Deuteronomy 17:7.
23. Maimonides, *Yad, Edut* 1:1.
24. Maimonides, *Yad, Sanhedrin* 21:6.
25. *Mishnah, Horiot* 13.
26. Leviticus 15:28.
27. *Ketubot* 72a; *Gittin* 2b.
28. *Ketubot* 88a.
29. *Hiddushei Ritva, Kiddushin* 35a.
30. Judges 5:6, see *Rashi.*
31. See *Mishnah, Niddah* 6:4; *JT Shevuot* 4:1; *Shulhan Aruch, Hoshen Mishpat* 7:4.
32. Moshe Meiselman, *Jewish Woman in Jewish Law* (New York: Ktav Publishing House, 1978), 88.
33. Except for creditors whose claim is prior to the marriage.
34. *Mishnah, Bava Batra* 9:1; *Ketubot* 13:3.
35. *Tosefta, Ketubot* 6:5.
36. *Shulhan Aruch, Even HaEzer* 112:18.
37. Ibid. 113:1.
38. *Bava Batra* 141a.
39. *Rabbeinu Gershom*, ad loc.
40. *Rama, Shulhan Aruch, Even HaEzer* 111:15.
41. See *Rama, Shulhan Aruch, Even HaEzer* 108:3.
42. *Ketubot* 80a; *Shulhan Aruch, Even HaEzer* 85:13, 17.

CHAPTER 12

1. Maimonides, *Sefer HaMitzvot*, Positive Commandments, end.
2. *Mishnah, Horayot* 3:7.
3. R. Meir Simha of Dvinsk, *Meshech Hochmah, Parashat Noah, Peru.*
4. *Pesahim* 43b.
5. *Pesahim* 109a.
6. *Berachot* 20b. According to some authorities, *Kiddush* on the festivals as well.
7. *Megillah* 4a.
8. *Shabbat* 23a.
9. *Pesahim* 108a.
10. *Mishnah, Kiddushin* 1:7
11. *Tosefta, Kiddushin* 1:10.
12. See *Sefer Abudarham*, Part III, "The Blessings over the Commandments"; see *Magen Avot* 2:6.
13. *Berachot* 17b.
14. *MaHaral, Drush al HaTorah* 15, *"Shuv amar."*

15. *Yalkut Shimoni, Samuel* 247:78. See *Berachot* 54a.

16. R. Samson Raphael Hirsch, *The Pentateuch* (Gateshead: Judaica Press, 1976), Leviticus 23:43.

17. *Niddah* 45b.

18. *Megillah* 16b.

19. *Numbers Rabbah* 21:11; *Exodus Rabbah* 28:2; *Pirkei d'Rabbi Eliezer* 45.

20. *Berachot* 10a; *Mishnah, Makkot* 2:6; *Sanhedrin* 43a.

21. *Pesahim* 48b; *Midrash Rabbah*, Exodus 28:2.

22. *Maimonides, Yad, Mamrim* 2:9, and see *Raavad. Rashi*, however, disagrees (*Rosh HaShanah* 33a, "*Hanashim me'akvin*") and maintains that a woman performing a *mitzvah* from which she has been excused transgresses on the negative precept of *Bal tosif*, which forbids "adding on" to the Torah (Deuteronomy 13:1).

(However, see the *MaHarsha* on *Rashi*, who states that the prohibition of *Bal tosif* does not apply to accepting the obligation of performing a *mitzvah*, but applies to amending an existing *mitzvah* by attaching additions to it, e.g., adding a fifth Torah verse to the four verses in the *tefillin*.)

Rashi repeats this view elsewhere, in a comment on the talmudic statement, in *Eruvin* 96a, that Michal, daughter of King Saul, donned *tefillin*, where he says ("*Velo mihu*"): "For her act is like an addition to the words of the Torah, since the Torah excused women from time-dependent Positive Commandments." However, *Tosafot* ("*Michal bat Kushi*") does not share *Rashi*'s view.

23. *Kiddushin* 31a; *Bava Kamma* 38a, 87a.

24. This is based on the idea that the most important act an individual can do is to fulfill God's wishes. See *Tosafot, Kiddushin* 31a, "*Gadol hametzuvah ve'oseh.*"

25. Maimonides, *Yad, Talmud Torah* 1:13.

26. Ibid.; see also Maimonides, *Yad, Tzitzit* 3:9; *Rama, Shulhan Aruch, Orah Hayim* 589:6; *Birkei Yosef, Shulhan Aruch, Orah Hayim* 654:2.

27. *Rama, Shulhan Aruch, Orah Hayim* 589:6; see *Rabbeinu Tam, Tosafot, Kiddushin* 31a, "*Delo*": "*Denashim mevarchot al mitzvot asey shehazeman gerama af-al-gaf dipeturot legamri . . . ve'ein kahn mishum lo tisa et shemo lashav.*"

28. *Levush*, 17:2, 589:6; *Haye Adam* 11:43; *Shulhan Aruch, Orah Hayim* 589:6: *Shulhan Aruch HaRav*; *Aruch HaShulhan*; *Mateh Ephraim*; *Mishnah Berurah*; *Hatam Sofer, Sha'ar HaGedilim VeHakelaim* 23: "*Uneshei didan nahagu levarech al-pi hachraat HaRama, vehalilah leharher.*"

29. *Shulhan Aruch, Orah Hayim* 70:1.

30. *Magen Avraham, Orah Hayim* 489:1.

31. *Haye Adam* 141:7.

32. *Taz, Shulhan Aruch, Orah Hayim* 648:6; *Aruch HaShulhan, Orah Hayim* 70:1.

33. Ibid.

34. S. R. Hirsch, *The Pentateuch*, Leviticus 10:1–3.

35. I Samuel 15: 19–22.

36. *Mishnah, Kiddushin* 1:7.

37. *Mishnah, Shabbat* 2:6.

CHAPTER 13

1. See *Kitzur Shulhan Aruch* 75:2.

2. *Rabbeinu Bahya, Midrash*, Exodus 19:4; *Mishnah Berurah, Shulhan Aruch, Orah Hayim* 263:1.

3. *Shabbat* 23b.
4. Proverbs 6:23.
5. *Rashi, Shabbat* 23b.
6. Maimonides, *Yad, Shabbat* 5:3.
7. *Shulhan Aruch, Orah Hayim* 263:2, 3.
8. *Mishnah Berurah*, ad loc.
9. *Shulhan Aruch, Orah Hayim* 263:3.
10. *Rama, Shulhan Aruch, Orah Hayim* 264:10 and *Mishnah Berurah*, ad loc.
11. *Mishnah Berurah, Shulhan Aruch, Orah Hayim* 262:2.
12. Apparently, originally only one candle was lit, and this is the original requirement; see *Berachot* 31a; *Shabbat* 23b, 25b, 34a, 119b; *Genesis Rabbah* 11; *Mishnah Berurah, Shulhan Aruch, Orah Hayim* 263:5, n. 22.
13. *Shulhan Aruch, Orah Hayim* 263:1.
14. R. David Auerbach *Halichot Betah* (Jerusalem: Machon Shaarei Ziv, 1983), 14:18.
15. *Halichot Betah* 14:21.
16. See *Halichot Betah* 14:32.
17. See *Shulhan Aruch, Orah Hayim* 263:4.
18. Ibid.
19. *Haye Adam, Shabbat* 5:9.
20. Numbers 15:19–20.
21. See Ezekiel 44:28–31.
22. Tamar Frankiel, *The Voice of Sarah* (San Francisco: Harper San Francisco, 1990), 74.
23. Ibid., 75.
24. Ibid., 78–79.
25. Exodus 20:8.
26. Deuteronomy 5:12.
27. *Berachot* 20b.
28. *Shulhan Aruch, Orah Hayim* 271:2. See *Halichot Betah* 15:10.
29. *Shulhan Aruch, Orah Hayim* 291:6. The *Levush* (291:1) maintains that the eating of the three Sabbath meals is not merely a rabbinic precept, but is of scriptural origin.
30. *Rabbeinu Nisim* to R. Isaac Alfasi (*Rif*), *Shabbat* 445.
31. Exodus 16:22.
32. Maimonides, *Yad, Shabbat* 29:1.
33. *Pesahim* 102b.
34. *Levush* 296:1.
35. *Kuntres Aharon, Ta'amei HaMinhagim U'Mekorei HaDinim*, 511.
36. *Kol Bo*, q. in *Ta'amei HaMinhagim U'Mekorei HaDinim*, 511.
37. See *Tosafot, Pesahim* 102b, *"Rav."*
38. *Shulhan Aruch, Orah Hayim* 296:8.
39. See *Magid Mishneh* to Maimonides, *Yad, Shabbat* 29:1; *Magen David* to *Shulhan Aruch, Orah Hayim* 296:8.
40. *Rama, Shulhan Aruch, Orah Hayim* 296:8.
41. *Rama, Shulhan Aruch, Orah Hayim* 299:10.
42. See *Magen Avraham, Shulhan Aruch, Orah Hayim* 296:8, who refers to the opinion of the *Ba"h* (quoted by the *Mishnah Berurah*) and concludes that the *Halachah* is in accordance with the opinion of the *Ba"h*, i.e., that women may recite the entire *Havdalah* service.
43. *Mishnah Berurah, Shulhan Aruch, Orah Hayim* 296:8.

44. *Shulhan Aruch, Orah Hayim* 300:1 and *Mishnah Berurah,* ad loc.
45. *Shabbat* 123a; *Shulhan Aruch, Orah Hayim* 675:3.
46. *Megillah* 4a; *Shulhan Aruch, Orah Hayim* 689:1.
47. *Pesahim* 128a; *Shulhan Aruch, Orah Hayim* 472:14.
48. *Pesahim* 108b, *Rashi,* and *Rashbam, "She'af."*
49. *Sotah* 11b.
50. *Shabbat* 23a; see *Rashi, "Hayu."*
51. Deuteronomy 16:14.
52. *Kiddushin* 34b; *Rosh HaShanah* 7b.
53. Deuteronomy 16:14.
54. *Rashi, Kiddushin* 34b, *"Ba'alah mesamhah"*; see *Tosafot, "Ishah ba'alah mesamhah."*
55. *Pesahim* 109a.
56. *Shulhan Aruch, Orah Hayim* 529:2.
57. *Halichot Betah* 17:6.
58. Exodus 19:19.
59. *Rosh HaShanah* 30a; *Shulhan Aruch, Orah Hayim* 589:3.
60. *Mishnah, Kiddushin* 29a.
61. However, *Rashi* disagrees. In *Rosh HaShanah* 33a (*"Hanashim meakvin"*), *Rashi* writes: "Since women are totally exempt [from the *mitzvah* of *shofar*] as it is a time-dependent Positive Precept, if they do sound the *shofar* they transgress on the prohibition of *Bal Tosif,* not adding to the *mitzvot.*" (Deuteronomy 13:1: "Everything that I command you, you shall carry out punctiliously; you must not add anything to it nor subtract anything from it.") The *MaHarsha* (ad loc.) takes issue with *Rashi,* stating that the transgression of *Bal Tosif* applies not to the voluntary acceptance of the obligation of a *mitzvah,* but to adding on to an existing one, e.g., adding a fifth passage of the Torah to the four required in the *tefillin.* See Maimonides, *Yad, Mamrim* 2:9, and *Raavad.*
62. *Shulhan Aruch, Orah Hayim* 589:6.
63. *Rama, Shulhan Aruch, Orah Hayim* 589:6.
64. *Shulhan Aruch, Orah Hayim* 589:1.
65. *Ben Ish Hai, Parashat Nitzvaim,* 17.
66. See *Sukkah* 28b.
67. *Rosh HaShanah* 9a–9b.
68. *Teshuvot Ktav Sofer, Shulhan Aruch, Orah Hayim* 112; *Yabia Omer, Shulhan Aruch, Orah Hayim* 37.
69. *Shulhan Aruch, Orah Hayim* 617:1.
70. Ibid.
71. *Shulhan Aruch, Orah Hayim* 617:4.
72. *Mishnah Berurah,* ad loc.
73. Ibid.
74. *Halichot Betah* 21:20.
75. Ibid.
76. Ibid.
77. Ibid.
78. *Shulhan Aruch, Orah Hayim* 640:1.
79. *Rama, Shulhan Aruch, Orah Hayim* 658:9; *Mishnah Berurah, Shulhan Aruch, Orah Hayim* 654:1.
80. See *Halichot Betah* 22:5, 9.

81. Maimonides, *Yad, Yom Tov* 6, 7; *Shulhan Aruch, Orah Hayim* 530.
82. See *Shulhan Aruch, Yoreh De'ah* 282:9.
83. See R. Moshe Meiselman in *Jewish Woman in Jewish Law*, 146, who quotes R. Joseph B. Soloveitchik as telling him that women's *hakafot* would be in conflict with the "respect and awe owed to the synagogue," and would be "a violation of synagogue etiquette."
84. *Shabbat* 23a. See *Pesahim* 108b, *Megillah* 4a, *Arachin* 3a.
85. In some households it is customary for all members of the family to light individually.
86. Maimonides, *Yad, Hanukkah* 3:4; *Shulhan Aruch, Orah Hayim* 675:3.
87. *Mishnah Berurah, Shulhan Aruch, Orah Hayim* 675:3; *Halichot Betah* 23:5.
88. Ibid., 675:9.
89. *Halichot Betah* 23:3.
90. *Shulhan Aruch, Orah Hayim* 679.
91. *Shulhan Aruch, Orah Hayim* 670:1, and *Mishnah Berurah.*
92. *Shulhan Aruch, Orah Hayim* 689:1.
93. *Megillah* 4a.
94. *Rashi* and *Rashbam, Pesahim* 108b, *"She'af."*
95. A statement in the Jerusalem Talmud (*JT Megillah* 2:5) indicates that the reason women are obligated to hear the *Megillah* is that the survival of all Jews, women as well as men, was in doubt until the Jews were saved.
96. *Mishnah Berurah, Shulhan Aruch, Orah Hayim* 689:1.
97. *Arachin* 2b.
98. See *Piskei HaRosh, Megillah* 1:4; *Shulhan Aruch, Orah Hayim* 689:2, and *Magen Avraham*, and *Biur HaGra; Havat Yair,* 10; *Avnei Nezer, Orah Hayim* 511; *Halichot Betah* 24:12.
99. See *Halichot Betah* 24:13.
100. *Megillah* 23a; *Shulhan Aruch, Orah Hayim* 282:3.
101. *Halichot Betah* 24:17; see *Rama, Shulhan Aruch, Orah Hayim* 690:18 and *Mishnah Berurah.*
102. *Halichot Betah* 24:17.
103. *Halichot Betah* 24:20.
104. Esther 9:22.
105. *Shulhan Aruch, Orah Hayim* 695:4.
106. Ibid.
107. *Halichot Betah* 24:23.
108. *Halichot Betah* 24:24.
109. Deuteronomy 16:3.
110. *Pesahim* 43b.
111. *Shulhan Aruch, Orah Hayim* 472:14.
112. *Shulhan Aruch, Orah Hayim* 472:14; *Halichot Betah* 18:15–26.
113. *Shulhan Aruch, Orah Hayim* 472:14, and *Mishnah Berurah.*
114. *Sotah* 11b.
115. Psalms 68:14.
116. Song of Songs 8:5.
117. Exodus 38:8.
118. *Rashi,* Exodus 38:8, citing *Midrash Tanhuma.* See *Ramban,* Exodus 38:8.
119. Leviticus 23:15.

120. Maimonides, *Yad, Temidin U'Musafin* 7:24.
121. *Ramban* to *Kiddushin* 34a.
122. *Shulhan Aruch, Orah Hayim* 489:1.
123. *Shulhan Aruch, Orah Hayim* 549:6, 550:1, and *Mishnah Berurah*. The Fast of Esther is less obligatory than the other fasts and the halachic regulations regarding fasting are therefore less stringent. See *Halichot Betah* 26:4.
124. *Shulhan Aruch, Orah Hayim* 554:1–3, 7.
125. See *Halichot Betah* 25:2, n. 2, *"Vehayom mekubal."*
126. *Shulhan Aruch, Orah Hayim* 554:6.
127. *Mishnah Berurah, Orah Hayim* 554.6.
128. Ibid.
129. See *JT Pesahim* IV, 1:30d; *JT Taanit* I, 6:64c; *Rokeah*, 228; *Shulhan Aruch, Orah Hayim* 417:1.
130. *Shulhan Aruch, Orah Hayim* 417: 1; see *Pri Hadash*.
131. *Shulhan Aruch, Orah Hayim*, 417:1.
132. *Halichot Betah* 16:3.
133. Ibid., n. 8.
134. *Halichot Betah* 16:4.
135. *Pri Hadash, Orah Hayim* 417:1.
136. *Halichot Betah* 16:8.
137. *Halichot Betah* 16:10.
138. *Shulhan Aruch, Orah Hayim* 418:1.
139. *Shulhan Aruch, Orah Hayim* 419:1, and *Halichot Betah* 16:2.
140. See *Midrash Tanhuma, Ki Tisa* 19 and *Zohar*, Exodus 192a.
141. *Pirkei d'Rabbi Eliezer* 45; see *JT Pesahim* 4:1; *JT Taanit* 1:6.
142. *Tur, Orah Hayim* 417.
143. *Turei Zahav, Shulhan Aruch, Orah Hayim* 417:1.
144. Exodus 35:22; 25, 26, 29.
145. Nahmanides, Exodus 35:22.
146. *Sotah* 11b.
147. See *Exodus Rabbah* 51:8.
148. *Baalei Tosafot*, ad loc.
149. From the Blessing for the New Moon.

CHAPTER 14

1. Deuteronomy 11:13.
2. *Taanit* 2a.
3. Psalms 106:1.
4. *Berachot* 6a.
5. *Berachot* 8a.
6. Psalms 82:1.
7. Maimonides, *Yad, Tefillah* 8:1.
8. *Berachot* 6a.
9. Ibid.
10. Maimonides, *Yad, Tefillah* 1:1.

11. Many of these are blessings. Strictly speaking, *Tefillah*, or formal prayer, refers to the *Amidah* (*Shmoneh Esrei*) prayer recited thrice daily.
12. *Berachot* 20b.
13. I Samuel 1:13.
14. *Berachot* 31b.
15. *Berachot* 31a.
16. See *Yalkut Shimoni*, sec. 80; see *Midrash Tanhuma, Vayera* 1.
17. *Berachot* 27b; *Shulhan Aruch, Orah Hayim* 106:2. *Halichot Betah* cites the *Hafetz Hayim* as having given permission to his wife not to pray regularly because she was involved in the rearing of her children. He also cites the *responsa* of the *Hazon Ish*, who states that women who are involved with their children are excused for prayers. (*Halichot Betah* 6:1:1, n. 1, end.)
18. Maimonides, *Yad, Tefillah* 1:6.
19. See *Halichot Betah* 6:2.
20. Deuteronomy 8:10.
21. *Berachot* 21a; *Shulhan Aruch, Orah Hayim* 126:1.
22. *Berachot* 20a,b.
23. *Shulhan Aruch, Orah Hayim* 70:1. "And they should read at least the first verse, and some say also the first portion of verses (*Ve'ahavta*). However, it is customary today that women read all three portions of verses [of the *Shema*]" (*Halichot Betah* 5:1). The recitation of the blessings preceding the *Shema* are optional (*Halichot Betah* 5:4).
24. See *Berachot* 14a; *Pesahim* 118a; *Taanit* 28b; Maimonides, *Yad, Hanukkah* 3:5–6, and commentaries.
25. See *Shulhan Aruch, Orah Hayim* 101:4, and *Mishnah Berurah*.
26. Maimonides, *Yad, Tefillah* 1:1.
27. Exodus 23:25.
28. Maimonides, *Yad, Tefillah* 1:1, 2.
29. *Shulhan Aruch, Orah Hayim* 55:1; *Halichot Betah* 10:2, and n. 4.
30. *Halichot Betah* 6:8:13.
31. *Shulhan Aruch, Orah Hayim* 55:1. For a discussion of the halachic view of women and congregational prayer, see Meiselman, 135–146.
32. *Mishnah Berurah, Shulhan Aruch, Orah Hayim* 55:1.
33. J. David Bleich, *Contemporary Halachic Problems*, vol. 3 (New York: Ktav and Yeshiva University Press, 1989), 115–116. R. Bleich refers (116 n. 1) to published reactions on the parts of the halachic authorities R. Moses Feinstein, R. Joseph B. Soloveichik, and R. Herschel Schachter. The two leading halachic authorities of the second half of the twentieth century have been R. Joseph B. Soloveitchik, who served as the revered teacher of generations of Orthodox rabbis ordained at Yeshiva University, and R. Moses Feinstein, the master of *Halachah*, whose work of *responsa*, *Igrot Moshe*, is the preeminent twentieth-century supplement to the Code of Jewish Law, and an important compendium of modern day halachic decisions.

R. Avraham Weiss, an advocate of women's prayer groups, in his book *Women at Prayer* (New York: Ktav: 1990), 107–110, refers to a statement by R. Saul Berman of Lincoln Square Synagogue in New York who quoted a colleague as saying that R. Soloveitchik "responded very positively" to such groups, and suggested textual changes in prayers to make such prayer services halachically acceptable. He also states that R. Shlomo Riskin "on numerous occasions indicated that Rav Soloveitchik had told him that women's *tefillah* groups are halachically permissible."

Rabbi Weiss cites a statement by R. Herschel Schachter of Yeshiva University: "It is well known that the two great sages of our generation . . . R. Soloveitchik, and . . . R. Feinstein, both oppose the practices . . . [of] *hakafot* specifically designated for women, *minyanim* [for women] for prayer, the reading of the Torah scroll, and the reading of the Megillah."

R. Weiss also cites a *teshuvah* (halachic decision; *responsum* of Jewish law) of R. Moses Feinstein issued by his grandson, R. Mordechai Tendler, which states:

> In reality, it is hard to find a situation where this problem [of women whose motivation is insincere] does not exist. Therefore, it is hard for us to say that any "women's *minyan*" does not have this problem.
>
> And [therefore] only in the theoretical realm itself can one say that if there is a group of righteous women whose intention is purely for the sake of Heaven without intending to undermine God's Torah or Jewish practice, then, of course, why prevent them from praying together?
>
> And they may also read from the Torah Scroll, provided that they take care not to do it in such a way that one might erroneously believe it to be actually a public reading, i.e., they should not say the Torah blessings in public. They should rely on the blessings which they said earlier, or in the event that they have not yet said the blessings, they may say them to themselves. There are, of course, additional details included in our *Igrot Moshe* which one should take careful note of in this matter. Each *baal horaah* [arbiter of *Halachah*] should conduct himself in this matter in a way which is in line with this outlook.

R. Weiss states that R. Feinstein's concern about sincere motivation relates to the possibility of *ziyuf haTorah*, the falsification or distortion of the Torah, which should be prevented at all cost. This could come about if women's prayer group participants or the public are led to believe that their Torah reading of the Torah is a public, rather than private, act and that the prayer service is perceived as a *minyan*–as is indeed the general perception.

R. Feinstein says that theoretically there should be no objection to women's prayer groups, but makes clear that the likelihood of a group of women meeting all the criteria necessary "does not exist." This is confirmed by a "clarification" (cited by R. Weiss) that R. Feinstein issued through his grandson, lest there be a possibility of his *teshuvah* being misunderstood:

> As stated in my letter, the detailed discussion was *purely in a theoretical sense*. My grandfather pragmatically feels that the possibility of a group of women or, for that matter, men, existing in any one community which will fill the lengthy philosophical criteria mentioned in his printed *teshuvah* is extremely remote. Therefore, realistically speaking, he doesn't commend or actually condone the establishment of women's prayer groups.

On the basis of the information cited by R. Weiss, it is evident that–although R. Weiss concludes otherwise–R. Feinstein clearly opposes the establishment of women's prayer groups, both in his original halachic *teshuvah* and in the subsequent clarification. While he maintains the theoretical possibility for such prayer groups if properly halachically constituted, he emphasizes that "realistically speaking" the possibility for doing so at present is either "extremely remote" or that it "does not exist."

34. Bleich, ibid. R. Bleich concludes that this is why "knowledgeable rabbis" do not encourage women's prayer groups. "Such encouragement would be tantamount to *lifnei iver*–advising a less advantageous mode of action when a parallel and much more advantageous course of conduct is readily available.

"Many participants in women's *minyanim* speak and write movingly of the religious experience such participation brings them. Presumably, some may argue that the religious experience in which they share is sufficient reason to sacrifice the incontrovertible advantage of *tefillah betzibbur* (congregational prayer). That position is predicated on a fundamental error–if not an error of *Halachah,* then an error of *hashkafah,* or religious perspective. "Let these comments not be understood as denigrating the value of religious experience. *Kavanah* (devotion) is certainly a form of religious experience and its value cannot be extolled too greatly. But Judaism recognizes a hierarchy of values, and *kavanah, deveikut,* religious experience or "attachment," desirable and laudable as they may be, should never be permitted to supplant other [more important] values. The fulfillment of a *mitzvah* in an optimal manner, albeit without extraordinary *kavanah,* is to be favored over less optimal fulfillment accompanied by fervent religious experience."

35. *Megillah* 23a.

36. R. Meiselman (197 n. 64) quotes R. Joseph B. Soloveitchik as having informed him that "he is opposed such *aliyot* and has never told any rabbi that they are permitted."

37. See *Shulhan Aruch, Yoreh De'ah* 22:10.

38. *Magen Avraham, Orah Hayim* 282:3. Women are exempted from the obligation to listen to the Torah and *Haftarah* readings on the festivals (*Halichot Betah* 9:3).

39. See *Mishnah Berurah, Shulhan Aruch, Orah Hayim* 282:3.

40. *Shulhan Aruch, Orah Hayim* 55:1.

41. *Sedei Hemed,* Collection of Laws, Mourning, 160. *Mishpetei Uziel* (2, *Orah Hayim* 13) says that the exclusion is based on a son being able to assume the.role of his father to publicly sanctify God and thus "elevate" the soul of the departed, but a daughter, who is not expected to take her father's place in the synagogue, is able to perform the same thing on the basis of her good deeds. *Halichot Betah* quotes *Mateh Ephraim* to the effect that a daughter's answering of *Amen* to the recitation of *Kaddish* is considered the equivalent of her recitation of *Kaddish.*

42. *Shaarei Teshuvah,* to *Rama, Shulhan Aruch, Orah Hayim* 132:2, cites the opinion of *Shevut Yaakov,* II, 53, who states that in the absence of a son a daughter may recite *Kaddish* (with a proper *minyan*) in her home. *Kitzur Shulhan Aruch* 26:20 mentions this as well but also cites *Havat Yair* 262, where this is not permitted. *Halichot Betah* 10:8–9 also cites halachic authorities who allow the recitation of *Kaddish* by a woman at her home in the presence of a proper *minyan* in the absence of a son who can recite it.

43. On the right arm for left-handed people.

44. Exodus 13:9, 16; Deuteronomy 6:4–9; 11:13–20.

45. There is also a tradition that a daughter of *Rashi* wore *tefillin.*

46. See *Rashi, Eruvin* 96b, "*Velo mihu bah hachamim,*" and *Tosafot,* ad loc., "*Michal bat Kushi.*"

47. Deuteronomy 11:19.

48. *JT Berachot* 2:3; see also *Pesikta Rabbati,* section 22.

49. *Targum Jonathan ben Uziel* to Deuteronomy 22:5.
50. See Meiselman, 150.
51. See *Tosafot, Eruvin* 96a, *"Dilma"*; *Tosafot, Hagigah* 16b, *"Laasot"*; *Tosafot, Rosh HaShanah* 33a, *"Ha Rabbi Yehudah."*
52. *Responsa* of R. Meir of Rothenburg, ed. Kalman Kahana (Jerusalem), 1:34, 143.
53. *Yoma* 7b.
54. *Ravad, Torat Kohanim*, chap. 2.
55. *Shulhan Aruch, Orah Hayim* 38:3.
56. *Rama, Shulhan Aruch, Orah Hayim* 38:3. *"Ve'im hanashim rotzin lehahmir al atzman, mohin beyadan."*
57. Numbers 15:37–40.
58. Maimonides, *Yad, Tzitzit* 13:11.
59. *Menahot* 43a
60. Maimonides, *Yad, Tzitzit* 3:9; *Shulhan Aruch, Orah Hayim* 17:2.
61. Maimonides, *Yad, Tzitzit* 3:9.
62. *Rama, Shulhan Aruch, Orah Hayim* 17:2.
63. Ibid.
64. *Sefer MaHaril*, 7.
65. Deuteronomy 22:5.
66. *Targum Jonathan ben Uziel*, ad loc.
67. *Halichot Beitah* 2:2.
68. Meiselman, 154.
69. *Berachot* 35a.
70. *Shulhan Aruch, Orah Hayim* 202–230.
71. Deuteronomy 8:10.
72. *Berachot* 20b.
73. *Shulhan Aruch, Orah Hayim* 186:1.
74. *Berachot* 45b and *Rashi*, ad loc.
75. *Piskei HaRosh* 4:16.
76. *Arachin* 3a.
77. *Tosafot, Berachot* 45b, *"Sheani."*
78. *Piskei HaRosh, Berachot* 7:4.
79. *Menahot* 43b; *Shulhan Aruch, Orah Hayim* 46:4.
80. See *Levush, Shulhan Aruch, Orah Hayim* 46:4.
81. R. Dovid Gottlieb, in discussion with the author, refers to the *Otzar HaTefilot*, who understands the negative formulation of the man's blessing to be derived from the talmudic philosophical judgment, *"noah lo le'adam shelo nivra yoter mishenivra"* (*Eruvin* 13b), "better would it have been for man not to have been created at all than to have been created," since man, who, in large measure, was created in order to be obedient to God, does not fulfill his duties and responsibilities to God. Consequently, men cannot easily proclaim in full confidence their appreciation for receiving more responsibilities through a blessing containing a positive formulation when they are aware that they cannot be certain that they will fulfill those responsibilities. The blessing women recite, however, is not of a parallel nature to the one recited by men; it is not a blessing for their *responsibilities* but in appreciation of *their feminine nature*. Women thank God for having created them, in accordance with the divine will, as women, with innate characteristics and traits that are uniquely feminine.
82. *Tosefta, Berachot* 6:23.

83. *The Hirsch Siddur* (Jerusalem and New York: Feldheim, 1978), 13.

84. Meiselman, 51. *Halichot Betah* quotes the *Yeshuot Yaakov* as maintaining that *kiretzono*, according to His will, refers to God having created woman on the basis of His will alone, and not, as man was made according to the Midrash, after first consulting with the angels. (*Halichot Betah* 3 n. 16.)

CHAPTER 15

1. *Mishnah, Pe'ah* 1:1; *Shabbat* 127a.
2. *Avot* 5:26.
3. *Avot* 6:2.
4. *Shabbat* 31b.
5. *Kiddushin* 29b; *Shulhan Aruch, Yoreh De'ah* 245:1.
6. *Kiddushin*, ibid.; *Yoreh De'ah*, ibid.
7. Deuteronomy 11:19.
8. *Ketubot* 29b.
9. *Mishnah, Sotah* 3:2.
10. See *Birkei Yosef, Shulhan Aruch, Yoreh De'ah* 246:7.
11. Deuteronomy 5:1.
12. *The Daily Prayer Book*, blessing preceding the *Shema.*
13. *Sefer Hasidim*, 313.
14. *Sefer Mitzvot Katan*, intro.
15. *Horeb, A Philosophy of Jewish Laws and Observances*, vol. 2, trans. from the German original with introduction and annotation by Dayan Dr. I. Grunfeld (London: Soncino, 1962), 371.
16. *The Hirsch Siddur* (New York: Feldheim, 1978), commentary to the *Shema*, 122.
17. *Shemirat Shabbat Kehilchata, "Hinuch HaBanim Lemitzvot,"* 13–14.
18. *Halichot Betah* 27:4.
19. Maimonides *Yad, Yesodei Torah* 4:13.
20. Maimonides *Yad, Talmud Torah* 1:13.
21. Ibid.
22. *Tuv Ayin*, sec. 4.
23. Ibid.
24. *Perishah* to *Tur, Yoreh Deah* 246:15.
25. M. Meiselman, *Jewish Woman in Jewish Law* (New York: Ktav, 1978), 38–39.
26. *Hafetz Hayim, Likutei Halachot, Sotah* 21b.
27. *Moznayim LaMishpat* (Jerusalem, 1968), sec. 42.
28. Ibid.
29. Genesis 30:1.
30. *"Ukamohu tuchal lehavin ulehaskil bedivrei sechel vehasidut, kemo she'asu ha'imahot vekama tzidkaniyot uneviot, vekaasher yoreh peshat parashat Eishet Hayil."*
31. See *Rashi*, Genesis 6:9.
32. *Akedat Yitzhak*, Genesis 30:1.
33. *Halichot Betah* 28:3. See n. 3.
34. Meiselman, 39–40.
35. N. Geschwind and A. M. Galaburda, "Cerebral Lateralization: Biological

Mechanisms, Associations and Pathology," in *Archives of Neurology*, No. 42, 428–459, 521–552, 634–654; Doreen Kimura, "Are men's and women's brains really different?" in *Canadian Psychology* 28:2 (1987): 133–147; "Sex differences in cerebral organization for speech and praxic functions," in *Canadian Journal of Psychology*, No. 37, 19–35; Jeanette McGlone, "Sex Differences in Human Brain Assymetry: A Critical Survey," in *The Behavioral and Brain Sciences* 3 (1980): 215–264.

36. Sandra Witleson, professor of psychiatry at McMaster University, Hamilton, Ontario, q. in *Time* (September 9, 1991), 55.

37. Ralph Holloway and Christine de Lacoste-Utamsing, "Sexual Dimorphism in the Human *Corpus Callosum*," in *Science* 216 (June 25, 1982): 1431.

38. See Dianne McGuinness, *When Children Don't Learn* (New York: Basic Books, 1985), 21, 115–119; Eleanor Maccoby and Carol Jacklin, *The Psychology of Sex Differences* (Stanford: Stanford University Press: 1974), 75–85.

39. K. Rosenthal, "Hormonal influence on cognitive ability patterns," Research Bulletin 653, Department of Psychology, University of Ontario (London, Ontario, March 1987).

40. Doris F. Jonas and A. David Jonas, "Gender Differences in Mental Function: A Clue to the Origin of Language," in *Current Anthropology* 16 (December 1975): 626–630.

41. *Time*, ibid.; Alice Rossi, "Gender and Parenthood," in *American Sociological Review* 49 (February 1984): 1:19.

42. See Camilla Benbow and Julian C. Stanley, "Sex Differences in Mathematical Ability: Fact or Artifact," in *Science* 222 (1983): 1029–1031.

43. L. J. Harris, "Sex differences in spatial ability: possible environmental, genetic and neurological factors," in M. Kinsbourne, ed., *Asymmetrical Function of the Brain* (Cambridge: Cambridge University Press, 1978), 405–522; "Sex-Related Variations in Spatial Skills," in S. Liben, et al., eds., *Spatial Representation and Behavior across the Life Span* (New York: Academic Press, 1981), 83–112.

44. Anne Moir and David Jessel, *Brain Sex: The Real Differences between Men and Women* (London: Michael Joseph, 1989), 186.

45. See *U. S. News and World Report* (August 8, 1988), 54.

46. See Maccoby and Jacklin, vii, 351–352.

47. See Richard Restak, *The Brain. The Last Frontier* (New York: Doubleday, 1979), 205; Maccoby and Jacklin, 351–352, 368; James Q. Wilson and Richard Hernnstein, *Crime and Human Nature* (New York: Simon & Schuster, 1985), 124–125; K. E. Moyer, "The Physiology of Aggression and the Implications for Aggression Control," in J. L. Singer, ed., *The Control of Aggression and Violence* (New York: Academic Press, 1971), 61–92; Robert T. Robin, June M. Reinisch, and Roger Haskett, "Postnatal, Gonadal Steroid Effects on Human Behavior," in *Science* 211 (1981): 1318–1324; Mary Knudsen, in Carl Degler, *In Search of Human Nature–The Decline and Revival of Darwinism in American Social Thought* (New York and Oxford: Oxford University Press, 1991), 300.

48. See Dennis L. Krebs, "Altruism–An Examination of the Concept and a Review of the Literature," in *Psychology Bulletin* 73 (1970): 258–302; Maccoby and Jacklin, 354; Norma Deitch Feschbach, "Studies of Empathetic Behavior in Children," in B. A. Maher, ed., *Progress in Experimental Personality Research*, vol. 8 (New York: Academica Press, 1978), 1–47; Martin L. Hoffman and Laura E. Levine, "Early Sex Differences in Empathy," in *Developmental Psychology* 12:6 (1976): 557–558; E. Mark Cummings, Barbara Hollenback *et al.*, in Carolyn Zahn-Wexler, E. Mark Cummings, and Ronald

J. Ionnotti, eds., *Altruism and Aggression: Social and Biological Origins* (Cambridge: Cambridge University Press, 1986), 167–168.

49. *Igrot Moshe, Shulhan Aruch, Orah Hayim* 1:104.

50. Ibid.

51. See R. Jehiel Jacob Weinberg in *HaPardes, Nisan* 5723; R. Hanoch Zundel Grossberg in *HaMaayan* 13:2 (*Tevet* 5733); *Kol Mevaser* 2:44.

52. *Seridei Eish* 3:93.

53. *Halichot Betah* 13:20. When reciting the *Sheheheyanu* the *bat mitzvah* should do so at the same time as she dons a new dress or eats a new fruit (ibid.).

Glossary

Abba–Father; daddy.

Admor–(Plural, *Admorim*) Hasidic rabbi; acronym for "our master, teacher, and rabbi."

Agunah–"Anchored woman." A woman who cannot obtain a divorce because her husband is missing, or because uncertainty exists whether her husband is alive, or because he refuses to cooperate by granting her a legal Jewish divorce.

Ahavah–Love.

Aleph-Bet–The first two letters of the alphabet; the "ABC's."

Aliyah–(Plural, *aliyot*) Going up; in the synagogue, the process of going–or being "called"–up to read the Torah.

Am haaretz–Ignoramus or boor.

Av–Father.

Bar kayama–Viable; a viable human being.

Bar/bat mitzvah–Literally, "son/daughter of the commandment," that is, one under obligation to fulfill the commandments; a term denoting both religious majority and the occasion at which this status is formally assumed–age thirteen years and one day for boys, and twelve years and one day for girls.

Bet Din–Rabbinic court. In ancient times, a court of law. In modern times, an ecclesiastic court dealing primarily with religious matters such as *kashrut* and divorce.

Binah–Understanding; discernment; insight; perception.

Birkat HaMazon–Grace after meals.

Birkat HaZimun–The invitation to participate in a group recitation of *Birkat HaMazon*, grace after meals.

Derech eretz–Literally, "the way of the land." Proper comportment and behavior in keeping with accepted social and moral practice: courtesy, politeness, honor of elders, good manners, etiquette, respect, and consideration for others.

Derashah–Sermon; interpretation; homily; moral oration.

Devar mitzvah–An act of kindness.

Eishet Hayil–Women of Valor, that is, the Jewish wife and mother; the title and opening words of the traditional hymn of exaltation in praise of the Jewish wife and mother sung at the inauguration of the weekly family Sabbath eve feast, from Proverbs 31.

Em–Mother.

Etrog–Citron. One of the "Four Species" held during part of morning prayer during the Sukkot festival.

Gadol–(Plural, *gedolim*) Great, or the great one; a leading Torah authority.

Gaon–(Plural, *Geonim*) Literally, "genius"; the head of the academy in the posttalmudic period.

Genizah–Storage room for old religious books, documents, and ritual objects.

Get (*Get Piturin*)–The Jewish bill of divorce.

Gemara–Commentary and discussions on and a supplement to the *Mishnah* and, together with the *Mishnah*, forming the Talmud.

Gematria–The numerical equivalent of Hebrew letters.

Gemilut hasadim–Acts of love performed for one's fellow (See *Hesed*).

Gezerat HaKatuv–Divine decree.

Hachnasat orhim–Literally "bringing guests into one's home"; hospitality to strangers–one expression of *gemilut hasadim*.

Haggadah–The Passover *seder* guidebook.

Hakafot–Circular processions with the Torah on Simhat Torah.

Halachah–Jewish law.

Hallah–The taking of the dough portion when baking; braided Sabbath bread loaf.

Halipin–A form of exchange that serves as a legal consideration.

Halitzah–A biblically prescribed ritual (Deuteronomy 25:9–10) conducted between a childless widow and her late husband's brother, which obviates the necessity for levirate marriage.

Hametz–Leaven; ordinary bread.

Hanukkah–The eight-day Feast of Lights.

Hanukkiyah–Hanukkah lamp, used during the Hanukkah festival.

Hasidism–In modern times, a movement of religious revival founded by R.

Israel Baal Shem Tov (1700–1770), which emphasizes finding God through joy and prayer. Followers are called *hasidim.*

Hatan–Groom.

Havdalah–Literally, "separation." The ceremony marking the end of the Sabbath.

Herem–Excommunication.

Hesed–Acts of love performed for one's fellow.

Hinuch–Education.

Hok–(Plural, *hukim*) Scriptural statute.

Hol HaMoed–The intermediate days of the Passover and Sukkot festivals.

Imma–Mother; mommy.

Ish–Man.

Ishah–Woman.

Kabbalah–Literally, "received," or "received lore." The term used for the esoteric teachings and mystic lore of Jewish tradition.

Kaddish–Prayer recited in memory of the deceased.

Kallah–Bride.

Kashrut–Fitness. Usually applied to the laws relating to food considered to be fit for eating, because the source of the food is "kosher" or because the food is properly prepared.

Kavanah–Proper intent; spiritual and mental concentration and devotion accompanying prayers or when performing a precept.

Kedeshah–A harlot.

Kedushah–Holiness.

Ketubah–Literally, "her writ." The marriage document containing the husband's obligations and guarantees to his wife presented at the marriage ceremony.

Kinyan–A formal acknowledgment of an agreement; acquisition.

Kiddush–The Sabbath and festival "sanctification" ritual, usually conducted over wine.

Kiddushin–Literally, "sanctification." Marriage betrothal.

Kohen (*Cohen*)–A Jew of priestly (Aaronic) descent.

Kohen Gadol–High priest.

Kollel–An institution for advanced Torah study, usually for married students.

Kos–Cup.

Lapid–Torch.

Lashon HaKodesh–The holy tongue; Hebrew.

Lulav–Palm, one of the "Four Species" held during part of the morning services during the Sukkot festival.

Mamzer–(Plural, *mamzerim*) The offspring of certain prohibited adulterous or incestuous relationships.

Matzah–Unleavened bread.

Mazal tov (Mazeltov)–Good luck.

Megillah–Scroll; the Book of Esther.

Mehitzah–Separation; the divider between the men's and the women's section in the traditional synagogue.

Mideoraita–A precept ordained by the Torah.

Miderabanan–A rabbinically ordained precept.

Midrash–Rabbinic exegetical and homiletical literature forming a study of and commentary on the Torah, composed primarily during the first millennium of the Common Era.

Mikveh (Mikvah)–(Plural, *mikvaot*) Ritual bath.

Minhag–Custom.

Minyan–A quorum for Jewish public prayer.

Mishlo'ah manot–The custom of sending gifts during the Purim festival.

Mishnah–The Oral Law, composed in six "orders" or divisions (*Shishah Sidrei Mishnah*–accronym: SH'AS), originally taught orally. Codified, edited, and committed into writing at the beginning of the third century and, together with the *Gemara*, the commentary and discussion on the *Mishnah*, forming the Talmud.

Mitzvah–(Plural, *mitzvot*) A biblical or rabbinic precept or commandment; a good deed.

Moch–Contraceptive tampon.

Musar–Jewish ethics and morals.

Nasi–President; leader of the community.

Neder–Religious vow.

Negia–Physical contact (in particular, between men and women).

Niddah–Menstruant; the status of the woman from the onset of her menstrual period until her immersion in a *mikveh*.

Olam HaBa–The world to come; paradise.

Omer–The biblical wave-offering.

Onah–Literally, "season." The husband's obligation for marital relations with his wife.

Oral Law–The term used for the law that was originally transmitted orally and handed down from generation to generation and eventually committed to writing as the *Mishnah* and *Gemara*, together known as the Talmud.

Passover–The eight-day festival celebrating freedom.

Paytan–Liturgical poet.

Piryah verivyah–Procreation.

Peru urevu–Be fruitful and multiply. The biblical command to procreate.

Pesak Din–Rabbinic decision on Jewish law.

Purim–The Feast of Lots; the Esther Festival.

Rahmanut–Compassion.

Rodef–Pursuer.

Rosh HaShanah–The Jewish New Year.

Rosh Hodesh–Festival celebrating the beginning of a new month.

Sanhedrin–Assembly of rabbinic scholars that functioned as both high rabbinical court and legislature in ancient Israel.

Seder–Order; the Passover eve feast.

Sephardi–Spanish; Jews of Spanish/Portugese or of non-European origin.

Shechinah–The Divine Presence; the Spirit of God on earth.

She'ilah–Query regarding *Halachah,* Jewish law.

Shalom bayit–The peaceful home; harmony between husband and wife.

Shema Yisrael–"Hear O Israel." The first words of the prayer "Hear O Israel, the Lord our God is One" (Deuteronomy 6:4), Judaism's confession of faith, which proclaims the absolute unity of God and which is recited twice daily by the believing Jew.

Shabbat–The Sabbath.

Shabbat Shalom–Sabbath greeting: "Peaceful Sabbath."

Shadchan–(Plural, *shadchanim*) Matchmaker, marriage broker.

Shochet–Authorized slaughterer for kosher meat.

Shofar–The horn of an animal, usually a ram, sounded on Rosh HaShanah and following the Yom Kippur fast, and on other occasions.

Shtraimel–(Yiddish) Wide cylindrical fur hat worn by hasidic men on Sabbaths, festivals, and certain festive occasions.

Shulhan Aruch–Literally, "The Prepared Table." The Code of Jewish Law.

Siddur–The Jewish Prayer Book.

Simhat Torah–The festival celebrating the conclusion of the annual cycle of Torah Pentateuchal readings.

Sofer–Scribe of Hebrew books and documents.

Sukkot–The eight-day festival of booths.

Seudah Shelishit–The third Sabbath meal.

Sukkah–Temporary dwelling outside the home in which the Jew resides during the eight-day fall Sukkot festival.

Taharat HaMishpahah–The Purity of Family Life; the laws and way of life that govern marital relations between husband and wife, especially those relating to *niddah* and *mikveh.*

Takkanah–Rabbinical enactment.

Tallit–Four-cornered, fringed, capelike garment worn by the married man during morning prayers.

Tallit Katan–(*"Arba Kanfos"*) Small *tallit,* usually worn beneath the shirt, but often worn above the shirt by *hasidim.*

Talmid hacham–(Plural, *talmidei hachamim*) A Torah scholar.

Talmud–Study; the oral teachings of the Torah, including the Mishnah and the *Gemara.*

Tanach–Acronym for *Torah, Nevi'im, Ketuvim*–the Hebrew Bible.

Tanna–(Plural, *Tannaim*) Rabbinic scholar and teacher or the early (mishnaic) period of the Talmud.

Targum–Aramaic translation of the Bible.

Tefillah–Prayer.

Tefillah Betzibbur–Communal prayer.

Tefillin–Leather cubes containing biblical passages, worn by Jewish males on the arms and upper forehead during daily morning prayers.

Torah–Literally, "The Teaching." The Pentateuch, or the Five Books of Moses.

Torah She baal Peh–The Oral Torah–the Talmud and the Codes.

Torah She bichtav–The Written Torah–the Bible.

Tosafists–Rabbinic glossarists of the Talmud, mainly French and German, who during the twelfth to fourteenth centuries composed the *Tosafot* glosses to the Talmud.

Tosefta–Collection of rabbinic teachings on the Oral Law of the early talmudic period not included in the Mishnah.

Terumot and *Ma'asrot*–Biblically ordained gift offerings and tithings.

Tevilah–Immersion in a *mikveh*.

Tzaddik–Righteous person; hasidic rabbi.

Tzedakah–Charity; righteousness.

Tzelem Elohim–The image of God.

Tzitzit–Fringes on the four-cornered *tallit* worn in accordance with biblical injunction as a reminder to perform God's precepts.

Tzeniut–Modesty.

Ubar–Fetus.

Yeshivah–Academy for the study of Torah.

Yoharah–Excessive pride; exhibitionism.

Yom Kippur–The Day of Atonement.

Bibliography

Selected Hebrew Sources

The works are classified by the principal texts followed by the commentaries on them, listed chronologically.

BIBLE AND COMMENTARIES

Mikraot Gedolot. The text of the Hebrew Bible, with Aramaic *Targum* translations and various commentaries. Jerusalem, 1977.

Rashi (R. Solomon Yitzhaki, 1040–1105).

Rashbam (R. Samuel ben Meir, c. 1080-1085–1158).

R. Abraham *Ibn Ezra* (1092–1167).

Radak (R. David Kimhi, c. 1160–c. 1235).

Ramban (R. Moses ben Nahman – Nahmanides, c. 1195–1270).

R. Ovadiah *Sforno* (1470–1550).

Vilna Gaon (R. Elijah, Gaon of Vilna, 1720–1797). *Aderet Eliyahu*.

R. Samuel David Luzzatto (*Shadal*, 1800–1865). *Perush Shadal*. Tel Aviv, 1965.

R. Meir Leibush *Malbim* (1809–1879).

Meshech Hochmah (R. Meir Simhah HaKohen of Dvinsk, 1843–1926), 1927.

TARGUM – MIDRASHIM

Targum Jonathan ben Uziel, first century B.C.E.–first century C.E. A midrashic translation of the Prophets into Aramaic. In *Mikraot Gedolot*.

Targum Onkelos, second century C.E.. The standard Aramaic translation and paraphrase of the Bible. In *Mikraot Gedolot*.
Midrash Mechilta. Philadelphia, 1949.
Midrash Torat Kohanim.
Sifra. Jerusalem, 1959.
Sifri. Liepzig, 1917.
Midrash Rabbah. Tel Aviv, 1968.
Midrash Tanhuma. Berlin, 1927.
Pesikta Rabbati. Vienna, 1880.
Tana d'Bei Eliyahu. Vienna, 1902.
Yalkut. Vilna, 1898.
Pirkei D'Rabbi Eliezer. London, 1916.
Pesikta D'Rabbi Kahana. Philadelphia, 1975.

TALMUD AND COMMENTARIES

Mishnah. New York, 1963.
Shmonah Perakim (Maimonides–R. Moses ben Maimon, The *Rambam*, 1135–1204). With most editions of the *Mishnah*.
Avot D'Rabbi Nathan. London, 1887.
Babylonian Talmud. Jerusalem, 1970.
Rishonim - Early talmudic commentators, tenth–fifteenth centuries.
Rabbeinu Hananel (tenth–eleventh centuries). With many standard editions of the Babylonian Talmud.
Rashi (see above). In all standard editions of the Talmud.
Tosafot. Analyses and commentary by French and German scholars of the twelfth and thirteenth centuries, among which *Rabbeinu Tam*, *Rashi*'s grandson, was the leading member. With all standard editions of the Talmud.
Ramban (see above). Jerusalem, 1928.
Mordechai (R. Mordecai ben Hillel, d. 1298). With most editions of the Talmud.
Tosafot Rid (R. Nissim Gerondi, d. 1380). New York, 1946.
Shitah Mekubetzet (R. Bezalel Ashkenazi, c. 1520–1592). Tel Aviv, 1954.
MaHarsha (R. Samuel Edels, 1555–1631). With most standard editions of the Talmud.
Palestinian Talmud (Jerusalem Talmud; all references to the Jerusalem Talmud in notes are preceded with "JT"). Jerusalem, 1975.

CODES AND COMMENTARIES

Rif (R. Isaac Alfasi, 1013–1103). In most editions of the Talmud.
Mahzor Vitri (R. Simhah ben Samuel, eleventh century).
Even HaEzer (Eliezer ben Nathan, d. 1165). Prague, 1610.
Maimonides (see above). *Mishneh Torah* (or *Yad HaHazakah*–referred to in notes as "*Yad*"). New York, 1956.
Hasagot HaRavad (R. Abraham ben David, c. 1125–1198). With all standard editions of the *Mishneh Torah*.
Hagahot Maimoniot (R. Meir HaKohen, thirteenth century). With all standard editions of the *Mishneh Torah*.

Kesef Mishneh (R. Joseph Caro, 1488–1575). With all standard editions of the *Mishneh Torah*.
Magid Mishneh (R. Yom Tov Vidal, fourteenth century). With all standard editions of the *Mishneh Torah*.
Lehem Mishneh (R. Abraham di Boton, c. 1545–1588). With all standard editions of the *Mishneh Torah*.
Sefer HaRokeah (R. Elazar ben Judah, c. 1165–c. 1230). Fano, Italy, 1505.
Rosh (R. Asher ben Jehiel, 1250–1327).
Kol Bo (Anonymous, thirteenth century). New York, 1945.
Sefer HaHinuch (Attributed to R. Aaron HaLevi of Barcelona, fourteenth century). Jerusalem, 1951.
Sefer Mitzvot Gadol (S'mag–R. Moses ben Jacob of Coucy, thirteenth century). Venice, 1522.
Sefer Mitzvot Katan (S'mak–R. Isaac ben Joseph of Corbeil, d. 1280). Ladi, 1805.
Tur (R. Jacob ben Asher, c. 1270–1340). Vilna, 1900. This work has four divisions: *Orah Hayim, Yoreh De'ah, Hoshen Mishpat, Even HaEzer*. Vilna, 1900.
Bet Yosef (R. Joseph Karo, 1488–1575). With standard editions of the *Tur*.
Darchei Moshe (R. Moses Isserles, c. 1520–1572). With standard editions of the *Tur*.
MaHaril (R. Jacob Halevi Mollin, c. 1360–1427). Lvov, 1860.
Shulhan Aruch (R. Joseph Karo, 1488–1575). An abridged version of the *Bet Yosef* Commentary on the *Tur*, divided into four major divisions. Vilna, 1911.
Rama (R. Moses Isserles, see above). With standard editions of the *Shulhan Aruch*.
Turei Zahav (*Taz*–R. David HaLevi, 1586–1667). With standard editions of the *Shulhan Aruch*.
Helkat Mehokek (R. Moses Lima, 1605–1658). With standard editions of the *Shulhan Aruch*.
Magen Avraham (R. Abraham Gombiner, 1637–1683). With standard editions of the *Shulhan Aruch*.
Mor Uketzia (R. Jacob Emden, 1697–1776). With standard editions of the *Shulhan Aruch*.
Ba'er Hetev (R. Judah Ashkenazi, eighteenth century). With standard editions of the *Shulhan Aruch*.
Biur HaGra (R. Elijah ben Solomon Zalman–The *Vilna Gaon*, 1720–1797). With standard editions of the *Shulhan Aruch*.
Pri Megadim (R. Joseph ben Meir Teomim, c. 1727–1792). With standard editions of the *Shulhan Aruch*.
Birkei Yosef (R. Haim Joseph–Hidah, 1724–1806). Vienna, 1860.
Mishneh Berurah (R. Israel Meir HaKohen–Hafetz Hayim, 1838–1933). Tel Aviv, 1955.
Hazon Ish (R. Isaiah Karelitz, 1878–1953). Bnei Brak, 1958.
Igrot Moshe (R. Moses Feinstein, 1895–1986). New York, 1961.
Levush (R. Mordecai Jaffe, c. 1535–1612). Venice, 1620.
Haye Adam (R. Abraham Danzig, 1748–1820). Warsaw, 1908.
Hochmat Adam (R. Abraham Danzig, see *Haye Adam*). Warsaw, 1899.
Kitzur Shulhan Aruch (R. Shlomo Ganzfried, 1804–1886). Lublin, 1888.
Aruch HaShulhan (R. Yehiel Michel Epstein, 1829–1908). Warsaw, 1911.
Halichot Betah (R. Davi Auerbach). Jerusalem: Shaarei Ziv, 1983.
Shemirat Shabbat KeHilchata (R. Joshua Neuwirth). Jerusalem: Feldheim, 1979. (English edition, 1984.)

EXTRALEGAL LITERATURE: ETHICAL, PHILOSOPHICAL, AND MYSTIC

Zohar. Jerusalem, 1960.

Emunot VeDe'ot (Saadia Gaon, d. 942). Constantinople, 1562.

Hovat HaLevavot (R. Bachya ibn Pakuda, eleventh century). Tel Aviv, 1949.

Moreh Nevuchim (Maimonides–the *Rambam*, see the preceding). Jerusalem, 1959.

Baalei HaNefesh (R. Abraham ben David–*Ravad*, c. 1125–1198). Warsaw, 1863.

Sefer Hasidim (R. Judah HeHasid, d. 1217). Jerusalem, 1964.

Igeret HaKodesh (Ascribed to *Ramban*, R. Moses ben Nahman–Nahmanides, see the preceding). Jerusalem, 1955.

Maalot HaMidot (R. Y'hiel ben Y'kutiel HaRofe, thirteenth century). Jerusalem.

Kad HaKemah (R. Bachya ben Asher, thirteenth century). New York, 1980.

Menorat HaMaor (R. Israel Al-Nakawa, c. 1340–1391). New York, 1932.

Menorat HaMaor (R. Isaac Aboab, second half fourteenth century). Jerusalem.

Nefesh Yehudah (R. Moses Frankfurt, 1672–1762). With many editions of *Menorat HaMaor*.

Orhot Tzadikim (fifteenth century). New York, 1974.

Reshit Hochmah (R. Elijah de Vidas, sixteenth century). Venice, 1579.

Pele Yoetz (R. Eliezer Papo, seventeenth century). Jerusalem.

Shevet Musar (R. Elijah HaKohen Itamari, d. 1729). Amsterdam, 1734.

Siddur Bet Yaakov (R. Jacob Emden, see the preceding). Lemberg, 1904.

Likutei MoHaran (R. Nahman of Bratzlav, 1772–1811). Ostroy, 1806.

Likutei Etzot HaShalom. Warsaw, 1913.

Hupat Hatanim (Raphael Meldola, 1754–1828). Venice, 1797.

Shaarei Rahamim. Vilna, 1871.

Ahavath Hessed (R. Israel Meir HaKohen–Hafetz Hayim, see the preceding); English translation by Leonard Oschry, New York and Jerusalem: Feldheim, 1976.

Shemirat HaLashon (R. Israel Meir HaKohen–Hafetz Hayim, see the preceding); English adaptation by R. Zelig Pliskin, *Guard Your Tongue*. Jerusalem and New York: Feldheim, 1975.

Taamei HaMinhagim (R. Abraham Isaac Sperling, 1851–1921), Jerusalem.

Michtav MeEliyahu (R. Elijah Eliezer Dessler, 1891–1954). London, 1955. Abridged version published in English by Aryeh Carmel, *Strive for Truth*! New York: Feldheim, 1978.

Binyan Adei Ad (R. Solomon Wolbe, twentieth century), Jerusalem, 1979.

Musar Avicha U'Midot HaRe'iyah. Jerusalem: Mossad Harav Kook, 1973.

Ahavas Yisrael. Brooklyn, New York: Kehot, 1977.

Mitzvot HaBayit (R. Joseph D. Epstein, twentieth century). Brooklyn, New York, 1966.

HaIshah VeHamitzvot (Elyakim G. Ellinson). Jerusalem: The World Zionist Organization, 1981.

Halichot Betah (R. David Auerbach). Jerusalem, 1983.

HaIshah BeYahadut Shavah Yoter (Ayala Glicksberg). Tel Aviv: Aleph Hotzaat S'farim, 1983.

HaPeninah (Dov Raphel, editor). Jerusalem, 1989.

RESPONSA

Teshuvot R. Meir of Rothenburg (R. Meir of Rothenburg, d. 1293). Lemberg, 1860.

Teshuvot Rashba (R. Solomon ben Adret, 1235–1310). Several editions.
Tashbatz (R. Simon ben Zemach Duran, 1361–1444). Amsterdam, 1739.
Teshuvot Giv'at Pinhas. Lvov, 1837.
Teshuvot MaHarik (R. Joseph Colon, 1420–1480).
Teshuvot Radvaz (R. David ben Solomon ibn Avi Zimra, 1480–1574).
Teshuvot of MaHaram of Lublin (R. Meir ben Gedalyah, 1558–1616).
Teshuvot R. Akiva Eiger (1761–1837).
Teshuvot Hatam Sofer (R. Moses Sofer, 1762–1839). Vienna, 1855.
Teshuvot MaHarit (R. Joseph of Trani). Lemberg, 1861.
Teshuvot MaHaram Schick (R. Moses Schick, 1807–1879). Muncacz, 1881.

Selected English and Other Sources

Abramov, Tehilla. *The Secret of Jewish Femininity: Insights into the Practice of Taharat HaMishpachah*. Jerusalem: Targum Press and Feldheim Publishers, 1988.

Aguilar, Grace. *Women of Israel*. New York: D. Appleton and Co., 1854.

———. *The Spirit of Judaism*. Cincinnati: Bloch Publishing Co., 1842.

Alfasi, Isaac. *HaHasidut*. Tel Aviv: Maariv, 1974.

Aristotle. *Generation of Animals*. Trans. A. L. Peck. Cambridge, MA: Harvard University Press, 1943.

Aristotle. *Politics and Poetics*. Trans. B. Jowett and I. Twining. New York: Viking Press, 1957.

Barth, Aron. *The Jew Faces Eternal Problems*. Jerusalem: The Jewish Agency, 1965.

Baum, Charlotte, Hyman, Paula, and Michel, Sonya. *The Jewish Woman in America*. New York: Dial Press, 1976.

Bleich, J. David. *Contemporary Halachic Problems*. New York: Ktav and Yeshiva University Press, 1983.

Brayer, Menachem M., *The Jewish Woman in Rabbinic Literature: A Psychohistorical Perspective*. Hoboken, NJ: Ktav, 1986.

Breuer, Joseph. *The Jewish Marriage: Source of Sanctity*. New York: Philipp Feldheim, 1956.

Daly, Mary. *The Church and the Second Sex*. New York: Harper & Row, 1975.

De Beauvoir, Simone. *The Second Sex*. Trans. and ed. H. Parshley. New York: Alfred Knopf, 1972.

Degler, Carl. *In Search of Human Nature: The Decline and Revival of Darwinism in American Social Thought*. New York and Oxford: Oxford University Press, 1991.

Eisenberg, Dov. *A Guide for the Jewish Woman and Girl*. Monsey, NY: Dov Eisenberg, 1981.

Elman, Peter, ed. *Jewish Marriage*. London: Soncino, 1967.

Encyclopaedia Judaica. Jerusalem: Keter, 1971.

Feldman, David M. *Health and Medicine in the Jewish Tradition*. New York: Crossroad, 1987.

Feldman, David M. *Marital Relations, Birth Control and Abortion in Jewish Law*. New York: Schocken Books, 1974.

Frankiel, Tamar. *The Voice of Sarah*. San Francisco: HarperCollins, 1990.

Gilligan, Carol. *In a Different Voice*. Cambridge and London: Harvard University Press, 1982.

Goldwurm, Hersh, ed. *The Rishonim*. New York: Mesorah Publications, 1982.
Graetz, H. *History of the Jews*. Philadelphia: The Jewish Publication Society of America, 1894.
Hertz, J. H. *The Pentateuch and Haftorahs*. London: Soncino, 1981.
Hirsch, Samson Raphael. *Collected Works* (German). Frankfurt: I. Kaufmann, 1902.
______. *Horeb: A Philosophy of Jewish Laws and Observances, Translated from the German Original with Introduction by I. Grunfeld*. London: Soncino, 1962.
______. *Judaism Eternal*. London: The Soncino Press, 1959.
______. *The Hirsch Siddur*. Jerusalem and New York: Feldheim, 1978.
______. *The Pentateuch, Commentary and Translation*. Rendered into English by Isaac Levy. Gateshead, England: Judaica Press, 1976.
______. *The Pentateuch*. Trans. S. R. Hirsch and excerpts from *The Hirsch Commentary*, ed. Ephraim Oratz and English trans. from the German Gertrude Hirschler. New York: Judaica Press, 1986.
Isaacs, A. S. *Young Champion, One Year in Grace Aguilar's Girlhood*. London, 1933.
Jacob, H. E. *The World of Emma Lazarus*. New York: Schocken Books, 1949.
Josephus: Complete Works. Grand Rapids, MI: Kregel Publications, 1978.
Kaplan, Aryeh. *Waters of Eden*. New York: NCSY/Orthodox Union, 1976.
Kaufman, Michael. *Love, Marriage, and Family in Jewish Law and Tradition*. Northvale, NJ: Jason Aronson, 1991.
Kayserling, M. *Die Jüdishchen Frauen in der Geschichte Literatur und Kunst*. Leipzig, 1879.
Kitov, A. E. *The Jew and His Home*. Trans. with an introduction by Nathan Bulman. New York: Shengold, 1963.
Lamm, Norman. *A Hedge of Roses*. New York: Feldheim Publishers, 1966.
Lepon, Shoshana. *No Greater Treasure: Stories of Extraordinary Women Drawn from the Talmud and Midrash*. Jerusalem: Targum Press and Feldheim Publishers, 1990.
Levi, Leo. *Man and Woman, The Torah Perspective*. Jerusalem: Ezer Layeled, 1980.
Maccoby, Eleanor, and Jacklin, Carol. *The Psychology of Sex Differences*. Stanford: Stanford University Press, 1974.
Maimonides. *The Commandments*. Trans. Charles B. Chavel. London and New York: Soncino, 1967.
Meiselman, Moshe. *Jewish Woman in Jewish Law*. New York: Ktav, 1978.
Miller, Yisroel. *In Search of the Jewish Woman*. Jerusalem and New York: Feldheim Publishers, 1984.
Modder, F. *The Jews in the Literature of England*. London, 1939.
Moir, Anne, and Jessel, David. *Brain Sex: The Real Difference between Men and Women*. London: Michael Joseph, 1989.
Montesquieu, Charles-Louis de. *The Spirit of Laws*. London, 1750.
Moore, George Foot. *Judaism in the First Centuries of the Christian Era*. New York: Schocken Books, 1971.
National Jewish Population Survey. New York: Council of Jewish Federations, 1991.
Radcliffe, Sarah Chana. *Aizer K'negdo: The Jewish Woman's Guide to Happiness in Marriage*. Jerusalem: Targum Press and Feldheim Publishers, 1988.
Ranke-Heinemann, Uta. *Eunochs for the Kingdom of Heaven*. New York: Doubleday, 1990.
Remy, Nahida. *The Jewish Woman*. Trans. Louise Mannheimer. New York: Bloch Publishing Co., 1916.
Restak, R. *The Brain: The Last Frontier*. New York: Doubleday, 1979.
Rossi, Alice. *The Feminist Papers*. New York and London: Columbia University Press, 1973.

Roth, Cecil. *The House of Nasi: Joseph, Duke of Naxos*. Philadelphia: The Jewish Publication Society of America, 1948.

———. *The House of Nasi: Dona Gracia*. London, 1947.

———. *The Jews in the Renaissance*. Philadelphia: The Jewish Publication Society of America, 1959.

———. *History of the Jews in Venice*. Philadelphia: The Jewish Publication Society of America, 1930.

Schappes, Morris U., ed. *Emma Lazarus: Selections from Her Poetry and Prose*. New York: Cooperative Book League, 1944.

Schmelz, U. O., and DellaPergola, Sergio. *Basic Trends in American Jewish Demography*. New York: The American Jewish Committee, 1988.

———.*Papers in Jewish Demography*. Jerusalem: The Institute of Contemporary Jewry and the Hebrew University, 1989.

Spiro, Melford E. *Gender and Culture: Kibbutz Women Revisited*. New York and London: Harcourt, Brace, Jovanovich, 1975.

———.*Kibbutz: Venture in Utopia*. Cambridge, MA: Harvard University Press, 1955, 1971.

Tavard, George H. *Women in the Christian Tradition*. Notre Dame and London: University of Notre Dame Press, 1973.

Tendler, Moshe. *Pardes Rimonim*. New York: The Judaica Press, 1979.

The Life of Gluckel of Hameln, 1646–1724, Written by Herself. Trans. original Yiddish and ed. Beth-Zion Abrahams. New York: Thomas Yoseloff, 1963.

The Poems of Emma Lazarus. Boston and New York: Houghton Mifflin and Co., 1889.

Tiger, Lionel, and Shepfer, Joseph. *Women in the Kibbutz*. New York and London: Harcourt, Brace, Jovanovich, 1975.

Weiss-Rosmarin, Trude. *Jewish Women through the Ages*. New York: The Jewish Book Club, 1940.

Index

Abba Hilkiya, 31
Aboab, Isaac, 160
Abortion. *See also* Birth control
  Jewish law and, 165
  medical problems of fetus, 168–169
  rates of, in modern Israel, 172
  severity by which viewed, in Judaism, 165–166
  when permitted, in Judaism, 167–168
Abrabanel, Benvenida, 87–88
Abraham ben David, 130, 159–160, 241
Abraham Meir of Worms, wife of, 75
Abstinence. *See also* Birth control
  birth control, 162–163
  sexuality, 133–134
Acquinas, Saint Thomas, xxiii, xxiv
Adel of Belz, 83
Adel the Tzadikah, 82
Adornment, during *niddah*, 148
Adultery, divorce and, 186
Aggression, marriage as optional for women, 13–14
Aguilar, Grace, 9, 101–103
Agunah
  alleviation of, 193–194
  problem of, 191–193
  women's evidence in court, 199
AIDS, abortion, medical problems of fetus, 168–169
Akiva, 3, 9, 39, 68–69, 148, 156, 185
Alexander the Great, 29
Antiquity. *See* Classical world
Arama, Isaac, 254, 255
Aristotle, xxiii
Aryeh Leib Sarahs, mother of, 83
Asaf, S., 120
Asher ben Yehiel, 192
Ashkenazi, Boula, 78
Assimilation, Jewish survival and, 175–176
Augustine, Saint, xxiii, xxiv
Azulai, Hayim Yosef David, 253

Baal HaTanya, Freda, daughter of the, 83–84
Baal Shem Tov, 81
Bacharach, Havah, 79–80
Barazani, Osnat bat Samuel, 80
Barth, Aron, 147
Bat mitzvah, 256–258

Beauvoir, Simone de, xxvi
Beilinson, Shechter, 154
Benedictions, 244–245
Berkowitz, Gila, 150
Biblical women, 45–64. *See also* Torah
  Deborah and Yael, 56
  Esther, champion of Jews of the Persian Empire, 61–62
  Hanah, prayer and devotion, 59–60
  Huldah, 54
  inspirational role, 45
  Judith
    commemoration of, on Hanukkah, 63
    holiness of sensuality, 63
    savior of Jews, 62
  marriage without dowry, 51–52
  matriarchs, 47–51
    Rachel and Leah, 51
    Rebeccah, 49–51
    Sarah, 47–49
  Miriam, 54–55
  motherhood in ancient Israel, 46–47
  prophetesses, 53–54
  redemption, women's role in, 55–56
  Ruth the Moabite, 60–61
  Song of Deborah, 57–59
  Tamar
    initiative and, 52–53
    mother of Kings of Israel, 53
Biology, gender differences, xxx–xxxi, 255–256
Birkat Hamazon, 245–246
Birth control, 159–172
  abortion
    Jewish law and, 165
    medical problems of fetus, 168–169
    rates of, in modern Israel, 172
    severity by which viewed, 165–166
    when permitted, 167–168
  abstinence, 162–163
  biblical reference to, 159–160
  "family planning," 163–164
  Jewish/Christian positions compared, 164, 169–172
  Jewish view of, 160–161, 172
  permission, rules for, 162
  sterilization, 161–162
  Torah commandment to be fruitful and multiply, 159, 160
Birth rates, of Jews, 178
Blessings, 244–245
Blood taboos, *mikveh* as medium for elevated life, 145–146
Brachah, Hanah, 85
Bruriah, Torah study, example of, 253–254

Caesarian section, 171
Calvin, John, xxiv
Capital punishment, court testimony of women, 201
Caro, Joseph, 15, 218
Catholicism, birth control, Jewish/Christian positions compared, 164, 169–172. *See also* Christianity
Ceba, Ansaldo, 94
Character, child rearing, gender role and, 27
Childbearing. *See also* Pregnancy; Procreation
  biblical women
    initiative and, 52–53
    mother of Kings of Israel, 53
  fast days, 228
  health hazard
    abortion and, 169, 170–172
    exemption to procreation, 160
  Yom Kippur, fasting on, 221
Child rearing, gender role and, 27
Christianity
  birth control, Jewish/Christian positions compared, 164, 169–172
  gender roles, Jewish/Christian attitudes compared, 36–37
  sexuality and, 123
  women's status in, xxiii–xxv
Circumcision, morality and, 3–4
Civil and criminal law, 197–202
  court testimony, 200–202
  credibility of women in court, 199–200

women and, 197
women as witnesses, 198–199
Classical world, women's status in, xxii–xxiii
Cleanliness, family purity and, 155–157. *See also* Family purity
Compassion, of women, 30–31
Conjugal neglect, protection of women against, 131–132
Consent, marriage requirement, 112–113
Counting the *Omer*, 228
Court testimony, of women, civil and criminal law, 200–202
Creation
equality at, 35
gender role and, 23
male and female characteristics equal, 20
marriage as path to giving, 11–12
marriage as transcendental wholeness, 18
woman's dependence on man, 35–36
Credibility, of women in court, 199–200
Criminal law. *See* Civil and criminal law

David of Imola, 93
Day of Atonement. *See* Yom Kippur
Death of husband
divorce, *agunah* problem, 191–194
inheritance law, 202–203
marriage, *ketubah* support requirements, 116
women's evidence in court, 199
DellaPergola, Sergio, 173, 178, 179
Demography, 172–179
abortion, rates of, in modern Israel, 172
assimilation and, 175–176
future prospects, 178–179
intermarriage, in U.S., 174
Jewish demographic losses, 174–175
Jewish education and, 173
Jewish family and, in U.S., 173–174
Jewish population loss, in U.S., 172–173
Jewish posterity and, 177
replenishment and, 176–177
vanishing Jew, 177–178
Dependence
marriage
dependence or independence is woman's choice, 114
ketubah support requirements, 116
woman's dependence on man, 35–36
Depersonalization, sexuality, humanization versus, 129–130
Discernment, Rebeccah and, 49–50
Disrespect, as ground for divorce, 189–190
Divine precepts. *See Mitzvot*
Divorce, 181–194
agunah
alleviation of, 193–194
as problem, 191–193
assimilation and, Jewish survival, 175–176
blame not apportioned in, 187
community militates against, 182–183
discouragement of, 181–182
disrespect as ground for, 189–190
get and, 184–185
husband and wife make decision, not courts, 186–187
husband may compel, instances of, 190
ketubah support requirements, 116
liberal attitude toward, 185–186
maltreatment and abuse of wife, 188–189
rabbinic courts and aid to women, 187–188
story of Zusya of Hanipoli, 183–184
truth and concealment, 182
when only option, 184
wife may compel, instances of, 191
Down's syndrome, abortion, medical problems of fetus, 168–169
Dowry, marriage without, biblical women, 51–52

Education. *See* Jewish religious education
Elazar ben Azarya, 32

Embracing, sexuality, single persons, 126–127
Emden, Jacob, 137, 139, 166, 168
Enabler role
wife role and, 39
women and, 38–39
Equality, at creation, 35
Estates and wills. *See* Death of husband
Ethics
Jewish religious education and, 5–6
moral living and, 6
Evil, women and, in Christianity, xxiv

Falk, Beilah, 78–79, 253
Family, 9–20. *See also* Marriage
as basic institution, 19
child rearing, gender role and, 27
gender roles
complementarity, 25–26
nature of, in Judaism, 24–25
intermarriage, in U.S., 174
Jewish family and, in U.S., 173–174
love and, 9–10
love of God, attainment of, 10
male and female characteristics equal humanity, 19–20
marriage as optional for women, 13–14
marriage as path to giving, 11–12
marriage as reward of the woman, 15–16
marriage as transcendental wholeness, 18
marriage as wholeness, 12–13
marriage ideal, 17–18
procreation duty, women exempt from, 15
self and other, xxvii–xxviii
single persons and, 13
social duties versus self-fulfillment, 18–19
"walking" after God and, 10–11
women's role and, xxxiii
"Family planning," birth control, 163–164
Family purity, 143–158
biblical sources for, 144–145
cleanliness and, 155–157
concern for woman and marriage, 146–147
consideration for woman, 147
contemporary revival of *niddah* and *mikveh*, 150
health benefits, 153–154
hedge of roses image, 150–151
hygiene and, 154–155
mikveh as medium for elevated life, 145–146
mikveh in tradition, importance of, 157–158
rules of *niddah* and *mikveh*, 143–144
separation
ensuring against being taken for granted, 149–150
medium for refreshing the relationship, 148–149
reunion freshness, 151–152
spirituality and, 147–148
tranquillity and repose, 152
time and woman, 153
Fast days, festivals, 228
Feige bat Adel, 82
Feinstein, Moses, 257
Feldman, David M., 132
Femininity, family purity and, 143–158. *See also* Family purity
Feminism
contemporary society, xxvi–xxvii
demography, Jewish demographic losses, 174–175
gender differences and, xxix–xxx
self and, xxvii–xxix
Festivals, 218–231. *See also* Religious laws and customs; Sabbath
counting the Omer, 228
fast days, 228
hakafot, rejoicing with the Torah on Simhat Torah, 221–222
Hanukkah lamp, 223
Hanukkah lights, kindling of, 223–224
man's *mitzvah* to please wife during, 219
obligation to keep, 218–219
Passover
four cups of wine, 226–227

hametz and *matzah*, 226
Purim, 224
Purim gifts to the poor, 225–226
reading the *Megillah*, 224–225
Rosh Hodesh, 228–231
shofar and, 219–220
Sukkot, dwelling in the *sukkah*, 221
Yom Kippur, fasting on, 220–221
Fishel, Royzil, 76–77
Frankiel, Tamar, xxxiii, 25, 63–64, 215–216
Freda, daughter of the Baal HaTanya, 83–84
Freud, S., xxxi
Friedan, Betty, 175
Friedman, M. A., 120
Fulgentius of Ruspe, Saint, 169–170

Gamliel, 28–29
Gender differences. *See also* Gender roles; Sexuality
Judaism and, xxix–xxx
male and female characteristics equal humanity, 19–20
natural cause and, xxx–xxxi
sex drive, 126
sociology and, xxxi–xxxii
Torah study, modern discoveries, 255–256
Gender roles, 23–41. *See also* Gender differences; Marriage; Sexuality
equality at creation, 35
family life and, 25–26
Hirsch, Samson Raphael, on, 26–27
Jewish/Christian attitudes compared, 36–37
Judaism's rationale for, 24
marriage as optional for women, 13–14
mother of a sage, 39
nature of, in Judaism, 24–25
physiological and psychological differences, 23–24
relative significance question and, 26
Torah and, 37
wife role as enabler, 39
woman and the golden rule, 31
woman as enabler, 38–39
woman as source of national moral strength, 33–35
woman as Torah educator, 32–33
woman of torches, 40
woman of valor, 40–41
woman's dependence on man, 35–36
woman's influence, 32
woman's mercy and compassion, 30–31
woman's traits, 28–29
woman's understanding, 29
woman's wisdom, 29–30
Gerondi, Nissim, 16
Gershom, Rabenu, 203
Get, divorce and. *See also* Divorce
Gilligan, Carol, xxxi
Gluckel of Hameln, 95–98
Gnostic gospels, women and, xxiv
God
gender role and, 23, 24
love of, attainment of, 10
mitzvot and, 7–8
morality and, 3–4, 5
as role model, 4–5
self and other, xxvii–xxviii
"walking" after, 10–11
Goitein, S. D., 120
Golden Rule, 9, 31
Goldman, Emma, xxxii, xxxiii
Gracia Nasi, Dona, 88–92
Graetz, Heinrich, 92
Gratz, Rebecca, 100
Greece. *See* Classical world

HaCohen, Israel Meir, 254
Halachah, prayer, women's congregations, 237
HaLevi, David, 230
Hallah, Sabbath, 215–216
Hametz, Passover and, 226
Hand-holding, sexuality, single persons, 126–127
Hanukkah
Hanukkah lamp, 223
Hanukkah lights, kindling of, 223–224
Haring, Bernard, 171
Hasidic women, Torah study, 81–86

Havah, Hanah, 84
Havdalah, separating holy from profane, Sabbath, 217–218
Health benefits, family purity, 153–154
Hedge of roses image, family purity, 150–151
HeHasid, Judah, 163, 251
Heilpern, Edel, 79
Hertz, J. H., 158
Hewlett, Sylvia Ann, xxxii
Hillel, 185
Himmelfarb, Milton, 174
Hirsch, Samson Raphael, xxi, xxii, 26–27, 40, 47, 124, 148, 156, 210, 211–212, 246, 251
Holocaust, Jewish survival and, 177
Homosexuality, prohibition, 127–128
Horowitz, Sarah Rebeccah Rachel Leah, 77
Horowitz-Sternfeld, Surele, 84
Humanity, male and female characteristics equal, 19–20
Humanization
  depersonalization versus, 129–130
  sexuality, 124–125
Hunt, Mortimer, 131
Husband, obligations to his wife, 113
Hygiene, family purity and, 154–155

Influence
  Sarah and, 48–49
  of women, 32
Inheritance law, 202–204
  daughters preferred in support and maintenance, 203–204
  generally, 202–203
  property rights, 203–204
Insight, Rebeccah and, 50–51
Intelligence
  wisdom of women, 29–30
  woman's understanding, 29
Intermarriage, in U.S., Jewish family and, 174
Isaac ben Moses of Vienna, mother-in-law of, 75
Isaac of Corbeil, 131, 251
Ishmael, 166
Israel, kibbutz, gender differences and, xxxi–xxxii
Isserles, Moses, 203–204, 244
Isserlin, Redel, 75
Italian Renaissance, 92–93

Jesus, women and, xxiv
Jewish religious education
  ethics and, 5–6
  Jewish survival and, 173
  prayer, religious school prayer for girls, 237–238
  Schenirer, Sarah, 108
  woman as Torah educator, 32–33
  women and, xxxiii–xxxiv
Jewish survival
  assimilation and, 175–176
  future prospects, 178–179
  intermarriage, in U.S., 174
  Jewish education and, 173
  Jewish population loss, in U.S., 172–173
  Jewish posterity and, 177
  replenishment and, 176–177
  vanishing Jew, 177–178
Josephus, 67
Joshua ben Hananiah, 32
Judah HeHasid, 139
Judah Loew of Prague, 11
Judaism
  gender differences and, xxix–xxx
  masculofeminism and, xxvii–xxix
  women's education and, xxxiii–xxxiv
  women's status and, xxii, xxv

Kaddish, synagogue, separation of sexes in, 240
Kant, I., xxxi
Kaplan, Aryeh, 146–147
Karo, Joseph, 168, 189
Katz, Hanah, 77
Ketubah. *See also* Marriage
  ancient forms of, 117–119
  document of women's rights, 114–115
  enforcement provisions, 116–117
  importance of, 117

origin and purpose of, 120–121
support requirements, 116
tradition of, 117
variations in text of, 119–120
Kevod hatzibbur, prayer, *Aliyot* to the Torah for women, 238–239
Kibbutz, gender differences and, xxxi–xxxii
Kiddush, Sabbath, 216
Kiera, Esther, 92
Kissing, sexuality, single persons, 126–127
KiTov, Eliyahu, 37, 155

Lamm, Norman, 153
Landau, Yehezkel, 166
Law. *See* Civil and criminal law; Inheritance law; Religious law and custom
Lazarus, Emma, 103–107
Legal contract, marriage, 111–112
Lesbianism, prohibition, 127–128
Levi Yitzhak of Berditchev, 11
Liens, inheritance law, 202
Light unto the nations, morality, 8
Liguori, Alphonsus, 171
Loew, Judah, 210
Love
family and, 9–10
of God, attainment of, 10
Rebeccah and, 49–50
Luria, Solomon, 162
grandmother of, 75
Luther, Martin, xxiv–xxv

Magnus, Albertus, xxiv
Maimonides, 15, 113, 114, 135, 139, 140, 156, 157, 167, 188, 189, 194, 198, 207, 214, 217, 218, 234, 243, 244, 252, 253
Malkah of Belz, 83
Malkah the Triskerin, 85
Mamzerim, Jewish survival and, 176
Marriage, 111–122. *See also* Family; Sexuality; Single persons
consent requirement, 112–113
economics in, dependence or independence is woman's choice, 114
guarantee of rights and privileges to wife, 121–122
husband's obligations to his wife, 113
ideal of, partnership not merger, 17–18
Jewish idea of, 111
ketubah
ancient forms of, 117–119
document of women's rights, 114–115
enforcement provisions, 116–117
importance of, 117
origin and purpose of, 120–121
support requirements, 116
tradition of, 117
variations in text of, 119–120
legal contract, 111–112
obligation to respect the wife, 121
as optional for women, 13–14, 15
as path to giving, 11–12
as reward of the woman, 15–16
sexuality, men's obligations to gladden his wife, 129
successful marriage, requirements for, 20
as transcendental wholeness, 18
wholeness and, 12–13
wife's obligations to her husband, 113–114
without dowry, biblical women, 51–52
Mar Ukba, 31
Masculofeminism, self and, xxvii–xxix. *See also* Feminism
Matriarchs, 47–51
Rachel and Leah, 51
Rebeccah, 49–51
Sarah, 47–49
Matzah, Passover and, 226
Mausbach, Joseph, 170
Megillah, reading of, 224–225
Meir, 31, 181–182
Meir of Rothenburg, 188, 241
Meirosh, daughter of Elimelech of Lizhensk, 82

Meiselman, Moshe, 202, 244, 246, 254, 255
Mercy, of women, 30–31
Mikveh. *See also* Family purity
  biblical sources for, 143–144
  contemporary revival of, 150
  family purity rules, 143–144
  as medium for elevated life, 145–146
  tradition and, importance of, 157–158
Minyanim, prayer, women's congregations, 237
Mitzvot
  God and, 7–8
  morality and, 6–7
Modena, Bathsheba, 75–76
Modena of Ferrara, Pomona da, 75, 93
Moderation, in sexuality, 139–140
Modesty. *See also* Privacy
  Sarah and, 48–49
  woman's traits, 28
Montefiore, Judith, 98–99
Montesquieu, xxi
Moore, George Foot, xxv
Morality
  basis of, 3–4
  God and, 4
  God as role model, 4–5
  Judaism as guide to, 6
  light unto the nations, 8
  mitzvot and, 6–7
  woman as source of national moral strength, 33–35
  women's role and, xxxii–xxxiii
Morpurgo, Rachel, 99–100
Motherhood, in ancient Israel, biblical women, 46–47. *See also* Child bearing; Child rearing

Nahmanides, 230
Namnah, daughter of Samuel ben Ali, 74
Natural cause, gender differences, xxx–xxxi
Nehamah the Tzadikah, 84
Neuwirth, Joshua, 251
Niddah. *See also* Family purity
  adornment during, 148
  contemporary revival of, 150
  family purity rules, 143–144
  hygiene and, 154–155

Omer, counting of, 228
Origen, xxiv
Ovadiah ben Jacob Sforno, 20

Pann, Toiba, 76–77
Paola dei Piatelli, 93
Partnership, marriage as, 17–18
Passover
  four cups of wine, 226–227
  hametz and *matzah*, 226
Paul, Saint, xxiii, xxiv
Paul IV (pope of Rome), 90–91
Paul VI (pope of Rome), 164
Perna, 93
Peter, Simon, xxiv
Physiology, gender role and, 23–24
Piaget, J., xxxi
Pious XII (pope of Rome), 164
Pleasure, as incentive, sexuality, 138–139
Positive Precepts, women excused from, 208–209
Poverty, Talmud, Queen Helena, 66–67
Power, Sarah and, 48–49
Prayer, 233–247
  Aliyot to the Torah for women, 238–239
  Birkat Hamazon, 245–246
  blessings and benedictions, 244–245
  separation of sexes in synagogue, 239–240
  tallit, 242–244
    mitzvah of *tzitzit*, 242
    as optional precept, 243
    women's exemption, 243–244
  tefillin, 240–242
    nature of, 240–241
    sanctity and *kavanah*, 241–242
  "That He has not made me a woman," 246–247
  women and, 233–236
    duty of men and women, 234–235
    Judaism and, 233–234

praying with congregation preferable, 235–236
women's congregations, 236–238
Halachah and *minyanim*, 237
religious school prayer for girls, 237–238
Pregnancy. *See also* Childbearing; Procreation
fast days, 228
health hazard
abortion and, 169, 170–172
exemption to procreation, 160
as physical hazard, pleasure and, 139
Yom Kippur, fasting on, 221
Privacy. *See also* Modesty
court testimony of women, civil and criminal law, 200–202
Sarah and, 48–49
woman's traits, 28
Procreation. *See also* Childbearing; Pregnancy
duty of, women exempt from, 15
marriage as reward of the woman, 15–16
Torah commandment to be fruitful and multiply, 159
Property rights
inheritance law, 203–204
marriage, *ketubah* support requirements, 116
Prophetesses, biblical women, 53–54
Protestantism, women and, xxiv–xxv. *See also* Catholicism; Christianity
Psychology, gender role and, 23–24
Purim
festival of, 224
gifts to the poor, 225–226
Purity. *See* Family purity

Ranke-Heinemann, Uta, 164, 171
Rape, sexuality, consent of woman required, 130–131
Rashi. *See* Solomon ben Isaac of Troyes (*Rashi*)
Reason, rejection of, as source of morality, 4
Redemption, women's role in, biblical women, 55–56
Religious laws and customs, 207–212. *See also* Festivals; Sabbath
obligation to fulfill all negative precepts, 212
performance of exempted precepts that are not optional, 211–212
precepts devolving upon women, 212
woman's option to perform exempted *mitzvot*, 210–211
women excused from fourteen positive precepts, 208–209
women's exemptions, 207–208
women's spirituality, 209–210
Replenishment, Jewish survival and, 176–177
Reserve, Sarah and, 48–49
Ritual, morality and, 5. *See also* Family purity; Festivals; Religious laws and customs
Roman Catholics. *See* Catholicism; Christianity
Rome. *See* Classical world
Rosh HaShanah, *Shofar*, listening to, festivals, 220
Rosh Hodesh, 228–231

Sabbath, 213–218. *See also* Festivals; Religious laws and customs
Hallah, 215–216
Havdalah, separating holy from profane, 217–218
Kiddush, 216
kindling the Sabbath lights, 213–214
precedence accorded the woman kindling the lights, 214–215
three meals, 217
Samuel ben Meir, 219
Sanchez of Cordoba, Thomas, 171
Sara, mother of Aryeh Leib Sarahs, 83
Sarah Bat-Tovim, 77–78
Sassoon, Flora, 81
Schenirer, Sara, 107–108
Schmelz, U. O., 173, 178
Scribes, 93
Seder, Passover, four cups of wine, 226–227

Self, feminism and, xxvii–xxix
Self-fulfillment, social duties versus, 18–19
Selfish state, single persons and, 16–17
Serr, David M., 153–154
Sexuality, 123–141. *See also* Gender differences; Gender roles; Marriage
  abstinence, 133–134
  advice to husband, 136–138
  biblical women
    Judith, holiness of sensuality, 63
    Tamar, initiative and, 52–53
  conjugal neglect, protection against, of woman, 131–132
  consent of woman required, 130–131
  emotional commitment required, 134
  harmonization of spiritual and sexual, 123–124
  humanization, 124–125
  humanization versus depersonalization, 129–130
  husband's duty to cater to wife's needs, 135–136
  lesbianism, 127–128
  mamzerim, 176
  man's obligations to gladden his wife, 129
  mastery of instincts, 125
  moderation in, 139–140
  mutual privileges and duties, 140–141
  obligation of man to ensure wife's satisfaction, 132–133
  pleasure as incentive, 138–139
  single persons
    permissions, 126–127
    prohibitions, 125–126
  wife's privileges, 134–135
  wife's satisfaction takes precedence, 138
  of women
    Christianity and, xxiv
    Judaism and, 128–129
Shabtai ben Meir HaCohen, mother of, 80
Shapira, Perele, 84
Shlomtzi, Sarah, 85
Shneur Zalman of Lyady, daughter of, 83–84
Shofar, listening to, festivals, 219–220
Simhah ben Samuel of Vitri, 189
Simhah of Dvinsk, Meir, 166
Simhat Torah, *Hakafot*, rejoicing with the Torah on, 221–222
Simon Bar Kochba, 118
Simon of Frankfurt, 210
Single persons
  rabbinic views of, 13
  selfish state and, 16–17
  sexuality
    permissions, 126–127
    prohibitions, 125–126
  unfortunate status, 16
Sixtus V (pope of Rome), 164
Society
  Judaism and, xxviii
  social duties versus self-fulfillment, 18–19
Sociology, gender differences and, xxxi–xxxii
Sofer, Moses, 162, 222
Solomon ben Adret, 241
Solomon ben Isaac of Troyes (*Rashi*), 48, 74, 167, 219, 227
Sonenfeld, Joseph Hayim, 252
Song of Deborah, 57–59
Sorotzkin, Zalman, 254
Sterilization, birth control, 161–162
Sukkot, dwelling in the *sukkah*, 221
Sullam, Sarah Coppio (Copia), 93–94
Survival. *See* Jewish survival
Synagogue, separation of sexes in, 239–240

Tallit, 242–244
  mitzvah of *tzitzit*, 242
  as optional precept, 243
  women's exemption, 243–244
Talmud, 64–71
  Bruriah, talmudic scholar, 69
  Ima Shalom, 70
  Kimchit, mother of high priests, 69–70
  Queen Helena, 66–67

Queen Salome, 64–66
Rachel bat Kalba Savua, 67–69
Tay-Sachs disease, abortion, medical problems of fetus, 168–169
Techines composers, 76
Tefillin, 240–242
nature of, 240–241
sanctity and *kavanah*, 241–242
Tendler, Moses, 154
Tertullian, xxiv
Tiktiner, Rebeccah, 76
Time, woman and, family purity, 153
Tischleder, Peter, 170
Tocqueville, Alexis de, xxxii
Torah. *See also* Biblical women
Abrabanel, Benvenida, 87–88
Abraham Meir of Worms, wife of, 75
Aguilar, Grace, 101–103
Ashkenazi, Boula, 78
Bacharach, Havah, 79–80
Barazani, Osnat bat Samuel, 80
Falk, Beilah, 78–79
Fishel, Royzil, 76–77
gender roles and, 37
Gluckel of Hameln, 95–98
Gracia Nasi, Dona, 88–92
Gratz, Rebecca, 100
hasidic women, 81–86
Heilpern, Edel, 79
Horowitz, Sarah Rebeccah Rachel Leah, 77
Isaac ben Moses of Vienna, mother-in- law of, 75
Isserlin, Redel, 75
Italian Renaissance, 92–93
Katz, Hanah, 77
Kiera, Esther, 92
Lazarus, Emma, 103–107
Luria of Poland, Solomon, grandmother of, 75
Modena, Bathsheba, 75–76
Modena of Ferrara, Pomona da, 75, 93
Montefiore, Judith, 98–99
Morpurgo, Rachel, 99–100
mother of a sage, 39
Namnah, daughter of Samuel ben Ali, 74
Pann, Toiba, 76–77
Rashi's daughters, 74
Salome and, 66
Sarah Bat-Tovim, 77–78
Sassoon, Flora, 81
Schenirer, Sara, 107–108
Shabtai ben Meir HaCohen, mother of, 80
Sullam, Sarah Coppio (Copia), 93–94
Tiktiner, Rebeccah, 76
woman as Torah educator, 32–33
Torah study, 249–256
emulation of forebears, 255
example of Bruriah, 253–254
gender differences, modern discoveries, 255–256
importance of, 249–250
in-depth Torah study, 252–253
modern times, 254–255
teaching of Torah to daughters, 250–252
woman as enabler of, 38–39
women and, 73
Torches, woman of, 40
Touching, sexuality, single persons, 126–127
Trani, Isaiah di, 139
Turnus Rufus, 3
Tzitzit
mitzvah of, 242
women's exemption from, 242

Understanding, of women, 29
Unmarried persons. *See* Single persons

Valor, woman of, 40–41
Virdimura di Medico of Catania, 93

Waldenberg, Eliezer, 168
"Walking" after God, family and, 10–11
Webermacher, Hanah Rachel (Maid of Ludomir), 85–86

Weinberg, Jehiel Jacob, 257–258
Wholeness
  male and female characteristics
    equal humanity, 19–20
  marriage and, 12–13, 18
Wills and estates. *See* Death of husband
Wisdom, of women, 29–30
Witch-hunts, Christianity and, xxv
Witnesses, women as, civil and criminal law, 198–199
Wife, obligations to her husband, 113–114. *See also* Marriage
Women
  influence of, on Jewish history, xxi
  sexuality of, 128–129
  time and, family purity, 153
Women's movement, demography, Jewish demographic losses, 174–175
Women's status
  Christianity, xxiii–xxv
  classical world, xxii–xxiii
  contemporary society, xxvi–xxvii
  Judaism and, xxii, xxv

Yadin, Yigael, 117, 118, 144
Yenta the Prophetess, 83
Yom Kippur
  fasting on, 220–221
  Shofar, listening to, festivals, 220

Zionism
  Lazarus, Emma, 106–107
Zusya of Hanipoli, 183–184

ABOUT THE AUTHOR

Dr. Michael Kaufman, a distinguished scholar and author, studied at Yeshiva and Mesivta Torah Vodaath, Telshe Yeshiva, Brooklyn College, and the University of Louisville. He has published numerous books and studies on Judaism and Jewish art and culture, including *Love, Marriage, and Family in Jewish Law and Tradition*, *The Art of Judaism*, *A Timeless Judaism for Our Time*, and *A Guide to Jewish Art*. He also served as a consultant to the *Encyclopaedia Judaica*. Dr. Kaufman resides with his family in Jerusalem opposite the Western Wall.